Medical Management of the Pregnant Patient

Karen Rosene-Montella
Editor

Medical Management of the Pregnant Patient

A Clinician's Handbook

Springer

Editor
Karen Rosene-Montella, MD
SVP Women's Services and Clinical Integration, Lifespan Corporation
Professor and Vice Chair of Medicine
Director of Obstetric Medicine
The Warren Alpert Medical School of Brown University
Providence, RI, USA

ISBN 978-1-4614-1243-4   ISBN 978-1-4614-1244-1 (eBook)
DOI 10.1007/978-1-4614-1244-1
Springer New York Heidelberg Dordrecht London

Library of Congress Control Number: 2014952774

© Springer Science+Business Media New York 2015
This work is subject to copyright. All rights are reserved by the Publisher, whether the whole or part of the material is concerned, specifically the rights of translation, reprinting, reuse of illustrations, recitation, broadcasting, reproduction on microfilms or in any other physical way, and transmission or information storage and retrieval, electronic adaptation, computer software, or by similar or dissimilar methodology now known or hereafter developed. Exempted from this legal reservation are brief excerpts in connection with reviews or scholarly analysis or material supplied specifically for the purpose of being entered and executed on a computer system, for exclusive use by the purchaser of the work. Duplication of this publication or parts thereof is permitted only under the provisions of the Copyright Law of the Publisher's location, in its current version, and permission for use must always be obtained from Springer. Permissions for use may be obtained through RightsLink at the Copyright Clearance Center. Violations are liable to prosecution under the respective Copyright Law.
The use of general descriptive names, registered names, trademarks, service marks, etc. in this publication does not imply, even in the absence of a specific statement, that such names are exempt from the relevant protective laws and regulations and therefore free for general use.
While the advice and information in this book are believed to be true and accurate at the date of publication, neither the authors nor the editors nor the publisher can accept any legal responsibility for any errors or omissions that may be made. The publisher makes no warranty, express or implied, with respect to the material contained herein.

Printed on acid-free paper

Springer is part of Springer Science+Business Media (www.springer.com)

Preface

There are over 62 million women of childbearing age in the United States, 85 % of whom will have given birth by age 33. At least one-third of these women are entering pregnancy with a chronic medical illness, and 50 % are overweight or obese. Most women will not have received any preventive or medical services in the year prior to conception. This translates into women entering pregnancy without preconception counseling about nutrition, high-risk behaviors, or safety of medications and often with chronic disease in suboptimal control. Looking at diabetes alone, there are 1.85 million women of reproductive age with diabetes and an even greater number with prediabetes. Preconception management of these women could potentially mitigate risk for 113,000 births. There are 1 million women on antiepileptic drugs, impacting 75,000 pregnancies, and 7 million women who describe themselves as frequent drinkers, affecting 577,000 births annually.

Medical Management of the Pregnant Patient is meant to draw attention to the many women of childbearing age before, during, and after pregnancy who have concomitant medical illness. The authors are all experts in the field of obstetric medicine, internists with special expertise and training in medical problems in pregnancy. All work collaboratively with obstetricians and maternal-fetal medicine physicians, understanding that care of this very vulnerable and rewarding population is best done with a highly motivated team. The rewards are enormous for all of us who have worked in this field.

Medical Management of the Pregnant Patient is a practical guide to the management of the most frequently encountered medical illnesses during pregnancy. We hope that it brings you, the providers asked to participate in the care of sick pregnant women, some measure of guidance and comfort. This book is dedicated to my mentors in the field, Drs. Peter Garner and Richard V. Lee, and to all of the patients who have entrusted their care to me over many years.

Providence, RI, USA   Karen Rosene-Montella

Contents

Part I Cardiac Disease

1 Cardiac Disease 3
   Michael F. Sorrentino and Athena Poppas

Part II Critical Care

2 Management Principles of the Critically Ill Obstetric Patient 21
   Elie Zouein and Ghada Bourjeily

Part III Depression and Anxiety

3 Mood Disorders 35
   Teri Pearlstein, Ellen Flynn, and Carmen Monzon

Part IV Diabetes and Obesity

4 Diabetes and Pregnancy 61
   Lucia Larson and Marshall Carpenter

Part V GI/Liver

5 The Gastrointestinal Tract and the Liver in Pregnancy:
   Normal Functions and Diseases 81
   Silvia Degli Esposti, Judy Nee, and Sumona Saha

Part VI Hematology

6 Thrombophilia and Thrombosis 133
   Courtney Bilodeau and Karen Rosene-Montella

7	**Special Hematologic Issues in the Pregnant Patient** Tina Rizack, Kimberly Perez, and Rochelle Strenger	149

Part VII Hypertension/Preeclampsia

8	**Hypertensive Disorders of Pregnancy** Margaret A. Miller and Marshall Carpenter	177

Part VIII Infectious Diseases

9	**Viral Infection in Pregnancy: HIV and Viral Hepatitis** Erica J. Hardy, Silvia Degli Esposti, and Judy Nee	197

Part IX Neurology

10	**Headaches and Seizures** Julie L. Roth and Courtney Bilodeau	219

Part X Pulmonary

11	**Pulmonary Disorders in Pregnancy** Mariam Louis, D. Onentia Oyiengo, and Ghada Bourjeily	235

Part XI Renal

12	**Renal Disease in Pregnancy** Lucia Larson	261

Part XII Rheumatology

13	**The Care and Management of Rheumatologic Disease in Pregnancy** Candice Yuvienco and Kerri Batra	275

Part XIII Thyroid Disease

14	**Thyroid Disease** Mae Whelan and Geetha Gopalakrishnan	321

Index 341

Contributors

Kerri Batra, MD Obstetric Medicine, Rheumatology, Women's Medicine Collaborative, The Miriam Hospital, Providence, RI, USA

The Warren Alpert Medical School of Brown University, Providence, RI, USA

Courtney Bilodeau, MD Obstetric Medicine, Women's Medicine Collaborative, Miriam Hospital, Providence, RI, USA

The Warren Alpert Medical School of Brown University, Providence, RI, USA

Ghada Bourjeily, MD Pulmonary, Critical Care and Medicine, Women's Medicine Collaborative, The Miriam Hospital, Providence, RI, USA

The Warren Alpert Medical School of Brown University, Providence, RI, USA

Marshall Carpenter, MD Women's Medicine Collaborative, The Miriam Hospital, Providence, RI, USA

Department of Obstetrics and Gynecology, Tufts University School of Medicine, Boston, MA, USA

Silvia Degli Esposti, MD Center for Women's Gastrointestinal Medicine, Women's Medicine Collaborative, The Miriam Hospital, Providence, RI, USA

The Warren Alpert Medical School of Brown University, Providence, RI, USA

Ellen Flynn, MD Women's Behavioral Medicine, Women's Medicine Collaborative, The Miriam Hospital, Providence, RI, USA

The Warren Alpert Medical School of Brown University, Providence, RI, USA

Geetha Gopalakrishnan, MD OB Medicine-Endocrinology and Diabetes in Pregnancy, Women's Medicine Collaborative, The Miriam Hospital, Providence, RI, USA

Hallett Center for Diabetes and Endocrinology, Rhode Island Hospital Providence, RI, USA

The Warren Alpert Medical School of Brown University, Providence, RI, USA

Erica J. Hardy, MD Women's Infectious Diseases Consultation, Women and Infants Hospital, Providence, RI, USA

The Warren Alpert Medical School of Brown University, Providence, RI, USA

Lucia Larson, MD Obstetric Medicine, Women's Medicine Collaborative, The Miriam Hospital, Providence, RI, USA

The Warren Alpert Medical School of Brown University, Providence, RI, USA

Katie Lester, RD, LDN Women's Medicine Collaborative, The Miriam Hospital, Providence, RI, USA

Mariam Louis, MD Division of Pulmonary, Critical Care and Sleep Medicine, College of Medicine, University of Florida, Jacksonville, FL, USA

Margaret A. Miller, MD Obstetric Medicine, Women's Medicine Collaborative, The Miriam Hospital, Providence, RI, USA

The Warren Alpert Medical School of Brown University, Providence, RI, USA

Carmen Monzon, MD Women's Behavioral Medicine, Women's Medicine Collaborative, The Miriam Hospital, Providence, RI, USA

The Warren Alpert Medical School of Brown University, Providence, RI, USA

Judy Nee, MD Internal Medicine, Beth Israel Deaconess Medical Center, Boston, MA, USA

Harvard Medical School, Boston, MA, USA

D. Onentia Oyiengo, MBChB Pulmonary and Critical Care Fellowship, Rhode Island Hospital, Providence, RI, USA

The Warren Alpert Medical School of Brown University, Providence, RI, USA

Teri Pearlstein, MD Women's Behavioral Medicine, Women's Medicine Collaborative, The Miriam Hospital, Providence, RI, USA

The Warren Alpert Medical School of Brown University, Providence, RI, USA

Kimberly Perez, MD Department of Hematology/Oncology, Rhode Island Hospital, Providence, RI, USA

The Warren Alpert Medical School of Brown University, Providence, RI, USA

Contributors

Athena Poppas, MD Cardiovascular Institute of Rhode Island, Providence, RI, USA

Echocardiography Laboratory, Department of Medicine, Section of Cardiology, Rhode Island, Miriam Hospitals, Providence, RI, USA

The Warren Alpert Medical School of Brown University, Providence, RI, USA

Tina Rizack, MD, MPH Department of Medicine, Women and Infants Hospital, The Warren Alpert Medical School of Brown University, Providence, RI, USA

Karen Rosene-Montella, MD SVP Women's Services and Clinical Integration, Lifespan Corporation, Providence, RI, USA

Obstetric Medicine, Women's Medicine Collaborative, The Miriam Hospital, Providence, RI, USA

The Warren Alpert Medical School of Brown University, Providence, RI, USA

Julie L. Roth, MD Department of Neurology, Comprehensive Epilepsy Program, Rhode Island Hospital, Providence, RI, USA

The Warren Alpert Medical School of Brown University, Providence, RI, USA

Sumona Saha, MD University of Wisconsin School of Medicine and Public Health, Madison, WI, USA

Greg Salgueiro, MS, RD, LDN Women's Medicine Collaborative, The Miriam Hospital, Providence, RI, USA

Michael F. Sorrentino, MD Internal Medicine, Rhode Island Hospital, Providence, RI, USA

Rochelle Strenger, MD Department of Hematology/Oncology, The Miriam Hospital, Providence, RI, USA

The Warren Alpert Medical School of Brown University, Providence, RI, USA

Mae Whelan, MD Endocrinology Fellow, Department of Internal Medicine, Rhode Island Hospital, Providence, RI, USA

The Warren Alpert Medical School of Brown University, Providence, RI, USA

Candice Yuvienco, MD Division of Rheumatology, Department of Internal Medicine, UCSF Fresno, Fresno, CA, USA

University Rheumatology Associates, Fresno, CA, USA

Elie Zouein, MD Department of Medicine, Respiratory Intensive Care Unit, Rhode Island Hospital, Providence, RI, USA

Part I
Cardiac Disease

Chapter 1
Cardiac Disease

Michael F. Sorrentino and Athena Poppas

Introduction

The management of the pregnant patient with heart disease continues to be a challenge to health-care providers. Currently, 0.2–4 % of pregnancies in western countries are complicated by coexisting cardiovascular disease, and both the severity of disease and the number of patients are increasing [1]. It is important to understand the risks and management issues to better advise patients preconception and provide appropriate treatment during pregnancy. Management plans should be made by multidisciplinary teams, taking into consideration both mother and fetus. Treatments for pregnant patients with higher-risk lesions should occur in specialized centers with broad experience. In general, outcomes are favorable and improved by early diagnosis, vigilant management, and thoughtful treatment.

M.F. Sorrentino, M.D. (✉)
593 Eddy Street, Providence, RI 02903, USA

Internal Medicine, Rhode Island Hospital, 593 Eddy Street, Providence, RI 02906, USA
e-mail: michael.f.sorrentino@gmail.com

A. Poppas, M.D.
Cardiovascular Institute of Rhode Island, 2 Dudley Street, Providence, RI 02905, USA

Echocardiography Laboratory, Department of Medicine, Section of Cardiology,
Rhode Island, Miriam Hospitals, 593 Eddy Street, Main Building, Room 209,
Providence, RI 02903, USA
e-mail: apoppas@lifespan.org

Background

Congenital and acquired cardiovascular disease in pregnancy ranges from relatively benign (mitral valve prolapse) to life-threatening (pulmonary arterial hypertension). Therefore, early identification of patients with cardiac disease and an accurate and complete diagnosis with assessment of ventricular function and clinical status are necessary so as to optimize thoughtful, individualized maternal and neonatal risks. Ideally, preconception evaluation and counseling should occur. There are a number of global risk indices which can be utilized to predict maternal and neonatal morbidity and mortality. The most widely used is the well-validated CARPREG study from Toronto [2] (Table 1.1). This should be combined with known lesion-specific risks as outlined in Table 1.2. There are certain cardiac

Table 1.1 Risk classification of conditions in patients with heart disease

High-risk conditions	Intermediate-risk conditions	Low-risk conditions
Severe systemic ventricular dysfunction (LVEF < 30 % OR NYHA III and IV)	Uncorrected cyanosis, repaired complex CHD	Repaired simple congenital heart disease without residual cardiac dysfunction
Significant pulmonary hypertension	Large left to right shunt	Small left to right shunts
Marfan syndrome with aortic root or aortic valve involvement		
Severe coarctation, aortic or mitral stenosis	Mild to moderate coarctation, aortic or mitral stenosis	Bicuspid aortic valve
	Prosthetic valves	Pulmonic stenosis
	Arrhythmias	Aortic or mitral regurgitation with good ventricular function

From References [1, 3]

Table 1.2

Predictors of maternal cardiovascular events and risk score from the CARPREG study
- Prior cardiac event (heart failure, TIA/CVA or arrhythmia)
- Baseline NYHA functional class > II or cyanosis
- Left heart obstruction (mitral valve area <2 cm2, aortic valve area <1.5 cm2, peak LV outflow tract gradient >30 mmHg by echocardiography)
- Reduced systemic ventricular systolic function (ejection fraction <40 %)

CARPREG risk score: for each predictor that is present, a point is assigned.

Risk of maternal events (arrhythmia requiring treatment, pulmonary edema, stroke, or cardiac death):

0 point	5 %
1 point	27 %
≥2 points	75 %

LV left ventricular; *TIA/CVA* transient ischemic attack/cerebrovascular accident; *NYHA* the New York Heart Association conditions in which the maternal risk of death is unacceptably high (25–50 %) and pregnancy is considered contraindicated [1–3].

- Severe pulmonary artery hypertension (75 % systemic)
- Severe systemic ventricular dysfunction (LVEF <30 %, NYHA III–IV)
- Aortic root dilation (>45 mm in Marfan, >50 mm in bicuspid aortic valve)
- Severe left-sided obstruction (aortic or mitral valve stenosis, coarctation)

A team of specialists with expertise in the cardiac disorders in pregnancy should be involved early and throughout the pregnancy. Intermediate- to high-risk cardiac patients have an increase in obstetric complications as well, including gestational hypertension and preeclampsia, preterm labor, and postpartum hemorrhage. There is also an increased risk of neonatal complications including intrauterine growth restriction and low birth weight, premature delivery, respiratory distress, intraventricular hemorrhage, and death [4].

Based upon outcomes reported in the literature which includes single center experience, registry data in Europe, and prospective studies in Canada, patients can be grouped into high-, intermediate-, and low-risk groups (Table 1.2). For a specific individual, the exact cardiac condition will dictate risk and management. It can be useful to categorize these diseases into groups, which behave similarly and are outlined in Table 1.3. Congenital defects include atrial septal defects, ventricular septal defects, tetralogy of Fallot, transposition of the great arteries, coarctation of the aorta, and several other illnesses; these represent a growing number of patients because of advanced care during childhood, so patients are now surviving into adulthood. Aortic diseases include Marfan syndrome, Ehlers-Danlos syndrome, Turner syndrome, and bicuspid aortic valve. Cardiomyopathies include peripartum and idiopathic. Arrhythmias encompass both tachycardias and bradycardias. Acute coronary syndrome can occur during pregnancy, both from unstable plaques and from dissection. Hypertension can become worse during pregnancy. Thrombosis can occur (both arterial and venous) because of increased hypercoagulability during pregnancy (refer to Heme chapter).

Table 1.3 Cardiovascular diseases with associated risks and management

Condition	Maternal risk	Obstetric and offspring risk	Management
Congenital defects			
Atrial septal defect	Thromboembolism, arrhythmias	Preeclampsia and SGA	Prevention of venous stasis during pregnancy
Ventricular septal defect	Small VSDs have low risk; large defects with pulmonary hypertension is high risk	Preeclampsia, prematurity	Follow-up twice during pregnancy

(continued)

Table 1.3 (continued)

Condition	Maternal risk	Obstetric and offspring risk	Management
Atrioventricular septal defect	Severe valve regurgitation and/or impaired ventricular function should be surgically corrected before pregnancy	Acute heart failure during or just after delivery. Offspring mortality (recurrent complex CHD)	Severe regurgitation or impaired ventricular function should have monthly or bimonthly f/u (with echo)
Coarctation of aorta	Well tolerated after repair. Aortic dissection	Hypertensive disorders and miscarriages	F/u every trimester following systemic blood pressure
Pulmonary valve stenosis/ regurgitation	Well tolerated unless severe: RV failure, arrhythmias	Preeclampsia	F/u every trimester; severe is monthly or bimonthly (including echo) Consider caesarean section
Tetralogy of Fallot	Repaired tolerated well unless RV dysfunction and/or severe PR. Heart failure, arrhythmias, thromboembolism, aortic root dilation	SGA, prematurity, recurrent CHD especially with 22q11 deletion	F/u every trimester, severe PR or RV dysfunction should be monthly
Ebstein anomaly	Well tolerated unless cyanotic or severe regurgitation. Heart failure and arrhythmias especially with WPW	Prematurity, SGA, and fetal mortality associated with cyanosis	F/u every trimester; severe is monthly or bimonthly
Transposition of great arteries after atrial or arterial* switch operation *Limited data	Arrhythmias and heart failure; 10 % irreversible decline in systemic ventricular function	Hypertensive disorders Pulmonary hypertension. Prematurity, SGA, fetal mortality	F/u every month or bimonthly (including echo). Early caesarean for decline in ventricular function
Congenitally corrected transposition of great arteries	Arrhythmias heart failure, 10 % irreversible decline in systemic ventricular function. Contraindicated with NYHA>II or EF<40 %	Hypertension, prematurity, fetal mortality	F/u monthly (including echo and ECG for heart block). Early caesarean for decline in ventricular function
Fontan circulation (for single ventricle)	High risk: atrial arrhythmias and heart failure. Contraindicated in cyanosis (oxygen saturation <85 %), EF<40 % or severe valvular regurgitation	Hypertensive disorders. Prematurity, SGA, and fetal death	F/u monthly (including echo) including postpartum. Consider therapeutic anticoagulation

(continued)

1 Cardiac Disease

Table 1.3 (continued)

Condition	Maternal risk	Obstetric and offspring risk	Management
Aortic disorders			
Marfan syndrome	Aortic root diameter >4 cm associated with dissection 10 % (vs. 1 %). Prepregnancy surgery when aorta is >45 mm	50 % hereditary risk	F/u monthly with echoes. Beta-blockers during pregnancy. Assisted 2nd stage of labor. Aorta>4 cm elective caesarean
Ehlers-Danlos syndrome	Contraindicated in type IV (aortic dissection and uterine rupture)	50 % hereditary risk 15q21 mutation	F/u monthly with echo beta-blockers
Valvular disorders			
Mitral stenosis (rheumatic)	Increase in NYHA class. Severe is poorly tolerated with pulmonary edema, atrial fibrillation, and deaths	Prematurity IUGR and stillbirth	F/u monthly or bimonthly (including echo). Beta-blockade and rest for symptoms. Diuretics for pulmonary edema. Anticoagulation for atrial fibrillation or large atria. Percutaneous mitral valvuloplasty if medical management fails
Aortic stenosis (congenitally bicuspid)	Well tolerated unless severe: heart failure and arrhythmias, aortic dissection with dilated aorta	Hypertension. IUGR, prematurity	Prepregnancy CT/MR imaging of aorta. Severe is monthly or bimonthly f/u and caesarean delivery Percutaneous aortic valvuloplasty if medical management fails or valve replacement after early caesarean section
Mitral/aortic regurgitation	Severe, asymptomatic regurgitation is well tolerated unless reduced ventricular function then: high risk of heart failure		F/u every trimester in mild/moderate, monthly in severe. Blood pressure control and diuresis for heart failure and cardiac surgery if refractory
Tricuspid regurgitation	Well tolerated in isolation If severe regurgitation: arrhythmias		Conservative management
Coronary artery disease			
Coronary artery disease	With good ventricular function well tolerated	Prematurity, fetal death	Ischemic evaluation prepregnancy. Continue ASA and beta-blocker but no statin or ACEI

(continued)

Table 1.3 (continued)

Condition	Maternal risk	Obstetric and offspring risk	Management
Acute myocardial infarction	Mortality between 10 and 20 %, the highest in early postpartum period	Fetal mortality and prematurity (related to maternal mortality)	Most new cases due to coronary dissection diagnosed by cardiac catheterization and treated with stenting or CABG
Cardiomyopathies			
Peripartum cardiomyopathy	Heart failure, ventricular arrhythmias, and sudden cardiac arrest. Over 50 % recover by 6 months. Subsequent pregnancies carries recurrence risk of 30–50 % and is contraindicated if persistent ventricular dysfunction	Prematurity	Diuretics, beta-blockers, no ACEI. If hemodynamically unstable, urgent delivery. Consider anticoagulation for LVEF < 30 % or known thrombus
Dilated cardiomyopathy	High risk in LVEF <40 %: worsening LVEF and heart failure, arrhythmias, death. Contraindicated if LVEF <20 % or class III–IV	Hypertensive disorders. Prematurity, fetal death	Treatment as above for heart failure. Follow-up monthly with trimester echoes
Hypertrophic cardiomyopathy	Increased risk in symptomatic patients and with an outflow tract gradient of >30 mmHg Heart failure and arrhythmias	Hereditary risks in autosomal dominant cases	Beta-blockers. Follow-up monthly with trimester echoes. ICD for high-risk patients. Avoid epidural anesthesia, assisted 2nd stage of labor.
Arrhythmias			
SVT	Well tolerated in structurally normal hearts. Hypotension, heart failure in valvular and congenital heart disease		Abort with vagal maneuvers, adenosine, IV beta-blockers, electrical cardioversion. Prophylaxis, with digoxin and metoprolol first, followed by sotalol, flecainide, or propafenone. Catheter ablation only in special circumstances

(continued)

1 Cardiac Disease

Table 1.3 (continued)

Condition	Maternal risk	Obstetric and offspring risk	Management
Atrial fibrillation/ flutter	Occurs in structurally abnormal hearts or hyperthyroidism causing hypotension, heart failure, and stroke		Rate control digoxin, beta-blockers, and non-dihydropyridine calcium channel antagonists Electrical cardioversion for instability. Full-dose anticoagulation
Ventricular tachycardia	Idiopathic right ventricular outflow tract tachycardia in normal hearts controlled with medications. VT with structural heart disease is associated with increased risk of sudden cardiac death		Unstable: electrical cardioversion. Stable: IV sotalol, procainamide, or amiodarone. Prophylaxis with beta-blockers. ICD implantation for high-risk patients
AV block	Second degree occurs rarely. Isolated congenital complete heart block typically has a favorable outcome		Temporary pacing during delivery in some women with complete heart block and symptoms

Epidemiology

In western countries, cardiovascular disease is a rare complication of pregnancy, but it is the major medical cause of maternal death [5–7]. Whereas maternal mortality from hemorrhage has decreased over time, the proportion due to cardiac causes (cardiomyopathy, myocardial infarction, pulmonary hypertension, aortic dissection) has increased. The number of patients who have or develop cardiac complications in pregnancy has been increasing for a number of potential reasons including delayed childbearing, increased prevalence of cardiovascular risk factors (diabetes, hypertension, obesity), and improved treatment and survival of patients with congenital heart disease. The spectrum of cardiovascular disease complicating pregnancies differs by geography and has also shifted over time. In western countries, congenital heart disease has increased in prevalence (64–82 %), and rheumatic valvular disease decreased, whereas the converse is true elsewhere [2, 6]. Acquired valvular, myocardial disease and arrhythmias make up the next most common disorders.

Pathobiology

Normal Physiologic Changes

Pregnancy is characterized by dramatic and reversible changes in cardiovascular hemodynamics. The normal heart is quite plastic and able to adapt to these alterations, but the diseased heart often does not have adequate reserve and may decompensate with the excess strain imposed. These changes begin early after conception and progress through gestation. Physiologic changes return to near baseline by 6 weeks postpartum, but adaptive, structural changes can take months to normalize [8].

Resting cardiac output increases 30–60 % (i.e., from 3.5 to 6.0 L/min) and begins early in pregnancy. Most of this excess output is delivered to the kidneys, placenta, and skin. There is a significant increase in preload or stroke volume and lesser increase in heart rate and decrease in systemic blood pressure and peripheral resistance [8]. Numerous mediators (including estrogens, prostaglandins, and nitric oxide) contribute to these changes. These changes produce an expected increase in myocardial oxygen demand. Myocardial contractility, when measured by load-independent parameters, appears unchanged. During labor and delivery, uterine contractions create an additional brief increase of cardiac output and blood pressure of 10–20 %. In early postpartum, there can be a further increase in preload and cardiac output due to relief of vena caval compression and autotransfusion from the emptied and contracted uterus [1, 7].

Effect of Pregnancy on the Disease and Disease on the Pregnancy

Given the known hemodynamic changes in pregnancy, one can anticipate how these alterations will affect various disease states. Cardiac conditions that have similar pathophysiologic underpinnings will respond similarly to the increase in preload and heart rate and decrease in afterload. Cardiac lesions which produce volume overload include congenital right to left shunts and acquired valvular regurgitation. The additional volume load of pregnancy is usually well tolerated unless shunt reversal, pulmonary hypertension, or ventricular dysfunction is present. Cardiac lesions which produce pressure overload on the preceding cardiac chamber include valvular stenosis and aortic coarctation. If the obstruction is not severe, these lesions are usually well tolerated. On the other hand, in severe aortic stenosis, syncope can occur from the expected decrease in afterload or heart failure from the increase in volume; patients with severe mitral valve stenosis will predictable worsen from the increase in heart rate and preload. Complex congenital cardiac lesions which produce cyanosis from right to left shunts include tetralogy of Fallot, univentricles, and transposition of the great arteries. These patients are usually corrected or palliated at a young age, and uncorrected patients rarely survive into adulthood.

Patients with completely corrected lesions with good ventricular function can usually tolerate the stress of pregnancy fairly well. Arrhythmias are more common, and these patients require close follow-up [2]. In the rare patient with persistent cyanosis, maternal and fetal outcomes are poor, correlating with maternal hematocrit and arterial pressure of oxygen [9]. In patients with dilated cardiomyopathy, the volume load of pregnancy and increase demands coupled with the inability to take ACE inhibitors usually lead to deterioration in cardiac function and worsening of heart failure symptoms. In patients with hypertrophic cardiomyopathy, the increase in preload and heart rate will cause a predictable worsening of symptoms but rarely decompensation. The hemodynamic burden and structural changes to the vasculature are deleterious to patients with Marfan disorder; the aortic root enlarges, and for those with preexisting aneurysm, the risk of aortic dissection is high (10 %) [1]. Detailed description of specific cardiac disorders with maternal and fetal effects is outlined in Table 1.3.

Diagnosis

Signs and Symptoms

The hemodynamic alterations noted above are reflected in the physical exam, making differentiating pathologic from normal findings more challenging. In general, pregnancy is a hypervolemic, hyperdynamic state mimicking disease states such as hyperthyroidism. Increase cardiac output creates normal systolic ejection flow murmurs; if ≥ 3/6 grade, it should be considered abnormal. Pulses are usually brisk and bounding. Jugular venous distension can be seen late in pregnancy at peak intravascular volume, but waveforms are normal. The diaphragm may be elevated due to the gravid uterus, but lung sounds should be clear. Lower extremity edema is frequently seen, particularly in late pregnancy and with advanced maternal age [1, 7].

Common symptoms in normal pregnancy can mimic cardiovascular disease, and a careful history and physical exam is crucial. Dyspnea is reported in half of women by the second trimester and three-fourths by the third trimester. Importantly, physiologic dyspnea does not progress, or occur at rest or interfere with activities of dialing living (ADLs). Orthopnea and paroxysmal nocturnal dyspnea (PND) are pathologic symptoms and rarely seen in normal pregnancy. If a constellation of signs and symptoms is suggestive of heart failure, then an echocardiogram can quickly and safely exclude peripartum cardiomyopathy. Palpitations are reported throughout gestation and in a structurally normal heart are rarely associated with arrhythmias. Palpitations that are persistent, associated with shortness of breath, chest discomfort, or dizziness, require evaluation. New onset chest pressure or pain, especially that radiates to the arm or jaw or associated with dyspnea, is abnormal and suggestive of coronary ischemia. Particularly in older patients with cardiac risk factors, prompt evaluation is important.

Differential Diagnosis

The differential diagnosis of most cardiac signs and symptoms noted above includes normal physiologic changes. Lower extremity edema if unilateral should raise concern for DVT which has an increased incidence in pregnancy. Similarly, because of the increased hypercoagulable state, pulmonary embolism is more common in pregnancy and should be excluded in patients with acute shortness of breath. Chronic chest pain, particularly if burning, is more likely related to the common occurrence of GERD in pregnancy. Acute, severe chest pain could indicate an aortic dissection particularly in patients with Marfan disease or congenital bicuspid aortic valve, coarctation, and/or aortopathy. Known heart disease should be taken into account when formulating a differential. A careful medical history is crucial in determining the etiology of cardiovascular symptoms. It is important to ask detailed family history including sudden death (especially for those with syncope and palpitations), along with premature myocardial infarction.

Diagnostic Evaluation

A thorough cardiac physical exam is indicated in all patients with new cardiovascular symptoms and should emphasize new onset murmurs (pathologic murmurs are systolic greater than grade 3/6 in intensity and all diastolic murmurs), development of cyanosis, persistent neck vein distension, cardiomegaly, sustained arrhythmia, a fixed split second sound, and left parasternal lift or loud P2 (suggestive of pulmonary hypertension). Echocardiography should be performed in all women who have new and unexplained cardiovascular symptoms. It can safely assess and follow ventricular and valvular function, aortic dimensions, exclude shunts and estimated pulmonary artery pressures. Transesophageal echo is occasionally required to assess for aortic dissection, prosthetic valve function, or endocarditis, and medications for conscious sedation are relatively safe in pregnancy. Cardiac MRI may be used when other imaging data is insufficient, and the data is crucial to care of the mother. Gadolinium may cross the placenta and has not been studied in pregnancy and hence should be avoided. Exercise testing is particularly useful in patients with congenital heart disease, coronary artery disease, and asymptomatic moderate to severe valvular heart disease; ideally this should be done preconception to assess for functional capacity and risks of pregnancy. An exercise test that shows a drop in blood pressure or drop in oxygen saturation can identify those at risk of developing symptoms or complications. Cardiac catheterization can be performed when necessary during pregnancy; however, one should shield the gravid uterus and take care to shorten fluoroscopic time to minimize radiation exposure. Fetal radiation exposure is still well below levels considered teratogenic particularly after organogenesis occurs in the first trimester [1]. Electrophysiology studies (such as those for ablation) or ICD placement is rarely indicated in pregnancy but can be performed with less radiation and more ultrasound guidance if other medical therapies have failed.

Management/Treatment

General considerations for both the mother and fetus are discussed below. For each of the various cardiac lesions, they have been grouped by similar pathophysiologic category with disease-specific recommendations outlined in Table 1.3.

General Maternal Considerations

Ideally, details of a patient's specific cardiac lesion, severity, and its effect on patient functioning should be assessed prior to pregnancy. Imaging, stress testing, and cardiac catheterization are employed to accurately define the extent and effects of the cardiac disorder. The most widely utilized system to characterize a patient's clinical status is the New York Heart Association (NYHA) functional classification (see below).

The New York Heart Association Functional Classification
• Class I: Asymptomatic
• Class II: Symptomatic at greater than normal activity level
• Class III: Symptomatic with normal activity level
• Class IV: Symptomatic at rest

To risk stratify pregnant women with cardiac disease, one should employ the lesion-specific assessment as outlined in Table 1.3, with global risk indices preferably CARPREG or alternatively ZAHARA for congenital lesions alone [2, 10]. In CARPREG, patients with increasing number of high-risk findings have increasing risk of major adverse events from 5 % for those without any to 75 % for those with more than one high-risk predators (see Table 1.1).

For those patients with the highest-risk lesions, in which maternal mortality may be over 20 %, termination of the pregnancy should be advised, and reliable methods to prevent pregnancy should be discussed (see section on prevention). If the patient wishes to continue with the pregnancy, then a carefully coordinated plan with all subspecialties should be discussed and includes antepartum, peripartum, and postpartum phases of care.

General Fetal Considerations

Up to a third of pregnancies of women with heart disease may have adverse fetal and neonatal outcomes. Genetic counseling, preferably preconception, is advised for women with congenital heart disease. Recurrence rates for most congenital cardiac lesions range from 3 to 5 % for first-degree relatives; children born to mother with tetralogy of Fallot carry a 13 % incidence of congenital heart disease, and autosomal dominant conditions such as Marfan syndrome carry a 50 % recurrence rate [1].

Fetal echocardiography can identify and characterize possible anomalies in utero. Infants of mothers with heart disease are more likely to be growth restricted and premature as well. General measures such as folic acid supplementation and immunization against rubella for susceptible individuals should commence several months prior to pregnancy. Reducing other known obstetric risk factors such as smoking or multiple gestations in the case of IVF may improve neonatal outcomes [4].

Antepartum Management

Antepartum surveillance is particularly important in preventing, identifying, and treating maternal complications in those who have cardiovascular disease. The key to safe pregnancy care in the patient with cardiovascular disease begins with prenatal assessment: a careful obstetric and cardiac history along with physical exam, laboratory assessment with hemoglobin and platelet count and specific cardiac testing (including electrocardiography, echocardiography, exercise testing) as indicated. Evaluation and treatment that include radiation (such as cardiac catheterization) or cardiopulmonary bypass surgery (for valve repair or replacement) can be performed if necessary for maternal well-being but optimally should be done before pregnancy to improve maternal and fetal outcomes [1, 3, 7].

The frequency and testing required for prenatal visits should be tailored to the specific patient and condition. For those who are at the highest risk for complications, prenatal visits with thorough history and physical examination to detect deterioration early may need to be every two weeks, with weekly visits after 32 weeks gestation. Echocardiograms should be performed for any significant worsening of symptoms and functional class as well as for regular monitoring of ventricular and valvular function to capture changes early. Patients with poor or worsening functional class (i.e., NYHA III/IV) as well as those with significant pulmonary hypertension may require inpatient admission during the mid-second trimester for the duration of the pregnancy and delivery in a critical care setting.

Fetal cardiac anomalies are best characterized by echocardiography at 18–22 weeks gestation though a few centers have reported screening for major anomalies sooner. Smoking cessation, correction of maternal anemia, and rest should be pursued to minimize the risks of intrauterine growth restriction and preterm birth. If the mother has cyanotic heart disease or pulmonary hypertension, reducing maternal activity along with oxygen therapy may lessen fetal growth restriction and preterm births. In the 3rd trimester, serial noninvasive biophysical testing of the fetus can detect hypoxemia and compromise early. The frequency of testing, one to two times per week, depends on the maternal cardiac condition and initial fetal findings. If preterm birth is anticipated, antenatal corticosteroids should be given prior to 32–34 weeks.

One special consideration is for women with mechanical heart valves. These patients are at increased risk for valve dysfunction, thromboembolism, and death (5–10 %). As per ACCP guidelines, patients with mechanical heart valves should have anticoagulant regimen and require close monitoring of efficacy [1, 11, 12]. The following regimens are acceptable and should be discussed with patients:

- Adjusted dose LMWH two times a day throughout pregnancy (goal anti-Xa level 4–6 h post-dose, 0.8–1.2 U/ml)
- Adjusted dose UFH every 12 h (goal aPTT ≥ 2× control)
- UFH or LMWH as above until the 13th week with substitution by vitamin K antagonists until close to delivery when UFH or LMWH is resumed
- If concerns exist about efficacy/safety of the above with very high risk of thromboembolism, vitamin K antagonists throughout pregnancy with replacement by UFH or LMWH close to delivery

Peripartum Management During Labor and Delivery

In the pregnant patient with cardiovascular disease, labor and delivery pose an additional stress on the heart which should be mitigated with optimal management. Spontaneous vaginal delivery is tolerated in most patients and is associated with less blood loss, infection, and venous thrombosis. Caesarean section should be reserved for obstetric indications [1, 7]. For those with left ventricular outflow obstruction or aortic disease, an assisted 2nd stage of labor may reduce Valsalva and stress on the heart. A planned, early caesarean delivery may be needed in those patients with deteriorating cardiac function and symptoms refractory to medical management (such as in congestive heart failure). In high-risk patients, elective induction is often advocated so that a team of specialists can be available for management of peripartum complications.

Patients with known arrhythmias can be monitored with telemetry. Treatment for arrhythmias is similar to that in the nonpregnant state and should not be withheld due to pregnancy, including adherence to ACLS protocols. In those with intracardiac shunts, air filters are placed in intravenous lines to prevent paradoxical air emboli. Invasive hemodynamic monitoring is rarely indicated except in the highest-risk patients for whom rapid correction of changes can be lifesaving. Arterial pressure monitoring is appropriate for severe aortic stenosis, pulmonary artery hypertension particularly with Eisenmenger syndrome, and large, bidirectional shunts. In those patients, epidural anesthetics and maternal systemic hypotension should be avoided. Swan-Ganz catheterization may be beneficial in severe aortic/mitral stenosis, NYHA class III–IV status, and significant ventricular dysfunction. When invasive monitoring is indicated, the volume shifts, and increased hemodynamic risks necessitate monitoring for at least 24–48 h postpartum in an intensive care setting.

Congestive heart failure also presents issues during labor, particularly because of the increase in maternal cardiac output during uterine contractions. Labor should proceed in the left lateral position. Carefully titrated epidural anesthesia is required for impaired ventricular function or poor NYHA status. Again, maternal expulsive efforts should be minimized in the second stage of delivery. The largest increase in cardiac output occurs during the period immediately after delivery, and hence, patients should be monitored closely in the first 24–48 h.

If the patient is receiving anticoagulation, delivery may need to be timed such that unfractionated heparin is stopped 4 to 6 h prior to induction of labor, caesarean delivery, and/or regional anesthesia, so that coagulation profiles have normalized [1, 11, 12]. In terms of antibiotic prophylaxis for infective endocarditis, there has been a lack of evidence of benefit and is therefore not recommended during vaginal or caesarean delivery.

Prevention

As discussed, several cardiac conditions confer significant morbidity and mortality risk to both mother and fetus, and in those cases, pregnancy should be discouraged (Table 1.2). However, in the majority of other cases, pregnancy is tolerated well, and these patients can be cautioned but reassured. Options for contraception include barrier methods, hormonal contraception, and sterilization. In those patients with high-risk lesions, a combination of barrier methods and hormonal contraception can be considered. All estrogen-containing contraceptives carry the risk of thrombosis, and caution should be exercised in patients with mechanical heart valves or cyanotic heart lesions (due to paradoxical embolism). Progestin-only contraceptives can be useful in these patients. Intrauterine devices (IUD) can be used, but should be used in caution in those with arrhythmias (due to reports of arrhythmias during insertion), with shunts (vagal response can occur during insertion), and with prosthetic material or valves who are at high risk of developing bacterial endocarditis (due to higher risk of bacteremia during placement) [1].

Postpartum Recommendations

Maternal and fetal outcome/general prognosis can be linked to NYHA functional status. For example, maternal mortality may be as high as 7 % when classes III and IV are combined, while classes I and II combined yield a mortality of 0.5 %. Likewise, fetal mortality may be as a high as 30 % in classes III and IV patients, in contrast to 2 % for classes I and II [2, 6, 9]. In addition to focusing on maternal functional status, it is also useful to consider several factors, including the type of cardiac abnormality, previous corrective surgery/procedure, other risk factors, and the heredity of the cardiac lesions in newborns.

In those situations where maternal mortality risks are significant, appropriate counseling and social support for the pregnant woman and her family is critical, including frank discussions about who will be involved in the care of the child should maternal demise occur.

References

1. Regitz-Zagrosek V, Blomstrom Lundqvist C, Borghi C, et al. ESC guidelines on the management of cardiovascular diseases during pregnancy: the task force on the management of cardiovascular diseases during pregnancy of the European society of cardiology. Eur Heart J. 2011; 32:3147–97.
2. Siu S, Sermer M, Colman JM, et al. Prospective multicenter study of pregnancy outcomes in women with heart disease. Circulation. 2001;104:515–21.
3. Bonow RO, Carabello BA, Chatterjee K, et al. ACC/AHA 2006 guidelines for the management of patients with valvular heart disease. J Am Coll Cardiol. 2006;146:e1–146.
4. Siu SC, Colman JM, Sorensen S, et al. Adverse neonatal and cardiac outcomes are more common in pregnant women with cardiac disease. Circulation. 2002;105:2179–84.
5. CEMACH. CEMACH Saving Mothers' Lives: Reviewing Maternal Deaths to Make Motherhood safer—2003–2005: The Seventh Report on Confidential Enquiries into Maternal Deaths in the United Kingdom. London: Centre for Maternal and Child Enquiries; 2008.
6. Roos-Hesselink JW, Ruys TPW, Stein JI, et al. Outcome of pregnancy in patients with structural or ischemic heart disease: results of registry of the European society of Cardiology. Eur Heart J. 2013;34(9):657–65.
7. Simpson LL. Maternal cardiac disease: update for the clinician. Obstet Gynecol. 2012;119: 345–59.
8. Poppas A, Shroff SG, Korcarz C, Hibbard J, Berger D, Lindheimer M, Lang RM. Serial assessment of the cardiovascular system in normal pregnancy: role of arterial compliance and pulsatile arterial load. Circulation. 1997;95(10):2407–15.
9. Drenthen W, Pieper PG, Roos-Hesselink JW, et al. Outcome of pregnancy in women with congenital heart disease. J Am Coll Cardiol. 2007;49:2303–11.
10. Drenthen W, Boersma E, Balci A, Moons P, Roos-Hesselink JW, Mulder BJ, Vliegen HW, van Dijk AP, Voors AA, Yap SC, van Veldhuisen DJ, Pieper PG. Predictors of pregnancy complications in women with congenital heart disease. Eur Heart J. 2010;31:2124–32.
11. Bates Sm, Greer IA, Middeldorp S et al. VTE, thrombophilia, antithrombotic therapy and pregnancy Antithrombotic and thrombolytic therapy ACCP Evidence-based Clinical Practice Guidelines (9th edition). Chest. 2012;141:e691s-736s
12. Elkayam U, Bitar F. Valvular heart disease and pregnancy: prosthetic valves. J Am Coll Cardiol. 2005;46:403–10.

Part II
Critical Care

Chapter 2
Management Principles of the Critically Ill Obstetric Patient

Elie Zouein and Ghada Bourjeily

Pregnant women constitute a small percentage of admissions to the intensive care units in most institutions. However, given the profound physiologic changes of pregnancy, these women present a challenge for most practitioners. Pregnancy physiology is discussed in the context of the various interventions described below. This chapter will review basic interventions in the ICU to help the clinician manage this unique population.

Pregnancy Physiology

Many anatomical and physiological changes occur during pregnancy that impact the management of critically ill gravidas.

E. Zouein, M.D. (✉)
Department of Medicine, Respiratory Intensive Care Unit,
Rhode Island Hospital, 593 Eddy Street,
Providence, RI 02903, USA
e-mail: ezouein@lifespan.org

G. Bourjeily, M.D.
Pulmonary, Critical Care and Medicine, Women's Medicine Collaborative,
The Miriam Hospital, 146 West River Street, Providence, RI 02904, USA

The Warren Alpert Medical School of Brown University, Providence, RI, USA
e-mail: Ghada_bourjeily@brown.edu

Respiratory Changes

Both the anteroposterior and the transverse diameters of the chest increase in pregnancy, and the diaphragm moves upward by about 4 cm [1]. Enlargement of the breasts may affect chest compliance and the ease of intubation [2]. The increase in blood and interstitial fluid volume is responsible for the development of mucosal edema especially in the oropharyngeal and laryngeal structures reducing the airway diameter. Hyperemia, which is possibly related to hormonal changes and the increase in plasma volume, makes the mucosa friable and prone to bleeding with minimal trauma. This increased friability may then compromise the visualization of the upper airway landmarks. Longitudinal upper airway assessment with Mallampati grading system suggests that airways become less patent with pregnancy progression (Pilkington). In addition, Mallampati grades I–II may progress to III–IV during labor and do not return to pre-labor grades for an additional 12 h [2].

During pregnancy, oxygen consumption is increased by 30–60 % [2]. There is a 20 % decline in functional residual capacity by term. An additional drop of nearly 25 % may be observed in the supine position [2]. The increase in oxygen consumption and the reduction in functional residual capacity in the supine position contribute to decreased oxygen reserve and lead to faster desaturations in response to apnea. A study by Choi et al. has shown that compared to nonpregnant controls and following sedation and the use of paralytics, pregnant women have a significantly faster decline in oxygenation and increase in PaCO2 in response to induced apneas [3]. Thus, intubation protocols should be modified in pregnant women to account for these changes.

Cardiovascular Changes

Pregnancy is associated with profound hemodynamic changes that prepare gravidas for the blood loss that is anticipated during delivery. Blood volume increases by 40–52 % by the end of gestation [4, 5]. This increase begins as early as 6 weeks gestation, peaks in the late second trimester, and then plateaus. Blood volume in pregnancy varies but is generally 1,200–1,600 ml greater than in a nonpregnant individual [6]. The rise in blood volume results from an expansion of erythrocytes as well as significant rise in plasma volume. The latter is due to an increase in sodium and water retention related to enhanced renin-angiotensin-aldosterone system activity, and an increase in the hepatic production of renin related to the hyperestrogenic state of pregnancy [1]. The disproportionate increase in red blood cells to plasma volume results in a physiologic anemia of pregnancy [7].

Heart rate increases by 10–20 % during gestation, but this increase usually occurs in the latter part of pregnancy. Cardiac output (CO) starts rising in the first trimester, peaking by the end of the second trimester [8, 9], and may be as high as 50 % above prepregnancy values. This rise is more pronounced in twin, compared to singleton pregnancies. The rise in CO is caused by a significant increase in preload and stroke volume in the early part of gestation. CO is then maintained in the second half of pregnancy primarily by an increase in heart rate. Nearly 17 % of cardiac output is directed to the uterine arteries to supply a flow of 500 ml/min to the placenta and the growing fetus. Both central venous and pulmonary capillary wedge pressure are unchanged in pregnancy.

Systemic vascular resistance falls early in pregnancy as a result of vasodilation in response to hormonal stimulation [10]. Despite an increase in cardiac output, the end result is a fall in blood pressure (BP) in the first trimester. Diastolic blood pressure falls are more pronounced than systolic blood pressure changes and result in a widened pulse pressure. Mean BP decreases by 10–15 mm Hg starting in the first trimester with a nadir in BP occurring at approximately 24–28 weeks [11]. Similar changes occur in the pulmonary circulation, leading to unchanged pulmonary pressures despite the increase in cardiac output.

Plasma colloid osmotic pressure (COP) falls during normal pregnancy from 23.2 mm Hg in the first trimester to 21.1 mmHg at term [12] to 16 mm after delivery and that fall is even more pronounced in PEC [13]. This drop in colloid osmotic pressure not only contributes to the development of pulmonary edema even in the absence of elevated hydrostatic pressures but also contributes to its higher incidence in the postpartum, compared to the antenatal period.

Aortocaval compression caused by the gravid uterus in the supine position may result in decreased venous return, reduced filling of the right heart cavities resulting in maternal hypotension and potential for uteroplacental insufficiency in women with tenuous intravascular status [2]. Combining these changes with the increased oxygen consumption observed in pregnancy and labor and delivery, the decrease in FRC in the supine position and limited oxygen reserve and the reduction in cardiac output in the supine position may all compromise placental perfusion in susceptible individuals [1].

Gastrointestinal Changes

Gastrointestinal physiologic changes occurring in pregnancy and around labor and delivery complicate airway intubation further. A generalized slowing of the gastrointestinal tract function occurs in pregnancy due to the effect of progesterone on smooth muscles. Lower esophageal sphincter tone is reduced with a subsequent increase of acid reflux frequency [14]. During labor, gastric emptying is slower [2]. The gravid uterus compresses the duodenum and the stomach increasing the chances of regurgitation. When opioids are administered during labor or added to the epidural analgesia, gastric emptying is further delayed, but the use of local anesthetics in epidural analgesia alone has no effect [2].

Airway Management

Airway management in pregnancy remains a true challenging task, and pregnant women are eight times more at risk for tracheal intubation failure than the general surgical population. In addition to the usual indications for airway intubation that are relevant for the nonpregnant population, airway intubation in pregnancy may need to be performed when regional anesthesia around delivery fails or is contraindicated in cases such as sepsis, local infection at the site, coagulopathy, or spine abnormalities [2].

As in the nonpregnant population, predicting a difficult intubation or anesthesia complications requires the evaluation of several criteria. These criteria include Mallampati or modified Mallampati score, receding mandible, protruding upper incisors, and a short neck. Part of this assessment may be affected by pregnancy physiology. The physiological and anatomical changes related to pregnancy contribute to complications with sedation or rapid sequence induction procedures, reduction in upper airway size and gastrointestinal changes that may predispose to a higher risk of aspiration. The risk is further augmented by the urgency of certain obstetric interventions. The presence of comorbid conditions such as obesity or preeclampsia may also increase the risk of difficult airway management. In addition, the huge reduction in general anesthesia practice and the shift toward the safer locoregional methods in obstetric populations implicate a major reduction in teaching this technique to the younger generations of obstetric anesthesiologists, possibly impacting the level of comfort and competency in performing this intervention [1].

Thus, to limit the complications of difficult airway management, it would be reasonable to use regional anesthesia when appropriate but to also adopt a thorough and repeated evaluation of the upper airway in pregnant women and access the most experience provider for intubation.

Pathological Conditions Associated with Increased Risk of Difficult Airway Management in Pregnancy

Obesity

Obesity is a major issue in the modern world and has reached heights of an epidemic in certain developed countries. Despite efforts to reduce obesity, women of reproductive age and pregnant women are no exception [1]. Obesity is associated with numerous pregnancy-related complications, including anesthesia-related complications. Obesity is a risk factor for difficult intubation in the general as well as in obstetric population: a BMI > 26 kg/m^2 is by itself a risk factor for difficult mask ventilation [1]. Morbidly obese parturients have a higher incidence of cesarean delivery necessitating anesthetic intervention [2].

Preeclampsia and Eclampsia

Preeclamptic parturients have narrowed upper airways secondary to soft tissue swelling. This is well observed in sitting and supine position [15, 16]. Neck, facial, and tongue edema may be cues for possible difficult airway. Moreover, thrombocytopenia in the settings of preeclampsia constitutes a major risk since it shifts the choice from regional to general anesthesia in the case of an operative delivery. In addition, the risk of bleeding during airway intubation is higher with thrombocytopenia which may significantly impact visualization of the upper airway landmarks and complicate airway intubation further.

Preoperative Evaluation of Airways in Obstetrics

Identification of patients who may require airway intubation is a joint responsibility of the anesthesiologist and the obstetrician. In these situations, early planning of anesthetic management can be initiated. Many findings on physical exam may help in predicting difficult airway management including a Mallampati grade above II, a mouth opening less than 3.5 cm, a thyroid-chin distance less than 6.5 cm, and a sternum-chin distance less than 13.5 cm [1]. In addition, cervical spine and mandibular mobility need to be assessed.

Patients considered at an intermediate to high risk should have a comprehensive discussion of their analgesia options as well as alternate plans after failed intubation, if general anesthesia is required.

Management Steps

In summary, key points in airway management of pregnant women include airway assessment prior to intubation even in urgent situations; aspiration precautions such as elevation of the head of the bed, cricoid pressure, and possibly administration of citric acid/sodium citrate; smaller endotracheal tube size may be necessary; and lower doses of sedatives and anesthetics may be needed.

Although preoxygenation is a necessary step, care should be taken with manual ventilation to avoid the risk of aspiration. In patients who are hemodynamically compromised, the gravida may need to be placed in a supine position with a left-sided tilt to relieve inferior vena cava obstruction and improve cardiac output and organ perfusion. The tilt may be achieved by using the Cardiff wedge or the human wedge [17] or simply by using a manual uterine displacement.

Given the potential difficulties in airway management in pregnant women, the provider most experienced in airway management should be performing airway intubation. A difficult airway cart should be available. Laryngeal mask airway (LMA) is the first option in the difficult to intubate patient.

Hemodynamic Monitoring

Not surprisingly, pregnant women have been excluded from many critical care trials. Hence, many of the data are based on either pregnancy-specific disorders or on expert opinion and logical decisions informed by pregnancy physiology. Indications for hemodynamic monitoring in obstetrics are similar to the non-obstetric population but also include some pregnancy-specific disorders such as severe preeclampsia with refractory hypertension or severe cardiovascular collapse such as in the setting of an acute amniotic fluid embolism. Other indications in obstetrics include structural heart disease with a potential for decompensation during labor and delivery. Indications for hemodynamic monitoring in adult respiratory distress syndrome (ARDS) or septic shock are unchanged in pregnancy compared to the nonpregnant population. In general, conditions requiring hemodynamic monitoring in pregnancy are uncommon. However, when they do occur, interpretation of hemodynamic data requires a good understanding of the physiologic changes associated with pregnancy.

Noninvasive Monitoring

Echocardiography and urinary diagnostic indices are noninvasive monitoring methods that have been evaluated in obstetric patients in small studies. A high correlation between echocardiography and invasive techniques has been seen in the measurement of cardiac output [18, 19], stroke volume, ventricular filling pressure, and pulmonary artery pressures [18] in obstetric patients. In a study of 14 obstetric patients with refractory hypertension and oliguria, the authors reported that 12 of the reported cases were successfully managed without the need for invasive monitoring suggesting that echocardiography may be an effective alternative to pulmonary artery catheterization in pregnancy [20]. In a study evaluating seven oliguric preeclamptic patients [21], urinary indices of volume status including fractional excretion of sodium and urine sodium were inconsistent with findings on pulmonary catheterization. These data suggest that urinary indices alone may be misleading in guiding fluid management in preeclamptic patients. Given the increased hydrostatic pressure, lowered oncotic pressure, and capillary leak associated with preeclampsia, these patients are at very high risk for pulmonary edema.

Invasive Monitoring

The value of the pulmonary artery catheter (PAC) in critically ill patients has been debated for decades, and recent trials have not demonstrated a clear benefit [22]. Data in pregnancy are scarce. Although there are a few studies evaluating the hemodynamic profiles of preeclamptic women [23], there are no randomized controlled trials evaluating the clinical usefulness of pulmonary artery catheters in pregnancy in general. Available data suggest a modest correlation between central venous pressures (CVP) and pulmonary capillary wedge pressure (PCWP) in untreated patients with preeclampsia. This is not true, however, in hypertensive patients that have undergone an intervention such as IV fluids or vasoactive agents, and wide variations in the range of the PCWP-CVP gradient have been reported in treated patients [24–26]. It is possible that this poor correlation following therapy is due to a delay in equilibration of intravascular fluid, with PCWP rising before CVP. These data suggest that although CVP may be an acceptable initial diagnostic tool in hypertensive gravidas, it may be less reliable in monitoring the hemodynamic status following therapeutic interventions.

Vasopressors

Etiologies of hemodynamic compromise in pregnancy are similar to those observed in the general population and include hemorrhage, infection and sepsis, or cardiogenic shock. However, circulatory collapse related to regional anesthesia is the most common cause in the pregnant population.

The overall principles of management of shock in the obstetric population should not differ much from the general population; however, it should take into consideration the physiology of pregnancy. Identifying pregnant patients in shock may be challenging as early signs of shock such as tachycardia and reduced blood pressure may also be observed in normal pregnancies. Changes in these measurements over time may be more helpful clues. One of the mainstays of the management of critically ill gravidas is maintaining adequate tissue perfusion and oxygenation of both the mother and the fetus. Placental blood flow is proportional to uterine blood flow. The latter is dependent on uterine perfusion pressure which is directly proportional to the maternal systemic blood pressure and cardiac output. Moreover, as uterine blood flow is at its maximal capacity under normal conditions, it is unable to adapt to low perfusion states.

Given the significant improvement in outcomes of sepsis with early goal-directed therapy, it would be reasonable to assume that similar interventions should be applied in pregnant women. However, it is not clear whether the same parameters should be used in pregnancy as in the nonpregnant population and whether this intervention truly improves outcomes in pregnant women. Until further data are available, it would be reasonable to intervene the same way, with some caveats. As discussed above, in the second trimester and beyond, the gravid uterus can hinder venous return and up to 25 % reduction in cardiac output by means of aortocaval compression. Hence, the first steps in the management of pregnant women with circulatory collapse should start by placing gravidas in a left lateral decubitus position which has been shown to improve cardiac output significantly [17]. Although fluid resuscitation is the first step in managing hemodynamic instability, the lower oncotic pressures associated with pregnancy and the tendency of pregnant and postpartum women to develop pulmonary edema at lower hydrostatic pressures should be considered. Therefore, careful monitoring should be performed in pregnant women being resuscitated with intravenous fluids. Despite the lower physiologic oncotic pressures, it is unclear whether pregnant women would benefit from being resuscitated with colloids as opposed to crystalloids.

In cases of severe hemodynamic compromise, where the patient remains unresponsive to volume repletion, vasopressors may be necessary to optimize the hemodynamic status. Owing to their potential to decrease uterine perfusion, the choice of vasoactive agents in pregnancy is important. However, the effect of these drugs on placental perfusion may not be an important factor in decision making since withholding such therapy will lead to persistence of severely low blood pressure, which will likely affect maternal morbidity and mortality and guarantee poor placental perfusion [27]. The optimal drug would be one with the least negative effect on placental perfusion but with equal or superior benefit to systemic pressures. There is a paucity of evidence about the optimal vasopressor in obstetric patients. The majority of data originate from animal studies as the majority of human studies have been performed in the setting of hypotension caused by regional anesthesia around labor and delivery. While these data are helpful, they are limited by the fact that cardiovascular physiology is different depending on the type of shock. Therefore, we may not be able to extrapolate data related to regional anesthesia to sepsis, for instance, or cardiogenic shock.

Dopamine is a dopaminergic, alpha-1 and beta-1 agonist. The action of this drug on these receptors is dose dependent. Multiple animal studies show that dopamine reduces uterine artery blood flow in pregnant baboons and sheep [28–30]. No studies looked at the possibility of fetal toxicity in humans, but cardiac abnormalities were reported in some animal studies [31, 32]. Though prolactin release is inhibited by dopamine [33], it is not clear whether exogenous dopamine impacts lactation significantly.

Dobutamine is mainly a beta-1 and beta-2 agonist. Though dobutamine use has been reported in human pregnancies following myocardial infarction or cardiopulmonary bypass [34, 35], there are no human studies looking its effect on placental perfusion. Based on experimental animal studies, dobutamine is not expected to increase the risk of congenital abnormalities.

Epinephrine is an alpha-1 and beta-1 and to a lesser extent a beta-2 agonist. The drug has been known to interfere with embryo development, likely through hemodynamic effects [36]. Epinephrine produced increased uterine activity and uterine vasoconstriction associated with impaired fetal gas exchange in monkeys [37]. In addition due to its beta-2 activity, epinephrine may induce uterine relaxation delaying the progression of labor. *Norepinephrine* is an alpha-1 and beta-1 agonist. No reproductive animal studies are available. The drug crosses the placenta, and thus its use in pregnancy may affect the fetus [38, 39]. Phenylephrine is a pure alpha-1 agonist. This drug is commonly used to treat maternal hypotension induced by spinal or epidural anesthesia during C-section. The use of this drug was not clearly associated with increased fetal risks, despite reports of small increase in unusual birth defects in the Collaborative Perinatal Project which included more than 4,000 women exposed to this agent during pregnancy. *Ephedrine* stimulates the release of norepinephrine, but this drug is less potent than norepinephrine. It is also used at delivery for the prevention and/or treatment of maternal hypotension associated with spinal anesthesia during C-section. Though it has comparable effect on blood pressure to phenylephrine, ephedrine is associated with a higher incidence of elevated heart rate, maternal nausea, and vomiting [40]. Both drugs are associated with reduced fetal pH, but neonatal Apgar scores and the incidence of fetal acidosis defined as umbilical arterial pH <7.2 were better in women treated with phenylephrine [40].

Vasopressin is a direct vasoconstrictor without inotropic or chronotropic activity. No animal reproductive studies were conducted. Based on animal data, the drug can produce necrosis of embryonic extremities through vasoconstriction [41, 42]. This drug may be helpful in cases of severe acidosis where other agents may be ineffective. It is not clear whether higher doses of this drug need to be used in pregnant women given possible increased metabolism by the placenta-secreted enzyme vasopressinase. However, recent recommendations by the American Heart Association [43] do not suggest dose modification in pregnancy.

Based on the above data, when faced with persistent hypotension after adequate fluid resuscitation, phenylephrine and ephedrine have the best effect on placental perfusion judged by their effect on fetal acidosis during pregnancy. However, if another drug is thought to have superior effects on outcomes in a given context, that drug should be chosen instead of phenylephrine and ephedrine.

In summary, management of critically ill pregnant women may be challenging. However, a thorough understanding of pregnancy physiology can help clinicians make informed decisions in the absence of evidence-based guidelines to help direct the care. Multidisciplinary approaches to this complex and unique population would likely yield the best outcomes.

References

1. Boutonnet M, Faitot V, Keita H. Airway management in obstetrics. Ann Fr Anesth Reanim. 2011;30:651–64.
2. Dennehy KC, Pian-Smith MC. Airway management of the parturient. Int Anesthesiol Clin. 2000;38:147–59.
3. Cheun JK, Choi KT. Arterial oxygen desaturation rate following obstructive apnea in parturients. J Korean Med Sci. 1992;7:6–10.
4. Elkus R, Popovich Jr J. Respiratory physiology in pregnancy. Clin Chest Med. 1992;13: 555–65.
5. Hytten F. Blood volume changes in normal pregnancy. Clin Haematol. 1985;14:601–12.
6. Pritchard JA. Changes in the blood volume during pregnancy and delivery. Anesthesiology. 1965;26:393–9.
7. Lund CJ, Donovan JC. Blood volume during pregnancy. Significance of plasma and red cell volumes. Am J Obstet Gynecol. 1967;98:394–403.
8. Clark SL, Cotton DB, Lee W, et al. Central hemodynamic assessment of normal term pregnancy. Am J Obstet Gynecol. 1989;161:1439–42.

9. Katz R, Karliner JS, Resnik R. Effects of a natural volume overload state (pregnancy) on left ventricular performance in normal human subjects. Circulation. 1978;58:434–41.
10. Clapp 3rd JF, Seaward BL, Sleamaker RH, Hiser J. Maternal physiologic adaptations to early human pregnancy. Am J Obstet Gynecol. 1988;159:1456–60.
11. Moutquin JM, Rainville C, Giroux L, et al. A prospective study of blood pressure in pregnancy: prediction of preeclampsia. Am J Obstet Gynecol. 1985;151:191–6.
12. Oian P, Maltau JM. Transcapillary forces in normal pregnant women. Acta Med Scand Suppl. 1985;693:19–22.
13. Benedetti TJ, Starzyk P, Frost F. Maternal deaths in Washington state. Obstet Gynecol. 1985;66:99–101.
14. Habr F, Raker C, Lin CL, Zouein E, Bourjeily G. Predictors of gastroesophageal reflux symptoms in pregnant women screened for sleep disordered breathing: a secondary analysis. Clin Res Hepatol Gastroenterol. 2013;37:93–9.
15. Izci B, Riha RL, Martin SE, et al. The upper airway in pregnancy and pre-eclampsia. Am J Respir Crit Care Med. 2003;167:137–40.
16. Izci B, Vennelle M, Liston WA, Dundas KC, Calder AA, Douglas NJ. Sleep-disordered breathing and upper airway size in pregnancy and post-partum. Eur Respir J. 2006;27:321–7.
17. Ramsay G, Paglia M, Bourjeily G. When the heart stops: a review of cardiac arrest in pregnancy. J Intensive Care Med. 2013;28(4):204–14.
18. Belfort MA, Rokey R, Saade GR, Moise Jr KJ. Rapid echocardiographic assessment of left and right heart hemodynamics in critically ill obstetric patients. Am J Obstet Gynecol. 1994;171:884–92.
19. Easterling TR, Watts DH, Schmucker BC, Benedetti TJ. Measurement of cardiac output during pregnancy: validation of Doppler technique and clinical observations in preeclampsia. Obstet Gynecol. 1987;69:845–50.
20. Belfort MA, Mares A, Saade G, Wen T, Rokey R. Two-dimensional echocardiography and Doppler ultrasound in managing obstetric patients. Obstet Gynecol. 1997;90:326–30.
21. Lee W, Gonik B, Cotton DB. Urinary diagnostic indices in preeclampsia-associated oliguria: correlation with invasive hemodynamic monitoring. Am J Obstet Gynecol. 1987;156:100–3.
22. Sandham JD, Hull RD, Brant RF, et al. A randomized, controlled trial of the use of pulmonary-artery catheters in high-risk surgical patients. N Engl J Med. 2003;348:5–14.
23. Young P, Johanson R. Haemodynamic, invasive and echocardiographic monitoring in the hypertensive parturient. Best Pract Res Clin Obstet Gynaecol. 2001;15:605–22.
24. Bolte AC, Dekker GA, van Eyck J, van Schijndel RS, van Geijn HP. Lack of agreement between central venous pressure and pulmonary capillary wedge pressure in preeclampsia. Hypertens Pregnancy. 2000;19:261–71.
25. Cotton DB, Lee W, Huhta JC, Dorman KF. Hemodynamic profile of severe pregnancy-induced hypertension. Am J Obstet Gynecol. 1988;158:523–9.
26. Wallenburg HC. Invasive hemodynamic monitoring in pregnancy. Eur J Obstet Gynecol Reprod Biol. 1991;42 Suppl: S45–51.
27. Miller M, Bourjeily G. Management of the critically ill pregnant patient. Volume 23 (Lession 8). Pulmonary and Critical Care Update (PCCSU) [Internet]. April 2009.
28. Callender K, Levinson G, Shnider SM, Feduska NJ, Biehl DR, Ring G. Dopamine administration in the normotensive pregnant ewe. Obstet Gynecol. 1978;51:586–9.
29. Fishburne Jr JI, Dormer KJ, Payne GG, Gill PS, Ashrafzadeh AR, Rossavik IK. Effects of amrinone and dopamine on uterine blood flow and vascular responses in the gravid baboon. Am J Obstet Gynecol. 1988;158:829–37.
30. Rolbin SH, Levinson G, Shnider SM, Biehl DR, Wright RG. Dopamine treatment of spinal hypotension decreases uterine blood flow in the pregnant ewe. Anesthesiology. 1979;51:37–40.
31. Borkowf A, Kolesari GL. Uptake and blood pressure studies in the chick embryo following treatment with a teratogenic dose of dopamine. Teratology. 1986;34:97–102.
32. Kuhlmann RS, Kolesari GL, Kalbfleisch JH. Reduction of catecholamine-induced cardiovascular malformations in the chick embryo with metoprolol. Teratology. 1983;28:9–14.

33. Petraglia F, De Leo V, Sardelli S, et al. Prolactin changes after administration of agonist and antagonist dopaminergic drugs in puerperal women. Gynecol Obstet Invest. 1987;23:103–9.
34. Stokes IM, Evans J, Stone M. Myocardial infarction and cardiac arrest in the second trimester followed by assisted vaginal delivery under epidural analgesia at 38 weeks gestation. Case report. Br J Obstet Gynaecol. 1984;91:197–8.
35. Strickland RA, Oliver Jr WC, Chantigian RC, Ney JA, Danielson GK. Anesthesia, cardiopulmonary bypass, and the pregnant patient. Mayo Clin Proc. 1991;66:411–29.
36. Jost A. Degeneration of the extremities of the rat fetus induced by adrenaline. C R Hebd Seances Acad Sci. 1953;236:1510–2.
37. Adamsons K, Mueller-Heubach E, Myers RE. Production of fetal asphyxia in the rhesus monkey by administration of catecholamines to the mother. Am J Obstet Gynecol. 1971;109: 248–62.
38. Minzter BH, Johnson RF, Paschall RL, Ramasubramanian R, Ayers GD, Downing JW. The diverse effects of vasopressors on the fetoplacental circulation of the dual perfused human placenta. Anesth Analg. 2010;110:857–62.
39. Wang L, Zhang W, Zhao Y. The study of maternal and fetal plasma catecholamines levels during pregnancy and delivery. J Perinat Med. 1999;27:195–8.
40. Lee A, Ngan Kee WD, Gin T. A quantitative, systematic review of randomized controlled trials of ephedrine versus phenylephrine for the management of hypotension during spinal anesthesia for cesarean delivery. Anesth Analg. 2002;94:920–6 (table of contents).
41. Davies J, Robson JM. The effects of vasopressin, adrenaline and noradrenaline on the mouse foetus. Br J Pharmacol. 1970;38:446P.
42. Love AM, Vickers TH. Vasopressin induced dysmelia in rats and its relation to amniocentesis dysmelia. Br J Exp Pathol. 1973;54:291–7.
43. Vanden Hoek TL, Morrison LJ, Shuster M, et al. Part 12: cardiac arrest in special situations: 2010 American heart association guidelines for cardiopulmonary resuscitation and emergency cardiovascular care. Circulation. 2010;122:S829–61.

Part III
Depression and Anxiety

Chapter 3
Mood Disorders

Teri Pearlstein, Ellen Flynn, and Carmen Monzon

Depression During Pregnancy

Definition and Prevalence

10 to 15 % of pregnant women are depressed, approximately half having major depressive disorder (MDD) and half having minor depressive disorder. This prevalence rate is similar to prevalence rates reported in reproductive age women outside of the perinatal period. The diagnostic criteria for MDD include depressed mood or loss of interest or pleasure along with other criteria (Table 3.1). Minor depressive disorder constitutes fewer symptoms or less impairment in functioning. Concurrent anxiety symptoms and stress are common in many women who have MDD during pregnancy.

Screening Measures

Depression during pregnancy is often measured by the Edinburgh Postnatal Depression Scale (EPDS) [2] or the Patient Health Questionnaire (PHQ-9) [3]. The EPDS (Table 3.2) is a 10-item self-report scale developed as a screen for postpartum depression (PPD); it is widely used during pregnancy as well. The top line of questions 1, 2, and 4 is scored "0," the top line of the other questions is scored "3," and the maximum possible score is 30. A score of 12 or above would warrant a clinical

T. Pearlstein, M.D. (✉) • E. Flynn, M.D. • C. Monzon, M.D.
Women's Behavioral Medicine, Women's Medicine Collaborative, The Miriam Hospital,
146 West River Street, 3rd floor, Providence, RI 02904, USA

The Warren Alpert Medical School of Brown University, Providence, RI, USA
e-mail: Teri_Pearlstein@brown.edu

Table 3.1 Summary of DSM-5 diagnostic criteria for major depressive disorder [1]

A.	Five (or more) of the following symptoms have been present during the same 2-week period and represent a change from previous functioning; at least one of the symptoms is either (1) or (2)
	(1) Depressed mood most of the day, nearly every day, as indicated by either subjective report (e.g., feels sad, empty, hopeless) or observation made by others (e.g., appears tearful)
	(2) Markedly diminished interest or pleasure in all, or almost all, activities most of the day, nearly every day
	(3) Significant weight loss when not dieting or weight gain (e.g., a change of more than 5 % of body weight in a month), or decrease or increase in appetite nearly every day
	(4) Insomnia or hypersomnia nearly every day
	(5) Psychomotor agitation or retardation nearly every day (observable by others, not merely subjective feelings of restlessness or being slowed down)
	(6) Fatigue or loss of energy nearly every day
	(7) Feelings of worthlessness or excessive or inappropriate guilt (which may be delusional) nearly every day (not merely self-reproach or guilt about being sick)
	(8) Diminished ability to think or concentrate, or indecisiveness, nearly every day
	(9) Recurrent thoughts of death (not just fear of dying), recurrent suicidal ideation without a specific plan, or a suicide attempt or a specific plan for committing suicide
B.	The symptoms cause clinically significant distress or impairment in social, occupational, or other important areas of functioning
C.	The episode is not due to the physiological effects of a substance or a general medical condition
D.	The occurrence of the major depressive episode is not better explained by schizoaffective disorder, schizophrenia, delusional disorder, or other psychotic disorders
E.	There has never been a manic episode or a hypomanic episode

interview for depression. The EPDS includes questions about both mood and anxiety; it does not include questions about fatigue, oversleeping, or changes in appetite which can be common during pregnancy. The PHQ-9 (Table 3.3) is a 9-item self-report scale widely used in primary care settings as a screen for MDD [3]. The questions mirror the DSM-5 criteria for MDD. A score of 10 or above would warrant a clinical interview for depression. A positive answer on the question about suicidal ideation on either the EPDS or PHQ-9 would warrant further evaluation of suicidality.

Similar to the findings for screening for depression in adult populations in primary care, screening for depression during pregnancy in ob-gyn clinics does not necessarily lead to patient referral to treatment, patient access of treatment, or improvement in depression and anxiety. Barriers include availability of treatment, cost, child care, stigma of referral to a mental health clinician, as well as clinician time constraints and expertise with psychiatric disorders. Recent studies suggest

Table 3.2 Edinburgh Postnatal Depression Scale (EPDS) [2]

In the past 7 days:	6. Things have been getting on top of me
1. I have been able to laugh and see the funny side of things	___ Yes, most of the time I haven't been able to cope at all
___ As much as I always could	___ Yes, sometimes I haven't been coping as well as usual
___ Not quite so much now	___ No, most of the time I have coped quite well
___ Definitely not so much now	___ No, I have been coping as well as ever
___ Not at all	7. I have been so unhappy that I have had difficulty sleeping
2. I have looked forward with enjoyment to things	___ Yes, most of the time
___ As much as I ever did	___ Yes, sometimes
___ Rather less than I used to	___ Not very often
___ Definitely less than I used to	___ No, not at all
___ Hardly at all	8. I have felt sad or miserable
3. I have blamed myself unnecessarily when things went wrong	___ Yes, most of the time
___ Yes, most of the time	___ Yes, quite often
___ Yes, some of the time	___ Not very often
___ Not very often	___ No, not at all
___ No, never	9. I have been so unhappy that I have been crying
4. I have been anxious or worried for no good reason	___ Yes, most of the time
___ No, not at all	___ Yes, quite often
___ Hardly ever	___ Only occasionally
___ Yes, sometimes	___ No, never
___ Yes, very often	10. The thought of harming myself has occurred to me
5. I have felt scared or panicky for not very good reason	___ Yes, quite often
___ Yes, quite a lot	___ Sometimes
___ Yes, sometimes	___ Hardly ever
___ No, not much	___ Never
___ No, not at all	

that acceptance of and adherence to treatment is increased when mental health care is integrated in the ob-gyn or primary care setting.

Effect of Pregnancy on MDD Prevalence

Although the prevalence of MDD during pregnancy is the same as the prevalence in nonpuerperal women, pregnancy may be a time of risk of developing an episode in vulnerable women. It has been reported that rates of completed suicide may be lower in pregnant women; however, some studies report that rates of suicidal ideation may be higher compared to nonpuerperal women.

Table 3.3 Patient Health Questionnaire (PHQ) [3]

PHQ-9	Over the *last 2 weeks*, how often have you been bothered by any of the following problems?	Not at all	Several days	More than half the days	Nearly every day
1.	Little interest or pleasure in doing things	0	1	2	3
2.	Feeling down, depressed, or hopeless	0	1	2	3
3.	Trouble falling or staying asleep or sleeping too much	0	1	2	3
4.	Feeling tired or having little energy	0	1	2	3
5.	Poor appetite or overeating	0	1	2	3
6.	Feeling bad about yourself—or that you are a failure or have let yourself or your family down	0	1	2	3
7.	Trouble concentrating on things, such as reading the newspaper or watching television	0	1	2	3
8.	Moving or speaking so slowly that other people could have noticed or the opposite—being so fidgety or restless that you have been moving around a lot more than usual	0	1	2	3
9.	Thoughts that you would be better off dead or of hurting yourself in some way	0	1	2	3

Risk Factors for MDD During Pregnancy

Previous MDD, poor social support, single status, adolescence, intimate partner violence, poor relationship quality, anxiety, life stress, unintended pregnancy, lower education, lower income, smoking, diabetes, high preconception body mass index, chronic medical conditions, previous miscarriage or stillbirth, obstetric risk.

Effect of MDD on Pregnancy

Women with MDD are reported to demonstrate poor health behaviors such as poor nutrition, lack of exercise, not taking prenatal vitamins and prescribed medications, poor compliance with prenatal care, increased smoking, and increased use of alcohol and over-the-counter and illicit drugs.

Effects of Untreated Prenatal MDD, Anxiety, and Stress on the Fetus

Altered fetal response to vibroacoustic stimulation, altered fetal heart rate variability, changed movement and sleep patterns, altered attention, delayed fetal head and overall growth, decreased maternal-fetal attachment, increased maternal and fetal cortisol- and corticotropin-releasing hormone (CRH), increase in C-reactive protein and pro-inflammatory cytokines, and possible epigenetic changes to placental glucocorticoid receptor promoter gene and 11-beta-hydroxysteroid dehydrogenase-2 gene.

Effects of Untreated Prenatal MDD, Anxiety, and Stress on Birth Outcome

- Preterm birth (PTB) [4]
- Low birth weight (LBW) [4]
- Small-for-gestational age (SGA)
- Low Apgar scores
- Cesarean delivery

Some of these effects are thought to be related in part to increased maternal and fetal cortisol levels, elevated fetal CRH, and increased norepinephrine. Low folate levels can add to the risk of depression on LBW and SGA.

Effects of Untreated Prenatal MDD, Anxiety, and Stress on the Infant and Child

- Infant: Altered neonatal behavioral scores, altered cortisol reactivity, greater relative right frontal EEG asymmetry, decreased vagal tone, altered reactivity to pain or stress, altered temperament, altered attention, delayed neuromotor development, and sleep problems.
- Toddler: Delayed motor and cognitive development, altered executive function, internalizing and externalizing disorders, and altered response to stress.
- Child and Adolescent: Increased risk of depression, anxiety disorders, ADHD, psychosis, and altered response to stress.

Prenatal programming effects may be modified by postpartum caregiving and may be exacerbated by continued maternal depression or childhood adversity.

Antidepressant Use During Pregnancy

Approximately 7 % of women in the United States take an SSRI at some point during their pregnancy. Sertraline is currently the most prescribed antidepressant during pregnancy, followed by fluoxetine.

Many women discontinue their antidepressant once the pregnancy is recognized, either on their own or at the advice of a clinician. Discontinuation of antidepressants may lead to an increased risk of relapse of MDD, particularly in women with more previous episodes, longer length of illness, and an episode in the 6 months prior to conception. The risk of relapse is highest during the first trimester.

There is a risk of relapse of recurrent MDD even if antidepressants are maintained during pregnancy.

Pregnancy Outcomes with Antidepressant Use

Fetal exposure to antidepressants occurs through the umbilical cord, across the placenta by transporter genes, and through absorption from amniotic fluid. Antidepressant exposure in the fetus is influenced by the cord-to-maternal ratio of the antidepressant level; half-life of antidepressant; peak and trough levels of antidepressant; cytochrome P450 genetic polymorphisms in the mother, fetus, and placenta; and the unbound fraction of antidepressant in the fetus [5]. Adverse birth outcomes have not been clearly associated with timing of SSRI exposure (e.g., first vs. third trimester), length of SSRI exposure (e.g., part of pregnancy vs. throughout pregnancy), or dose of SSRI.

Spontaneous Miscarriage

Approximately 12 % of clinically recognized pregnancies under 20 weeks undergo spontaneous miscarriage, usually during the first trimester. Exposure to antidepressants during the first trimester increases the risk of spontaneous miscarriage by approximately 65 %. Maternal depression is a confounding factor in most studies to date.

Preterm Birth

PTB occurs in 12 % of births in the United States. Many cohort and case-control studies have reported an increased risk of PTB (pooled OR of 1.55) with prenatal exposure to selective serotonin reuptake inhibitors; [6] some studies have controlled for maternal depression but most have not. A recent review commented that the risk of PTB averages 3 days shorter gestational age, considered a small effect [6].

Birth Weight

LBW occurs in 8 % of births in the United States. Many cohort and case-control studies have reported an increased risk of LBW (pooled SMD of −0.10) with prenatal exposure to selective serotonin reuptake inhibitors; [6] some studies have controlled for maternal depression but most have not. A recent review commented that the risk of lowered LBW averages 2.6 ounces, considered a small effect [6].

Lower 1 min and 5 min Apgar scores with SSRIs have been reported [6]. PTB and LBW have also been reported with prenatal exposure to tricyclic antidepressants. The mechanism by which antidepressants might increase risk for PTB and LBW is not clear. Some studies suggest that the effects of antidepressants on birth outcome may be additive to the effects of untreated or underlying maternal depression and anxiety on birth outcome.

Congenital Malformations

Mixed results have been reported about increased risks of congenital malformations with first trimester exposure to antidepressants. If an increased risk does exist, it is a small increase in absolute risk (approximately 0.5 % with antidepressants vs. 0.3 % in unexposed pregnancies) and no consistent organ malformation has been reported with antidepressants as a class [7, 8]. There is a possibility of increased cardiac septal defects with paroxetine (1 % vs. 0.7 % in unexposed pregnancies) [9] and left outflow tract heart defects with bupropion [8]. The mechanism by which antidepressants might increase cardiac malformations is not clear, but altered serotonergic influence on cardiac development is hypothesized. Study results have been inconsistent, and the small absolute increased risks could be due to the antidepressant, the underlying illness, or unknown factors associated with either or both [8].

Persistent Pulmonary Hypertension of the Newborn

Persistent pulmonary hypertension of the newborn (PPHN) occurs in 1–2 infants per 1,000 live births. PPHN occurs when there is failure of the normal relaxation in the fetal pulmonary vascular bed during the circulatory transition that occurs shortly after birth. The elevated pulmonary hypertension causes right-to-left shunting of extrapulmonary blood through the ductus arteriosus and foramen ovale, which can lead to hypoxemia, respiratory distress, acidosis, and right heart failure. There is a 10–20 % mortality risk which varies with etiology.

Risk Factors: Meconium aspiration or other lung injury, prematurity, postmaturity, hypoglycemia, cold stress, inflammation, sepsis, pulmonary hypoplasia, nonsteroidal anti-inflammatory drug use, lower socioeconomic status, diabetes, urinary tract infections, tobacco use, smoking, cesarean section delivery, increased maternal weight, and fetal male gender.

Potential Etiologies: Increased vasoconstriction of smooth muscle cells and/or decreased production of nitric oxide, a potent vasodilator. SSRIs may influence serotonin effects on pulmonary vascular smooth muscle endothelium [10].

Increased Risk with SSRIs

Three of 6 studies have reported increased risk (risk ratio up to 5) of PPHN with SSRI use in the second half of pregnancy; the 3 studies reporting an increased risk have large sample sizes [11]. The absolute risk is approximately 0.3 % with SSRI use after week 20 of pregnancy [12]. This increased risk has been noted with fluoxetine, sertraline, paroxetine, and citalopram. PPHN may represent the severe end of a spectrum of respiratory difficulties with SSRI exposure.

The mortality rate with SSRIs (in the one study that had mortality from PPHN in babies exposed to SSRIs) was reported equal to the mortality rate without exposure to SSRIs [12].

In July 2006, the FDA issued a Public Health Advisory stating that in one study, PPHN was six times more common in babies whose mothers took an SSRI antidepressant after the 20th week of the pregnancy compared to babies whose mothers did not take an antidepressant. The FDA advised careful consideration of the potential benefits and risks of the medication for each individual pregnant patient.

In December 2011, the FDA issued a Safety Announcement advising health-care professionals not to alter their current clinical practice of treating depression during pregnancy due to conflicting findings of studies of SSRI use during pregnancy and the development of PPHN.

Postnatal Adaptation Syndrome

An FDA Alert in 2004 warned that neonates exposed to SSRIs or SNRIs late in the third trimester may develop complications following delivery requiring prolonged hospitalization, respiratory support, and tube feeding.

Neonatal symptoms include respiratory distress, cyanosis, apnea, seizures, temperature instability, feeding difficulty, vomiting, hypoglycemia, hypotonia, hypertonia, hyperreflexia, tremor, jitteriness, irritability, and constant crying.

Prevalence: 10–30 % of newborns exposed to SSRIs and SNRIs. Postnatal adaptation syndrome (PNAS) has been most frequently associated with fluoxetine, paroxetine, and venlafaxine third trimester exposure.

Potential Etiologies: Serotonin toxicity due to accumulation of antidepressant in the neonate, cholinergic overdrive, and discontinuation syndrome from abrupt discontinuation of neonate exposure to antidepressant [13].
Course: Symptoms usually transient with spontaneous resolution within 2 weeks.
Treatment: Observation of neonate and supportive treatment as needed; intensive care may be indicated for a few days. Although the FDA made a suggestion in 2004 to taper antidepressants prior to expected delivery, there is no evidence that tapering the dose of antidepressant prior to expected delivery lessens neonatal adaptation symptoms, and this strategy could increase the risk of postpartum depression (PPD).

Long-Term Effects on Child Development

- SSRI use in pregnancy has been associated with mild developmental delays in motor development and attention in 1–3 yo children; these delays are within normal limits and seem to resolve with age.
- Exposure to prenatal depression, not prenatal exposure to antidepressants, has been associated with problematic behaviors in 3–6 yo children.
- SSRI use in pregnancy has been associated with 2–3 times increased risk of autism spectrum disorders in some but not all studies [14].

Continued exposure to untreated maternal depression beyond the first postpartum year continues to be a critical risk for cognitive and behavioral problems in childhood and contributes to long-term psychopathology in the child and adolescent.

Other Possible Negative Effects from Antidepressant Use During Pregnancy

- New onset hypertension or preeclampsia
- Prolonged QT interval in the newborn
- Increased mortality in the first month or year of life

Each of these possible increased risks need further study and may be partially explained by confounding factors, particularly major depression or its related health behaviors.

Possible Beneficial Effects from SSRI Use During Pregnancy

- Accelerated infant speech perception
- Increased attention as measured by infant P50 auditory sensory gating

Medications for Anxiety or Insomnia

Many women with depression during pregnancy have comorbid anxiety symptoms and/or insomnia. Women must also consider the safety of anxiolytics and sleep medications while pregnant.

Benzodiazepines

- Most studies do not report an increased risk of major malformations, although an increased risk of anal atresia with lorazepam has been reported. Case-control studies have suggested an increased risk of oral cleft, but this has not been reported in cohort studies.
- Concurrent SSRIs may increase risk of cardiac defects.
- Increased risk of PTB.
- Increased risk of neonatal symptoms with concurrent SSRIs

Hypnotic Benzodiazepine Receptor Agonists

- No evidence of increased risk of congenital malformations
- High dose associated with neural tube defect in one case report
- Increased risk of PTB and LBW
- Increased risk of neonatal symptoms with concurrent SSRIs

Table 3.4 Non-pharmacological treatment of depression for the perinatal woman

Interpersonal psychotherapy
Cognitive behavioral therapy
Light therapy
Exercise
Fish oil
Yoga
Mindfulness/meditation
Massage
Acupuncture
Heart rate variability feedback (HRVB)
Repetitive transcranial magnetic stimulation (rTMS)
Electroconvulsive therapy (ECT)

Non-pharmacological Treatment of Depression

Many perinatal women choose non-pharmacological treatments for their depressive symptoms to avoid exposure to antidepressant medication during pregnancy or while breast-feeding (see Table 3.4). Many of these treatments have not undergone systematic study, or studies have resulted in mixed results. Interpersonal psychotherapy (IPT) has received systematic study in women with PPD, both in individual and group formats. IPT involves 12–16 sessions targeting role transitions, interpersonal conflicts, grief and loss, and interpersonal sensitivity while maximizing social support. Cognitive behavioral therapy (CBT) is another short-term evidence-based psychotherapy for MDD, but it has received less study in perinatal women. CBT techniques include cognitive reframing, problem solving, goal setting, and homework. CBT can be administered in individual and group formats, and it can be combined with relaxation training, exposure therapy, and mindfulness techniques [15].

Treatment Dilemmas During Pregnancy

Treatment decisions need to be individualized and involve the woman, her partner, and her clinicians. A woman's current symptom severity, previous disease course and treatment history, stage of pregnancy, and plans to breast feed must be considered. Additionally, a woman's perceptions, expectations, and wishes about treatment must be taken into account. Clinicians need to present the latest research findings about both the short-term and long-term risks of untreated depression, anxiety, and stress as well as reports about risks of antidepressant exposure. Women with mild or moderate depression may want to taper and discontinue their antidepressant prior to or after conceiving to avoid risks of antidepressant exposure. Non-pharmacological strategies can be pursued. Women with severe, recurrent depression who have a history of relapsing when they discontinue their antidepressant should consider maintenance of antidepressant treatment during pregnancy even if they are asymptomatic or minimally symptomatic when they conceive [16].

Postpartum Blues

Postpartum blues include depressed mood, tearfulness, emotional lability, irritability, anxiety, fatigue, and insomnia. These symptoms can be experienced by 80 % of newly postpartum mothers, symptoms peak at days 4–5, and they generally resolve spontaneously within the first two postpartum weeks.

Potential etiologic factors include the rapid fall in estrogen, increase in monoamine oxidase A levels, altered HPA axis functioning, and altered serotonin functioning.

There is no specific treatment for postpartum blues except for support and reassurance. Women who have persistent symptoms should contact their ob-gyn or PCP since postpartum blues are considered a risk factor for the development of postpartum depression.

Postpartum Depression (PPD)

Definition and Prevalence

Approximately 15 % of postpartum women are depressed, approximately half having major depressive disorder (MDD) and half having minor depressive disorder. This prevalence rate is similar to prevalence rates reported in reproductive age women outside of the perinatal period, but the postpartum period is considered a time of increased risk of developing MDD. The diagnostic criteria for MDD include depressed mood or loss of interest or pleasure along with other criteria (Table 3.1). The strict definition of PPD is MDD with onset within the first month postpartum; however, many clinicians and researchers consider the first 6 months postpartum as a potential time of onset. The signs and symptoms of PPD are the same as nonpuerperal MDD; however, anxiety symptoms are frequently concurrent. Minor depressive disorder constitutes fewer symptoms or less impairment in functioning. Many women with PPD hide their symptoms due to cultural expectations that new motherhood should be a time of happiness.

Screening Measures

PPD is usually measured by the Edinburgh Postnatal Depression Scale (EPDS) [2], a 10-item self-report scale developed for the screening of PPD (Table 3.2). A score of 12 or above would warrant a clinical interview for depression. The EPDS includes questions about both mood and anxiety; it does not include questions about fatigue or changes in appetite, which can be common after delivery. Several other screening measures exist for PPD, and the Patient Health Questionnaire (PHQ-9) [3] is also used in postpartum women. The PHQ-9 (Table 3.3) is a 9-item self-report scale widely used in primary care settings as a screen for MDD. The questions mirror the DSM-IV criteria for MDD. A score of 10 or above would warrant a clinical interview for depression. A positive answer on the question about suicidal ideation on either the EPDS or PHQ-9 would warrant further evaluation of suicidality. Postpartum women presenting with depression should also have anemia and thyroid abnormalities ruled out.

Similar to the findings for screening for depression in adult populations in primary care, screening for PPD in ob-gyn, primary care, and pediatric clinics does not necessarily lead to patient referral to treatment, patient's accessing treatment, or improvement in depression and anxiety. Barriers include clinician time constraints and lack of experience with psychiatric disorders, as well as availability of treatment, cost, child care, and stigma of referral to a mental health clinician. Recent studies suggest that acceptance of and adherence to treatment is increased when mental health care is integrated in the ob-gyn or primary care setting. Screening for PPD and referring for treatment in pediatric clinics during well-baby visits has not been widely adopted to date.

Risk Factors

Prior MDD, prior PPD (25–50 % risk), MDD during pregnancy, anxiety during pregnancy, thyroid abnormality, prior PMS/PMDD, poor social support, poor partner relationship, postpartum blues, and recent life stressor.

Potential Etiologies

- Abrupt and rapid fall of estrogen following delivery
- Elevated monoamine oxidase A binding in CNS leading to decreased monoamine levels
- HPA axis dysregulation
- Thyroid abnormality
- Oxytocin dysregulation
- Prolactin dysregulation
- Altered GABA, serotonin, β-endorphin, or BDNF
- Genetic polymorphisms in estrogen receptor and serotonin transporter genes
- Sleep deprivation

Risks of Untreated PPD

- Impaired mother-infant attachment
- Decreased initiation and maintenance of breast-feeding
- Suicide
- Infanticide
- Negative effects on child development

- Infant: Excessive crying, colic, sleep problems, temperament difficulties, and poor self-regulation.
- Toddler: Delayed motor and cognitive development, altered executive function, behavioral inhibition, externalizing disorders, poor emotion regulation, and conduct problems.
- Child and Adolescent: Increased risk of depression, anxiety disorders, conduct disorders, ADHD, and medical disorders.

A new mother has the challenges of increased demands from care of her newborn, sleep deprivation, and providing continued care for the rest of the family. A major depressive episode is associated with suffering and morbidity, and if it remains untreated, it can lead to chronic depression and recurrent illness. Some studies have suggested that even when maternal depression improves, the negative effects on child development may not always improve.

Pharmacotherapy Treatment of PPD

Antidepressants are the first-line choice for moderate to severe postpartum depression, with or without concurrent psychotherapy. Choice of antidepressant treatment follows the guidelines of nonpuerperal patients, which takes into account a patient's prior response to a particular medication and the side effect profile. In addition, the breast-feeding status of the mother must be taken into account. Few placebo-controlled studies with antidepressants for PPD exist. Three studies reported efficacy for fluoxetine, sertraline, and paroxetine, each compared to placebo. Sertraline has also been reported to be equivalent to nortriptyline, and there are open-label case series reported with sertraline, venlafaxine, fluvoxamine, and bupropion [17].

Preliminary reports suggest that transdermal estradiol may improve symptoms of PPD, but systematic studies are lacking. Estradiol treatment may decrease breast milk production in the immediate postpartum period, and it carries health risks and need for progestin use with long-term administration [17].

Antidepressants and Breast-Feeding

The antidepressant exposure risk with breast-feeding is much lower than during pregnancy. Antidepressant levels in the infant are influenced by the infant's age and capacity to metabolize the drug through the hepatic enzymes, and premature infants may be more vulnerable to adverse effects [18]. Poor feeding, irritability, sedation, and sleeping problems are possible adverse effects. A relative infant dose of 10 % or less is generally considered low risk [19]. Although the number of mother-infant pairs studied is few for many antidepressants, most studies report a relative infant dose less than 10 % for almost all antidepressants examined to date. In particular, sertraline, paroxetine, fluvoxamine, and nortriptyline levels in breast-feeding infants yield low to undetectable infant serum levels [19]. Fluoxetine is less preferred with breast-feeding due to higher infant serum levels presumably due to the long half-life of fluoxetine and its metabolites, and high infant levels have also been reported with citalopram [18]. There is one case report of seizure activity with bupropion 300 mg PO daily. Doxepin is contraindicated with breast-feeding. Overall, breast-feeding can be safely compatible with antidepressants; sertraline or paroxetine should be considered first-line choices if efficacious for the mother [18].

Non-pharmacological Treatment Options

Many postpartum women, particularly if breast-feeding, may choose to use non-pharmacological treatments for the management of PPD to avoid exposure risk from antidepressants in breast milk. Many of the proposed treatments in Table 3.4 have not undergone systematic study in women with PPD, and the evidence base for most is sparse. In addition to the treatments listed in Table 3.4, home visits, peer support, and couples therapy may be beneficial for women with PPD.

Bipolar Disorder

Bipolar disorder is a chronic psychiatric illness that is characterized by relapsing and remitting vacillations in mood as well as alterations in behavior and function. Affective symptoms range from periods of stable and euthymic mood to episodes of mania, hypomania, and/or depression. Sometimes a bipolar episode includes symptoms of the opposite pole, leading to mixed features (i.e., simultaneous combination of depressive and manic symptoms). Bipolar illness carries a high morbidity and mortality; 25–50 % attempt suicide and 15 % complete suicide.

A critical component of the disorder is that the alteration in mood, functional ability, and behavior represents *a change* from usual baseline and impacts multiple domains in a woman's life. The average age of onset of bipolar disorder is 20 years of age. 10 to 15 % of adolescents diagnosed with MDD will go on to develop bipolar disorder. It is important that the correct diagnosis be made in the pregnant or postpartum woman since this has significant implications for the management of the disorder in pregnancy and the postpartum period.

Definition and Prevalence

The prevalence of bipolar disorder type I (see Box 3.1) is 0.4–1.6 % and occurs equally in men and women. However, women experience more depressive episodes and rapid cycling (4 or more discreet mood episodes in a 12-month period) than men. Bipolar disorder type II (see Box 3.2) occurs in 10–20 % of people with bipolar disorder, and it is more common in women (70–90 %) than in men (10–30 %).

Box 3.1 Bipolar I disorder [1]

Essential diagnostic feature: manic episode which may or not be preceded by or followed by a hypomanic or major depressive episode.

Manic episode is characterized by at least 1 week of abnormally and persistently elevated, expansive, or irritable mood and increased goal-directed activity or energy, associated with at least 3 of the following:

- Inflated self-esteem or grandiosity
- Decreased need for sleep
- More talkative than usual
- Flight of ideas or sense that thoughts are racing
- Distractibility
- Increase in goal-directed activity (either socially, at work or school, or sexually) or psychomotor agitation
- Excessive involvement in activities that have a high potential for painful consequences (e.g., unrestrained buying sprees, sexual indiscretions, or foolish business investments)

Box 3.2 Bipolar II disorder [1]

Essential diagnostic feature: current or past hypomanic episode and a current or past major depressive episode. The episode is not severe enough to cause marked impairment or to necessitate hospitalization and does not include psychotic features

Hypomanic episode is characterized by at least 4 days of abnormally and persistently elevated, expansive, or irritable mood and increased activity or energy, associated with at least 3 or more of the following:

- Inflated self-esteem or grandiosity
- Decreased need for sleep
- More talkative than usual
- Flight of ideas or sense that thoughts are racing
- Distractibility
- Increase in goal-directed activity (either socially, at work or school, or sexually) or psychomotor agitation
- Excessive involvement in activities that have a high potential for painful consequences (e.g., unrestrained buying sprees, sexual indiscretions, or foolish business investments)

Differential Diagnosis

- Mood disorder due to a general medical condition
- Substance-induced mood disorder and/or acute intoxication, substance withdrawal
- Delirium due to an underlying medical condition
- Major depressive disorder with psychotic features
- Schizoaffective disorder

Diagnostic Evaluation

- Toxicology
- Thyroid function tests
- Parathyroid
- CBC
- Chem 7
- VDRL/HIV
- B12, folate
- Medication review

Effect of Pregnancy on Bipolar Disorder

Pregnancy is *not* protective against relapse or symptom exacerbation of bipolar illness. Adding to the challenge of managing this severe form of mental illness, many women considering pregnancy, or who are currently pregnant, are encouraged by family, friends, and clinicians to discontinue effective medication out of concern for risks to the fetus. However, discontinuation of medication places women at even higher risk of psychiatric decompensation which has a direct impact on fetal well-being and outcomes. Relapse rates of pregnant women who discontinue mood-stabilizing medication are as high as 80 %. Even in women who continue medication during pregnancy, relapse rates are approximately 35 %, with the highest rate of relapse during the first trimester.

Effect of Bipolar Disorder on Pregnancy

Relapse of bipolar illness is associated with poor maternal self-care, poor engagement with prenatal care, smoking, substance abuse, increased risk taking (e.g., hypersexual behavior), impaired judgment, suicidality, and psychosis. Each of these, alone, is known to negatively impact fetal well-being and affect fetal outcome. Both treated and untreated bipolar disorders have been associated with

PTB. Infants of women with untreated bipolar disorder have an increased risk of microcephaly and neonatal hypoglycemia.

Risk Factors for Relapse During Pregnancy with Medication Discontinuation

- Younger age
- Earlier onset of bipolar disorder
- Recent mood episode
- Frequent recurrent episodes
- Unplanned pregnancy
- Use of antidepressants

Postpartum Period

A recent study reported that 14 % of women with first-time psychiatric contact during the first postpartum month converted to a bipolar diagnosis over the next 15 months, suggesting that depressive symptoms that present in the first postpartum month may be a marker for underlying bipolarity. Among women with no prior history of affective illness, 7.6 % will have their first bipolar episode in the postpartum period. For women with known bipolar disorder, the postpartum period is a time of very high risk of relapse or decompensation. In women being treated with medication, relapse rates are as high as 52 %, and among women who are untreated or discontinue mood-stabilizing medication, relapse rates may exceed 80 %.

Risk Factors for Postpartum Relapse

- Women under 30 years
- Earlier age of onset of bipolar disorder
- Unstable mood in pregnancy
- Medication discontinuation
- Prior psychiatric decompensation in the postpartum period

The majority of women with bipolar disorder who relapse postpartum experience postpartum depression. A mixed presentation is also common whereby women present with a combination of depressive and manic symptoms. The greatest concern is postpartum psychosis.

Postpartum psychosis occurs in 1 to 2 per 1,000 births. Risk factors include previous psychosis, family history of puerperal psychosis, primiparity, and pregnancy or delivery complications. However, in women with bipolar disorder, the risk is 100 times greater, occurring after 25–50 % of deliveries. Among women with bipolar disorder, having a family history of bipolar disorder increases the risk or postpartum psychosis to 75 vs. 30% in bipolar women with no family history.

The onset of postpartum psychosis is abrupt and rapid, most often within 2 weeks of delivery. Studies report that many of these women contacted a health-care provider for concerns about postpartum depression, and manic or psychotic symptoms were missed. Of particular concern is that many women with bipolar disorder type II are often misdiagnosed as having postpartum depression and treated solely with

> **Box 3.3 Symptoms of postpartum psychosis**
>
> Mood lability
>   Agitation and restlessness
>   Anxiety—extreme fearfulness around the infant or in allowing others to help with care
>   Insomnia
>   Cognitive dysfunction including confusion, difficulty attending to basic tasks
>   Psychotic symptoms
>   Delusions most commonly religious
>   Auditory hallucinations
>   Ideas of reference—receiving messages from radio, TV, computer, etc.
>   Paranoid ideation

> **Box 3.4 Clinical Point**
>
> Postpartum psychosis is a psychiatric emergency requiring psychiatric hospitalization for safety of the patient and her family

antidepressants with the potential of precipitating a manic and/or psychotic episode with negative consequences for the mother, infant, and family (see Box 3.3).

Women with postpartum psychosis are at risk of infanticide, filicide, and suicide (see Box 3.4). Approximately 4 % of women with postpartum psychosis commit infanticide.

It has been reported that women who have had psychotic episodes during the postpartum period only may be well between and during subsequent pregnancies, but mood-stabilizing and/or antipsychotic medications should be started immediately after delivery as prophylaxis. However, for women who have had bipolar episodes outside of the puerperium, given the high rates of bipolar episodes during pregnancy, and particularly following delivery, it is imperative that these women remain on prophylactic medication through pregnancy that is efficacious in managing their bipolar symptoms. It is also critical that bipolar women receive psychiatric care prior to (if possible) and throughout pregnancy and the postpartum period in order to optimize psychotropic medications, for referral to psychotherapy and resources for postpartum women with severe mental illness and for encouraging establishment of social supports for the patient. As in pregnancy, communication between the patient, ob-gyn, mental health clinician, therapist/case manager (if involved), pediatrician, and the patient's larger support network is imperative.

Mood Stabilizers and Antipsychotics in the Perinatal Woman

The gold standard in the treatment of bipolar disorders is mood-stabilizing medications which include lithium, antiepileptic medications, and antipsychotic medications.

Lithium

Earlier reports suggested that there was a 20-fold increase in Ebstein's anomaly with fetal exposure to lithium in the first trimester, a risk of 0.1 % (vs. 0.005 %), and 1.2–7.7 increased risk for any cardiac malformation. However, more recent reports have failed to demonstrate an increased risk of Ebstein's anomaly or other congenital malformations [20].

Because lithium is exclusively metabolized and cleared through the kidney, lithium levels and renal function need to be monitored throughout pregnancy due to increased fluid volume and GFR in the second and third trimesters. Thyroid function tests and fetal growth also need to be monitored through pregnancy.

First Trimester:

- Baseline lithium level, Bun/Cr, TSH

Second Trimester:

- Lithium level, Bun/Cr, TSH
- Level II U/S and fetal echocardiogram

Third Trimester:

- Lithium level, Bun/Cr, TSH

Postpartum:

- Lithium level and close monitoring for signs/symptoms of toxicity in mother due to postpartum diuresis and temporary reduction of lithium dose near delivery.
- Aggressive hydration and avoidance of nephrotoxins such as NSAIDs.
- Close monitoring of infant for signs/symptoms of toxicity such as hypotonicity, arrhythmia, respiratory distress, nephrogenic diabetes insipidus, and neonatal hypothyroidism.
- Cord blood lithium level, if possible.
- Breast-feeding is generally contraindicated since serum lithium levels in infant can be 10–50 % maternal level. However, breast-feeding can be done with close monitoring of the infant for signs of toxicity including hypotonia, hypothermia, cyanosis, T-wave inversions, and lethargy. In addition, the neonate will require close monitoring of lithium level, renal function, and thyroid status by the pediatrician.

Valproate

Multiple studies have reported that valproate is associated with high rates of malformations, (approximately 10 %) with first trimester exposure, and extensive types of malformations, e.g., neural tube defects, hypospadias, cardiac defects, and oral clefts. Risks of malformations increase with increased doses of valproate and with use of multiple antiepileptic medications. Recent data has confirmed that exposure to valproate in pregnancy leads to lower IQ and delayed neurocognitive development [21]. An FDA Drug Safety Communication in June 2011 warns that children born to mothers that took valproate during pregnancy have lower cognitive test scores than children who were unexposed to valproate.

Carbamazepine

Studies generally do not report significantly increased teratogenicity with carbamazepine, except for an increased risk of spina bifida (1 % vs. 0.1% without exposure). The use of folic acid before pregnancy and during the first trimester may reduce the risk of neural tube defects. Carbamazepine has been associated with neurodevelopmental delay, but less than with valproate.

First Trimester:

- Baseline VPA or CBZ drug levels, LFTs, CBC, B12, and folate.
- Folic acid supplementation: 4 mg daily through week 12 of pregnancy, then decrease to 0.4mg daily.

Second Trimester:

- Monitor VPA or CBZ drug level, CBC, and LFTs.
- Level II U/S for morphology and growth monitoring.
- Alpha-fetoprotein (AFP) level in amniotic fluid or maternal serum at 18–22 weeks gestation

Third Trimester:

- VPA or CBZ drug level, CBC, and LFTs

Postpartum:
Close observation of infant for adverse effects and morphological exam.

Both valproate and carbamazepine are considered to be compatible with lactation. Breast-fed infants may exhibit transient hypotonia, irritability or sedation, anemia, thrombocytopenia, or hepatic dysfunction. Infant will require close monitoring by a pediatrician. To date, prospective studies do not report long-term worsening of neurobehavioral status with breast-feeding.

Lamotrigine

Early reports had suggested an increased risk of oral clefts, but recent reports from multiple international registries fail to demonstrate an increased risk of congenital malformations with lamotrigine. To date, prospective studies have not reported cognitive or developmental delay with exposure during pregnancy.

Management during pregnancy is similar to monitoring of valproate and carbamazepine, but lamotrigine levels are not routinely monitored.

Lamotrigine is considered compatible with breast-feeding, particularly if the maternal dose is not high. Infant serum levels have been reported up to 40 % of maternal levels, and apnea was reported in one neonate whose mother was on high-dose lamotrigine. Thus far, there have not been reports of neurocognitive or developmental delay in children with lamotrigine exposure through breast milk.

Topiramate exposure during pregnancy has been associated with increased risk of oral clefts, hypospadias, and LBW.

Newer antiepileptic medications such as levetiracetam, oxcarbazepine, and gabapentin have little data regarding safety in pregnancy. There are also few reports about newer antiepileptic medications and breast-feeding.

Antipsychotic Medications [22]

First Generation Antipsychotics (FGAs):

- Major malformations are either not above the baseline rate or minimally increased; there is no specific pattern of malformations.
- Risk of transient neonatal complications—extrapyramidal symptoms, motor restlessness, tremor, hypertonicity, dystonia, and withdrawal symptoms. FDA issued a Drug Safety Communication in February 2011 about potential risk of abnormal muscle movements and withdrawal symptoms in newborns whose mothers were treated with antipsychotics during the third trimester of pregnancy.
- Lower neuromotor performance reported in 6-month-old infants.
- Minimal information available about child neurocognitive development.

Second Generation Antipsychotics (SGAs):

- Increased risk of metabolic syndrome, obesity, gestational diabetes, and hypertension.
- Major malformations are either not above the baseline rate or minimally increased; there is no specific pattern of malformations.
- Olanzapine and/or clozapine associated with macrocephaly.
- Olanzapine has been associated with large-for-gestational-age infants and heavier birth weight.
- Risk of transient neonatal complications—extrapyramidal symptoms, motor restlessness, tremor, hypertonicity, dystonia, and withdrawal symptoms. FDA issued

a Drug Safety Communication in February 2011 about potential risk of abnormal muscle movements and withdrawal symptoms in newborns whose mothers were treated with antipsychotics during the third trimester of pregnancy.
- Concern about agranulocytosis with clozapine, no reports to date.
- Lower neuromotor performance reported in 6-month-old infants.
- Minimal information available about child neurocognitive development.

Breast-Feeding [23]

- Sporadic case reports of adverse effects in infants reported with FGAs and SGAs, no consistent patterns.
- In few case reports with infant serum levels, level of antipsychotics considered low.
- Concern about agranulocytosis with clozapine, no reports to date.
- Use minimum effective dose with regular pediatrician follow-up to monitor infant.

Treatment Dilemmas for Perinatal Woman with Bipolar Disorder

During pregnancy and the postpartum period, there are no risk-free decisions for a woman with bipolar disorder. The severity of the bipolar illness must be considered along with the developmental stage of the fetus or neonate, bearing in mind the risks associated with treatment vs. no treatment vs. suboptimal treatment. Valproate should be avoided unless that is the only mood stabilizer the woman responds to. While bipolar disorder is a serious chronic illness, it can be very responsive to treatment, and the best outcomes are associated with active collaboration between the patient, her family, her obstetrician, and her mental health clinicians.

References

1. American Psychiatric Association. Diagnostic and statistical manual of mental disorders. 5th ed. Arlington, VA: American Psychiatric Publishing; 2013.
2. Cox JL, Holden JM, Sagovsky R. Detection of postnatal depression. Development of the 10-item Edinburgh postnatal depression scale. Br J Psychiatry. 1987;150:782–6.
3. Kroenke K, Spitzer RL, Williams JB. The PHQ-9: validity of a brief depression severity measure. J Gen Intern Med. 2001;16:606–13.
4. Grote NK, Bridge JA, Gavin AR, Melville JL, Iyengar S, Katon WJ. A meta-analysis of depression during pregnancy and the risk of preterm birth, low birth weight, and intrauterine growth restriction. Arch Gen Psychiatry. 2010;67:1012–24.
5. Sit D, Perel JM, Wisniewski SR, Helsel JC, Luther JF, Wisner KL. Mother-infant antidepressant concentrations, maternal depression, and perinatal events. J Clin Psychiatry. 2011;72:994–1001.
6. Ross LE, Grigoriadis S, Mamisachvili L, VonderPorten EH, Roerecke M, Rehm J, et al. Selected pregnancy and delivery outcomes after exposure to antidepressant medication: a systematic review and meta-analysis. JAMA Psychiatry. 2013;70:436–43.
7. Jimenez-Solem E, Andersen JT, Petersen M, Broedbasek K, Jensen JK, Afzal S, et al. Exposure to selective serotonin reuptake inhibitors and the risk of congenital malformations: a nationwide cohort study. BMJ Open. 2012;2.

8. Byatt N, Deligiannidis KM, Freeman MP. Antidepressant use in pregnancy: a critical review focused on risks and controversies. Acta Psychiatr Scand. 2013;127:94–114.
9. Alwan S, Friedman JM. Safety of selective serotonin reuptake inhibitors in pregnancy. CNS Drugs. 2009;23:493–509.
10. Occhiogrosso M, Omran SS, Altemus M. Persistent pulmonary hypertension of the newborn and selective serotonin reuptake inhibitors: lessons from clinical and translational studies. Am J Psychiatry. 2012;169:134–40.
11. 't Jong GW, Einarson T, Koren G, Einarson A. Antidepressant use in pregnancy and persistent pulmonary hypertension of the newborn (PPHN): A systematic review. Reprod Toxicol 2012;34:293–7.
12. Kieler H, Artama M, Engeland A, Orjan E, Furu K, Gissler M, et al. Selective serotonin reuptake inhibitors during pregnancy and risk of persistent pulmonary hypertension in the newborn: population based cohort study from the five Nordic countries. BMJ. 2012;344:d8012.
13. Moses-Kolko EL, Bogen D, Perel J, Bregar A, Uhl K, Levin B, et al. Neonatal signs after late in utero exposure to serotonin reuptake inhibitors: literature review and implications for clinical applications. JAMA. 2005;293:2372–83.
14. Harrington RA, Lee LC, Crum RM, Zimmerman AW, Hertz-Picciotto I. Prenatal SSRI use and offspring with autism spectrum disorder or developmental delay. Pediatrics. In press 2014.
15. Brandon AR, Freeman MP. When she says "no" to medication: psychotherapy for antepartum depression. Curr Psychiatry Rep. 2011;13:459–66.
16. Yonkers KA, Wisner KL, Stewart DE, Oberlander TF, Dell DL, Stotland N, et al. The management of depression during pregnancy: a report from the American Psychiatric Association and the American College of Obstetricians and Gynecologists. Obstet Gynecol. 2009;114:703–13.
17. Kim DR, Epperson CN, Weiss AR, Wisner KL. Pharmacotherapy of postpartum depression: an update. Expert Opin Pharmacother. 2014;15:1223–34.
18. Berle JO, Spigset O. Antidepressant use during breastfeeding. Curr Womens Health Rev. 2011;7:28–34.
19. Rowe H, Baker T, Hale TW. Maternal medication, drug use, and breastfeeding. Pediatr Clin North Am. 2013;60:275–94.
20. McKnight RF, Adida M, Budge K, Stockton S, Goodwin GM, Geddes JR. Lithium toxicity profile: a systematic review and meta-analysis. Lancet. 2012;379:721–8.
21. Meador KJ, Baker GA, Browning N, Cohen MJ, Bromley RL, Clayton-Smith J, et al. Fetal antiepileptic drug exposure and cognitive outcomes at age 6 years (NEAD study): a prospective observational study. Lancet Neurol. 2013;12:244–52.
22. Gentile S. Antipsychotic therapy during early and late pregnancy. A systematic review. Schizophr Bull. 2010;36:518–44.
23. Klinger G, Stahl B, Fusar-Poli P, Merlob P. Antipsychotic drugs and breastfeeding. Pediatr Endocrinol Rev. 2013;10:308–17.

Part IV
Diabetes and Obesity

Chapter 4
Diabetes and Pregnancy

Lucia Larson and Marshall Carpenter

Introduction

Diabetes in pregnancy has important implications for both maternal and fetal health. The increasing prevalence of diabetes requires that providers caring for women of childbearing age understand how to counsel and manage women with diabetes. In women with type 1 and type 2 diabetes mellitus (DM), pregnancy outcome can be improved by pregestational intervention to insure euglycemia during conception and the embryonic period. In gravidas whose glucose intolerance is discovered during pregnancy [i.e., gestational diabetes (GDM)], glucose surveillance during pregnancy and diabetic and other metabolic screening following pregnancy positively impact fetal and maternal health. The aim of this chapter is to describe the effect of pregnancy on glucose metabolism, discuss the clinical importance of diabetes in pregnancy, summarize screening and diagnostic testing models for GDM, and highlight important clinical issues that impact on pregestational and gestational diabetes management.

L. Larson, M.D. (✉)
Obstetric Medicine, Women's Medicine Collaborative, The Miriam Hospital,
146 West River Street, Ste 11C, Providence, RI 02904, USA

The Warren Alpert Medical School of Brown University, Providence, RI USA
e-mail: Lucia_larson@brown.edu

M. Carpenter, M.D.
Women's Medicine Collaborative, The Miriam Hospital,
146 West River Street, Providence, RI 02904, USA

Department of Obstetrics and Gynecology, Tufts University School of Medicine,
Boston, MA, USA

© Springer Science+Business Media New York 2015
K. Rosene-Montella (ed.), *Medical Management of the Pregnant Patient*,
DOI 10.1007/978-1-4614-1244-1_4

Epidemiology

Driven in large part by the obesity epidemic, diabetes is a major increasing public health issue. Recent population-based glycosylated hemoglobin (HbA1c) screening has shown that prediabetes (HbA1c ranging 5.7–6.4 %) affects 35 % of all women in the United States aged ≥19 years old and diabetes affects an additional 10.8 % in the same age group [1]. Further, the prevalence of diabetes in developed countries is expected to rise 20 % by 2030 based on obesity and age demographics [2]. Thus, diabetes in pregnancy can be expected to be increasingly common. In a southern California population of insured pregnant women, the prevalence of diabetes of any form increased from 8.3 per 100 pregnancies in 1999 to 9.2 per 100 pregnancies in 2005 [3]. Of note, the prevalence of chronic diabetes among gravidas is increasing. In the interval from 1999 to 2005, the proportion of diabetic gravidas with pregestational diabetes in this same group of women rose from 11 to 26 %. Since approximately 3.7 % of adults aged 20–44 years old have undiagnosed diabetes [1], many women will be first diagnosed in pregnancy.

The prevalence of GDM generally reflects the prevalence of type 2 DM in the population. It is higher in Asians, African-Americans, Native Americans, and Hispanics as compared to non-Hispanic Whites [3]. Increased maternal age, family history, previous history of GDM or poor obstetric outcomes, ethnicity, polycystic ovarian syndrome, hypertension, and obesity are all risk factors. GDM has been found to occur in approximately 4 % of pregnancies (range of 1–14 %) [4], but if the diagnostic criteria for GDM that is recommended by the IADPSG and ADA are used, the proportion of pregnancies affected by GDM could be as high as 18 % [5].

Pathobiology

Pregnant women undergo a number of physiologic changes to meet the metabolic needs of the growing products of conception. Early in pregnancy, glucose crosses the placenta by facilitated diffusion and amino acids are shunted to the fetoplacental unit by active transport. Maternal fasting glucose levels decline, beginning early in the first trimester [6]. As pregnancy progresses, the maternal energy source switches from glucose based to lipid based so that glucose is further freed for fetal use. Maternal insulin needs increase due to increased maternal cortisol levels and placental production of the contrainsulin hormones, human placental lactogen, prolactin, estrogen, and progesterone. Because of this, both fasting and postprandial insulin levels rise during pregnancy. Women with pregestational diabetes usually require increasing doses of insulin throughout pregnancy. Gravidas whose insulin secretion may have been adequate to maintain euglycemia in the nonpregnant state but lack adequate pancreatic reserve may develop both fasting and postprandial hyperglycemia and, thus, be diagnosed as having gestational diabetes.

Pregestational Diabetes

The likelihood of developing maternal and fetal complications related to pregestational diabetes during pregnancy is linked to both glucose control and the degree of preexisting end-organ disease. The goal of preconception care is to institute measures resulting in a normal A1c prior to conception and to identify and optimally treat end-organ disease.

Maternal complications of type 1 and type 2 DM include microvascular and macrovascular disease. Over the long term, the risk of microvascular complications from DM has not been shown to be increased by pregnancy but its presence does have important immediate implications during pregnancy. The development of diabetic retinopathy has been found to be accelerated by improved glycemic control in nonpregnant patients, and pregnancy has been associated with progression of retinopathy [7–9]. Whether this association is related to institution of better metabolic control in pregnant women or to associated physiologic changes in pregnancy is not clear. Though not adequately studied in pregnancy, this likely predisposition to advancing retinopathy among successfully treated gravidas and the often uncertain duration of diabetes prior to pregnancy suggest benefit from retinal examination prior to pregnancy or early in newly diagnosed pregnancy. The opportunity for possible early treatment likely provides safety for the patient and avoids early delivery due to later ocular complications.

Approximately one third of patients with a 10-year history of diabetes will develop diabetic nephropathy with attendant hypertension, proteinuria, and renal insufficiency. The presence of renal disease increases the risk for both maternal and fetal adverse outcomes (see Renal Chapter). Forty percent of women entering pregnancy with a serum creatinine of 1.4–1.9 mg/dL, from any cause, experience a pregnancy-related decline in renal function which persists postpartum in 50 % [10, 11]. Approximately one third of women with serum creatinine ≥2 mg/dL progress to end-stage renal disease during pregnancy or in the postpartum period [10]. Baseline microalbuminuria and proteinuria increase during pregnancy and may reach the nephrotic range as pregnancy progresses, though it generally improves after delivery [12]. Angiotensin-converting enzyme (ACE) inhibitors and angiotensin II receptor blockers (ARBs) are shown to be more effective in preserving renal function and delaying the progression of proteinuria in nonpregnant diabetic patients. Among those who anticipate pregnancy and can be relied on to identify its onset in the first trimester, the continued use of these agents is preferable during the period of months leading up to pregnancy. These drugs should not be used after pregnancy is diagnosed because of their association with fetal growth restriction, renal failure, and oligohydramnios. Calcium channel blockers such as diltiazem appear to be safe during pregnancy and likely provide protection of maternal renal function. Since the combination of proteinuria and hypertension is an essential hallmark of preeclampsia, it is often unclear whether the patient with diabetic nephropathy is demonstrating the physiologic effect of pregnancy that increases proteinuria and a deterioration of maternal renal function, or such changes reflect the development of superimposed preeclampsia. Consequently, case series of such patients demonstrate a significantly increased risk of preeclampsia and iatrogenic premature delivery among diabetic gravidas with nephropathy [13]. These findings underscore the importance of establishing baseline data regarding renal and hepatic function and metabolic correlates of preeclampsia early in pregnancy for later comparison.

The prevalence of ischemic heart disease (IHD) among pregnant diabetic patients is unknown, but increased metabolic demands of pregnancy increase cardiac work and the shift toward a prothrombotic balance during pregnancy may increase risk of coronary insufficiency. The criteria that would warrant cardiac evaluation in a pregnant woman with diabetes are undefined. However, in women with symptoms suggestive of coronary disease and those with additional predisposing factors, cardiac evaluation prior to or early in pregnancy is advisable. During pregnancy, a stress ECG or stress echocardiogram can be safely performed (see Cardiac Chapter).

Diabetic gastropathy may compromise maternal nutrition among those with longstanding disease. Our approach to excessive emesis in the diabetic patient includes intravenous fluids, antiemetics, endoscopic evaluation, and parenteral feeding (see GI Chapter).

Diabetic ketoacidosis (DKA) can be seen at lower glucose concentrations during pregnancy than in nonpregnant women and should be considered even if glucoses are not over 250 mg/dL in the appropriate clinical setting [14, 15]. Whether the risk of DKA is increased in pregnancy is unknown. Even controlled series may be subject to surveillance and reporting biases. Factors that may predispose to DKA in pregnancy include patient failure to medicate in the context of nausea and vomiting, the development of urinary tract infection, or administration of beta sympathomimetic medications and corticosteroids, often employed during pregnancy. Treatment with crystalloid replacement and insulin should be both urgent and aggressive. The fetus is very sensitive to maternal acidemia, hypovolemia, and hyperglycemia, the latter increasing the fetoplacental oxygen requirements. Treatment should be initiated before electrolyte and blood gas data are available. The young pregnant women may not display signs of hypovolemia readily and can readily accept 2 l of normal saline or lactated Ringers solutions in the first hour of treatment. Because of the hormonal milieu of pregnancy and the accompanying hyperglycemia and hyperlipidemia, initial intravenous insulin infusion rates of 10–20 units per hour are common in the treatment of diabetic ketoacidosis in pregnancy. Generally, in utero resuscitation is preferable to the delivery of a metabolically compromised fetus. Often, prompt maternal treatment will allow continuation of pregnancy [16].

Fetal and Perinatal Risks Due to Maternal Diabetes

Hyperglycemia and diabetic end-organ disease, particularly nephropathy, cause increased risk of adverse fetal and neonatal outcomes. Hyperglycemia in the periconceptional period and during the early first trimester has been associated with the combined incidence of spontaneous abortion and congenital anomalies of 65 % [17].

Since the median interval for conception among fertile couples is six months, the patient who is anticipating pregnancy (and her physician) should be prepared for a lengthy interval of intensive treatment. All diabetic, sexually active women should be employing a reliable means of contraception.

The Pederson hypothesis [18] of the pathophysiology of diabetic fetopathy originally proposed that fetal overgrowth is caused by increased transplacental passage of glucose due to maternal hyperglycemia. This causes increased fetal insulin secretion with resulting increased deposition of fat and glycogen. This hypothesis has been supported by experimental models in several species and in human clinical observations [19]. Diabetic fetopathy causes increased operative delivery and fetal injury at birth and neonatal metabolic disturbances, including hypoglycemia, hypocalcemia, polycythemia, and hyperbilirubinemia. Maternal hyperglycemia has been shown to acutely increase fetoplacental oxygen requirement and may thereby contribute to the increased risk of death, found late in diabetic pregnancy among macrosomic fetuses. Restricted fetal growth may occur due to poor placental perfusion due to diabetic vasculopathy, chronic hypertension, renal dysfunction, and superimposed preeclampsia.

Later in life, the offspring of women with diabetes are at greater risk for obesity, hypertension, and diabetes, compared to those born of women who developed diabetes after their pregnancies and those who never developed diabetes [20]. Table 4.1 delineates the risks associated with diabetes.

Table 4.1 Some risks associated with diabetes in pregnancy

Fetal and infant risks	Maternal risks
Miscarriage or stillbirth[a]	Worsening or unmasking of end-organ disease related to diabetes[a]
Congenital anomalies[a]	
• Caudal regression syndrome	• Retinopathy
• CNS abnormalities—spina bifida, anencephaly, hydrocephalous	• Nephropathy
	• Neuropathy
• Cardiac	• Cardiac disease
Macrosomia	Hypoglycemia
Organomegaly	DKA in type 1[a]
Hypoxic events including intrauterine fetal demise	Infection, including pyelonephritis
	Pregnancy-induced hypertension/preeclampsia
Operative delivery	
Birth injury	
Respiratory distress	
Hypoglycemia	
Intrauterine growth restriction	
Cardiac hypertrophy with or without heart failure	
Hyperbilirubinemia	
Hypocalcemia	
Hypomagnesemia	
Polycythemia	
Hyperviscosity syndrome	
Preeclampsia	
Premature delivery	

[a]Risks specifically associated to pregestational diabetes

Pregnant women with diabetes require extra office visits and glucose surveillance. In our practice, the median number of visits for diabetes management is several times to once per month in addition to the routine visits to obstetrical caregivers. Additionally, we contact the patient by phone at a median of two times each week throughout pregnancy. We utilize daily fasting and 2-h postprandial glucose testing throughout pregnancy. Such intensive surveillance occurs in the context of a developing, open, and nonjudgmental relationship between patient and diabetes nurse-educator and physicians. We find a high degree of social burdens among our patients, such that often, social worker and psychiatric support are helpful in maintaining maternal and fetal health.

Gestational Diabetes

The American College of Obstetricians and Gynecologists (ACOG) defines GDM to be carbohydrate intolerance with onset or recognition during pregnancy [21]. Risk factors for GDM include obesity, family history of DM, age>25 years old, ethnicity (African-American, Hispanic, Native American, Asian, and Pacific Islander), previous delivery of a baby weighing over 9 pounds, polycystic ovarian syndrome, and personal history of glucose intolerance. Given the prevalence of risk factors in most populations in the United States, universal screening has been generally adopted. ACOG recommends a 2-step approach for the diagnosis of GDM. If the diabetic screen (a 50-g, 1-hour glucose challenge test) performed at 24–28 weeks' gestation results in a value of ≥ 140 mg/dl, a 100-g, 3-h diagnostic oral glucose tolerance test is recommended (see Table 4.4). An early diabetic screen at 12–14 weeks is recommended in women who are at increased risk for pregestational diabetes such as those with obesity, strong family history of diabetes, or a previous history of GDM. If its result is normal, screening should be repeated at 24–28 weeks' gestation.

Other professional organizations offer other diagnostic criteria for diabetes in pregnancy [22]. The International Association of Diabetes and Pregnancy Study Group (IADPSG) and American Diabetes Association (ADA) accept the following criteria for overt diabetes in pregnancy: fasting plasma glucose≥ 126 mg/dL, A1c≥ 6.5 %, or random plasma glucose≥ 200 mg/dL that is subsequently confirmed by elevated fasting glucose or A1c [23, 24]. Both organizations also recommended diabetes screening by employing a single 2-h, 75-g glucose tolerance test, with diagnostic thresholds noted in Table 4.4. This approach has been calculated to increase the number of gravidas diagnosed with gestational diabetes from 5–6 % to 15–20 % of pregnant women [5]. Given this, an NIH consensus development conference and ACOG have recommended continued use of the 2-step approach described above because of concern that the adoption of the new criteria "would increase the prevalence of GDM, and the corresponding costs and interventions, without clear demonstration of improvements in the most clinically important health and patient-centered outcomes" [25].

Treating Hyperglycemia in Diabetic Pregnancy

Maintaining euglycemia is paramount to mitigating the risks associated with hyperglycemia during pregnancy. In particular, treatment reduces risk for macrosomia, shoulder dystocia, and preeclampsia [26]. Among 25,000 gravidas in a worldwide prospective cohort study of gravidas without diagnosed diabetes, midpregnancy maternal glucose levels had a linear positive association with fetal birth weight, without evident threshold effect. In the United States, the ADA and ACOG recommend the goals of fasting and 2-h postprandial glucose concentrations of <95 mg/dL and <120 mg/dL [21, 27].

Among patients with newly diagnosed diabetes in pregnancy, we begin a regimen of glucose measurements in the fasting state and 2 h after each main meal. Concurrently, patients are provided dietary counsel to establish reduced carbohydrate intake (40 % of calories from carbohydrate, 20 %–30 % from protein, and 30–40 % from fat in 3 meals with planned snacks) in a stable diet as to timing, amount, and type of food. After 2–7 days of observation, those patients found to maintain normal fasting glucose values are encouraged to continue to pursue dietary change to lower postprandial values to target range. In the absence of obstetric contraindications, moderate physical activity is safe during pregnancy and may improve glucose control by enhancing insulin sensitivity.

For most women with GDM, these interventions will be sufficient without pharmacologic treatment. However, women with preexisting diabetes and some with GDM will require medication to achieve adequate glucose control. Insulin does not cross the placenta and its use offers two other advantages over oral agents during pregnancy. First, insulin treatment can be tailored to the timing of meals to minimize risk of hypoglycemia while achieving a euglycemic profile. Second, insulin treatment can generally achieve an acceptable euglycemic profile within two weeks even in an initially poorly controlled diabetic patient, a much shorter interval than is generally required by treatment with glyburide. A typical regimen includes either long- or intermediate-acting insulin in combination with short acting. NPH insulin and a short-acting insulin (regular (crystalline zinc) insulin or insulin lispro or insulin aspart) are prescribed prior to breakfast and the evening meal. Occasionally the evening dose of NPH insulin is moved to bedtime to more effectively treat fasting hyperglycemia. Limited data suggests that insulin detemir and insulin glargine may be safely used during pregnancy, but randomized trials comparing these agents to NPH are not available. However, if a woman has well-controlled pregestational diabetes on one of these agents and becomes pregnant, it is reasonable to continue it during pregnancy. Table 4.2 outlines the pharmacokinetics of different insulins.

The long-term effects of fetal exposure to sulfonylureas or metformin among offspring are unknown. Whether glyburide crosses the placenta in significant amounts is controversial, but it has not been shown to be associated with adverse fetal outcomes when compared to insulin. However, practical and theoretical limitations to its use are relevant to diabetes management. In one study, approximately 20 % of pregnant women with fasting glucoses over 110 mg/dL treated with glyburide failed to reach targeted glycemic control and ultimately required treatment

Table 4.2 Pharmacokinetics of different insulins [55]

Type of insulin	Onset of action	Peak action	Duration of action
Intermediate acting: NPH (isophane)	2–4 h	4–10 h	10–16 h
Short acting: regular	0.5–1 h	2–4 h	3–6 h
Rapid acting: Aspart Lispro Glulisine	< 0.25 h < 0.3–0.5 h < 0.25 h	0.5–1.0 h 0.5–2.5 h 1–1.5 h	3–5 h 3–6.5 h 3–5 h
Long acting: Glargine Detemir	2–4 h 0.8–2 h (dose dependent)	Relatively flat Relatively flat	20–24 h 12 h for 0.2 units/kg; 20 h for 0.4 units/kg, up to 24 h

switched to insulin [28]. Further, despite the attractive anticipation that frequent insulin adjustments can be avoided with glyburide use, it can cause hypoglycemia because of the inevitable mismatch between meal schedules and its pharmacodynamic effects. Metformin does cross the placenta but has not been shown to be associated with adverse perinatal outcomes. Up to 35 % of gravidas treated with metformin require insulin treatment to achieve adequate control, however [29]. We find that as compared with oral agents, insulin dosing can more nimbly respond to changing requirements due to increasing insulin resistance as pregnancy progresses and changes in diet due to early nausea, gastroparesis, or the patient's adoption of recommended diet. While this approach is more laborsome than using oral agents, we employ a diabetes nurse-educator in reviewing glucose data with patients at frequent intervals and find that most GDM and pregestational diabetic patients achieve euglycemic targets within 2 weeks of initiating treatment.

Collaboration Between Internist and Obstetric Offices

The interface between internist and obstetric offices is based on the expressed needs of obstetrical prenatal care providers, who must remain the primary site of care for pregnant women. This often requires the internist to actively define their services in a dialog with the obstetrical staff and physicians. The delegation of internist duties to the patient should be explicitly documented in initial correspondence from either party to provide the framework for subsequent patient education, treatment, and reciprocal reporting by both parties during and after pregnancy. Often, a third party physician, one who has been the primary prepregnancy caregiver, should participate in establishing roles as well. In our own practice, after initial conversations, we document our own understanding of each provider's role, while requesting any modification advised by the other party. We find that initial education and treatment of the diabetic gravida means more frequent visits with the obstetric internist.

This usually shifts to a more frequent interaction with the obstetrician as the pregnancy progresses. We provide the referring obstetrician with documentation of each visit with the internal medicine office.

Office visits are opportunities to assess glucose control face-to-face with patients. As observed by others [30], we frequently find the reported glucose values and those recorded in the memory of glucose meters to be discordant. Review of glucose data from the patient's meter also may provide insight into erratic timing of meals and lapses in glucose testing that allows for a more reality-based discussion of impediments to better glucose control. In order to develop a durable trust relationship with patients, we inform patients at the start of treatment that we will be reviewing glucose meter data at each office visit. We also emphasize that we view our therapeutic role as supportive and recognize the many physical, logistical, and psychological impediments to achieving glycemic control. Coexisting conditions such as hypertension, retinopathy, and nephropathy are addressed at these visits. After 20 weeks' gestation, evidence for possible superimposed preeclampsia should be sought. Tables 4.3 and 4.4 outline management steps from prior to and during pregnancy.

Table 4.3 Preconception assessment of diabetic women [50]

Key points	Specific recommendations
Assess glucose control • To prevent congenital anomalies and miscarriage, A1c should be as close to normal as possible without significant hypoglycemia before conception	• Measure A1c and patient to obtain self-monitoring of blood glucoses • Nutrition consult • Advise physical activity of 30 min or more daily on at least 5 days per week • Attain as close to normal BMI as possible prior to pregnancy. Recommend pregnancy weight gain according to the Institute of Medicine recommendations [51]
Assess degree of end-organ disease related to diabetes • Retinopathy • Nephropathy • Neuropathy • Cardiovascular disease	• Obtain dilated retinal exam by ophthalmologist and treat optimally prior to pregnancy. If pregnant, retinal evaluation should be obtained in the first trimester and followed throughout pregnancy depending on the findings. • Obtain BUN/creatinine and urine for microalbuminuria • Evaluate for gastroparesis • Foot exam, advise proper foot care • Evaluate awareness of hypoglycemia • EKG, consider evaluation for cardiac disease with appropriate stress test or cardiac echo as indicated • Consider testing for peripheral vascular disease if indicated by signs and symptoms or physical exam
Assess for and treat diseases associated with diabetes • Hypertension • Hyperlipidemia • Thyroid disease • Anemia, including pernicious anemia • Celiac disease • Depression • Liver disease	• Goal BP <130/80 mmHg • Fasting lipid profile • Obtain TSH, consider thyroid antibodies • Obtain CBC, ferritin, and consider vitamin B12 level in type 1 diabetics • Consider anti-tTG (tissue transglutaminase) and anti-EMG (endomysial antibody) to evaluate for celiac disease in type 1 DM • Obtain ALT/AST for evidence of nonalcoholic hepatosteatosis; consider liver ultrasound if indicated

(continued)

Table 4.3 (continued)

Key points	Specific recommendations
Review medications	• Treat with insulin during pregnancy and discontinue noninsulin regimen • During pregnancy discontinue ACE inhibitors, angiotensin II receptor blockers (ARBs), and statins • Continue 81-mg ASA if already taking, and consider beginning during pregnancy for preeclampsia prevention if not [52] • For pregnancy begin prenatal vitamin • For pregnancy begin 4-mg folic acid because diabetics are at increased risk for neural tube defects (recommended for women at high risk of neural tube defects though it is unclear if it is helpful in diabetics) [53]
Address increased risk for superimposed preeclampsia with pregnancy	• Obtain baseline preeclampsia labs including CBC/platelets, uric acid, AST, creatinine, urine protein to creatinine ratio, and 24-h urine collection for creatinine clearance and total protein • Consider 81-mg ASA for preeclampsia prevention
Additional measures	• Advise smoking cessation • Advise avoidance of alcohol for pregnancy

Table 4.4 Screening recommendations for diabetes in pregnancy

Professional society	Screening tests
IADPSG Consensus Panel [23] Endorsed by ADA	First prenatal visit (test all or only risk women depending on patient population) • Measure fasting plasma glucose (FPG), A1c, or random glucose, and treat and follow up as preexisting diabetes if FPG $\geq$ 126 mg/dL, A1c $\geq$ 6.5 %, random glucose $\geq$ 200 mg/dL with confirmation, diagnose as <u>overt diabetes</u> • If not diagnostic of overt diabetes and fasting plasma glucose $\geq$ 92 mg/dL but < 126 mg/dL diagnose as GDM • If not diagnostic of overt diabetes and FPG <92 mg/dL, test for GDM at 24–28 weeks' gestation 24–28 weeks' gestation: diagnosis of GDM Administer 2-h 75-g OGTT after overnight fast • Overt diabetes if FPG $\geq$ 126 mg/dL • GDM if one or more of the following values abnormal: FPG $\geq$ 92 mg/dL, 1-h plasma glucose $\geq$ 180 mg/dL, 2-h plasma glucose $\geq$ 153 mg/dL Normal if all values less than above
ACOG [21]	Diabetic screen—50-g 1-h glucose tolerance test • Cutoff threshold 130 mg/dL If abnormal, proceed to 3-h glucose tolerance test 100-g 3-h glucose tolerance test (diagnosis of GDM if 2 abnormal values)[b] • Fasting $\geq$ 95 mg/dL • 1 h $\geq$ 180 mg/dL • 2 h $\geq$ 155 mg/dL • 3 h $\geq$ 140 g/dL

[a]130 mg/dL cutoff has greater sensitivity than 140 mg/dL, also considered acceptable by ACOG [54]
[b]Carpenter and Coustan criteria [54]

Unless requested specifically by the referring obstetrical care office, we do not address issues of pregnancy viability and dating, screening for fetal disorders, and surveillance of fetal health and growth during pregnancy, as these issues are the general purview of obstetrical care. As pregnancy progresses, antenatal testing for fetal well-being and appropriate growth will be instituted. Types of tests of fetal well-being and the scheduling of fetal growth assessments will depend on individual pregnancy concerns. Fetal growth assessment at 28 gestational weeks' finding fetal abdominal circumference values in the upper quartile for gestational age increases the risk of fetal macrosomia at birth. More aggressive treatment of maternal hyperglycemia in this group has been shown to reduce the incidence of birth macrosomia [31].

Labor and Delivery

The risk for fetal acidosis and neonatal hypoglycemia has been associated with maternal hyperglycemia during labor and delivery. Management of maternal glucose concentrations among gravidas treated with insulin involves several considerations. Active labor is estimated to produce up to twice resting energy expenditure. Thus, labor is associated with insulin-independent glucose utilization that may appreciably reduce maternal insulin requirements in the fasting patient. ACOG recommends maintaining glucoses between 70 and 110 mg/dL during labor, though some authors suggest higher levels may be acceptable [32, 33]. Accomplishing this requires frequent glucose monitoring and, for some patients, insulin infusion. Type 1 diabetic patients require constant insulin infusion during labor, but often at less than one unit each hour during active labor. In such patients, we recommend that an insulin solution and a separate glucose solution be hung as ancillary to the main crystalloid line containing either lactated Ringers or normal saline solutions. We do not recommend subcutaneous insulin treatment during labor because of the unpredictable insulin requirements during this time. A suggested protocol for the management of insulin during labor and delivery is illustrated in Table 4.5.

Table 4.5 Diabetes mellitus management guideline for labor and postpartum

Background
• Patients in active labor require less insulin per hour than before they were in labor
• Recent doses of long-acting insulins may continue to affect maternal glucose values during labor
• Patients with type 1 diabetes mellitus require exogenous insulin (injection or infusion) at all times
• The main IV solution infused during labor should be lactated Ringer's or normal saline solution. IV solutions containing either glucose or insulin should be ancillary (piggy back) lines
• Diet during labor induction or spontaneous labor should be limited to clear liquids containing only artificial sweeteners until delivery or when the attempted labor inductions has been terminated

(continued)

Table 4.5 (continued)

Insulin doses prior to scheduled cesarean birth or labor induction

1. *Gestational and type 2 diabetic patients*
   - Pre-supper and bedtime insulins (regular CZI, aspart, lispro, and/or NPH) should be taken as routine
   - Bedtime glargine insulin doses should be halved the night before intervention
   - The patient should be admitted prior to usual breakfast time and capillary glucose value monitored hourly until steady-state values of 80–100 mg/dl are documented
   - An insulin infusion of not less than 0.5 units per hour should be started if values exceed 100 mg/dl. The dose should be adjusted at least hourly, until hourly steady-state (+/- 10 mg/dl) capillary glucose values of 80–100 mg/dl are obtained
   - Once steady-state glucose values are documented, the interval between glucose testing may be increased.

2. *Type 1 diabetic patient*
   - Pre-supper and bedtime insulins (regular CZI, aspart, lispro, and/or NPH) should be taken as routine
   - Bedtime glargine insulin doses should be halved the night before intervention
   - The patient should be admitted to the hospital in time to start an infusion of insulin prior to the time of the patient's usual breakfast
   - Insulin infusion in normal saline should be started at 0.5 to 1.0 units per hour
   - Glucose levels should be obtained by finger lancet or by indwelling venous catheter flushed with saline at each draw time. Glucose values should be assayed every 30 min for 1–2 h to allow adjustment of insulin infusion rate until hourly steady-state (+/- 10 mg/dl) capillary glucose values of 80–100 mg/dl are obtained.
   - Once steady-state glucose values are documented, the interval between glucose testing may be increased

Capillary glucose monitoring and insulin infusion during labor

1. *Gestational and type 2 diabetic patients*
   - Most patients with GDM or type 2 diabetes have significant insulin resistance during pregnancy, which immediately decreases following delivery. Their insulin requirements are often only a fraction of those required for strict glycemic control during pregnancy
   - Acceptable blood glucose values may range as high as 150 mg/dl, without intervention, in the postpartum patient since fetal effects are no longer relevant
   - The insulin infusion rate may be either terminated or adjusted downward based on the patient's prepregnancy glucose requirements and timing of next anticipated meal
   - Compared to prepregnancy doses, the exogenous insulin requirement may be reduced postpartum because the patient has recently been euglycemic and because of lactation effects
   - Patients with type 2 diabetes may resume 80 to 100 % of their insulin or oral mediation doses used prior to pregnancy when eating their usual diet
   - Gestational diabetes patients should have a fasting and a 2-h post-breakfast capillary glucose assay performed. If fasting is >140 or post-breakfast is >200 mg/dl is documented, treatment should be started prior to discharge and an appointment with a family practitioner, internist, or endocrinologist be scheduled. Patient's with lesser levels of hyperglycemia should be provided similar follow-up appointments but may not require immediate treatment

(continued)

4 Diabetes and Pregnancy

Table 4.5 (continued)

2. *Type 1 diabetic patients*	
	• Insulin infusion (in normal saline solution) should be continued at not less than 0.25 units per hour until two hours after first subcutaneous dose of regular or short-acting insulin is administered
	• Capillary glucose values should be assayed at least every four hours initially
	• The target range of capillary glucose concentrations is 80–150 mg/dl

Capillary glucose monitoring and insulin infusion immediately post-delivery

1. *Gestational and type 2 diabetic patients*
   - Most patients with GDM or type 2 diabetes have significant insulin resistance during pregnancy, which immediately decreases following delivery. Their insulin requirements are often only a fraction of those required for strict glycemic control during pregnancy
   - Acceptable blood glucose values may range to as high as 150 mg/dl, without intervention, in the postpartum patient since fetal effects are no longer relevant.
   - The insulin infusion rate may be either terminated or adjusted downward based on the patient's prepregnancy glucose requirements and timing of next anticipated meal
   - Compared to prepregnancy doses, the exogenous insulin requirement may be reduced postpartum because the patient has recently been euglycemic and because of lactation effects
   - Patients with type 2 diabetes may resume 80 to 100 % of their insulin or oral mediation doses used prior to pregnancy when eating their usual diet
   - Gestational diabetes patients should have a fasting and a 2-h post-breakfast capillary glucose assay performed. If fasting is >140 or post-breakfast is >200 mg/dl as documented, treatment should be started prior to discharge and an appointment with a family practitioner, internist, or endocrinologist be scheduled. Patient's with lesser levels of hyperglycemia should be provided similar follow-up appointments but may not require immediate treatment

2. *Type 1 diabetic patients*
   - Insulin infusion (in normal saline solution) should be continued at not less than 0.25 units per hour until two hours after first subcutaneous dose of regular or short-acting insulin is administered
   - Capillary glucose values should be assayed at least every four hours initially
   - The target range of capillary glucose concentrations is 80–150 mg/dl
   - Insulin requirement may be reduced postpartum because the patient has recently been euglycemic and because of lactation effects
     - Patients may resume their insulin doses, used prior to pregnancy, when eating their usual diet

Post-pregnancy preparation for chronic diabetes management

1. *Gestational diabetes patients without postpartum hyperglycemia*
   - Obtain nutrition counseling for patient
   - Glucose tolerance testing should be scheduled at approximately five weeks postpartum to occur one week before routine postpartum obstetrical care visit

2. *Patients with gestational diabetes, patients with postpartum hyperglycemia, and patients with type 1 and 2 diabetes*
   - Obtain nutrition counseling for patient
   - Schedule patient visit with established or new diabetes care provider (family practice physician, internist, or endocrinologist) within three weeks after discharge
   - Inform intended diabetes care provider regarding patient's mediation/insulin regimen

Pregestational Diabetes Management in the Postpartum Period

Women with pregestational diabetes usually demonstrate a marked reduction in exogenous insulin requirements within hours after delivery. At this time, the risk of hypoglycemia is higher than the risk of moderately elevated glucoses. We find it helpful to reinstate insulin at 2/3 prepregnancy doses in those known to enter pregnancy with acceptable glycemic control. In the common circumstance of unknown or poor glycemic control at time of conception, we generally provide half to two thirds the recent pregnancy insulin doses when the patient demonstrates the reliable ability to take meals. Breastfeeding should be encouraged in the diabetic parturient, but may decrease insulin needs. We generally liberalize glucose control targets in the postpartum woman who experience physiologic changes and multiple challenges in their eating and activity schedules as they care for their newborns. Table 4.6 summarizes the information on the use of diabetes medication in lactating women. Women with type 1 DM are at risk for postpartum thyroiditis. The Endocrine Society recommends obtaining a thyroid-stimulating hormone (TSH) assay 3 months postpartum [34].

We recommend that postpartum patient with prior GDM who has been treated with glyburide or insulin has a fasting and 2-h postprandial glucose assay during her birth hospitalization. Those who have persisting hyperglycemia, suggesting prediabetes, should have appropriate medical follow-up scheduled. Those who are euglycemic should undergo a 75-g 2-h glucose tolerance test at 6–12 weeks' postpartum, preferably prior to the scheduled postpartum obstetric office visit [35, 36]. Up to 20 % of those tested will have either impaired glucose tolerance or overt diabetes [37, 38]. Even those with normal results are at risk for subsequent diabetes. O'Sullivan found that approximately half of women with a history of gestational diabetes will develop type 2 diabetes within 20 years. Women with prior GDM also appear to have an increased risk for cardiovascular disease later in life compared to women with normal glucose tolerance during pregnancy [39, 40]. Even women who have a single abnormal value at 1 h on glucose tolerance testing have a cardiovascular profile with increased risk [41]. How much of this increased risk is due to the development of diabetes is uncertain. Given this, patients should be counseled on the importance of lifestyle modification. Evidence from studies like the Diabetes Prevention Program supports the use of diet and exercise or a pharmacologic agent to lower the incidence or delay the onset of diabetes in those at high risk for its development [42–45]. Specific recommendations include encouragement of breastfeeding, healthy nutrition, physical activity, weight loss of at least 5–7 % for overweight or obese patients, and appropriate cardiac risk factor modification including tobacco cessation and aggressive management of hyperlipidemia and hypertension [46]. The infants of gestational diabetic mothers (IDM), who are obese at birth, demonstrate higher BMI, blood pressure, insulin resistance, and lipid levels compared to IDMs with normal BMIs at birth. Assuming that such effects are true in other classes of diabetic mothers, it is reasonable to advocate that patients engage their families in similar modification of diet and exercise [47].

Table 4.6 Diabetes medication and breastfeeding

Drug	Hale lactation risk category[a] and review by American Academy of Pediatrics (AAP)	Comments
Insulin	L1, not reviewed by AAP	Insulin is large molecule that is not secreted into milk. However, even if it was secreted into the milk, the peptide would be destroyed in the GI tract and not absorbed
Metformin	Hale L1 Not reviewed by the AAP	Preferred oral agent in breastfeeding
Sulfonylureas • Glyburide • Glipizide	Glyburide—L2, not reviewed by AAP Glipizide—L3, not reviewed by AAP	Glyburide—milk levels undetectable, transfer to infant of clinically relevant amounts unlikely
Meglitinides • Repaglinide	Repaglinide L4, not reviewed by AAP	Rodent studies suggest repaglinide is transferred into milk and induce hypoglycemia and skeletal changes
Thiazolidinediones • Rosiglitazone • Pioglitazone	Rosiglitazone—L3, not reviewed by AAP Pioglitazone—L3, not reviewed by AAP	More data is needed
DPP-4 inhibitors • Sitagliptin	Sitagliptin—L3, not reviewed by AAP	More data needed
Glucagon-like peptide 1 agonist • Exenatide	Exenatide—L3, not reviewed by AAP	More data needed
Alpha glucosidase inhibitors • Acarbose Miglitol	Acarbose—L3, not reviewed by AAP Miglitol—L2, not reviewed by AAP	No data available in human milk but it is unlikely the drug would reach the milk compartment or be orally absorbed by the infant Miglitol—the manufacturer reports milk levels very small

[a]Hale Lactation Risk Categories—L1 Safest, L2 Safer, L3 Moderately Safe (Comment: New medications that have absolutely no published data are automatically categorized in this category regardless of how safe they may be), L4 Possibly Hazardous, L5 Contraindicated [56]

Euglycemic women with a history of GDM should be screened at regular intervals for diabetes. Women should be aware that the recurrence rate for GDM in subsequent pregnancies is between 30 and 84 % [48].

Contraception

We counsel patients to adopt reliable methods of contraception if they wish to maintain fertility. This will allow timely testing for diabetes prior to the next pregnancy. Oral contraceptives appear to be safe in diabetic patient without evident cardiovascular disease. Estrogen at daily doses of <35mcg does not appear to have adverse metabolic effects but, progestins (oral and injectable) are associated with insulin resistance and adverse lipid changes. The IUD does not have such metabolic effects, making it a good choice for many diabetics. While barrier methods also do not affect the metabolic profile, they must be used properly and consistently to be effective overall. Approximately 5 % of women of childbearing age had an unplanned pregnancy in 2006 which underscores the importance of contraception [49].

References

1. National Diabetes Statistics. National diabetes information clearinghouse. 2011. www.diabetes.niddk.nih.gov
2. Shaw JE, Sicree RA, Zimmet PZ. Global estimates of the prevalence of diabetes for 2010 and 2030. Diabetes Res Clin Pract. 2010;87(1):4–14.
3. Hunt KJ, Schuller KL. The increasing prevalence of diabetes in pregnancy. Obstet Gynecol Clin North Am. 2007;34(2):173–99. vii.
4. Baraban E, McCoy L, Simon P. Increasing prevalence of gestational diabetes and pregnancy-related hypertension in Los Angeles County, California, 1991-2003. Prev Chronic Dis. 2008; 5(3):A77.
5. Hypertension in pregnancy. Washington, DC: American College of Obstetricians and Gynecologists; 2013.
6. Mills JL, Jovanovic L, Knopp R, Aarons J, Conley M, Park E, et al. Physiological reduction in fasting plasma glucose concentration in the first trimester of normal pregnancy: the diabetes in early pregnancy study. Metabolism. 1998;47(9):1140–4.
7. Chew EY, Mills JL, Metzger BE, Remaley NA, Jovanovic-Peterson L, Knopp RH, et al. Metabolic control and progression of retinopathy. The Diabetes in Early Pregnancy Study National Institute of Child Health and Human Development Diabetes in Early Pregnancy Study. Diabetes care. 1995;18(5):631–7.
8. Diabetes C. Complications Trial Research G. Effect of pregnancy on microvascular complications in the diabetes control and complications trial. The Diabetes Control and Complications Trial Research Group. Diabetes Care. 2000;23(8):1084–91.
9. Sheth BP. Does pregnancy accelerate the rate of progression of diabetic retinopathy? An update. Curr Diab Rep. 2008;8(4):270–3.
10. Jones DC, Hayslett JP. Outcome of pregnancy in women with moderate or severe renal insufficiency. N Engl J Med. 1996;335(4):226–32.
11. Epstein FH. Pregnancy and renal disease. N Engl J Med. 1996;335(4):277–8.
12. Gordon M, Landon MB, Samuels P, Hissrich S, Gabbe SG. Perinatal outcome and long-term follow-up associated with modern management of diabetic nephropathy. Obstet Gynecol. 1996;87(3):401–9.
13. Ekbom P, Damm P, Feldt-Rasmussen B, Feldt-Rasmussen U, Molvig J, Mathiesen ER. Pregnancy outcome in type 1 diabetic women with microalbuminuria. Diabetes Care. 2001;24(10):1739–44.
14. Guo RX, Yang LZ, Li LX, Zhao XP. Diabetic ketoacidosis in pregnancy tends to occur at lower blood glucose levels: case-control study and a case report of euglycemic diabetic ketoacidosis in pregnancy. J Obstet Gynaecol Res. 2008;34(3):324–30.
15. Cullen MT, Reece EA, Homko CJ, Sivan E. The changing presentations of diabetic ketoacidosis during pregnancy. Am J Perinatol. 1996;13(7):449–51.
16. Parker JA, Conway DL. Diabetic ketoacidosis in pregnancy. Obstet Gynecol Clin North Am. 2007;34(3):533–43. xii.

17. Greene MF. Prevention and diagnosis of congenital anomalies in diabetic pregnancies. Clin Perinatol. 1993;20(3):533–47.
18. Pedersen J. Blood sugar of newborn infants. MD thesis. Copenhagen: Danish Science Press; 1952.
19. Bernstein IM, Catalano PM. Influence of fetal fat on the ultrasound estimation of fetal weight in diabetic mothers. Obstet Gynecol. 1992;79(4):561–3.
20. Pettitt DJ, Knowler WC, Bennett PH, Aleck KA, Baird HR. Obesity in offspring of diabetic Pima Indian women despite normal birth weight. Diabetes Care. 1987;10(1):76–80.
21. Committee on Practice B-O. Practice Bulletin No. 137: gestational diabetes mellitus. Obstetrics and gynecology. 2013;122(2 Pt 1):406–16.
22. Hartling L, Dryden DM, Guthrie A, Muise M, Vandermeer B, Aktary WM, et al. Screening and diagnosing gestational diabetes mellitus. Evid Rep Technol Assess. 2012;210:1–327.
23. International Association of D, Pregnancy Study Groups Consensus P, Metzger BE, Gabbe SG, Persson B, Buchanan TA, et al. International association of diabetes and pregnancy study groups recommendations on the diagnosis and classification of hyperglycemia in pregnancy. Diabetes care. 2010;33(3):676-82.
24. American DA. Diagnosis and classification of diabetes mellitus. Diabetes Care. 2013;36 Suppl 1:S67–74.
25. National Institutes of Health consensus development conference statement: diagnosing gestational diabetes mellitus, March 4-6, 2013. Obstetrics and gynecology. 2013;122(2 Pt 1): 358-69.
26. Hartling L, Dryden DM, Guthrie A, Muise M, Vandermeer B, Donovan L. Benefits and harms of treating gestational diabetes mellitus: a systematic review and meta-analysis for the U.S. Preventive Services Task Force and the National Institutes of Health Office of Medical Applications of Research. Ann Intern Med. 2013;159(2):123–9.
27. American DA. Standards of medical care in diabetes–2013. Diabetes Care. 2013;36 Suppl 1:S11–66.
28. Conway DL, Gonzales O, Skiver D. Use of glyburide for the treatment of gestational diabetes: the San Antonio experience. J Matern Fetal Neonatal Med. 2004;15(1):51–5.
29. Moore LE, Clokey D, Rappaport VJ, Curet LB. Metformin compared with glyburide in gestational diabetes: a randomized controlled trial. Obstet Gynecol. 2010;115(1):55–9.
30. Mazze RS, Shamoon H, Pasmantier R, Lucido D, Murphy J, Hartmann K, et al. Reliability of blood glucose monitoring by patients with diabetes mellitus. Am J Med. 1984;77(2):211–7.
31. Buchanan TA, Kjos SL, Montoro MN, Wu PY, Madrilejo NG, Gonzalez M, et al. Use of fetal ultrasound to select metabolic therapy for pregnancies complicated by mild gestational diabetes. Diabetes Care. 1994;17(4):275–83.
32. Practice ACOG. Bulletin. Clinical Management Guidelines for Obstetrician-Gynecologists. Number 60, March 2005. Pregestational diabetes mellitus. Obstet Gynecol. 2005;105(3): 675–85.
33. Kline GA, Edwards A. Antepartum and intra-partum insulin management of type 1 and type 2 diabetic women: Impact on clinically significant neonatal hypoglycemia. Diabetes Res Clin Pract. 2007;77(2):223–30.
34. De Groot L, Abalovich M, Alexander EK, Amino N, Barbour L, Cobin RH, et al. Management of thyroid dysfunction during pregnancy and postpartum: an Endocrine Society clinical practice guideline. J Clin Endocrinol Metab. 2012;97(8):2543–65.
35. American DA. Gestational diabetes mellitus. Diabetes Care. 2004;27 Suppl 1:S88–90.
36. Metzger BE, Buchanan TA, Coustan DR, de Leiva A, Dunger DB, Hadden DR, et al. Summary and recommendations of the Fifth International Workshop-Conference on Gestational Diabetes Mellitus. Diabetes Care. 2007;30 Suppl 2:S251–60.
37. Catalano PM, Vargo KM, Bernstein IM, Amini SB. Incidence and risk factors associated with abnormal postpartum glucose tolerance in women with gestational diabetes. Am J Obstet Gynecol. 1991;165(4 Pt 1):914–9.
38. Kjos SL, Buchanan TA, Greenspoon JS, Montoro M, Bernstein GS, Mestman JH. Gestational diabetes mellitus: the prevalence of glucose intolerance and diabetes mellitus in the first two months post partum. Am J Obstet Gynecol. 1990;163(1 Pt 1):93–8.

39. Retnakaran R, Qi Y, Connelly PW, Sermer M, Zinman B, Hanley AJ. Glucose intolerance in pregnancy and postpartum risk of metabolic syndrome in young women. J Clin Endocrinol Metab. 2010;95(2):670–7.
40. Kessous R, Shoham-Vardi I, Pariente G, Sherf M, Sheiner E. An association between gestational diabetes mellitus and long-term maternal cardiovascular morbidity. Heart. 2013;99(15):1118–21.
41. Retnakaran R, Qi Y, Sermer M, Connelly PW, Hanley AJ, Zinman B. The postpartum cardiovascular risk factor profile of women with isolated hyperglycemia at 1-hour on the oral glucose tolerance test in pregnancy. Nutr Metab Cardiovasc Dis. 2011;21(9):706–12.
42. Chiasson JL, Josse RG, Gomis R, Hanefeld M, Karasik A, Laakso M, et al. Acarbose for prevention of type 2 diabetes mellitus: the STOP-NIDDM randomised trial. Lancet. 2002; 359(9323):2072–7.
43. Knowler WC, Barrett-Connor E, Fowler SE, Hamman RF, Lachin JM, Walker EA, et al. Reduction in the incidence of type 2 diabetes with lifestyle intervention or metformin. N Engl J Med. 2002;346(6):393–403.
44. Pan XR, Li GW, Hu YH, Wang JX, Yang WY, An ZX, et al. Effects of diet and exercise in preventing NIDDM in people with impaired glucose tolerance. The Da Qing IGT and Diabetes Study. Diabetes care. 1997;20(4):537–44.
45. Tuomilehto J, Lindstrom J, Eriksson JG, Valle TT, Hamalainen H, Ilanne-Parikka P, et al. Prevention of type 2 diabetes mellitus by changes in lifestyle among subjects with impaired glucose tolerance. N Engl J Med. 2001;344(18):1343–50.
46. Gabbe SG, Landon MB, Warren-Boulton E, Fradkin J. Promoting health after gestational diabetes: a National Diabetes Education Program call to action. Obstet Gynecol. 2012;119(1):171–6.
47. Boney CM, Verma A, Tucker R, Vohr BR. Metabolic syndrome in childhood: association with birth weight, maternal obesity, and gestational diabetes mellitus. Pediatrics. 2005;115(3): e290–6.
48. Kim C, Berger DK, Chamany S. Recurrence of gestational diabetes mellitus: a systematic review. Diabetes Care. 2007;30(5):1314–9.
49. Finer LB, Zolna MR. Unintended pregnancy in the United States: incidence and disparities, 2006. Contraception. 2011;84(5):478–85.
50. Kitzmiller JL, Block JM, Brown FM, Catalano PM, Conway DL, Coustan DR, et al. Managing preexisting diabetes for pregnancy: summary of evidence and consensus recommendations for care. Diabetes Care. 2008;31(5):1060–79.
51. Rasmussen KM, Yaktine AL, editors. Weight gain during pregnancy: reexamining the guidelines. Washington, DC; 2009.
52. Duley L, Henderson-Smart D, Knight M, King J. Antiplatelet drugs for prevention of pre-eclampsia and its consequences: systematic review. BMJ. 2001;322(7282):329–33.
53. Cheschier N, Bulletins-Obstetrics ACoP. ACOG practice bulletin. Neural tube defects. Number 44, July 2003. (Replaces committee opinion number 252, March 2001). International journal of gynaecology and obstetrics: the official organ of the International Federation of Gynaecology and Obstetrics. 2003;83(1):123-33.
54. Coustan DR, Widness JA, Carpenter MW, Rotondo L, Pratt DC, Oh W. Should the fifty-gram, one-hour plasma glucose screening test for gestational diabetes be administered in the fasting or fed state? Am J Obstet Gynecol. 1986;154(5):1031–5.
55. Medical JL. Management of pregnancy complicated by diabetes. 4th ed. Alexandria, VA: American Diabetes Association; 2009.
56. Thomas H. Medications and Mothers' Milk: Hale Publishing. Texas: Amarillo; 2008.

Part V
GI/Liver

Chapter 5
The Gastrointestinal Tract and the Liver in Pregnancy: Normal Functions and Diseases

Silvia Degli Esposti, Judy Nee, and Sumona Saha

During pregnancy the change of hormonal and humoral milieu along with the displacement of intra-abdominal organs by the growing uterus causes profound modifications of the gastrointestinal tract, leading to altered gastric motility, altered intestinal transit time, and decreased gallbladder contraction [1].

Protein synthesis in the liver is remodeled, the bile composition changes toward a super saturated bile [2], and transport molecules located in the bile canaliculi are down-regulated while P450 enzymes and other phase reactant proteins are upregulated.

Systemic changes also affect the gastrointestinal system. The blood volume expands by 50 % causing hemodilution and promoting the formation of collateral vessels in the abdomen. Immunologic remodeling characterized by a shift toward the production of Th2 cytokines affects the course of autoimmune and infectious gastrointestinal diseases [3].

All together, these changes cause physiological alterations of laboratory values and cause common functional symptoms that many expectant mothers experience (Tables 5.1 and 5.2 summarize the effects of pregnancy on maternal gastrointestinal functions and laboratory values).

S. Degli Esposti, M.D. (✉)
Center for Women's Gastrointestinal Medicine, Women's Medicine Collaborative,
The Miriam Hospital, 146 West River Street, Providence, RI 02904, USA

The Warren Alpert Medical School of Brown University, Providence, RI, USA
e-mail: Silvia_Degli_Esposti@brown.edu

J. Nee, M.D.
Internal Medicine, Beth Israel Deaconess Medical Center, Boston, MA, USA

Harvard Medical School, Boston, MA, USA
e-mail: jnee@bidmc.harvard.edu

S. Saha, M.D.
University of Wisconsin School of Medicine and Public Health, Medical Foundation
Centennial Building, Rm 4224, 1685 Highland Avenue, 4th Floor, Madison, WI 53705, USA
e-mail: ssaha@medicine.wisc.edu

Table 5.1 Effects of pregnancy on maternal gastrointestinal functions

Physiological changes	Common symptoms
Decreased lower esophageal sphincter Decreased gastric empting Altered gastric and esophageal motility Increased intra-abdominal pressure	Esophageal reflux Nausea and vomiting of pregnancy
Increased intestinal transit Altered microbial flora Increased absorption Mechanical intra-abdominal organ displacement	Constipation Abdominal pain
Decreased gallbladder contractility Changes in bile composition	Bile crystal formation
Expansion of blood volume Collateral vessel formation Increased p450 enzymes Decreased bile transport	Altered drug metabolism Increased portal pressure Cholestasis

Table 5.2 The effects of pregnancy on laboratory values

Laboratory tests	Physiological alteration in pregnancy	Causes
Alkaline phosphates	Increased progressively ↑	Placental production
GGT	Decreased ↓	Decreased production
5′-nucleotidase	Normal	
AST and ALT	Normal	
Bilirubin	Normal or slightly increased ↑	Decreased excretion
Prothrombin time	Normal	
Albumin	Decreased ↓	Dilution
White blood cells	Increased ↑	Physiologic leukocytosis of pregnancy
Hemoglobin	Decreased ↓	Iron deficiency, dilution
Platelets	Decreased ↓	Dilution
Sedimentation rate	Increased ↑	
Biliary acid	Slightly increased ↑	Decreased excretion
Ferritin	Decreased ↓	Iron deficiency

Nutritional Requirements and Food Choices

Katie Lester and Greg Salgueiro

No other topics have generated more media attention and women concerns than nutrition in pregnancy.

Adequate nutrition and appropriate weight gain for healthy women can be easily achieved through a sensible diet rich in high-quality proteins, fresh fruits, vegetables, and the simple addition of a prenatal vitamin. The new weight guidelines issued in 2009 by the Institute of Medicine (IOM) are summarized in Table 5.3.

Table 5.3 Weight guidelines issued in 2009 by the Institute of Medicine (IOM)

Prepregnancy BMI	BMI + (kg/m^2) (WHO)	Total weight gain range (lbs)	Rates of weight gain second and third trimester (mean range in lbs/week)
Underweight	<18.5	28–40	1 (1–1.3)
Normal weight	18.5–24.9	25–35	1 (0.8–1)
Overweight	25.0–29.9	15–25	0.06 (0.5–0.7)
Obese (includes all classes)	≥30.0	11–20	0.5 (0.4–0.6)

Patients with underlying disease that might compromise the ability to consume and process food pose special challenges.

Patients affected by inflammatory bowel disorders (IBD), celiac disease, small bowel malabsorptive syndromes, gastric bypass, eating disorders, and liver disease will be particularly susceptible to nutritional deficiencies. In these at-risk conditions, restoration of adequate nutrition with replacement of vitamins and micronutrients is ideally achieved before conception. Some deficiencies will impact fetal and placental development irreversibly during the earliest stages of gestation compromising later outcomes.

Nutrition Requirements

Additional calories are needed during pregnancy for women who have a normal or low BMI prior to pregnancy. Women with a high prepregnancy BMI should be assessed individually to determine the appropriate amount of calories needed for a healthy pregnancy and to help prevent excess weight gain. The following calorie recommendations from the Academy of Nutrition and Dietetics are for women of normal weight prior to pregnancy:

First trimester: No additional calories are required.
Second trimester: Additional 340 calories/day are recommended.
Third trimester: Additional 450 calories/day are recommended.

Women with a low prepregnancy BMI may require more calories in addition to the above recommendations.

The most common nutritional requirements are summarized below.

Iron

Iron deficiency in pregnancy is very common as the requirements for iron progressively increase throughout the pregnancy in response to the expanding blood volume and the growing fetal demands. Maternal iron is responsible for fetal and early childhood stores up to 2 years of age, and iron deficiency in early childhood is linked to poor cognitive ability [4]. Several gastrointestinal disorders are associated with extreme iron deficiency: inflammatory disease, gastric bypass, and untreated celiac disease. These patients with prepregnancy depleted storages and impaired iron absorption respond poorly to oral supplementation and might require intravenous infusion.

Vitamin D

In 2012, the IOM recommended a daily intake of 600 international units of 25-hydroxyvitamin D (25-OH-D) for pregnant women. Maternal deficiency is linked to disordered fetal bone homeostasis, to newborn fractures, and possibly to premature birth and preeclampsia [5]. Women living in the northern hemisphere are prone to vitamin D deficiency, and many might not compensate for the lack of exposure to sunlight with an adequate oral intake. This is particularly true for patients with gastrointestinal and liver diseases that have impaired absorption of fats and fat-soluble vitamins. Given the lack of data and guidelines, moderate sunlight exposure and vitamin D supplementation of 2,000 IU daily are reasonable recommendations in pregnancy. The target level of total vitamin D considered "normal" is a circulating level of 25-OH-D of 32 ng/ml.

Folic Acid

Folic acid (folate) is responsible for fetal neurodevelopment, and 400 mg of folate is required daily during pregnancy.

In the United States, the decreased incidence of neural tube defects in newborns was achieved by adding folate to common food items and with an aggressive advertizing campaign promoting supplementation of folate in pregnancy. Folate is ubiquitous in fruits, vegetables, legumes, and grains. In addition, gut bacteria synthesize folate. Patients at risk for deficiency are patients with limited diet for personal and socioeconomic reasons, alcohol and substance abusers, and patients treated with chronic antibiotics or antifolate drugs.

Adequate amounts of folate are now added to all prenatal vitamins. Additional folate may be required in patients with a previously affected child with a neural tube defect and patients on antiepileptic drugs.

Essential Fatty Acid

Omega-6 polyunsaturated fatty acid and omega-3 polyunsaturated fatty acid, most notably docosahexaenoic acid (DHA), are essential for neural, visual, and cognitive development and contribute to immune system functioning. The usual western diet is deficient in these nutrients that are found in seeds, nuts, and cold-water oily fishes. Moreover, expectant mothers might avoid eating fish because of concerns about their mercury intake. The evidence supporting the need for DHA supplementation in pregnancy emerged over the last decade as a result of studies linking children's intellectual development to prenatal fatty acid intake of the mother. Current recommendations advise pregnant women to consume 500–600 mg of omega-3 fatty acid of which 200–300 mg of DHA daily [6]. It is important to stress that two servings weekly of low mercury content fish is safe in pregnancy and does not carry a risk of mercury toxicity. DHA is found in safe cold-water fish such as salmon and cod.

Calcium

Calcium is required for fetal bone formation along with vitamin D, so consumption of 1,000 mg of calcium is recommended daily in pregnancy. Patients with chronic malabsorption, short gut, and small bowel disease are at particular risk for calcium deficiency in pregnancy. Moreover, pregnancy can further deplete calcium stores worsening preexisting premature osteoporosis.

Food Choices

Certain foods and beverages can be unsafe if consumed during pregnancy [7, 8]. Here is a general list of items that should be avoided during pregnancy to help reduce the risk of fetal harm:

- Alcohol: Alcohol consumption in pregnancy may lead to adverse physical and neurodevelopmental outcomes for the infant.
- Fish that may contain high levels of mercury: Avoid fish with high levels of mercury such as shark, swordfish, king mackerel, tuna steak, marlin, grouper, and tilefish. It is safe to consume up to 12 ounces/week of other fish and shellfish that are lower in mercury.
- Soft cheese and ready-to-eat meats: Consuming soft cheese and ready-to-eat meats increases the risk for *Listeria* infection which is introduced during the preparation process. *Listeria* is killed by pasteurization and cooking. Pregnant women should avoid soft cheeses such as feta, Brie, blue-veined cheese, and goat cheese unless they have labels clearly stating they are made from pasteurized milk. Lunch meats, hot dogs, and food prepared from the deli counter should also be avoided unless they are reheated until hot and steamy throughout.
- Raw or uncooked fish, meats, and poultry: Consuming raw or uncooked items may increase the risk for foodborne illness.

Gastrointestinal Endoscopy in Pregnancy

Every year thousands of women have endoscopies while pregnant. Urgent diagnostic and therapeutic procedures if medically indicated should not be delayed because of theoretical concerns about fetal welfare [9]. A list of acceptable indications for endoscopy during pregnancy is provided in Table 5.4.

Pregnant women have undergone upper gastrointestinal tract endoscopy, colonoscopy, sigmoidoscopy, endoscopic retrograde cholangiopancreatography (ERCP), and percutaneous gastroscopy safely.

The fetus is extremely sensitive to hypoxia and acidosis; thus, special attention should be observed when performing endoscopy in pregnant patients. Hypotension, hypoxia, and prolonged abdominal pressure should be avoided. The presence of an anesthesiologist is recommended to titrate sedation and to manage airways that become edematous and easily collapsible in the second half of the pregnancy. ERCP should be performed only with therapeutic intent and by expert endoscopists to shorten the time of fetal exposure to radiation. Opioids (FDA category B) and propofol (FDA category B) effectively achieve moderate sedation during the procedure. Benzodiazepines (FDA category D) should be used with caution in the first trimester because of reports of cleft lip, cleft palate, and other fetal malformations caused by diazepam exposure prior to organogenesis [10].

Fetal monitoring during the procedure is recommended after 24 weeks of gestation when the fetus becomes viable. It requires that the procedure is performed in the presence of a team of experts including a high-risk obstetric specialist and in an appropriate facility where it is possible to perform immediate emergency cesarean section. Moreover, non-clinically significant or transient aberrations of the fetal tracing during endoscopy could lead to unnecessary emergency deliveries.

Lactating patients are advised to avoid breastfeeding the day of the procedure and to discard breast milk for at least 4 h after a procedure requiring sedation.

The following recommendations were published by the American Society for Gastrointestinal Endoscopy in 2012 (Table 5.5) [11].

Table 5.4 Indications for endoscopy in pregnancy

- Significant or continued GI bleeding
- Severe or refractory nausea and vomiting or abdominal pain
- Dysphagia or odynophagia
- Strong suspicion of colon mass
- Severe diarrhea with negative evaluation
- Biliary pancreatitis, symptomatic choledocholithiasis, or cholangitis
- Biliary or pancreatic ductal injury

Table 5.5 The following recommendations were published by the American Society for Gastrointestinal Endoscopy in 2012

- Consultation with an obstetrician is recommended regardless of fetal gestational age
- Always have a strong indication, particularly in high-risk pregnancies
- Defer endoscopy to second trimester whenever possible
- Use lowest effective dose of sedative medications
- Use category B drugs whenever possible
- Minimize procedure time
- Position patient in left pelvic tilt or left lateral position to avoid vena cava or aortic compression
- The decision to monitor fetal heart rate is individualized and will depend on gestational age of the fetus and available resources
- Before 24 weeks of fetal gestation, it is sufficient to confirm the presence of the fetal heart rate by Doppler before sedation is begun and after the endoscopic procedure
- After 24 weeks of fetal gestation, simultaneous electronic fetal heart and uterine contraction monitoring should be performed before and after the procedure. Ideally, procedures should be done at an institution with neonatal and pediatric services. If possible, a qualified individual, with obstetric support readily available in case of fetal distress or a pregnancy-related complication, should monitor before, during, and after the procedure the fetal heart rate and uterine contractions
- Endoscopy is contraindicated in placental abruption, imminent delivery, ruptured membranes, or uncontrolled preeclampsia

Source: Shergill AK, Ben-Menachem T, Chandrasekhara V, Chathadi K, Decker GA, et al. Guidelines for endoscopy in pregnant and lactating women. Gastrointestinal endoscopy. 2012;76(1):18-24. Epub 2012/05/15, with permission

Gastrointestinal Imaging and Radiation Exposure During Pregnancy

Fetal tissue is particularly susceptible to radiation damage. For this reason, before exposing a pregnant patient to any radiographic exams, the risks and the benefits have to be carefully weighed. The National Council on Radiation Protection and Measurements recommends limiting the total radiation exposure during gestation to less than 5 cGy [12]. Most of the plain films of the abdomen are well below this recommended threshold.

Computed tomography (CT) should be performed only when it is absolutely necessary and, if possible, after the first 12 weeks of gestation when organogenesis is near completion.

Other frequently ordered radiologic exams, barium swallow, upper gastrointestinal series, and small bowel fluoroscopy, can be substituted by safer diagnostic modalities such as endoscopic exams, magnetic resonance imaging (MRI), and ultrasound. Ultrasound remains the modality of choice for visualization of the liver. Recent advances in the field have made it possible to use ultrasound for the diagnosis of appendicitis with accuracy comparable to CT scan.

MRI without contrast can be ordered as an alternative to CT for workup intra-abdominal pathology. Magnetic fields are not harmful to living organisms but carry a theoretical risk of causing thermal injury in the early stage of gestation. However contrast media as gadolinium should be avoided because it crosses the placenta and recirculates non-excreted in the fetal compartment. The long-term safety of gadolinium exposure in uteri has not been established. MRI enterography utilizes an aqueous oral contrast solution, is safe, and is the modality of choice for the diagnosis of small bowel pathology [13].

Differential Diagnosis and Management of Common Gastrointestinal Complaints in Pregnancy

Gastrointestinal symptoms are very common in pregnancy due to physiological alteration of the gastrointestinal tract. They are often transitory, mild in nature, and easily controlled with conservative measures and reassurance. Nevertheless, significant medical problems can present in pregnancy, and prompt diagnosis and treatment should not be delayed. The presentation of differential diagnosis and diagnostic investigation of most frequent gastrointestinal complaints are similar for pregnant and nonpregnant patients (Table 5.6).

Table 5.6 Non-obstetric and obstetric causes of abdominal pain in pregnancy

Common GI complaints	Differential diagnosis	Diagnostic workup	Management	Potential risks
Nausea and vomiting	Common in 70–80 % of all pregnancies D/D: peptic ulcer, gastroenteritis, biliary colic, pancreatitis, bowel obstruction, migraines	If severe: abdominal ultrasound, CBC with diff, lipase, chem7, UA, liver panel, thyroid functions, *H. pylori* test	Symptomatic relief: ginger B6, dietary modification, antiemetic, intravenous hydration for most serious cases	Food avoidance, malnutrition, depression, dehydration
Heartburn	Common in 70–80 % all pregnancies D/D: viral or *Candida esophagitis*, biliary colic, pancreatitis	If severe, refractory with/or hematemesis and/or odynophagia: RUQ U/S, endoscopy	Aim to resolution: antacids, Sucralfate, H2 blockers, PPI	Food avoidance, esophageal stricture, malnutrition, persistence of GERD postpartum
Constipation	Common in 30 % all pregnancies D/D same as for nonpregnant: hypothyroidism, celiac disease, hyperparathyroidism, partial colonic obstruction	If severe: TSH, calcium, TTG, colonoscopy if colonic mass is suspected	Aims to resolution: fiber, osmotic laxatives, lactulose, avoid magnesium-containing laxatives	Obstruction, fecal impaction, ischemic colitis

(continued)

Table 5.6 (continued)

Common GI complaints	Differential diagnosis	Diagnostic workup	Management	Potential risks
Abdominal pain	Common For obstetric and non-obstetric causes see Table 5.7	If severe: CBC with diff., lipase, liver panel, UA, C-reactive protein, abdominal X-ray, abdominal ultrasound, MRI enterography if IBD is suspected	Treat underlying causes: IBS first line fibers, Dicyclomine, Amytriptiline	Appendicitis and other surgical and obstetric emergencies need to be promptly recognized, visceral perforation has high fetal loss
Chronic diarrhea	D/D same as for nonpregnant: IBS, celiac, lactose intolerance, IBD, pancreatic insufficiency	Work up as per nonpregnant: lactose tolerance test, TTG, stools studies, nutritional assessment, colonoscopy	Treat underlying causes: IBS first line fibers, Dicyclomine, Cholestyramine might cause vitamin K depletion and peripartum bleeding, nutrition supplements	Poor weight gain, malnutrition, fat-soluble vitamin deficiency
Acute diarrhea	D/D same as for nonpregnant: infectious gastroenteritis, drugs or toxin effect	Stool cultures	Symptomatic: aggressive hydration	Dehydration with hypovolemia, premature labor
Rectal bleeding	Common D/D same as for nonpregnant: hemorrhoids, fissures, rectal varices, colorectal cancers, ischemic colitis, IBD	Diagnostic sigmoidoscopy	Treat underlying causes: steroids, suppositories, fibers	Delayed diagnosis of potentially serious conditions
Hematemesis	Blood tinged vomit is common in N+V/HG and GERD D/D same as for nonpregnant: esophagitis, Mallory/Weiss tear, PUD, esophageal varices	Observation if minimal blood loss, CBC, endoscopy if therapeutic intervention is needed	Same as for nonpregnant: vigorous resuscitation, monitor anesthesia care recommended in emergency endoscopy	Anoxia, acidosis, hypotension can harm the fetus

Gastrointestinal Disorders and Pregnancy

Gastroesophageal Reflux Disease

Heartburn is a very common symptom during gestation with peak prevalence in the third trimester affecting nearly 80 % of all pregnant patients. Severe reflux might be predictive of reflux later in life.

Risk factors include multiparity, older maternal age, and history of Gastroesophageal Reflux Disease (GERD) before pregnancy, while the effect of obesity is still controversial. The etiology of esophageal reflux is likely multifactorial: changes in estrogen and progesterone levels affect gastrointestinal motility decreasing gastric emptying and altering esophageal motility. Progesterone promotes relaxation of the lower esophageal sphincter (LES) at rest favoring regurgitation of acid gastric content into the esophagus. The growing uterus exerts a mechanical pressure on the stomach and subdiaphragmatic organs that progressively increases throughout pregnancy.

However, GERD is often associated with nausea, vomiting, and regurgitation, and it is a contributing factor to hyperemesis gravidarum (HG) [14]. In addition, pulmonary complaints such as cough and asthma can be atypical manifestation of occult reflux.

Differential diagnosis includes infectious esophagitis, peptic ulcer disease, cholelithiasis, pancreatitis, gastroenteritis, and nephrolithiasis (Table 5.7).

In the absence of alarming symptoms such as weight loss, hematemesis, fever, dysphagia, and odynophagia, empirical acid-reducing measures can be implemented in a stepwise fashion reserving extensive workup for severe or refractory cases.

Table 5.7 Differential diagnosis of abdominal pain in pregnancy

Non-obstetric causes	Obstetric causes
• Peptic ulcer disease	• Preterm labor
• Appendicitis	• Chorioamnionitis
• Cholecystitis	• Ectopic pregnancy
• Hepatitis	• Pelvic vein thrombosis
• Pyelonephritis	• Uterine rupture
• Nephrolithiasis	• Acute fatty liver of pregnancy
• Inflammatory bowel disease	• Preeclampsia
• Irritable bowel syndrome	• Abruption placenta
• Gastroenteritis	
• Pancreatitis	

Source: Miller M. Gastrointestinal Disorders. In: Rosene-Montella K, Keely E, Barbour LA, Lee RV, eds. *Medical Care of the Pregnant Patient*. 2nd Edition. Philadelphia, PA: American College of Physicians. 2008;549-566

Therapy of GERD

Lifestyle Modification and Diet

Anti-reflux maneuvers and lifestyle modifications in pregnancy are still first-line intervention, and they follow the same principles as in the general population. They include dietary changes with preference for small frequent meals, avoidance of caffeine and chocolate, and limited consumption of fatty foods. Patients should avoid clothes tight at the waist and should sleep in semi-reclined position and on the left side to minimize nocturnal reflux.

Pharmacological Intervention

When nonpharmacological remedies fail, liquid antacids and sucralfate (FDA category B) can be used safely. Magnesium-containing antacids are avoided due to the theoretical risks of hypermagnesemia and impaired labor.

Among the H2 blockers, ranitidine (FDA category B) has been used extensively in pregnancy for the last 30 years, and no adverse effects have been reported.

On rare occasion, GERD symptoms will require long-lasting and complete acid suppression that can be achieved only with the newer class of drug: proton pump inhibitors (PPI). They have been introduced in the United States in the last 20 years and are still considered second line during pregnancy given the more recent introduction on the market. Nevertheless, in the last few years, their use in pregnancy has been studied in several large populations, and smaller studies have been compiled in an accurate meta-analysis [15]. The overall conclusion was that first trimester in utero exposure to PPI as a class of drug was not associated with any birth defects in the offspring [16]. The long-term effects on the growth and development of the exposed children are still unknown and will require studies designed for longer longitudinal follow-up.

Nausea and Vomiting of Pregnancy and Hyperemesis Gravidarum

While pregnancy has profound effects on the gastrointestinal tract as described above, nausea and vomiting of pregnancy (NVP) and hyperemesis gravidarum are the only two conditions unique to pregnancy.

Most cases of NVP are mild and resolve after the first trimester. Women with severe nausea and vomiting during pregnancy may have HG, an entity distinct from NVP but that shares many features, epidemiology, and underlying pathogenesis. NVP affects 70–80 % of pregnant women. HG is rare in comparison, occurring in 0.3–2 % of all pregnancies [17].

Risk factors for NVP include younger maternal age, primigravida, obesity, and multiple gestation. Low-income levels and a family history of NVP in a prior pregnancy have also been shown to be risk factors for its development in subsequent pregnancies [18].

Similarly, risk factors for HG include multiple gestations; trophoblastic disease; HG in prior pregnancy; family history of HG; fetal abnormalities such as triploidy, trisomy 21, and hydrops fetalis; and nulliparity. Cigarette smoking and male gender of the fetus may be protective.

Pathogenesis of Gestational Vomiting

Gestational vomiting that includes NVP and HG may result from various metabolic and endocrine factors, many of placental origin. The most implicated factor is human chorionic gonadotropin (hCG), which peaks in concentration around the peak time of symptoms. Several studies show that nausea and vomiting are worse in pregnant women with conditions associated with elevated hCG levels such as molar pregnancies, multiple gestations, and Down's syndrome and that concentrations of hCG correlate positively with symptom severity in women with HG. Other factors, such as estrogen, progesterone, placental prostaglandin E2, and leptin, may also contribute to the pathogenesis of NVP and HG.

Due to cross-reactivity between hCG and the thyroid-stimulating hormone (TSH) receptor, thyroid dysfunction has also been implicated in the pathogenesis of NVP and HG. In fact, abnormal thyroid function tests (typically low TSH and slightly elevate FT4) are found in two-thirds of women with HG. Despite these laboratory abnormalities, women with HG are generally euthyroid with no history of prior thyroid diseases, absent goiter, and negative antithyroid antibodies [19].

Alterations in lower esophageal sphincter (LES) resting pressure and esophageal peristalsis have been linked to NVP. While these changes are more typically associated with heartburn in pregnancy, gastroesophageal reflux disease (GERD) may also produce nausea and contribute to the symptoms of HG.

Despite the popular use of the term "morning sickness," NVP persists throughout the day in the majority of women and is limited to the morning in less than 2 % of women. It often begins within weeks of conceptions between 10 and 16 weeks and then resolves after 20 weeks. However, up to 10 % of women remain symptomatic beyond 22 weeks. While dehydration and orthostasis can occur in women with HG, most women with NVP have normal vital signs and a benign physical exam. The differential diagnosis for gestational vomiting includes gastroesophageal reflux disease, peptic ulcer disease (PUD), small bowel obstruction, acute cholecystitis, cholelithiasis, pancreatitis, as well as appendicitis, gastroenteritis, nephrolithiasis, pyelonephritis, and hepatitis.

Effect of NVP on Pregnancy Outcome

NVP is associated with a favorable outcome for the fetus with a decreased risk of miscarriage and no consistent associations with perinatal mortality.

Despite its favorable effects on the fetus, NVP causes substantial psychosocial morbidity in the mother. NVP impairs employment, performance of household duties, and parenting [20]. It is also associated with feelings of depression, consideration of termination of pregnancy, and impaired relationships with partners.

Hyperemesis Gravidarum

Hyperemesis gravidarum (HG) is severe nausea and vomiting during pregnancy leading to fluid, electrolyte, and acid–base imbalance, nutritional deficiency, and weight loss. HG is commonly defined as the occurrence of greater than 3 episodes of vomiting per day accompanied by ketonuria and a weight loss of more than 3 kg or 5 % of body weight. HG is the most common reason for hospitalization in early pregnancy and second only to preterm labor throughout pregnancy. In the United States, more than 36,000 women are admitted to the hospital each year due to HG [21]. Unlike NVP, which is associated with favorable fetal outcomes, HG poses significant health risks to the mother and fetus.

HG presents in the first trimester of pregnancy, usually starting at 4–5 weeks of gestation. In addition to severe nausea and vomiting, 60 % of women with HG experience excess salivation. Patients may also complain of GER symptoms such as retrosternal discomfort and heartburn. A pregnancy-unique quantification of emesis and nausea (PUQE) score can be used to track the severity of symptoms (Table 5.8).

Patients may present with signs of dehydration, and severely affected patients may also have muscle wasting and weakness and/or mental status changes.

Laboratory abnormalities in women with HG are characteristic of severe dehydration. Prealbumin levels may be low, reflecting poor protein nutrition status in the mother and possibly predicting lower fetal birth weights. Vitamin and mineral deficiencies such as vitamin B1 (thiamine), iron, calcium, and folate are also possible [22].

Liver function tests are abnormal in up to 50 % of hospitalized patients with HG. Mild hyperbilirubinemia (bilirubin < 4 mg/dl) and/or a rise in alkaline phosphatase to twice the upper limit of normal may be seen. A moderate transaminitis is the most common liver test abnormality with alanine aminotransferase (ALT) levels generally greater than aspartate aminotransferase (AST) levels. The transaminase elevation is usually two to three times the upper limit of normal. Serum amylase and lipase elevations are seen in 10–15 % of women. The amylase elevation may be due to excessive salivary gland production. As in NVP, TSH levels may be low in HG due to cross-reaction between the alpha subunit of HCG with the TSH receptor. HG is a clinical diagnosis based on symptoms and the exclusion of other conditions. Like NVP, no specific testing is needed to diagnose HG, but they are necessary to monitor the metabolic disturbances and the nutritional status. Ultrasound of the abdomen and pelvis may be helpful in excluding other causes such as gallbladder disease and hydatidiform mole and in assessing for multiple gestation. The differential diagnosis includes NVP, acute thyroiditis, eating disorders, biliary tract disease, viral hepatitis, and GERD.

Table 5.8 Motherisk-PUQE scoring system

1. In the last 12 h, for how long have you felt nauseated or sick to your stomach?	
Not at all	(n=1)
1 h or less	(n=2)
2 to 3 h	(n=3)
4 to 6 h	(n=4)
More than 6 h	(n=5)
2. In the last 12 h, have you vomited or thrown up?	
I did not throw up	(n=1)
1–2 times	(n=2)
3–4 times	(n=3)
5–6 times	(n=4)
7 or more times	(n=5)
3. In the last 12 h, how many times have you had retching or dry heaves without bringing anything up?	
At no time	(n=1)
1–2 times	(n=2)
3–4 times	(n=3)
5–6 times	(n=4)
7 or more times	(n=5)

Total score: no symptoms, 1–3; mild, 4–6; moderate, 7–12; severe, >13

Source: Miller M. Gastrointestinal Disorders. In: Rosene-Montella K, Keely E, Barbour LA, Lee RV, eds. *Medical Care of the Pregnant Patient*. 2nd Edition. Philadelphia, PA: American College of Physicians. 2008;549–566

Effect of HG on Pregnancy Outcome

Unlike NVP, HG is associated with both adverse maternal and fetal outcomes. In a study of over 150,000 singleton pregnancies, women with HG had increased rates of low pregnancy weight gain (<7 kg), low birth weight (LBW) babies, small for gestational age (SGA) babies, preterm birth, and poor 5-min Apgar scores [17].

Common maternal complications include weight loss, dehydration, micronutrient deficiency, and muscle weakness. More severe, albeit rare, complications include Mallory-Weiss tears, esophageal rupture, Wernicke's encephalopathy with or without Korsakoff's psychosis, central pontine myelinolysis due to rapid correction of severe hyponatremia, spontaneous pneumomediastinum, and vasospasm of the cerebral arteries. HG may also lead to psychological problems and result in termination of an otherwise wanted pregnancy and decreased likelihood to attempt a repeat pregnancy.

Various congenital malformations have been observed more in women with HG. Fetal coagulopathy and chondrodysplasia have also been reported from vitamin K deficiency with third trimester fetal intracranial hemorrhage [23].

Treatment

Treatment modalities for NVP and HG range from simple dietary modifications to drug therapy and total parental nutrition (TPN). Severity of symptoms and maternal weight loss are useful in determining the aggressiveness of treatment.

Currently, studies demonstrate that management of NVP is suboptimal. One recent prospective study of 283 women with NVP during the first trimester found that only half were asked about the intensity and severity of their symptoms and less than a quarter were asked if their symptoms interfered with their daily tasks and work [24].

Dietary Treatment

Affected women should avoid large meals and eat several small meals throughout the day. Meals that are bland and low in fat are preferred as fatty foods may further delay gastric emptying. Eating protein more than carbohydrates and taking in more liquids than solids may also help nausea by improving gastric dysrhythmias associated with NVP. Small volumes of salty liquids such as electrolyte replacement sport beverages are advised, and if the smell of hot foods is noxious, cold foods should be prepared.

Acupressure/Acupuncture

Acupressure of the Chinese acupuncture point P6 (Neiguan) has been found to decrease nausea in patients with chemotherapy-induced nausea and postoperative nausea and vomiting and may be helpful in treating HG [25]. Pressure may be placed manually or with elastic bands on the inside of the wrist. In addition, the ReliefBand, a battery-operated electrical nerve stimulator worn on the wrist can be used to stimulate the P6 site.

Ginger

Ginger is the single nonpharmacologic intervention recommended by the American College of Obstetrics and Gynecology. Ginger is believed to help improve NVP by stimulating GI tract motility and stimulating the flow of saliva, bile, and gastric secretions. A theoretical risk for bleeding, however, does exist due to its inhibitory effects on thromboxane synthetase and possibly on platelet function. Thus, ginger should not be used with anticoagulants [26].

Pharmacologic Treatment

Pyridoxine/Doxylamine

The combination of pyridoxine (vitamin B6) (pregnancy category A) and doxylamine (category B), now available in the United States as Diclegis, is the only medication that is specifically labeled for the treatment of NVP by the FDA. Although a prior doxylamine/B6 combination (Bendectin) was taken off the market in the 1980s in the United States due to reports of congenital malformations with first trimester use, it has been shown in several small randomized controlled trials to be effective [27] and in a meta-analysis which included 170,000 exposures to be safe to the fetus [28].

Antiemetics

Phenothiazines, chlorpromazine (Thorazine), and prochlorperazine (Compazine) are central and peripheral dopamine antagonists which have been shown to reduce symptoms in NVP and HG.

Promotility Agents

Metoclopramide (Reglan) is widely used for the treatment of NVP. It is pregnancy category B. Metoclopramide is believed to improve symptoms by increasing lower esophageal sphincter pressure and increasing gastric transit. It also corrects gastric dysrhythmias by stimulating antral contractions and promoting antroduodenal contractions. Studies have shown it to be not only as effective as promethazine in reducing symptoms and increasing well-being but also better tolerated [29].

With regard to safety, in a study of 81,703 births involving exposure to metoclopramide, no increased risk of major congenital malformations, low birth weight, preterm delivery, or perinatal death was found [30].

Despite its efficacy, metoclopramide use is limited by its side effect profile which includes dystonia, restlessness, and somnolence. In 2009, the FDA added a black box warning to metoclopramide due to the risk of tardive dyskinesia with chronic use.

Antihistamines and Anticholinergics

Antihistamines indirectly affect the vestibular system, decreasing stimulation of the vomiting center. Randomized controlled trials of antihistamine use in NVP are limited; however, meclizine (Antivert), dimenhydrinate (Dramamine), and diphenhydramine (Benadryl) have all been shown to control symptoms better than placebo [31]. A meta-analysis of more than 24 controlled studies with more than 200,000 pregnant women found that antihistamines (H1 blockers, in particular) given during the first trimester did not increase teratogenic risk [32].

Other Agents

Ondansetron (Zofran) (pregnancy category B) is widely used for the treatment of postoperative and chemotherapy-induced nausea and vomiting and is currently one of the most commonly prescribed antiemetics [33]. It is thought to work both centrally and peripherally by blocking serotonin receptors in the small bowel and the medullary vomiting center. Its safety in pregnancy was determined in a recent study which showed no significant increase in the number of miscarriages, major malformations, or birth weight between infants exposed to ondansetron and unexposed controls [34].

Oral and intravenous corticosteroids have been used for refractory cases of HG with variable results. They are believed to exert an antiemetic effect on the chemoreceptor trigger zone in the brain stem and are also postulated to correct the "relative adrenal insufficiency" induced by HG in which the hypothalamic-pituitary-adrenal axis is unable to respond to the increased demands of cortisol during early pregnancy.

There has been recent interest in acid-reducing medications (i.e., antacids, H2 blockers, and proton pump inhibitors) for NVP as one recent cohort study showed that women with NVP and heartburn and/or acid reflux had more severe nausea and vomiting than women without heartburn or acid reflux [14].

Intravenous Hydration and Nutritional Support

Women with intractable symptoms unresponsive to dietary modification and pharmacologic treatment whom are unable to maintain weight require additional support. For these patients, intravenous fluid therapy, enteral nutrition, or parenteral nutrition should be used to prevent fetal intrauterine growth restriction, maternal dehydration, and malnutrition.

Women requiring multiple hospitalizations may be considered for in-home intravenous hydration.

Enteral tube feeding and total parenteral nutrition should be considered if intravenous therapy is not successful in reducing symptoms and there is still a caloric deficit. In addition to nasogastric tubes, percutaneous endoscopic gastrostomy (PEG) tubes [35] have been used successfully to maintain nutrition in women with HG. Both of these modes of feeding are limited however by the risk of increased nausea and vomiting caused by intragastric feeding. Post-pyloric feeding tubes, both nasojejunal, and percutaneous endoscopic gastrojejunostomy have been attempted to reduce this risk; however, dislodgement of the tubes [36] and gastric coiling are common complications. In addition, nasoenteric tubes, either nasogastric or nasojejunal, are often poorly tolerated due to aesthetics and physical discomfort. Recently, surgical jejunostomy has been described as an alternative mode of nutrition delivery to women with HG [37].

For women unable to tolerate enteral feeding, parenteral nutrition should be considered. This therapy, however, is costly and associated with significant maternal morbidity [38] and reported a 9 % complication rate for parenteral nutrition via peripherally inserted central catheters in pregnancy and a 50 % complication rate for centrally inserted catheters. Infection and thrombosis were the two most frequently occurring complications and were hypothesized to result from pregnancy-associated hypercoagulability and immunologic suppression [38, 39]. Patients on parenteral nutrition also had higher rates of neonatal complications including admission to the neonatal intensive care unit, SGA, termination of pregnancy from HG, and fetal loss compared with women treated with enteral feeds [40]. Thus, although it may be more tolerable to patients, parenteral nutrition should be reserved for selected patients with HG.

Inflammatory Bowel Disease

Inflammatory bowel diseases (IBD), Crohn's disease (CD), and ulcerative colitis (UC) are chronic, waxing, and waning inflammatory conditions of the gastrointestinal tract with peaks in incidence during the reproductive years [41].

Symptoms of IBD include fatigue, diarrhea, hematochezia, abdominal pain, and weight loss leading to anemia and malnutrition. Patients with CD may pose additional challenges during gestation if they suffer from intestinal strictures, fistulas, intra-abdominal abscesses, and perianal disease. Although many therapies are available for the treatment of IBD, both CD and UC are associated with significant morbidity. The long-term side effects on the health of the newborn exposed in utero to these medications are unknown. Nevertheless, over the last decade, experts on the field reached the consensus that controlling the underlying disease and maintaining or inducing remission is the best strategy for these patients.

Fertility

In general, infertility rates for men and women with IBD, which range from 5 to 14 %, are no higher than in the general population. Initial epidemiologic data suggested higher infertility rates and smaller family size in individuals with Crohn's disease (CD); however, these studies predate the use of the more effective medical treatments used today [42]. They also did not account for higher voluntary childlessness rates in patients with IBD. Voluntary childlessness in IBD, although not fully understood, is likely the result of fears of IBD heritability, congenital abnormalities, and medication teratogenicity.

Notable subgroups of IBD patients do have compromised fertility, and patients should be aware that they may fall into this category. Women who have undergone ileal pouch-anal anastomosis (IPAA) comprise one of these subgroups. A recent systematic review found the infertility rate after IPAA to be about 30 % [43], likely due to adhesions and effect on tubal function.

Effect of Pregnancy on IBD

Pregnancy does not significantly alter the course of preexisting IBD or increase the risk for future complications. In fact, some studies suggest that pregnancy may lower the risk for future disease relapse [44]. Based on data showing similar risks of exacerbation during pregnancy (32–34 %) versus the fertile years in women with UC and CD, in general, women with IBD can be counseled that their risk of flaring during pregnancy is the same as when they are not pregnant.

Disease remission at the time of conception is very important for maintaining inactive disease during pregnancy. Women with inactive disease at conception had the same rate of relapse as nonpregnant IBD women. In contrast, other studies have shown that if conception occurs when IBD is active, two-thirds of women will suffer from persistent activity and, of these, two-thirds will worsen [45]. Thus, women with IBD should be advised to be in disease remission prior to conception.

Effect of IBD on Pregnancy

Women with IBD are at increased risk for certain adverse pregnancy outcomes. A recent meta-analysis combining 12 studies totaling 3907 patients with IBD found significantly increased risks for preterm birth [OR =1.87 (1.52, 2.31)], LBW [OR=2.1 (1.38, 3.19)], and cesarean section OR =1.5 (1.26, 1.79)] [43] but not of congenital anomalies when controlled for medication use. Whether disease activity during pregnancy increases the risk of adverse outcome or simply having IBD increases risk is still controversial. Earlier studies suggested that disease activity at conception was a predictor for spontaneous abortion and preterm birth [46] and disease activity during pregnancy increased the risk for low birth weight (LBW) and preterm birth [47]. However, several recent studies have found the increased risk of adverse events in women with IBD to be independent of disease activity [48].

Management of IBD During Pregnancy

Treatment of flares in pregnancy follows the same guidelines as for nonpregnant patients with the added goal of inducing a rapid remission to maintain a healthy pregnancy. Corticosteroids, antibiotics, cyclosporine, and antitumor necrosis factor alpha (TNF-α) agents can be initiated, if needed, to control disease activity in pregnancy. Women with medically refractory disease, toxic megacolon, or a high-grade stricture may require surgical intervention despite the risk inherent to surgery in pregnancy of miscarriages and premature birth.

The mode of delivery in women with IBD is dictated by obstetric considerations. One exception, however, is women with active perianal disease in whom cesarean section is advised [42]. Vaginal delivery in these patients may further disrupt the perineum and injure the anal sphincter. Notably, healed perianal disease and presence of an ileoanal pouch are not contraindications to vaginal delivery, although some experts advocate for cesarean section in the setting of an ileoanal pouch in order to preserve sphincter function. Pregnant women with IBD should see their physicians regularly to allow for monitoring of disease activity, nutritional status, and medication adherence. A successful pregnancy requires team effort with regular communication among the treating obstetrician and/or perinatologist and gastroenterologist.

Breastfeeding

Breastfeeding is unlikely to influence disease activity and may in fact be protective for the future development of IBD. However, many women with IBD choose not to breastfeed [49]. Physician recommendations, the fear of medication transmission, and personal preferences are the most common reasons cited. Physicians must therefore be aware of the actual risks so they can educate their patients.

IBD Medications in Pregnancy and Lactation

Most patients with IBD require pharmacologic therapy to maintain disease remission. Since controlled disease at conception is key to maintaining remission throughout pregnancy, medication discontinuation before attempting to conceive is not advised. With few exceptions, medications should be continued during the preconception period and pregnancy.

5-Aminosalicylates

5-Aminosalicylates (5-ASAs) are traditionally used as first-line therapy in patients with mild-to-moderate IBD. With the exception of olsalazine, the 5-ASAs and sulfasalazine are all FDA category B and considered low risk in pregnancy. As sulfasalazine inhibits folic acid metabolism, which may lead to neural tube defects, it is recommended that women taking sulfasalazine who are pregnant or considering pregnancy take 2 mg of supplemental folate daily [50]. In males, sulfasalazine use is associated with reversible oligospermia and adverse change in sperm motility and morphology. It is recommended that men taking sulfasalazine discontinue the drug for at least 3 months before attempting conception.

Both sulfasalazine and mesalamine are compatible with breastfeeding; however, nursing mothers should be aware of the rare association of watery diarrhea of the newborn with mesalamine use.

Corticosteroids

Corticosteroids (FDA category C) have been used extensively for the treatment of various inflammatory conditions in pregnancy. Many epidemiologic studies have reported a small increased risk for orofacial clefts in newborns exposed early in gestation.

In addition to monitoring for general side effects, pregnant women on corticosteroids should be monitored closely for hypertension and gestational diabetes mellitus. Fetal adrenal suppression has only been seen with corticosteroids that reach the fetus in the active form, betamethasone and dexamethasone, so it should not be an issue for commonly used steroids for IBD. Corticosteroids are considered safe in lactation.

Azathioprine/6-Mercaptopurine

The thiopurines (FDA category D), azathioprine, and 6-mercaptopurine (6-MP) are used as maintenance therapy in patients with moderate-to-severe IBD. Animal studies during organogenesis using doses of azathioprine no higher than twice the therapeutic range for humans did not find an increased risk for malformations. They did, however, show higher rates of miscarriage and intrauterine growth restriction. Similarly, 6-MP has also been shown to be teratogenic in rats exposed to supratherapeutic levels, but when 6-MP was given orally at no more than 12 times the maximum human dose, no fetal malformations were seen.

With regard to human data, thiopurine use by pregnant women for a variety of conditions, including IBD, was not associated with an increased risk of fetal malformations compared with the general population [51]. Similarly, data from women who have undergone solid-organ transplantation have neither reported higher rates of malformations nor any consistent patterns of congenital anomalies [52]. Transient anemia in the newborns was reported to be not correlated with mother anemia. Thus, most experts agree that the benefits of continuing these drugs in pregnancy far outweigh their potential risks.

Breastfeeding while taking a thiopurine is not recommended by the American Academy of Pediatrics (AAP) due to the hypothetical risk of immunosuppression in the exposed neonate. This recommendation does not reflect the results of recent studies which suggest that the transfer of azathioprine and 6-MP via breast milk is exceedingly low [53] and that no deleterious consequences of this low-level transfer in the newborn have been found [54].

Methotrexate

Methotrexate (FDA category X) is used for moderate or refractory IBD. Its use in pregnancy is associated with multiple congenital anomalies collectively called methotrexate embryopathy or fetal aminopterin-methotrexate syndrome [55]. As it can also induce fetal loss, methotrexate use is absolutely contraindicated in pregnancy. It should be used with extreme caution in young patients and discontinued for at least 3 to 6 months before conception [50].

Methotrexate is excreted into breast milk at low levels. Although the clinical significance of this is not known, given the absence of safety data and the potential danger of accumulation within neonatal tissues, the AAP does not recommend breastfeeding by mothers who are on methotrexate.

Thalidomide

Thalidomide (FDA category X) is occasionally used in the treatment of refractory CD. Its use in pregnancy is associated with fetal limb defects, central nervous system effects, and abnormalities of the respiratory, cardiovascular, gastrointestinal, and genitourinary system [50]. Its use in pregnancy is contraindicated. To monitor access to thalidomide and prevent teratogenicity, prescription of the drug in the United States requires registration by both the prescribing physician and the dispensing pharmacy with the System for Thalidomide Education and Prescribing Safety (STEPS) program.

Breastfeeding on thalidomide is contraindicated.

Cyclosporine

Cyclosporine (FDA category C) may be used in the treatment of fulminant UC. Although cyclosporine crosses the placenta, it has not been found to be teratogenic in animal models. A meta-analysis from the transplant literature did not find a significant increase in the risk of major malformations with cyclosporine use or an increased risk for preterm birth or low birth weight [56]. Its use in pregnancy for steroid-refractory UC has not been associated with an increased risk for congenital malformations; however, preterm birth and low birth weight have been reported [57]. Whether these outcomes are a reflection of the severity of the mother's underlying disease or of medication effects is not clear.

Cyclosporine is transferred at high levels into breast milk; however, no adverse effects have been reported in published case reports and case series of breastfed infants exposed to cyclosporine. Nevertheless, the AAP advises against breastfeeding while on cyclosporine due to potential alterations in cellular metabolism in the newborn.

Antibiotics

Prolonged antibiotics for the primary treatment of IBD are generally avoided during pregnancy. Patients with abdominal abscesses, phlegmons, impending perforation, or fulminant colitis may, however, require them. The antibiotics used most commonly in IBD, ciprofloxacin (FDA category C) and metronidazole (FDA category B), should be used with caution. Animal studies have shown a potential risk for the quinolones to cause cartilage defects [55], and metronidazole has been shown to cause fetal malformations when given during the first trimester [58].

Antitumor Necrosis Factor Alpha Agents

Several anti-TNF agents are FDA approved for the treatment of CD. All are FDA category B. Post-marketing surveillance studies and international registers have found infliximab to be of low risk of fetal malformation in pregnancy [59].

As infliximab and adalimumab are IgG class antibodies, they are actively transported across the placenta in the latter half of pregnancy. To minimize fetal exposure, experts recommend giving the last dose of infliximab around 32 weeks of gestation and the last dose of adalimumab between 34 and 36 weeks [60]. Dose adjustments are not felt to be necessary at this time for certolizumab pegol which is comprised of pegylated Fab' fragments only as placental transfer is minimal. Whether this strategy reduces the risk for future complications is topic of intense debate. Interruption of anti-TNF infusion might lead to antibody formation and loss of response to the therapy when reinstituted.

Breastfeeding while taking an anti-TNF agent is considered to be safe. Studies have either not detected infliximab in the breast milk of treated mothers or found infliximab to be present at low levels [61]. Adalimumab has been detected in breast milk, however, only at levels lower than 1 % of its level in serum [62]. Lactation data for certolizumab pegol is lacking.

Natalizumab

Natalizumab (FDA category B) is a monoclonal antibody of the IgG_4 class directed against alpha integrins that is approved for the treatment of refractory CD. Studies of pregnancy outcomes in natalizumab-treated mothers mainly have involved women with multiple sclerosis, for which the drug was first approved. These studies have not found any increased risk of teratogenicity. Nevertheless, given the recent introduction of natalizumab and the fact that it is first in its class, the safety of natalizumab is considered unknown [60]. It is recommended that women treated with natalizumab use sufficient contraception or stop the drug 3 months prior to conception.

Natalizumab is not recommended during breastfeeding due to lack of safety data (Table 5.9).

Table 5.9 Medications used to treat inflammatory bowel disease

Drug		FDA pregnancy category	Recommendations for pregnancy	Recommendations for lactation
Mesalamine		Generally category B	Low risk	Limited human data; potential diarrhea in breastfed infants
Sulfasalazine		B	Interferes with folate metabolism; give with 2 mg of folate	Limited human data; potential diarrhea in breastfed infants
Corticosteroids		C	Possible increased risk of oral clefts with first trimester use; risk for fetal adrenal insufficiency, macrosomia, premature rupture of membranes	Compatible
Antibiotics	Metronidazole	B	Safe	Safe
	Ciprofloxacin	C	Avoid long-term use as it binds to fetal cartilage and may cause arthropathy in children	Limited human data; probably compatible
Immunomodulators	Azathioprine/6-mercaptopurine	D	Probably safe; avoid starting de novo in pregnancy	Probably safe
	Methotrexate	X	Contraindicated due to teratogenicity; stop 6 months prior to conception	Contraindicated
	Thalidomide	X	Contraindicated due to teratogenicity	Contraindicated
	Cyclosporine	C	Probably safe	Not recommended
	Tacrolimus	C	Probably safe	Not recommended
Anti-TNF agents	Infliximab	B	Low risk; dose adjust Infliximab and Adalimumab in the third trimester to minimize fetal exposure	Compatible
	Adalimumab			
	Certolizumab pegol			
Natalizumab		C	No human data	Not recommended

Source: Modified by Kane S. Caring for women with inflammatory bowel disease. J Gender Specific Med 2001;4(1):54–9

Elevated Liver Function Tests (LFTs) in Pregnancy

Asymptomatic Moderate Elevation of LFTs

Asymptomatic moderate elevation of transaminases (LFTs) is a common event occurring in 8–11 % of the population. The laboratory abnormality is considered moderate if it does not exceed 4 times the normal value. Asymptomatic elevation of LFTs in pregnancy was found in 30 % of all patients at time of delivery, and more than 50 % of those had a pregnancy-related etiology [63, 64].

Liver functions are not obtained routinely in pregnancy, and abnormal values present often as an incidental finding. When the cause is not explained by the clinical context, a prompt workup should be ordered to exclude underlying occult liver disease (Table 5.10 summarizes the most common etiology of symptomatic and asymptomatic abnormal LFTs divided by trimesters).

The diagnostic workup for asymptomatic abnormal LFTs is the same in the pregnant and nonpregnant patients with few exceptions. It includes a detailed history and physical examination to assess personal and familial risk factors, hepatotoxic substances, comorbidities, and signs of chronic liver disease. Laboratory tests and liver imaging are tailored to the overall clinical situation and risk factors (Table 5.11). Three liver diseases unique to pregnancy can be minimally symptomatic in the early stages, and they need to be considered in the diagnostic differential:

Table 5.10 Etiology of liver function tests abnormality divided by trimesters

Etiology of abnormal transaminases in pregnancy	First trimester	Second trimester	Third trimester
	Asymptomatic		
	Systemic diseases Celiac disease, viral hepatitis acute, thyroid disease, right-sided heart failure, unknown		
	Underlying liver diseases Autoimmune hepatitis, Wilson's disease, hepatitis C and B, congenital liver disease, primary biliary cirrhosis, nonalcoholic fatty liver disease, alcoholic liver disease, drugs, toxins		
		Preeclampsia[a]	
			Acute fatty liver of pregnancy[a]
	Symptomatic		
Nausea, vomiting	*Hyperemesis gravidarum*[a]		
Itching	*Intrahepatic cholestasis of pregnancy*[a]		
			Acute fatty liver of pregnancy[a]
		Preeclampsia[a]	
Abdominal pain +/– nausea vomiting, fever	Cholelithiasis, cholecystitis, sepsis pancreatitis, acute viral hepatitis, portal vein obstruction, Budd-Chiari syndrome, alcoholic hepatitis, toxic hepatitis unknown causes		

[a]Diseases unique to pregnancy

Table 5.11 Workup of abnormal LFTs

• Viral hepatitis	• HCV, HCV Rna, HBsAG, HBcAG, IGM, EBV, HVS, HEV, CMV, HAV, IGM, EBV
• Autoimmune, genetic disease	
• Toxic	• ANA, SMA,AMA, SLA-LP, TTG, ceruloplasmin, ferritin, iron, TSH
• Gallstones	
• Vascular (Budd-Chiari, PVT)	• History of drug, poison, alcohol, medication ingestions
	• Right upper quadrant US with Doppler

intrahepatic cholestasis of pregnancy (ICP), preeclampsia, and more infrequently acute fatty liver of pregnancy (AFLP). They typically occur in the second half of the pregnancy, and their prompt diagnosis will improve the overall maternal and fetal outcome.

ICP is associated with elevated biliary acid preceding or following the onset of the typical pruritus. Fasting biliary acids should be included among the laboratory tests obtained routinely in the diagnostic workup.

The diagnosis of preeclampsia is more challenging since the presentation of the disease can be atypical with vague symptoms and isolated elevation of transaminases. Presence of hypertension, proteinuria, and elevation of uric acid help to confirm the diagnosis (see Hypertension chapter 9).

AFLP occurs in the third trimester. Compromised hepatic synthetic ability accompanies the elevation of transaminases and rapidly leads to acute liver failure. Liver imaging by ultrasound, magnetic resonance, and computer tomography demonstrates fat deposition in the hepatic parenchyma and might be of use in early diagnosis.

The etiology of abnormal LFTs cannot be found in a significant number of patients, so it is advisable to follow them through the pregnancy and postpartum to assure the normalization of laboratory abnormality.

Acute Hepatitis in Pregnancy

Acute hepatitis (AH) that occurs during gestation presents a challenge for the treating physician.

Acute viral hepatitis is considered the most common cause of jaundice in pregnancy. Viral hepatitis E and herpes simplex hepatitis have a particular severe course and can progress to acute liver failure (ALF) in pregnant patients. Infectious hepatitis is discussed in detail in Chapter 10 (HIV and Hepatitis chapter 10).

During the second and third trimester, the differential diagnosis of AH and ALF broadens including pregnancy-specific diseases: preeclampsia and acute fatty liver of pregnancy.

Table 5.12 summarizes differential diagnosis and management of severe acute AH and ALF in the latter part of the pregnancy.

Table 5.12 Etiology of acute hepatitis in the second and third trimester

Causes non-related to pregnancy	Causes pregnancy specific
• Acute viral hepatitis: HSV, HAV, HBV, HVD, HEV (See HIV chapter 10)	• Acute fatty liver of pregnancy (AFLP)
• Toxic: Suicidal attempt, drug overdose, accidental ingestion, alcoholic hepatitis	• Preeclampsia with/without hepatic rupture • HELLP
• Metabolic: Wilson's disease, autoimmune hepatitis	
• Vascular: Budd-Chiari, portal vein thrombosis	
Initial work up and management	
• History: Medications ingestion, toxin, sick contacts, IVD and substance abuse, travels. Family history of liver disease. Obstetric history • Physical: Vital signs, signs of preexisting liver disease, neurological assessment for hepatic encephalopathy • Initial work up: CBC with differential and smear for schistocytes, platelets, sodium, potassium, creatinine, magnesium, phosphorus, glucose, bicarbonate, transaminasis, bilirubin, alkaline phosphatase, arterial lactate, arterial gas measurement, urinalysis, coagulation parameter, viral serology (HSV PCR, HBsAgIGM core and HBV Viral DNA, HAV IGM, HCV PCR, HVD serology HEV serology), Acetaminophen adducts level, arterial ammonia level, auto antibodies (ANA, ASMA, SLA/LP), total gamma globulin, toxicology screen, blood typing, right upper quadrant ultrasound with Doppler • Supportive care: Correct hypoglycemia, correct hyponatremia, correct coagulophaty, intravenous H2blockers Consider antibiotics, steroids, lactulose, *N*-acetylcysteine • Assemble a multidisciplinary team: Maternal Fetal Medicine Specialist, Anesthesiologist, Obstetric Medicine Specialist, Transplant Hepatologist, Neonatologist, Intensive Care Specialist • Delivery • Early consultation with a transplantation center and immediate referral if signs of neurological impairment occurs (encephalopathy grade I)	

Pregnancy in Patients with Advanced Chronic Liver Disease

Chronic liver disease is associated with ovulatory failure, secondary amenorrhea, and infertility. However, normal fertility is maintained in a significant proportion of women with underlying liver disease, and today, patients are no longer advised against pregnancy for fear of complications. Thus, it is not uncommon to encounter pregnant patients with stable chronic liver diseases. Pregnancy is possible in liver transplant recipients [65] and in anovulatory patients, with assisted reproductive technologies. Portal hypertension can be seen in pregnant patients without underlying liver damage, as in the case of portal vein thrombosis. Such pregnancies are increasing and present unique medical challenges for both patients and clinicians.

Conception, Maternal, and Pregnancy Outcomes in Patients with Advanced Liver Disease

Conception Outcomes

It is estimated that half of all conceptions will result in live births. In a recent retrospective review of 69 pregnancies in patients with cirrhosis, the live birth rate was 58 % [66]. Miscarriage and elective termination rates did not differ from the average population rates of 19 % and 15 %, respectively, although half of the elective terminations were advised for medical reasons. In the same cohort, the stillbirth rate was increased by 6 %.

Pregnancy Outcomes

Advanced liver disease is associated with poor pregnancy outcomes, including an increased risk of premature birth and intrauterine growth restriction. In one study, 30 % of deliveries occurred before 30 weeks of gestation and 50 % before 35 weeks [66]. Other studies confirmed the same complications including preterm labor, intrauterine growth restriction, and infections [67]. The causes of stillbirth are not known and are most likely multifactorial. Maximizing nutritional status before and during pregnancy may improve outcomes. Patients with advanced liver disease, in particular, are prone to deficiencies in magnesium, phosphorus, and zinc and in fat-soluble vitamins such as vitamins D and K. Adequate levels should be carefully restored. A list of common medications used in the cirrhotic patient and their use in pregnancy is summarized in Table 5.13.

Maternal Outcomes

Liver failure, ascites, hepatic encephalopathy, and variceal bleeding are common complications in patients with cirrhosis and may occur during pregnancy. These complications are responsible for the high maternal mortality rate that occurs in this group of patients [68].

Pregnancy does not seem to exacerbate underlying liver disease or precipitate hepatic failure, but its effect on portal hypertension leads to an increased risk of variceal bleeding in the second half of gestation. Recently, the first prospective study addressing the natural history of post-hepatitic cirrhosis in pregnancy was published [68]. The data confirmed poor maternal outcomes for pregnant patients with cirrhosis; in this study, the increased maternal morbidity in comparison with nonpregnant control was secondary to variceal bleeding (78 % vs. 19 %). Maternal mortality was also increased (7.8 %). Other complications of advanced liver disease reported during gestation are described in Table 5.14.

Table 5.13 Common medications used in the cirrhotic patient

Medications	Use in pregnancy
Lactulose (FDA category B)	Frequently used without adverse effects
Spironolactone (FDA category C)	Contraindicated Feminization in rats
Hydrochlorazide (FDA category B)	Use if necessary Avoid hyponatremia
Furosemide (FDA category C)	Use if necessary Avoid hyponatremia
Ciprofloxacin (FDA category C)	Use only if absolutely necessary Associated to skeletal abnormalities
Metronidazole (FDA category B)	Use if necessary
Xifaxan (FDA category C)	No data available
Nonselective B-blocker (Propranolol category C)	Use if necessary Caution associated with newborn bradycardia

Table 5.14 Rare complications in the pregnant patient with advanced liver disease

Rupture of splenic aneurysms
Budd-Chiari syndrome
Portal vein thrombosis
Rupture of hepatic masses (hepatocellular carcinoma, adenoma)
Disseminated hepatic abscesses (schistosomiasis, amebiasis)

The model for end-stage liver disease (MELD), which is used to grade the severity of liver disease for transplant purposes, seems to predict the likelihood of complications in pregnant patients with cirrhosis with increased risk seen in patients with a MELD score higher than 10 [66].

Management of Portal Hypertension and Variceal Bleeding in Pregnancy

Esophageal variceal rupture has been observed to occur in up to half of the cases, with a high maternal mortality rate of 10 to 50 % [69]. This is caused by worsening of the portal hypertension due to the systemic and intra-abdominal physiological changes of pregnancy.

During gestation, compensatory dilation of collateral veins connecting the portal circulation and the azygos vein can occur. This is aggravated by increased circulating blood volume, which in the normal gestation will increase by 50 % peaking between 28 and 32 weeks. Moreover, the expanding uterus may compress the inferior vena cava (IVC) and increases intra-abdominal pressure. Rupture of esophageal varices or splenic artery aneurysm may occur. The major cause of maternal morbidity and mortality in pregnant patients with cirrhosis is increased portal hypertension and variceal bleeding in the third trimester and during labor and delivery. Bleeding is worsened by thrombocytopenia and coagulopathy, secondary to underlying hepatic dysfunction and vitamin K malabsorption.

Successful management of acute variceal bleeding in pregnant patients does not differ from nonpregnant patients and includes endoscopic band ligation (EVL), transjugular intrahepatic portosystemic shunt, and endoscopic injection sclerotherapy [70, 71]. The safety of octreotide infusion has not been established and carries a theoretical risk of uterine ischemia and therefore should be used only if absolutely necessary.

Many experts advocate for primary prevention of variceal bleeding in pregnancy, arguing its high mortality risk, despite the lack of available data supporting the efficacy of this strategy. In following this recommendation, pregnant patients with cirrhosis should undergo an upper endoscopy for detection and possible prophylactic EVL of high-risk varices. Endoscopy should be timed to coincide with maximum volume expansion (28 weeks of gestational age) [69, 72]. Nonselective beta-blockers typically used for primary and secondary variceal bleeding prophylaxis are indicated in all patients. Although intrauterine growth restriction, bradycardia, and hypoglycemia in the newborn have been reported with the use of beta-blockers, they should be continued in pregnancy to avoid rebound variceal bleeding; however, EVL is preferred for primary prophylaxis. Patients who did not undergo obliteration of varices should be considered for elective operative delivery because of the very high risk of bleeding during labor and delivery. Patients who have vaginal deliveries should be considered for early epidural anesthesia, shortening of the second stage, and assisted delivery. Correction of the international normalized ratio (INR) prior to operative or assisted delivery should be considered, and fresh frozen plasma and platelets should be available. If a cesarean section is performed, antibiotic coverage should be administered as prophylaxis for acute bacterial peritonitis.

When encountering a woman with chronic liver disease who wishes to become pregnant, clinicians must have a frank discussion regarding the associated risks, including the increased risk of complications of liver disease—especially variceal hemorrhage—and the increased risk of intrauterine fetal demise (Table 5.15).

Table 5.15 Care of pregnant patient with advanced liver disease

Preconception evaluation
- Assess liver disease function and portal hypertension and MELD calculation
- Advise patient with MELD > 10 of high maternal risk and poor outcome
- Maximize nutrition: replace fat-soluble vitamins and minerals
- Endoscopic variceal eradication (large varices)

Pregnancy
- Nonselective β-blockers should be continued
- Upper endoscopy and EVL of high-risk varices at 28 weeks
- Continue monitoring nutrition

Delivery
- C-section or operative delivery if risk of esophageal varices rupture
- Blood products as needed
- Antibiotic prophylaxis after C-section

Special Considerations in Patients with Preexisting Liver Disease

The treatment of the most common liver diseases in pregnancy is summarized in Table 5.16.

In general, pregnancy does not alter the course or treatment of chronic liver disease.

Wilson's Disease

Wilson's disease is a rare autosomal recessive disease of copper metabolism presenting in the first four decades of life with neurologic damage, hemolytic anemia, and liver disease. The accumulation of copper in the liver leads to progressive liver damage or acute fulminant hepatitis. Fulminant hepatitis is more common in female patients with a ratio of 4 to 1. When it presents acutely in pregnancy with hemolytic anemia, thrombocytopenia, and liver failure, it can be easily confused with HELLP syndrome. Diagnosis requires serum copper and 24-h urine for urinary copper excretion. Ceruloplasmin is often increased in pregnancy and thus of little value. Ultimately, liver biopsies might be necessary. Treated patients are fertile, and several cases of successful pregnancy with Wilson's disease are described in the literature [73, 74]. However, untreated Wilson's disease might lead to spontaneous abortion, fetal demise, and recurrent miscarriage. Treatment consists of lifelong administration of copper chelants: penicillamine, trientine, and tetrathiomolybdate. Scarce data exist regarding their safety in pregnancy. There are no reports of increased teratogenicity in small case series. The 2011 EASL recent guidelines recommended continuing chelating in pregnancy to avoid the risk of rebound liver damage upon discontinuation. Reduction and optimization of dosage of chelators might be useful

Table 5.16 Common causes of chronic liver disease and their therapy in pregnancy

Common chronic liver disease	Pregnancy considerations	Therapy
Alcoholic liver disease (ALD)	Causes fetal alcohol syndrome in the newborn	Abstinence Antabuse not safe
Non-alcoholic fatty liver disease	Increased prevalence with gestational diabetes	Glucose control Diet and exercise
Viral hepatitis B	Causes flares in pregnancy/postpartum	Antiretroviral probably safe
Viral hepatitis C	3 % vertical transmission Obstetric outcomes controversial	Nonoperative delivery Limit rupture of membrane time
Autoimmune hepatitis	May present acutely in pregnancy	Prednisolone, Azathioprine
Wilson's disease	May present in pregnancy	Zinc effective and well tolerated
Primary biliary cirrhosis	Course not altered by pregnancy	Ursodeoxycholic acid well tolerated
Primary sclerosis cholangitis	Course not altered by pregnancy	Ursodeoxycholic well tolerated
Hemochromatosis	Rare in fertile years Decreasing iron storages improves the disease	
Biliary atresia	Pregnancy is common in patient on a waiting list for liver transplant	Replace fat-soluble therapy Treat portal hypertension
Budd-Chiari syndrome	May present acutely precipitated by pregnancy in hypercoagulable patients	Anticoagulation Liver transplant
Portal vein thrombosis	May present acutely in pregnancy Important cause of portal hypertension in pregnancy	Anticoagulation Treat portal hypertension

in the third trimester to maintain adequate copper supply to the growing fetus. Zinc salt is also prescribed effectively to treat this condition, and its use is considered first line in pregnancy and women wishing to conceive [75].

Autoimmune Hepatitis

Autoimmune hepatitis (AIH) is a common disease occurring in 100,000 to 200,000 patients/year in the United States. It is more common in women than in men and often presents in patients during their childbearing age; thus, autoimmune hepatitis in pregnancy is a common condition. The mainstay treatment for autoimmune hepatitis is immunosuppression, usually with prednisone/prednisolone alone or in combination with azathioprine [76].

Table 5.17 Serological markers of autoimmune hepatitis

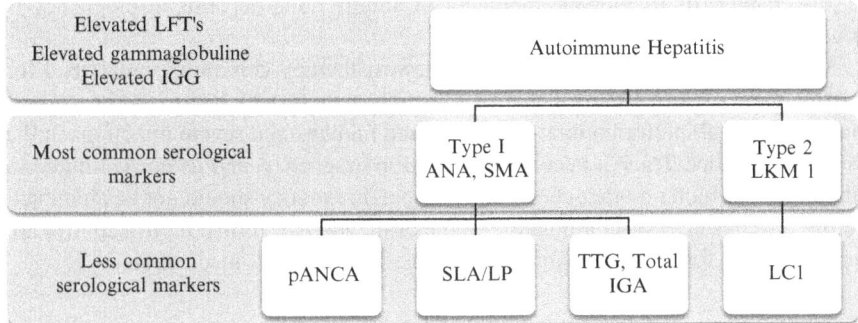

Fertility and Pregnancy Outcome and Natural History of the Disease in Pregnancy

While it has long been hypothesized that women with autoimmune hepatitis have difficulty with conceiving, this myth has since been debunked [77, 78]. The natural history of the disease is a fluctuating course, but the majority of patients will require lifelong immunosuppressant therapy. Successful spontaneous remissions have been described in pregnancy; however, worsening with poor maternal outcome and liver decompensation has been reported as well [78]. Therapy should be continued because relapse is associated with progression of the liver disease.

A recent case series showed an increase in risk of adverse outcomes, including prematurity and maternal hepatic decompensation. Poor outcome has been associated with poor disease control prior to conception [79].

Autoimmune hepatitis can present de novo in pregnancy and should be suspected in any patient with acute elevation of transaminases, positive autoimmune markers, and elevated gamma globulin (Table 5.17).

When autoimmune hepatitis is suspected, a confirmatory liver biopsy is justified in order to make appropriate management decisions. The disease may flare with the return of normal immunity after the pregnancy ends, and patients should be followed with care for the first 4 to 6 months postpartum as the immune system reconstitutes. Acute liver failure secondary to autoimmune hepatitis has been described in pregnancy.

Therapy

Prednisone (FDA category C), prednisolone (FDA category C), and azathioprine (FDA category D) have been used extensively in pregnancy for many decades. They are still the cornerstone of immunosuppressant therapy for a variety autoimmune and allergic conditions. Prednisolone is partially inactivated by the placenta resulting in reduced fetal exposure. Azathioprine teratogenicity was discussed in detail elsewhere in this chapter. Its use for the treatment of autoimmune hepatitis in pregnancy is considered appropriate when necessary.

Mycophenolate mofetil is among the newest therapy commonly prescribed for the treatment of autoimmune hepatitis. It is FDA category D; its use has been associated with fetal malformations in animals and humans and severe infections in the expectant mother. Thus, it is contraindicated in pregnancy, and its use is limited to situations in which no other choice is available. Pregnancy should not be attempted before 6 weeks after discontinuation of the drug, and two forms of birth control are recommended for women of childbearing age who take this medication.

Gallstone Disease

The prevalence of asymptomatic gallstones in pregnant women is between 2.5 % and 12 % [80]. Gallstones form because of the physiological changes that occur in pregnancy: decreased gallbladder motility and changes in bile composition. Despite the high prevalence, only 0.1 % of women develop symptoms of biliary colic and cholecystitis. The symptoms are the same as in the general population including nausea, vomiting, and abdominal pain. After the first attack, the likelihood of recurrence during pregnancy is high. Gallstone disease can present complicated by choledocolythiasis, ascending cholangitis, and pancreatitis.

Diagnosis is achieved with ultrasound and MRI without contrast. ERCP is also performed routinely both for diagnostic and therapeutic indications when common bile duct exploration with possible stone removal is necessary.

A conservative approach with fluids, antibiotic, and pain medications has been recommended fearing the complications of surgery during gestation. However, a recent study demonstrated that laparoscopic cholecystectomy can be performed safely in any trimester and that surgery is associated with fewer recurrences, hospitalizations, preterm labor, and morbidity than conservative therapy [81]. Laparoscopic cholecystectomy is now the second most common surgery in pregnancy.

Liver Diseases Specific to Pregnancy

Intrahepatic Cholestasis of Pregnancy

Intrahepatic cholestasis of pregnancy (ICP) is a condition characterized by pruritus, abnormal liver function tests, and elevated serum bile acids, all of which resolve after birth. The clinical significance of obstetric cholestasis is due to the potential risks to the fetus, which may include spontaneous or iatrogenic preterm birth and fetal death. Maternal morbidity, on the other hand, is low: intense pruritus may lead to significant sleep deprivation.

Pathogenesis

While previous studies have shown that genetic, hormonal, and exogenous factors play a role in the pathogenesis of ICP, the pathogenesis is still not completely understood. These factors are likely to act together altering the transport of biliary acids across the hepatocyte's canalicular membrane causing mild cholestasis. As a consequence, pruritus results from the accumulation of substances in the blood circulation. Decreased availability of biliary salts in the intestine will lead to malabsorption of fat and fat-soluble vitamins.

Findings of genetic mutations leading to ICP were discovered in the 1990s [82].

Estrogen and progesterone have been clearly linked to the pathogenesis of ICP. Initiation of oral contraceptives has been observed to precipitate cholestasis. Moreover, progesterone therapy in pregnancy is associated with the development of cholestasis. It is thought that estrogens decrease the uptake of bile acids. Genetic mutations may also predispose women to altered metabolism of estrogens. Abnormally high levels of progesterone have been found in women with ICP [83]. Particularly, sulfated progesterone metabolites may oversaturate transporter proteins needed to translocate phosphatidylcholine.

While genetic predisposition plays a role, exogenous factors leading to the development of ICP are less clear. Seasonal variations have been observed in different countries: ICP commonly occurs in the winter months. In a recent study, the underlying presence of liver disease was demonstrated for a subset of patients suggesting the presence of an intrahepatic cholestasis of pregnancy secondary to multifactorial liver damages [84]. The strongest association was found with hepatitis C infection, as 25 % of patients are positive for the HCV antibody and cholelithiasis [85].

Epidemiology

Worldwide cholestasis affects from fewer than 1 % to nearly 2.4 % of pregnancies in Chile. In the United States, 1 % of pregnancies are affected by the condition.

Diagnosis

Cholestasis of pregnancy usually presents in the third trimester but may be seen in atypical cases as early as the first trimester. Pruritis is the cardinal symptom of this clinical entity. Pruritis is generally intense, typically worse at night, and involves the palms of the hands and/or soles of the feet. Risk factors for development of intrahepatic cholestasis include those who develop cholestasis after use of oral contraceptives, personal or family history of cholestasis, or gallstones and underlying liver disease, especially hepatitis C.

Diagnosis is confirmed by the presence of elevated serum bile acids with or without abnormal LFTs. Liver function tests may show abnormal transaminases; bilirubin is infrequently elevated. Of note the mild elevation of alkaline phosphatase is usually placental in origin. Total bile acids (BA) are considered elevated if they exceed 10 umol/L in the fasting state. Postnatally, pruritis and liver function test normalization should be confirmed. Liver biopsy is generally not required for diagnosis but, if obtained, typically shows signs of cholestasis with bile plugs in the canaliculi, particularly in zone 3 [86]. Fat-soluble vitamins and vitamin K-dependent coagulation factors can be altered resulting in nutritional deficiency and bleeding complications. Vitamin A, vitamin D, vitamin E, and vitamin K level as well as prothrombin time should be obtained during the evaluation.

It is important to exclude other causes of liver disease. Upon initial evaluation of abnormal liver function tests and pruritis, viral screen for hepatitis A, B, and C; EBV; CMV; autoimmune hepatitis; and PBC (ANA, anti-smooth muscle, anti-LKM, and anti-mitochondrial antibodies) and right upper quadrant ultrasound should be investigated. Atypical preeclampsia and acute fatty liver of pregnancy should be part of the differential diagnosis.

Monitoring

Whether bile acids lead to fetal injury and death or not is debated. Based on previous research of 60 cases of intrahepatic cholestasis of pregnancy, it was observed that a value >40 mmol/L may be an indicator of severe elevation and higher risk of fetal demise [87]. However, this was not a randomized control study, and attempts to use these cutoffs have been inconsistent. One should not be reassured by a low level of bile acid nor plan for emergent intervention in higher levels. Nevertheless, periodic monitoring of LFTs, BA level, and PT/INR is recommended after the diagnosis is established.

Complications

Maternal and fetal complications continue to be debated in the literature. The table below shows the observed rates of spontaneous preterm birth, meconium passage, low APGAR scores, and fetal or neonatal death in several studies organized by year (Table 5.18). The most feared consequence of intrahepatic cholestasis is the risk of intrauterine death or stillbirth [88]. Based on recent literature, the perinatal mortality rate ranges from 5.7/1000 to 11/1000. The earlier the onset of cholestasis during pregnancy, the greater is the likelihood of spontaneous preterm birth. Possibly secondary to active management such as fetal monitoring, frequent laboratory testing, and also ursodiol administration, intrauterine death rates have now dropped to 3.5 %. Active management focuses highly on the observation that stillbirth in ICP typically occurs at weeks 37–39, so delivery by week 37 is often recommended.

Efforts to use bile acid cutoffs to indicate higher risk of stillbirth are unreliable.

Intrahepatic cholestasis has also been linked to increased passage of meconium. The incidence of meconium staining is approximately 15 % and usually a sign of fetal distress. Additionally, studies report a 40 % risk of preterm labor without

Table 5.18 Summary of the major studies of fetal outcome in ICP

	No. of cases	IUD and/or NND (%)	Meconium-stained liquor (%)	Preterm labor (%)	Planned delivery <37–38/40[a]
1964–1969	87	9	–	54	No
1965–1979	56	11	27	36	No
Post-1969	91	3	–	–	Yes
1988	83	4	45	44	Yes
1994	320	2	25	12	Yes
1990–1996	91	0	15	14.3	Yes
1999–2001	70	0	14	6	Yes

Adapted from Kumar S, Balki M, Williamson C (with Eliana Castillo and Deborah M. Money contributing to the section on viral hepatitis). Disorders of the liver, biliary system and exocrine pancreas in pregnancy. In: Powrie RO, Greene MF, Camann W, eds. *de Swiet's Medical Disorders in Obstetric Practice*, 5 Edition. Wiley-Blackwell: Oxford, England. 2010;223–255
NND neonatal death, *IUD* intrauterine death rate as a percentage of all births
[a]i.e., in the majority of cases in the study

active management. However, to avoid fetal demise, the majority of preterm delivery at 37 weeks is iatrogenic.

Maternal prognosis has generally thought to be excellent. Morbidity during ICP usually involves intense pruritis associated with the disease. However, a recent study from Finland has shown long-term outcomes that suggest otherwise. From 1972 to 2000, 10,504 women with ICP were matched to normal pregnancy controls: hepatitis C, gallstones and cholecystitis, nonalcoholic pancreatitis, and nonalcoholic liver cirrhosis including cases of primary biliary cirrhosis (17 cases among the 10,504 patients with ICP vs. two cases in the control group); this study illustrates the importance of excluding other causes of liver disease as ICP may be the first manifestation of chronic liver disease in these patients [89].

Maternal and Obstetric Management

Ursodiol has been shown to improve symptoms of pruritis as well as abnormal liver function tests in ICP, likely by increasing biliary excretion. It prevents damage to the canalicular membranes by increasing cellulization of cholesterol. Although it has been shown to decrease cholestasis, its positive effect on obstetric outcome is less convincing. A recent meta-analysis included 9 randomized controlled trials and concluded that maternal pruritis, ALT, and bile acids improved with ursodiol therapy. The small decrease in fetal premature births, respiratory distress, and need for ICU monitoring rates [90] failed to reach statistical significance. We recommend a treatment regimen beginning with UDCA 10–15 mg/kg daily and titrated up to 25 mg/kg daily, divided into two doses. Diarrhea is the most common, though rare, side effects and no adverse fetal effects have been demonstrated.

Table 5.19 Intrahepatic cholestasis of pregnancy

At diagnosis
- Exclude other causes of liver diseases
- Check liver functions/PT/INR, albumin
- Check fat-soluble vitamins
- Replace vitamins
- Start UDCA
- Pruritus relief agents

32 weeks to 39 weeks
- Monitor LFTs, BA
- PT/INR, albumin
- Fetal monitoring twice/week
- Frequent follow-up
and
- Deliver if rising LFTs, fetal distress, BAO 40mmol/L
- Amniocentesis for lung maturity

Low vitamin K level and abnormal coagulation parameter should be corrected before delivery to avoid bleeding complications, so patients should be supplemented with 10 mg of vitamin K daily.

There is still considerable debate about the best time to deliver a woman with ICP. No studies have addressed this issue specifically. The majority of recorded intrauterine deaths occurred between 37 and 39 weeks of gestation. Most experts recommend delivery in all women with ICP at 37 weeks. Others recommend delivery between 37 and 39 weeks only if there is fetal distress, rising of liver function tests, and/or biliary acids exceeding 40 mmol/L despite appropriate URSO therapy (Table 5.19).

Acute Fatty Liver of Pregnancy

Acute fatty liver of pregnancy (AFLP) is rare and potentially life threatening, otherwise unexplained liver failure in the third trimester of pregnancy. This is characterized by the accumulation of microvascular fat within the liver and thought to be a family of disorders related to impairment of fatty acid transport or mitochondrial oxidation.

Pathogenesis

The microvesicular fat deposition seen in biopsies resembled those of Reye's syndrome, a pathology known to result from mitochondrial dysfunction. A key to understanding the role of inherited defects in fatty acid transport and mitochondrial oxidation in AFLP has come from families afflicted with long-chain 3-hydroxyacyl

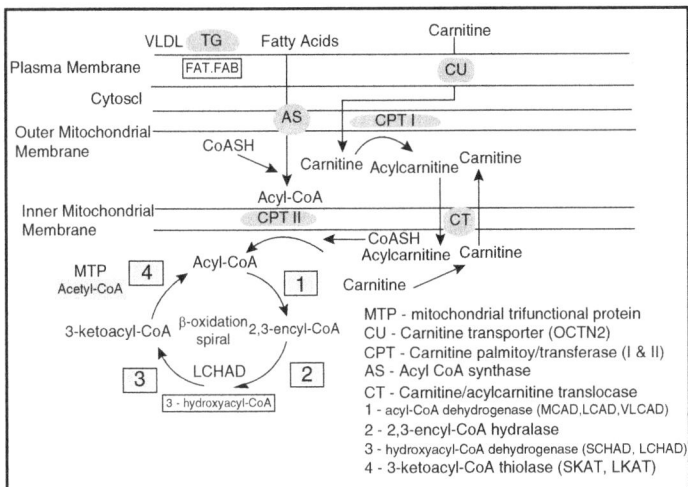

Fig. 5.1 Fatty acid transport and mitochondrial oxidation. From Degli Esposti S, Goodwin TM, Pickard J, Reily CA, Reyes H. Liver Disease. In: Rosene-Montella K, Keely E, Barbour LA, Lee RV, eds. *Medical Care of the Pregnant Patient*. 2nd Edition. Philadelphia, PA: American College of Physicians. 2008; 567-593, with permission

coenzyme A dehydrogenase (LCHAD) deficiency (Fig 5.1). A partial (such as in LCHAD deficiency) or complete deficiency of MTP (all three enzymes including LCHAD, MCHAD, SCHAD) leads to the accumulation of straight-chain fatty acids and their metabolites. Fetal fatty acid recirculates into the maternal circulation where it deposits and leads to fatty liver. Clinically, hours or months after birth, children present with nonketotic hypoglycemia and hepatic encephalopathy [91].

LCHAD mutations have also been associated with the HELLP syndrome. After case reports of LCHAD in patients with fatty liver, a larger series of families with known LCHAD mutations was reported [92]. LCHAD deficiency in the fetus was associated with a 79 % chance of developing either acute fatty liver of pregnancy or HELLP syndrome. It appears that although AFLP and even HELLP syndrome occur more commonly in cases where both the mother and fetus are affected with LCHAD deficiency, in certain situations, even the heterozygous state of LCHAD deficiency in the mother can be sufficient to predispose to fatty liver [93]. Maternal stressors may include fever, viral infection, toxic or drug ingestion (aspirin), reduced antioxidant intake, and obesity. In addition, throughout pregnancy and particularly in the third trimester, the pathway of fatty acid transport and mitochondrial oxidation decreases in efficiency. LCHAD in particular shows a steady decrease in activity from early to late pregnancy [94]. A proposed mechanism of acute fatty liver development is multifactorial: in the setting of maternal and/or fetal genetic predisposition with LCHAD or MTP deficiency, an increase in metabolic stress, decrease in mitochondrial oxidation, and environmental stress lead to the development of AFLP.

Table 5.20 Disorders of fatty acid transport and mitochondrial oxidation (FATMO) related to maternal complication

Maternal complication	Disorders of fatty acid transport and mitochondrial oxidation						
	LCHAD	TFP (MTP)	CPT I	CACT	MCAD	SCAD	Unknown[a]
Acute fatty liver of pregnancy	+++	++	+	−	−	+	++
HELLP syndrome	+++	−	−	−	+	+	++
Preeclampsia	+++	−	+	+	−	−	−
Hyperemesis	++	−	+	−	−	−	+
ICP	+	−	−	−	−	−	+

Modified from Rinaldo P. et al. Prenatal Diagnosis 2001; 21-52-4
From: Degli Esposti S, Goodwin TM, Pickard J, Reily CA, Reyes H. Liver Disease. In: Rosene-Montella K, Keely E, Barbour LA, Lee RV, eds. *Medical Care of the Pregnant Patient*. 2nd Edition. Philadelphia, PA: American College of Physicians. 2008; 567–593, with permission
+++, association reported in multiple cases; ++, association reported in more than one case; +, association reported in one case, possibly a coincidental event; -, association not reported
[a]Mothers of children with unspecified disorders but with clinical manifestations and strong biochemical evidence in vivo and vitro of an underlying FATMO disorder (P. Rinaldo et al., unpublished observations)

At present, genetic screening of newborn babies with white mothers with AFLP for fatty acid transport and mitochondrial oxidation disorders is warranted. Indeed, infants found to have LCHAD may develop sudden infant death months later due to a metabolic crisis. Acylcarnitine profiles show characteristic LCHAD, which is now included in the newborn screen in most states, is a convenient screen for these disorders [95].

Table 5.20 shows the spectrum of disorders of fatty acid transport and mitochondrial oxidation that has been associated with various pregnancy complications, primarily manifesting as liver disease. Preeclampsia, which is seen in 50 % or more of patients with AFLP, may play a role as a possible precipitant in the pathogenesis of AFLP, but this is unclear.

Clinical Presentation

Patients with AFLP present in the third trimester with symptoms and signs that vary widely (Table 5.21). Patients typically present with a nonspecific prodrome of malaise, anorexia, nausea, and vomiting that is often mistaken for viral illness. Jaundice is a frequent symptom. In severe cases, symptoms progress to liver failure and evidence of asterixis (hepatic encephalopathy) and coma may develop. Hypoglycemia, coagulopathy with frank bleeding, and sepsis may occur. Many affected patients have preeclampsia, but blood pressures remain deceptively low due to liver failure and a resultant further decrease in systemic vascular resistance.

Table 5.21 Acute fatty liver of pregnancy

Signs and symptoms	
Nausea, vomiting, lethargy, jaundice, or none	
Laboratory test results	
Elevated aminotransferases level but <1,000 U	
Increased prothrombin time	
Decreased fibrinogen level	
Concerns	
Potentially lethal to both the mother and fetus (DNA testing of family indicated)	
Management	
Prompt delivery	
Maximal support	

From: Degli Esposti S, Goodwin TM, Pickard J, Reily CA, Reyes H. Liver Disease. In: Rosene-Montella K, Keely E, Barbour LA, Lee RV, eds. *Medical Care of the Pregnant Patient*. 2nd Edition. Philadelphia, PA: American College of Physicians. 2008; 567–593, with permission

Thrombocytopenia in the third trimester should always prompt monitoring of liver function tests. Aminotransferase levels are elevated but are usually less than 1000 U. Bilirubin is almost always elevated. Patients with AFLP and severe hepatic failure have disseminated intravascular coagulation with thrombocytopenia and may meet the diagnostic criteria for the HELLP syndrome. Liver biopsy is generally not needed for diagnosis. However, liver biopsy specimens from patients with AFLP show microvesicular fatty infiltration that is most prominent in the central region. Fat may be seen in the biopsy specimens of patients with the HELLP syndrome, but it is not microvesicular and is not restricted to the centrilobular areas [96].

Improvement begins with delivery. Leukocytosis and bilirubin elevations may persist longer, even as the patient recovers clinically. In severe cases, the patient needs maximum support as the liver recovers and must be monitored for a host of possible complications, including acute respiratory failure, renal failure, gastrointestinal hemorrhage, acute pancreatitis, or nephrogenic diabetes insipidus [97]. Fetal demise is common. Surviving patients return to full health with no hepatic sequelae. Studies have described a subset of women who suffer from recurrent AFLP in subsequent pregnancies, but most patients have uncomplicated gestations after an affected gestation. Liver transplantation has been done for patients with AFLP, but prompt recognition and management of AFLP should obviate this need.

Management

The course of AFLP may progress rapidly to coma and death. A multidisciplinary approach is essential: consultation with the anesthesia, hepatology, intensive care, and hematology teams is needed in anticipation of complications. Cornerstones of therapy include 1) early identification and diagnosis; 2) supportive treatment by reversing coagulopathy with FFP, platelets, cryoprecipitate, avoiding hypoglycemia with glucose infusion, and intense monitoring of fluid status; and 3) delivery. Fatty liver of pregnancy in previously healthy women should resolve without requiring liver transplantation.

Prior to the 1970s, maternal mortality from AFLP was as high as 90 %. Fetal mortality was also marked at 50 %. Improvement in early detection of this fatal disease and early delivery has led to decrease in maternal mortality to less than 10 %. Infants born alive are generally thought to have an excellent prognosis, though should be monitored given the risk of possible poor outcome if found to be LCHAD deficient. Maternal risks include hemorrhage and acute liver failure. The fetus is at risk of intrauterine death.

Laboratory studies should include a coagulation panel, ammonia, viral hepatitis serologies (including hepatitis E in endemic regions and herpes simplex), glucose, complete blood count, and liver panel. Intravenous (IV) dextrose infusion, such as D10, may be required to maintain the glucose level. Given the low antithrombin levels associated with AFLP, some have advocated antithrombin infusions in cases of fatty liver [98], but randomized trials for this have not occurred, and as yet, the role of antithrombin infusion in treating fatty liver of pregnancy is unknown.

Prior to delivery, coagulopathy should be treated aggressively, without waiting for overt hemorrhage. Maternal and fetal glucose status should be monitored regularly. In the event of vaginal delivery, episiotomy should be avoided if possible; in the case of abdominal delivery, a midline incision in the skin is advocated, as the patient may have a significant risk of bleeding and altered coagulation. The same measures, including correction of coagulopathy and laboratory assessment, are recommended in the postpartum phase with close observation until all signs of liver function and coagulation have returned to normal. Maternal and newborn testing for LCHAD deficiency should be undertaken in the white population.

Preeclamptic Liver Disease (HELLP Syndrome)

Women who die from preeclampsia have a unique liver lesion: a hemorrhage and fibrin deposition most prominent in the zone immediately adjacent to the portal triads. While clinically observed for much longer, it was only in the early 1980s that HELLP syndrome, a variant of severe preeclampsia, was defined by Dr. Weinstein. It is defined by the presence of hemolysis, elevated liver enzyme levels, and low platelet in its complete form. The HELLP syndrome occurs in only 0.5–0.9 % of pregnancies yet comprises 10–20 % of those with severe preeclampsia.

Diagnosis and Clinical Manifestations

70 % of cases occur between the 27th and 37th week of gestation, but 10 % occur before the 27th week of gestation and 20 % after the 37th week. Women typically present with severe epigastric or right upper quadrant pain, often accompanied by

malaise, nausea, and vomiting. Vague viral-like illness complaints, as well as symptoms of preeclampsia, such as headache and excessive thirsts, are common complaints. A recent systematic review of symptoms in women with HELLP syndrome showed that the presence of headache, pain, visual disturbance, nausea, and vomiting predicts worse outcomes [99].

On physical examination, the patient almost always demonstrates discrete tenderness of the right upper quadrant or is completely asymptomatic. Preeclampsia findings of hypertension and proteinuria may be present. Generalized edema develops in >50 % of women prior to the development of HELLP. Ascites and jaundice may be present if severe liver disease has developed.

Pathogenesis and Diagnosis

Red cell hemolysis occurs through high-velocity flow through damaged endothelium, where intimal damage, fibrin deposition, and endothelial dysfunction occur. This process of microangiopathic hemolytic anemia leads to the presence of burr cells and schistocytes on peripheral smear. Damaged red cells release lactate dehydrogenase and are either conjugated by haptoglobin and quickly cleared from the circulation or converted to unconjugated bilirubin by the spleen. Thus, the findings of elevated LDH, increased unconjugated bilirubin, and low haptoglobin support the diagnosis of hemolysis. Typically, transaminases become elevated in HELLP syndrome due to liver injury. Thrombocytopenia, often the first manifestation of HELLP syndrome, is caused by increased consumption: platelets are activated by damaged endothelium and are cleared quickly leading to shorter lifespan.

Currently, there are two major classifications for the diagnosis of HELLP syndrome. The Tennessee classification requires 1) platelets<= 100 x 10^9, 2) AST>=70, and 3) LDH>=600. The Mississippi classification identifies different platelet, liver function, and LDH levels. Class 3, considered a clinical transition phase, is typified by platelets <150,000, AST>40, and LDH>600. Class 2 is characterized by platelets <100,000, AST>40, and LDH>600. Finally, class 3 (the complete form) is characterized by severe thrombocytopenia platelets <50,000, AST>70, and LDH>400. In general, elevated transaminases, AST and ALT, do not exceed 400 IU/L. Again bilirubin may be elevated due to hemolysis and increase in unconjugated bilirubin, but usually not more than twice normal. In contrast to acute fatty liver, synthetic liver function is preserved. Diagnosis is made on clinical grounds; liver biopsy shows the typical findings of preeclampsia but is usually not necessary for the diagnosis.

Complications

As is true of preeclampsia, complications of HELLP syndrome usually have a progressive course, with increased risk until delivery. Expectant management may be possible if fetal maturity is needed, particularly before 34 weeks. More common maternal complications include disseminated intravascular coagulation (DIC), postpartum hemorrhage, and abruptio placentae.

In <2 % of cases of HELLP, patients with preeclampsia may have intrahepatic hemorrhage or infarction. Abrupt, severe epigastric and/or right upper quadrant pain radiating to the back accompanied by transaminases greater than 500 IU/mL should be a tip off. Hypotension or dropping hematocrit in the presence of HELLP syndrome should trigger a search for a liver capsule hematoma or, in the event of liver rupture, free blood in the abdominal cavity. Magnetic resonance imaging and computed tomography (CT) are imaging techniques generally more reliable than ultrasound. Imaging reveals a wedge-shaped hypodensity on CT scan [100]. Affected women tend to be older and multigravid. Biopsy shows necrosis, with periportal hemorrhage and leukocyte infiltration in the periphery of the lesions. Although appearance of the liver injury can be dramatic, complete recovery is usually seen in the postpartum period, although rare cases require liver transplantation.

Management

Management is primarily supportive and consists of prompt delivery. In the presence of nonreassuring fetal monitoring, maternal disease, or gestation >34 weeks, delivery remains the cornerstone of treatment. For those at 27–34 weeks of gestation, conservative management, or "temporizing," for greater than 48–72 h may be a possible management option [101, 102]. Large studies comparing active management against conservative management are lacking, but prolongation of gestation to allow for fetal maturation must be weighed against maternal risk.

Steroids may have multiple roles to play in the HELLP syndrome. Before 32 weeks of gestation, it is generally acceptable to administer dexamethasone or betamethasone to accelerate fetal maturity and then to deliver shortly thereafter. Maternal recovery from HELLP syndrome may be achieved through administration of multiple doses of corticosteroids. Steroids are thought to decrease endothelial dysfunction and the inflammatory cascade present in HELLP. Although the literature is divided, at least one randomized trial has shown more rapid improvement in platelet levels as well as maternal morbidity in those with HELLP syndrome who received dexamethasone 10 mg every 12 h for 2 doses, followed by 5 mg every 12 h for 2 doses in the postpartum period [103]. The largest randomized controlled trial with 162 HELLP syndrome patients could not confirm the positive results observed in smaller studies [104].

Management of hepatic rupture or infarct should include a surgical consultation with someone with expertise in trauma. Contained hematoma usually presenting in a hemodynamically stable woman should be treated with supportive care. If rupture occurs with continued hemodynamic instability despite resuscitation, emergency radiologic and surgical intervention is warranted. At surgery, the hematoma below the Glisson capsule around the liver is found to have lifted the capsule up, leaving the underlying liver bleeding from multiple tears. A reasonable first-line treatment appears to be hepatic artery embolization [105, 106]. Rarely, in severe cases, management includes liver transplantation. Like the HELLP syndrome, hepatic hematoma has been reported to recur in subsequent pregnancies [107].

References

1. Kline LW, Karpinski E. Progesterone inhibits gallbladder motility through multiple signaling pathways. Steroids. 2005;70(9):673–9. Epub 2005/05/27.
2. Ko CW, Beresford SA, Schulte SJ, Matsumoto AM, Lee SP. Incidence, natural history, and risk factors for biliary sludge and stones during pregnancy. Hepatology. 2005;41(2):359–65. Epub 2005/01/22.
3. Koch CA, Platt JL. T cell recognition and immunity in the fetus and mother. Cell Immunol. 2007;248(1):12–7. Epub 2007/10/09.
4. Beard JL. Why iron deficiency is important in infant development. J Nutr. 2008;138(12):2534–6. Epub 2008/11/22.
5. Weinert LS, Silveiro SP. Maternal-fetal impact of vitamin d deficiency: a critical review. Matern Child Health J. 2014. Epub 2014/04/19.
6. Greenberg JA, Bell SJ, Ausdal WV. Omega-3 fatty acid supplementation during pregnancy. Rev Obstet Gynecol. 2008;1(4):162–9. Epub 2009/01/29.
7. Fit for Two: healthy eating & physical activity across your lifespan. Department of Health and Human Services NIH Publication No 06-5130: NIH; 2009.
8. Rippe JM, editor. Lifestyle medicine. 2nd ed. Boca Raton, FL: CRC Press; 2013.
9. Cappell MS. Risks versus benefits of gastrointestinal endoscopy during pregnancy. Nat Rev Gastroenterol Hepatol. 2011;8(11):610–34. Epub 2011/10/06.
10. Dolovich LR, Addis A, Vaillancourt JM, Power JD, Koren G, Einarson TR. Benzodiazepine use in pregnancy and major malformations or oral cleft: meta-analysis of cohort and case-control studies. BMJ. 1998;317(7162):839–43. Epub 1998/09/25.
11. Committee ASoP, Shergill AK, Ben-Menachem T, Chandrasekhara V, Chathadi K, Decker GA, et al. Guidelines for endoscopy in pregnant and lactating women. Gastrointest Endosc. 2012;76(1):18–24. Epub 2012/05/15.
12. Practice ACoO. ACOG Committee Opinion. Number 299, September 2004 (replaces No. 158, September 1995). Guidelines for diagnostic imaging during pregnancy. Obstet Gynecol. 2004;104(3):647–51. Epub 2004/09/02.
13. Patenaude Y, Pugash D, Lim K, Morin L, Diagnostic Imaging C, Lim K, et al. The use of magnetic resonance imaging in the obstetric patient. J Obstet Gynaecol Can. 2014;36(4):349–55.
14. Gill SK, Maltepe C, Koren G. The effect of heartburn and acid reflux on the severity of nausea and vomiting of pregnancy. Can J Gastroenterol. 2009;23(4):270–2.
15. Nikfar S, Abdollahi M, Moretti ME, Magee LA, Koren G. Use of proton pump inhibitors during pregnancy and rates of major malformations: a meta-analysis. Dig Dis Sci. 2002;47(7):1526–9. Epub 2002/07/27.
16. Pasternak B, Hviid A. Use of proton-pump inhibitors in early pregnancy and the risk of birth defects. N Engl J Med. 2010;363(22):2114–23. Epub 2010/11/26.
17. Dodds L, Fell DB, Joseph KS, Allen VM, Butler B. Outcomes of pregnancies complicated by hyperemesis gravidarum. Obstet Gynecol. 2006;107(2 Pt 1):285–92. Epub 2006/02/02.
18. Gadsby R, Barnie-Adshead AM, Jagger C. Pregnancy nausea related to women's obstetric and personal histories. Gynecol Obstet Investig. 1997;43(2):108–11. Epub 1997/01/01.
19. Kuscu NK, Koyuncu F. Hyperemesis gravidarum: current concepts and management. Postgrad Med J. 2002;78(916):76–9. Epub 2002/01/25.
20. Smith C, Crowther C, Beilby J, Dandeaux J. The impact of nausea and vomiting on women: a burden of early pregnancy. Aust N Z J Obstet Gynaecol. 2000;40(4):397–401. Epub 2001/02/24.
21. Jiang HG EA, Nicholas J, et al. Care of Women in U.S. hospitals, 2000. Agency for Healthcare Research and Quality, 2002 HCUP Fact Book No 3 AHRQ Pub No 02-0044. 2002.
22. Koch R, Hanley W, Levy H, Matalon K, Matalon R, Rouse B, et al. The maternal phenylketonuria international study: 1984–2002. Pediatrics. 2003;112(6 Pt 2):1523–9. Epub 2003/12/05.

23. Eventov-Friedman S, Klinger G, Shinwell ES. Third trimester fetal intracranial hemorrhage owing to vitamin K deficiency associated with hyperemesis gravidarum. J Pediatr Hematol Oncol. 2009;31(12):985–8. Epub 2009/12/04.
24. Lacasse A, Rey E, Ferreira E, Morin C, Berard A. Determinants of early medical management of nausea and vomiting of pregnancy. Birth. 2009;36(1):70–7. Epub 2009/03/13.
25. Davis M. Nausea and vomiting of pregnancy: an evidence-based review. J Perinat Neonatal Nurs. 2004;18(4):312–28. Epub 2005/01/14.
26. Backon J. Ginger in preventing nausea and vomiting of pregnancy; a caveat due to its thromboxane synthetase activity and effect on testosterone binding. Eur J Obstet Gynecol Reprod Biol. 1991;42(2):163–4. Epub 1991/11/26.
27. Niebyl JR, Goodwin TM. Overview of nausea and vomiting of pregnancy with an emphasis on vitamins and ginger. Am J Obstet Gynecol. 2002;186(5 Suppl Understanding):S253–5. Epub 2002/05/16.
28. McKeigue PM, Lamm SH, Linn S, Kutcher JS. Bendectin and birth defects: I. A meta-analysis of the epidemiologic studies. Teratology. 1994;50(1):27–37. Epub 1994/07/01.
29. Tan PC, Khine PP, Vallikkannu N, Omar SZ. Promethazine compared with metoclopramide for hyperemesis gravidarum: a randomized controlled trial. Obstet Gynecol. 2010;115(5):975–81. Epub 2010/04/23.
30. Matok I, Gorodischer R, Koren G, Sheiner E, Wiznitzer A, Levy A. The safety of metoclopramide use in the first trimester of pregnancy. N Engl J Med. 2009;360(24):2528–35. Epub 2009/06/12.
31. Leathem AM. Safety and efficacy of antiemetics used to treat nausea and vomiting in pregnancy. Clin Pharm. 1986;5(8):660–8. Epub 1986/08/01.
32. Seto A, Einarson T, Koren G. Pregnancy outcome following first trimester exposure to antihistamines: meta-analysis. Am J Perinatol. 1997;14(3):119–24. Epub 1997/03/01.
33. Rubenstein EB, Slusher BS, Rojas C, Navari RM. New approaches to chemotherapy-induced nausea and vomiting: from neuropharmacology to clinical investigations. Cancer J. 2006;12(5):341–7. Epub 2006/10/13.
34. Pasternak B, Svanstrom H, Hviid A. Ondansetron in pregnancy and risk of adverse fetal outcomes. N Engl J Med. 2013;368(9):814–23. Epub 2013/03/01.
35. Godil A, Chen YK. Percutaneous endoscopic gastrostomy for nutrition support in pregnancy associated with hyperemesis gravidarum and anorexia nervosa. JPEN J Parenter Enteral Nutr. 1998;22(4):238–41. Epub 1998/07/14.
36. Barclay BA. Experience with enteral nutrition in the treatment of hyperemesis gravidarum. Nutr Clin Pract. 1990;5(4):153–5. Epub 1990/08/01.
37. Saha S, Loranger D, Pricolo V, Degli-Esposti S. Feeding jejunostomy for the treatment of severe hyperemesis gravidarum: a case series. JPEN J Parenter Enteral Nutr. 2009;33(5):529–34. Epub 2009/06/27.
38. Russo-Stieglitz KE, Levine AB, Wagner BA, Armenti VT. Pregnancy outcome in patients requiring parenteral nutrition. J Matern Fetal Med. 1999;8(4):164–7. Epub 1999/07/16.
39. Cape AV, Mogensen KM, Robinson MK, Carusi DA. Peripherally inserted central catheter (PICC) complications during pregnancy. JPEN J Parenter Enteral Nutr. 2013;38(5):595–601. Epub 2013/05/28.
40. Holmgren C, Aagaard-Tillery KM, Silver RM, Porter TF, Varner M. Hyperemesis in pregnancy: an evaluation of treatment strategies with maternal and neonatal outcomes. Am J Obstet Gynecol. 2008;198(1):56 e1–4. Epub 2008/01/02.
41. Garland CF, Lilienfeld AM, Mendeloff AI, Markowitz JA, Terrell KB, Garland FC. Incidence rates of ulcerative colitis and Crohn's disease in fifteen areas of the United States. Gastroenterology. 1981;81(6):1115–24. Epub 1981/12/01.
42. Dubinsky M, Abraham B, Mahadevan U. Management of the pregnant IBD patient. Inflamm Bowel Dis. 2008;14(12):1736–50. Epub 2008/07/16.
43. Cornish J, Tan E, Teare J, Teoh TG, Rai R, Clark SK, et al. A meta-analysis on the influence of inflammatory bowel disease on pregnancy. Gut. 2007;56(6):830–7. Epub 2006/12/23.

44. Riis L, Vind I, Politi P, Wolters F, Vermeire S, Tsianos E, et al. Does pregnancy change the disease course? A study in a European cohort of patients with inflammatory bowel disease. Am J Gastroenterol. 2006;101(7):1539–45. Epub 2006/07/26.
45. Alstead EM. Inflammatory bowel disease in pregnancy. Postgrad Med J. 2002;78(915):23–6. Epub 2002/01/18.
46. Morales M, Berney T, Jenny A, Morel P, Extermann P. Crohn's disease as a risk factor for the outcome of pregnancy. Hepato-Gastroenterology. 2000;47(36):1595–8. Epub 2001/01/10.
47. Bush MC, Patel S, Lapinski RH, Stone JL. Perinatal outcomes in inflammatory bowel disease. J Matern Fetal Neonatal Med. 2004;15(4):237–41. Epub 2004/07/29.
48. Norgard B, Hundborg HH, Jacobsen BA, Nielsen GL, Fonager K. Disease activity in pregnant women with Crohn's disease and birth outcomes: a regional Danish cohort study. Am J Gastroenterol. 2007;102(9):1947–54. Epub 2007/06/19.
49. Kane S, Lemieux N. The role of breastfeeding in postpartum disease activity in women with inflammatory bowel disease. Am J Gastroenterol. 2005;100(1):102–5. Epub 2005/01/19.
50. Mahadevan U, Kane S. American gastroenterological association institute technical review on the use of gastrointestinal medications in pregnancy. Gastroenterology. 2006;131(1):283–311. Epub 2006/07/13.
51. Akbari M, Shah S, Velayos FS, Mahadevan U, Cheifetz AS. Systematic review and meta-analysis on the effects of thiopurines on birth outcomes from female and male patients with inflammatory bowel disease. Inflamm Bowel Dis. 2013;19(1):15–22. Epub 2012/03/22.
52. Norgard B, Puho E, Pedersen L, Czeizel AE, Sorensen HT. Risk of congenital abnormalities in children born to women with ulcerative colitis: a population-based, case-control study. Am J Gastroenterol. 2003;98(9):2006–10. Epub 2003/09/23.
53. Christensen LA, Dahlerup JF, Nielsen MJ, Fallingborg JF, Schmiegelow K. Azathioprine treatment during lactation. Aliment Pharmacol Ther. 2008;28(10):1209–13. Epub 2008/09/03.
54. Angelberger S, Reinisch W, Messerschmidt A, Miehsler W, Novacek G, Vogelsang H, et al. Long-term follow-up of babies exposed to azathioprine in utero and via breastfeeding. J Crohn's Colitis. 2011;5(2):95–100. Epub 2011/04/02.
55. Briggs GGFR, Yaffe SJ. Drugs in pregnancy and lactation. 7th ed. Philadelphia, PA: Lippincott, Williams & Wilkins; 2005.
56. Bar Oz B, Hackman R, Einarson T, Koren G. Pregnancy outcome after cyclosporine therapy during pregnancy: a meta-analysis. Transplantation. 2001;71(8):1051–5. Epub 2001/05/26.
57. Branche J, Cortot A, Bourreille A, Coffin B, de Vos M, de Saussure P, et al. Cyclosporine treatment of steroid-refractory ulcerative colitis during pregnancy. Inflamm Bowel Dis. 2009;15(7):1044–8. Epub 2009/01/13.
58. Czeizel AE, Rockenbauer M. A population based case-control teratologic study of oral metronidazole treatment during pregnancy. Br J Obstet Gynaecol. 1998;105(3):322–7. Epub 1998/04/09.
59. Lichtenstein GR, Feagan BG, Cohen RD, Salzberg BA, Diamond RH, Chen DM, et al. Serious infections and mortality in association with therapies for Crohn's disease: TREAT registry. Clin Gastroenterol Hepatol. 2006;4(5):621–30. Epub 2006/05/09.
60. Mahadevan U, Cucchiara S, Hyams JS, Steinwurz F, Nuti F, Travis SP, et al. The london position statement of the world congress of gastroenterology on biological therapy for IBD with the European Crohn's and Colitis Organisation: pregnancy and pediatrics. Am J Gastroenterol. 2011;106(2):214–23. quiz 24. Epub 2010/12/16.
61. Ben-Horin S, Yavzori M, Kopylov U, Picard O, Fudim E, Eliakim R, et al. Detection of infliximab in breast milk of nursing mothers with inflammatory bowel disease. J Crohn's Colitis. 2011;5(6):555–8. Epub 2011/11/26.
62. Ben-Horin S, Yavzori M, Katz L, Picard O, Fudim E, Chowers Y, et al. Adalimumab level in breast milk of a nursing mother. Clin Gastroenterol Hepatol. 2010;8(5):475–6. Epub 2009/12/17.
63. Ch'ng CL, Morgan M, Hainsworth I, Kingham JG. Prospective study of liver dysfunction in pregnancy in Southwest Wales. Gut. 2002;51(6):876–80. Epub 2002/11/13.
64. Rathi U, Bapat M, Rathi P, Abraham P. Effect of liver disease on maternal and fetal outcome–a prospective study. Indian J Gastroenterol. 2007;26(2):59–63. Epub 2007/06/15.

65. McKay DB, Josephson MA. Pregnancy in recipients of solid organs–effects on mother and child. N Engl J Med. 2006;354(12):1281–93. Epub 2006/03/24.
66. Westbrook RH, Yeoman AD, O'Grady JG, Harrison PM, Devlin J, Heneghan MA. Model for end-stage liver disease score predicts outcome in cirrhotic patients during pregnancy. Clin Gastroenterol Hepatol. 2011;9(8):694–9. Epub 2011/05/17.
67. Sandhu BS, Sanyal AJ. Pregnancy and liver disease. Gastroenterol Clin N Am. 2003;32(1):407–36, ix. Epub 2003/03/15.
68. Rasheed SM, Abdel Monem AM, Abd Ellah AH, Abdel Fattah MS. Prognosis and determinants of pregnancy outcome among patients with post-hepatitis liver cirrhosis. Int J Gynaecol Obstet. 2013;121(3):247–51. Epub 2013/03/23.
69. Zeeman GG, Moise Jr KJ. Prophylactic banding of severe esophageal varices associated with liver cirrhosis in pregnancy. Obstet Gynecol. 1999;94(5 Pt 2):842. Epub 1999/11/05.
70. Savage C, Patel J, Lepe MR, Lazarre CH, Rees CR. Transjugular intrahepatic portosystemic shunt creation for recurrent gastrointestinal bleeding during pregnancy. J Vasc Interv Radiol. 2007;18(7):902–4. Epub 2007/07/05.
71. Kochhar R, Goenka MK, Mehta SK. Endoscopic sclerotherapy during pregnancy. Am J Gastroenterol. 1990;85(9):1132–5. Epub 1990/09/01.
72. Ghidirim G, Mishin I, Dolghii A, Lupashcu A. Prophylactic endoscopic band ligation of esophageal varices during pregnancy. J Gastrointest Liver Dis. 2008;17(2):236–7. Epub 2008/06/24.
73. Malik A, Khawaja A, Sheikh L. Wilson's disease in pregnancy: case series and review of literature. BMC Res Notes. 2013;6:421. Epub 2013/10/22.
74. Furman B, Bashiri A, Wiznitzer A, Erez O, Holcberg G, Mazor M. Wilson's disease in pregnancy: five successful consecutive pregnancies of the same woman. Eur J Obstet Gynecol Reprod Biol. 2001;96(2):232–4. Epub 2001/06/01.
75. Brewer GJ, Johnson VD, Dick RD, Hedera P, Fink JK, Kluin KJ. Treatment of Wilson's disease with zinc. XVII: treatment during pregnancy. Hepatology. 2000;31(2):364–70. Epub 2000/02/03.
76. Czaja AJ. Autoimmune hepatitis in special patient populations. Best Pract Res Clin Gastroenterol. 2011;25(6):689–700. Epub 2011/11/29.
77. Kosar Y, Kacar S, Sasmaz N, Oguz P, Turhan N, Parlak E, et al. Type 1 autoimmune hepatitis in Turkish patients: absence of association with HLA B8. J Clin Gastroenterol. 2002;35(2):185–90. Epub 2002/08/13.
78. Schramm C, Herkel J, Beuers U, Kanzler S, Galle PR, Lohse AW. Pregnancy in autoimmune hepatitis: outcome and risk factors. Am J Gastroenterol. 2006;101(3):556–60. Epub 2006/02/09.
79. Westbrook RH, Yeoman AD, Kriese S, Heneghan MA. Outcomes of pregnancy in women with autoimmune hepatitis. J Autoimmun. 2012;38(2–3):J239–44. Epub 2012/01/21.
80. Date RS, Kaushal M, Ramesh A. A review of the management of gallstone disease and its complications in pregnancy. Am J Surg. 2008;196(4):599–608. Epub 2008/07/11.
81. Othman MO, Stone E, Hashimi M, Parasher G. Conservative management of cholelithiasis and its complications in pregnancy is associated with recurrent symptoms and more emergency department visits. Gastrointest Endosc. 2012;76(3):564–9. Epub 2012/06/27.
82. Jacquemin E, Cresteil D, Manouvrier S, Boute O, Hadchouel M. Heterozygous non-sense mutation of the MDR3 gene in familial intrahepatic cholestasis of pregnancy. Lancet. 1999;353(9148):210–1. Epub 1999/01/29.
83. Meng LJ, Reyes H, Axelson M, Palma J, Hernandez I, Ribalta J, et al. Progesterone metabolites and bile acids in serum of patients with intrahepatic cholestasis of pregnancy: effect of ursodeoxycholic acid therapy. Hepatology. 1997;26(6):1573–9. Epub 1997/12/16.
84. Marschall HU, Wikstrom Shemer E, Ludvigsson JF, Stephansson O. Intrahepatic cholestasis of pregnancy and associated hepatobiliary disease: a population-based cohort study. Hepatology. 2013;58(4):1385–91. Epub 2013/04/09.
85. Paternoster DM, Fabris F, Palu G, Santarossa C, Bracciante R, Snijders D, et al. Intra-hepatic cholestasis of pregnancy in hepatitis C virus infection. Acta Obstet Gynecol Scand. 2002;81(2):99–103. Epub 2002/04/12.

86. Ropponen A, Sund R, Riikonen S, Ylikorkala O, Aittomaki K. Intrahepatic cholestasis of pregnancy as an indicator of liver and biliary diseases: a population-based study. Hepatology. 2006;43(4):723–8. Epub 2006/03/25.
87. Glantz A, Marschall HU, Mattsson LA. Intrahepatic cholestasis of pregnancy: Relationships between bile acid levels and fetal complication rates. Hepatology. 2004;40(2):467–74. Epub 2004/09/16.
88. Geenes V, Chappell LC, Seed PT, Steer PJ, Knight M, Williamson C. Association of severe intrahepatic cholestasis of pregnancy with adverse pregnancy outcomes: a prospective population-based case-control study. Hepatology. 2014;59(4):1482–91.
89. Laatikainen T, Tulenheimo A. Maternal serum bile acid levels and fetal distress in cholestasis of pregnancy. Int J Gynaecol Obstet. 1984;22(2):91–4. Epub 1984/04/01.
90. Bacq Y, Sentilhes L, Reyes HB, Glantz A, Kondrackiene J, Binder T, et al. Efficacy of ursodeoxycholic acid in treating intrahepatic cholestasis of pregnancy: a meta-analysis. Gastroenterology. 2012;143(6):1492–501. Epub 2012/08/16.
91. Pons R, Cavadini P, Baratta S, Invernizzi F, Lamantea E, Garavaglia B, et al. Clinical and molecular heterogeneity in very-long-chain acyl-coenzyme A dehydrogenase deficiency. Pediatr Neurol. 2000;22(2):98–105. Epub 2000/03/30.
92. Ibdah JA, Bennett MJ, Rinaldo P, Zhao Y, Gibson B, Sims HF, et al. A fetal fatty-acid oxidation disorder as a cause of liver disease in pregnant women. N Engl J Med. 1999;340(22):1723–31. Epub 1999/06/03.
93. Blish KR, Ibdah JA. Maternal heterozygosity for a mitochondrial trifunctional protein mutation as a cause for liver disease in pregnancy. Med Hypotheses. 2005;64(1):96–100. Epub 2004/11/10.
94. Rakheja D, Bennett MJ, Foster BM, Domiati-Saad R, Rogers BB. Evidence for fatty acid oxidation in human placenta, and the relationship of fatty acid oxidation enzyme activities with gestational age. Placenta. 2002;23(5):447–50. Epub 2002/06/14.
95. Rector RS, Ibdah JA. Fatty acid oxidation disorders: maternal health and neonatal outcomes. Semin Fetal Neonatal Med. 2010;15(3):122–8. Epub 2009/11/21.
96. Barton JR, Riely CA, Adamec TA, Shanklin DR, Khoury AD, Sibai BM. Hepatic histopathologic condition does not correlate with laboratory abnormalities in HELLP syndrome (hemolysis, elevated liver enzymes, and low platelet count). Am J Obstet Gynecol. 1992;167(6):1538–43. Epub 1992/12/01.
97. Kennedy S, Hall PM, Seymour AE, Hague WM. Transient diabetes insipidus and acute fatty liver of pregnancy. Br J Obstet Gynaecol. 1994;101(5):387–91. Epub 1994/05/01.
98. Castro MA, Goodwin TM, Shaw KJ, Ouzounian JG, McGehee WG. Disseminated intravascular coagulation and antithrombin III depression in acute fatty liver of pregnancy. Am J Obstet Gynecol. 1996;174(1 Pt 1):211–6. Epub 1996/01/01.
99. Thangaratinam S, Gallos ID, Meah N, Usman S, Ismail KM, Khan KS, et al. How accurate are maternal symptoms in predicting impending complications in women with preeclampsia? A systematic review and meta-analysis. Acta Obstet Gynecol Scand. 2011;90(6):564–73. Epub 2011/03/02.
100. Barton JR, Sibai BM. Hepatic imaging in HELLP syndrome (hemolysis, elevated liver enzymes, and low platelet count). Am J Obstet Gynecol. 1996;174(6):1820–5. discussion 5-7. Epub 1996/06/01.
101. Visser W, Wallenburg HC. Temporising management of severe pre-eclampsia with and without the HELLP syndrome. Br J Obstet Gynaecol. 1995;102(2):111–7. Epub 1995/02/01.
102. van Pampus MG, Wolf H, Westenberg SM, van der Post JA, Bonsel GJ, Treffers PE. Maternal and perinatal outcome after expectant management of the HELLP syndrome compared with pre-eclampsia without HELLP syndrome. Eur J Obstet Gynecol Reprod Biol. 1998;76(1):31–6. Epub 1998/03/03.
103. Sibai BM, Barton JR. Dexamethasone to improve maternal outcome in women with hemolysis, elevated liver enzymes, and low platelets syndrome. Am J Obstet Gynecol. 2005;193(5):1587–90. Epub 2005/11/02.

104. Fonseca JE, Mendez F, Catano C, Arias F. Dexamethasone treatment does not improve the outcome of women with HELLP syndrome: a double-blind, placebo-controlled, randomized clinical trial. Am J Obstet Gynecol. 2005;193(5):1591–8. Epub 2005/11/02.
105. Erhard J, Lange R, Niebel W, Scherer R, Kox WJ, Philipp T, et al. Acute liver necrosis in the HELLP syndrome: successful outcome after orthotopic liver transplantation. A case report. Transpl Int. 1993;6(3):179–81. Epub 1993/05/01.
106. Hunter SK, Martin M, Benda JA, Zlatnik FJ. Liver transplant after massive spontaneous hepatic rupture in pregnancy complicated by preeclampsia. Obstet Gynecol. 1995;85(5 Pt 2):819–22. Epub 1995/05/01.
107. Greenstein D, Henderson JM, Boyer TD. Liver hemorrhage: recurrent episodes during pregnancy complicated by preeclampsia. Gastroenterology. 1994;106(6):1668–71. Epub 1994/06/01.

Part VI
Hematology

Chapter 6
Thrombophilia and Thrombosis

Courtney Bilodeau and Karen Rosene-Montella

Abbreviations

APTT	Activated partial thromboplastin time
APC	Activated protein C
APS	Antiphospholipid antibody syndrome
CT	Computed topography
CVT	Cerebral vein thrombosis
DVT	Deep vein thrombosis
EKG	Electrocardiogram
FVL	Factor V Leiden
IUGR	Intrauterine growth restriction
IUFD	Intrauterine fetal demise
IVC	Inferior vena cava
LMWH	Low-molecular-weight heparin
MRI	Magnetic resonance imaging
MRV	Magnetic resonance venography
MTHFR	5,10-Methylenetetrahydrofolate reductase

C. Bilodeau, M.D. (✉)
Department of Obstetric Medicine, Women's Medicine Collaborative, Miriam Hospital,
146 West River Street, Ste. 11C, Providence, RI 02904, USA

The Warren Alpert Medical School of Brown University, Providence, RI, USA
e-mail: cbilodeau1@lifespan.org

K. Rosene-Montella, M.D.
SVP Women's Services and Clinical Integration, Lifespan Corporation,
Providence, RI 02903, USA

Obstetric Medicine, Women's Medicine Collaborative, The Miriam Hospital,
Providence, RI 02903, USA

The Warren Alpert Medical School of Brown University, Providence, RI, USA

© Springer Science+Business Media New York 2015
K. Rosene-Montella (ed.), *Medical Management of the Pregnant Patient*,
DOI 10.1007/978-1-4614-1244-1_6

PAI	Plasminogen activator inhibitor
PE	Pulmonary embolism
PGM	Prothrombin gene mutation G20210A
PTS	Post-thrombotic syndrome
TAFI	Thrombin activatable fibrinolytic inhibitor
UFH	Unfractionated heparin
US	Ultrasonography
V/Q	Ventilation-perfusion
VTE	Venous thromboembolism

Thrombophilia

Background/Definition

Thrombophilia is an inherited or acquired predisposition for thrombosis due to alterations in the coagulation system. Greater than 50 % of patients with thrombophilia who develop a VTE have additional thromboembolic risk factors. Pregnancy alone can be this additional risk factor. Addition of other factors such as advanced maternal age (>35 years), race (black), certain medical conditions (diabetes), and mode of delivery (cesarean section) further increases this risk [1]. Table 6.1 highlights the risk factors for thrombosis in pregnancy. Placenta-mediated pregnancy

Table 6.1 Peripartum risk factors for VTE

Maternal risk factors
Age >35 years
BMI > 30 kg/m^2
Black race
Cigarette smoker
IV drug user
Medical comorbidities:
Infection, dehydration, diabetes, malignancy, autoimmune disease, varicose veins, sickle cell, nephrotic syndrome, hypertension
Personal or family history of VTE
Cesarean delivery or other surgery
Three or more previous deliveries
Obstetric hemorrhage
Preterm delivery (<37 weeks' gestation)
Stillbirth
Thrombophilia
Multiple pregnancy
Prolonged immobility
Prolonged labor (>24 h)
Preeclampsia/eclampsia

Sources: [2, 3]

complications may also increase with certain thrombophilias. This potential correlation is controversial and will be further discussed below.

The inherited thrombophilias include factor V Leiden mutation (FVL), prothrombin gene mutation G20210A (PGM), protein C deficiency, and protein S deficiency. Antiphospholipid antibody syndrome (APS) is an acquired thrombophilia which may occur alone or in association with systemic lupus erythematosus (SLE) [4]. Antithrombin III deficiency can be either an inherited disorder or acquired, such as with nephrotic syndrome when levels fall via urinary excretion of the protein [5].

The 5,10-methylenetetrahydrofolate reductase (MTHFR) gene polymorphism is very common in individuals of European decent and causes modest elevations of plasma homocysteine. Elevated plasma homocysteine levels are themselves associated with a mild increased risk for VTE; however, studies in pregnant and nonpregnant individuals with the 5,10-MTHFR gene polymorphism do not reveal a significantly increased risk for VTE [6, 7]. Therefore, the 5,10-MTHFR gene polymorphism is no longer considered by many to be an inherited thrombophilia, and maternal evaluation for the gene mutation or homocysteine levels is not recommended [8].

Epidemiology

The prevalence of inherited thrombophilias in the general population ranges between 0.03 and 15 %, with FVL being the most common [9]. One half of VTEs in pregnancy are associated with thrombophilia [10]. The absolute risk for VTE in pregnancy is 1–2:1,000 [2] in women with thrombophilia such as heterozygous FVL or PGM and no prior VTE, this risk rises to 1:400 [11]. Homozygous FVL is the highest risk inherited thrombophilia for VTE with an absolute VTE risk of 3.4 % [12]. Antithrombin deficiency and compound heterozygotes (e.g., FVL/PGM) represent higher-risk groups in pregnancy as well. Women with thrombophilia and a history of VTE are at even higher risk for developing a VTE in pregnancy.

Pathobiology

Normal Physiologic Changes

In pregnancy, there is a natural increase in the procoagulants fibrinogen, von Willebrand antigen, and factors VII, VIII, and X. Anticoagulant activity is decreased with lower total protein S levels and increased activated protein C (APC) resistance. The elevation of estrogen levels in pregnancy is a major contributor to the APC resistance [13]. Fibrinolytic activity is also inhibited from an increase in plasminogen activator inhibitor type 1 (PAI-1) and PAI-2 and decreased thrombin activatable fibrinolytic inhibitor (TAFI) [14, 15]. These changes contribute to the natural increased risk for maternal thrombosis.

Effect of Pregnancy on the Disease

The normal physiologic changes in pregnancy described above magnify the thrombosis risk of thrombophilia. In fact, pregnancy is often the precipitant to first identifying thrombophilia. When anticoagulant medication is needed for a patient with thrombophilia, the practitioner must consider physiologic changes in pregnancy and balance thrombosis with hemorrhage risk around delivery. Anticoagulant medication in pregnancy will be further discussed in Section "Thrombosis" of this chapter.

Effect of Disease on the Pregnancy

Beyond increasing risk for a VTE in pregnancy, thrombophilias have been suspected to decrease placental efficiency and thereby increase risk for obstetric complications. These placenta-mediated complications include intrauterine growth restriction (IUGR), intrauterine fetal demise (IUFD)/stillborn, abruption, and early, severe, or recurrent preeclampsia. The data to support the association of thrombophilias with poor pregnancy outcomes is conflicting and often gathered from small cohorts or retrospective studies. Routine screening for thrombophilias is not currently recommended, and therefore this data is often not available. Women with poor pregnancy outcomes when tested are more likely to have a thrombophilia compared to women with a normal pregnancy [16, 17]. The specifics on which thrombophilia and which poor outcomes remain undefined. At this time, there appears to be a stronger association for FVL and for late (>10 weeks) pregnancy loss [18, 19] compared with other thrombophilia and poor pregnancy outcome associations. A large, prospective study is needed to confirm the suggested causality and furthermore the utility of anticoagulation for the prevention of poor pregnancy outcomes with thrombophilia.

Unlike the inherited thrombophilias discussed above, the antiphospholipid syndrome (APS) has been definitively associated with both thrombosis and poor obstetric outcomes. APS is an acquired thrombophilia characterized by laboratory features (see Table 6.2) and clinical events. Diagnosis requires at least one laboratory finding and one clinical event. These events include thrombosis, recurrent (three or more) miscarriages, late (>10 weeks) pregnancy loss, preeclampsia, IUGR, and placental abruption [20]. The pathogenesis of the obstetric outcomes in APS remains unclear but is unlikely due entirely to placental thrombosis. Several observational studies of placentas affected by APS reveal no

Table 6.2 Inherited and acquired thrombophilias

Type	Thrombosis risk in pregnancy	Diagnostic test
Inherited		
Factor V Leiden mutation	High—homozygous Lower—heterozygous	APC resistance assay not accurate in pregnancy so DNA analysis is required
Prothrombin gene mutation G20210A	High—homozygous Lower—heterozygous	DNA analysis
Antithrombin III deficiency	High	Antithrombin III activity (<60 %)
Protein C deficiency	Lower	Protein C activity (<50 %)
Protein S deficiency	Lower	Protein S functional antigen assay (<55 %). If abnormal follow-up with protein S free antigen, <30 % second trimester, <24 % third trimester
Acquired		
Antiphospholipid antibody syndrome	High	Antiphospholipid antibodies, anticardiolipin antibodies, lupus anticoagulant, beta-2 glycoprotein (if abnormal repeat to confirm in 12 weeks)
Antithrombin III deficiency	High	Antithrombin III activity (<60 %)

Sources: [8, 17]

Table 6.3 Indications for thrombophilia evaluation

Unprovoked VTE at any age
Family hx of VTE or thrombophilia
Thrombosis at unusual site
Recurrent thrombosis
Recurrent IUGR
IUFD
Early severe or recurrent preeclampsia
Abruption

Sources: [8, 17]

evidence of thrombosis, and other studies point to a complement-mediated inflammatory process [4].

Table 6.2 lists inherited and acquired thrombophilias along with thrombosis risk category (high or lower) and the laboratory tests recommended for diagnosis of thrombophilia.

Diagnosis and Management

The laboratory studies currently used to identify thrombophilias are listed in Table 6.2. Indications for thrombophilia evaluation are listed in Table 6.3. Testing is not recommended if the results will not change clinical management or if results would not be as reliable, such as around the time of acute thrombosis (factor may be consumed leading to falsely low levels), in pregnancy or on oral contraceptives (lowers protein S), or on anticoagulation therapy (protein C and S lowered by Coumadin, antithrombin by heparins).

When a woman with a known thrombophilia desires to or becomes pregnant, recommended anticoagulation management strategies are based on severity of thrombophilia risk, maternal history of VTE, and other VTE risk factors. Anticoagulation management in pregnancy including recommended strategies for thrombophilia in pregnancy is detailed in the Thrombosis section and in Table 6.5. Specified guidelines regarding fetal assessment and timing of delivery in pregnancies affected by thrombophilia are not currently available. The individual patient's history and risk assessment should be taken into account and may warrant frequent fetal assessment and delivery at 39 weeks in the absence of obstetric complications such as IUGR or preeclampsia. Pneumatic compression boots or elastic compression stockings should be considered in the peripartum until the patient is ambulatory. Women with thrombophilia should consider non-estrogen-containing contraception, especially with a higher-risk thrombophilia [21].

Thrombosis

Background/Definition

Pregnancy increases risk for thrombosis, including deep vein thrombosis (DVT), pulmonary embolism (PE), and cerebral vein thrombosis (CVT). A PE is an obstruction of the pulmonary artery or one of its branches. A DVT is defined as proximal or distal depending upon location of the thrombus. Distal vein thrombosis is confined to the deep calf veins. Proximal vein thrombosis is located in the popliteal, femoral, or iliac veins. In pregnancy, the incidence of DVT is three times higher than incidence of PE. DVT is left sided in close to 85 % of cases [2, 22]. Isolated pelvic DVTs are much more common in pregnancy, 11 % [2] versus 1 % in the nonpregnant [23]. CVT is a thrombosis in the cerebral vein or dural sinus. CVT is a rare occurrence in the general population, and 75 % of adult patients with CVT are female. Peripartum CVT affects 12 per 100,000 deliveries [24]. Thrombosis can occur at any time during gestation and into the postpartum. Very commonly, the event in pregnancy is the patient's first VTE, as the hypercoagulability associated with pregnancy acts as a stress test for VTE. Maternal and fetal well-being are dependent on prompt diagnosis and management of acute thrombosis and when possible prevention of thrombotic events in pregnancy.

Epidemiology

VTE is at least four times more common in the pregnant versus nonpregnant state [1, 25]. Some retrospective cohort studies [26, 27] when compared to age-/gender-/time-matched controls [28] suggest the risk may be up to ten times higher in pregnant patients compared with nonpregnant patients. The risk is further increased by the presence of additional risk factors which are listed in Table 6.1. Most DVTs occur antepartum, and the events are evenly distributed throughout gestation [22]. The day-to-day risk for VTE is greatest in the postpartum [25, 27]. PE may be more common postpartum [29].

Pathobiology

Normal Physiologic Changes and Effect of Pregnancy on the Disease

The natural pregnancy state is hypercoagulable and prothrombotic. The coagulation changes in pregnancy (see Section "Thrombophilia" of this chapter) promote clot formation and decrease clot dissolution. In addition to normal coagulation system changes, there are numerous vascular alterations in pregnancy which contribute to thrombosis risk through promotion of venous stasis and increased vascular damage. Causes of venous stasis in pregnancy include the large vein compression by the gravid uterus, the right iliac artery overlying and compressing the left iliac vein, hormonally mediated venous dilation, and immobilization. Vascular damage occurring from vascular compression at delivery and assisted or operative delivery also promotes thrombosis.

Effect of Disease on the Pregnancy

VTE in pregnancy causes significant morbidity and mortality [30]. In the UK Confidential Inquiry on Maternal Mortality, the most common error leading to death from PE was failure to make the diagnosis; this occurred in over half of the 28 cases reviewed. Typical errors were to only consider infection as a cause of symptoms and failure to investigate because of mistaken belief that radiological testing is contraindicated in pregnancy. Two thirds of the deaths would potentially have been prevented with proper thromboprophylaxis [31]. The hospital mortality

Table 6.4 Common VTE signs and symptoms in pregnancy

VTE	Signs	Symptoms
PE	Tachycardia, tachypnea, hypoxia, abnormal heart and lung sounds, hypotension	Chest pain, dyspnea, hemoptysis, cough
DVT	Leg edema (especially unilateral), palpable cord, warmth, erythema, tenderness, skin changes	Swelling, pain, warmth
CVT	Abnormal neurologic exam, seizures, altered consciousness	Headache, stroke-like symptoms

of untreated PE is 30 %, making prompt and accurate diagnosis critical [32]. The diagnosis of VTE in pregnancy affects labor and delivery plans due to the added risk of bleeding with anticoagulation. Complications from DVT which extend beyond the pregnancy include post-thrombotic syndrome (PTS). Up to half of patients with proximal DVT outside of pregnancy experience this condition of limb pain, edema, discoloration, and ulcers [21]. Long-term follow-up of women who experienced DVT in pregnancy finds that 40–80 % develop PTS and 65 % have objectively confirmed deep vein insufficiency [33, 34]. Women with a history of VTE are also more limited by their contraceptive choices as estrogen-containing contraceptives are generally contraindicated.

Diagnosis

Common pregnancy complaints increase the challenge of VTE diagnosis. For example, symptoms of leg edema, dyspnea, or headache may be misinterpreted as due to normal pregnancy changes instead of as a clinical sign of a DVT, PE, or CVT, respectively. Furthermore, diagnosis may be delayed by physician and patient reluctance to perform a diagnostic study due to concern for fetal risk to radiation exposure. In the nonpregnant population, there are validated clinical assessment and diagnostic imaging procedures to guide the diagnosis of VTE [35]. These validated tools are not currently available for the pregnant patient. Guidance for VTE diagnosis in pregnancy is based on validated evidence from nonpregnant patients and information from small studies in pregnancy. Table 6.4 lists the most common signs and symptoms which can be associated with VTE in pregnancy.

PE Diagnosis

In pregnancy, the laboratory studies of D-dimer and alveolar-arterial gradient are not useful for PE diagnosis. D-dimer is an estimate of blood coagulation and ongoing fibrinolysis and is elevated throughout pregnancy [36]. No diagnostic cohort studies are currently available using D-dimers in the diagnostic approach of suspected PE in pregnancy. An abnormal arterial blood gas can be a clinical sign of PE. However, a normal alveolar-arterial gradient has been shown in 60 % of documented PEs [37]. Part of the initial work-up when a pregnant patient presents with signs and symptoms of a PE includes an electrocardiogram (EKG) and chest x-ray, although neither of these tests should be used to definitively rule in or rule out a PE [38]. In nonpregnant patients, the incidence of sinus tachycardia and evidence of right heart strain (i.e., RBBB) were found to be slightly increased in patients with PE. Chest x-rays may find possible alternative diagnoses such as pneumothorax, pulmonary edema, or pneumonia. If a pregnant patient presents with symptoms of both a DVT and PE, a reasonable first evaluation would be a compression ultrasonography (US) as the anticoagulation regimens for acute DVT and submassive PE are the same. This approach would limit fetal and maternal radiation exposure. However, a negative compression US for DVT alone should not be used to rule out the presence of a suspected PE due to low sensitivity. In one study, only thirty percent of patients with PE had a radiographically proven DVT at the time of presentation [39]. Therefore, a ventilation-perfusion (V/Q) scan or computed topography (CT) pulmonary angiography with US leg studies is recommended for PE diagnosis in pregnancy. There are advantages and disadvantages to either test, and prompt availability of the study varies by medical facility. The V/Q scan when compared to CT angiography has been studied more extensively in pregnancy, with a high (75 %) diagnostic value [40], and does not require contrast administration. V/Q scan results are interpreted through pretest probability; therefore, its negative predictive value is highest when results are normal or low probability [41]. In comparison to a V/Q scan, a CT angiography study when combined with a chest radiograph can offer an alternative diagnosis if no PE is present but also increases breast radiation exposure [42].

DVT Diagnosis

The test of choice for diagnosis of DVT in pregnancy is serial compression US. The test is inexpensive and noninvasive and does not expose subjects to radiation [43, 44]. Pelvic DVTs are more common in pregnancy; therefore, the US protocol should include the iliac veins and inferior vena cava at the level of the liver. Magnetic resonance imaging (MRI) and magnetic resonance venography (MRV) should be considered if a pelvic or iliac vein DVT is suspected and the US is negative. MRI does not require ionizing radiation and is generally considered to be safe in pregnancy, although fetal safety data is limited.

CVT Diagnosis

The patient with cerebral vein thrombosis is ill and only rarely has focal findings. Diagnosis can be difficult—she will often otherwise appear to have aseptic meningitis, but the risks are much higher (i.e., seizure or bleeding). MRI/V will confirm the diagnosis in most cases. In cases where MRI is not readily available, a CT scan may be considered for initial diagnosis, especially to evaluate for an alternative diagnosis such as cerebral infarcts or hemorrhages. However, the CT scan can appear normal in cases of CVT [24].

Management/Treatment

Treatment of Acute Thrombosis

Management of VTE in pregnancy is similar to the principles used in the nonpregnant patient, with the added complexity of avoiding harm to the fetus and maternal hemorrhage on anticoagulation. The suggested treatment plans are based predominantly on retrospective studies in pregnancy as no prospective trials have evaluated the efficacy and safety of different treatment modalities. Coumarins are not recommended for VTE treatment or prevention in pregnancy because they cross the placenta and can lead to fetal harm. Coumarins are associated with a distinctive embryopathy between 5 and 12 weeks' gestation, and after 12 weeks there is a 2–3 % risk of CNS abnormalities. Furthermore, coumarins increase the risk of fetal hemorrhage throughout the pregnancy. Heparins do not cross the placenta and therefore do not increase risk for teratogenicity or fetal hemorrhage. Both unfractionated heparin (UFH) and low-molecular-weight heparin (LMWH) are considered safe in pregnancy. The maternal risks associated with the heparins include heparin-induced thrombocytopenia and osteopenia leading to increased risk for vertebral fractures; these risks are higher with UFH than with LMWH [45]. The multidose vials used with UFH also pose a potential threat for contamination [46], and drawing up an individual dose may be more cumbersome for patient self-administration. Prior to starting anticoagulation, obtaining baseline complete blood count and renal and hepatic function is recommended.

Dosing requirements for UFH and LMWH increase with increasing gestation. A concern with UFH dosing is that there is no validated therapeutic range for the activated partial thromboplastin time (APTT) in pregnancy. The APTT can be affected by pregnancy due to the physiologic increase in coagulation factors and heparin-binding proteins [47]. Pregnancy concerns with LMWH dosing are related to variation in weight gained, changes to volume of distribution, and increases in plasma volume, creatinine clearance, and extracellular volume. When monitoring therapeutic level for LMWH, the target anti-Xa activity level is 0.6–1.0 IU/ml for twice a day dosing or 1.0–2.0 IU/ml for once daily administration (4–6 h after injection). The therapeutic target heparin anti-Xa level with UFH is 0.3–0.7 IU/ml [48]. For example, the typical therapeutic dose of the LMWH enoxaparin is 1 mg/kg every 12 h.

LMWH is currently the heparin of choice for treating acute thrombosis in pregnancy [48, 49]. If a patient has renal dysfunction, UFH may be the preferred anticoagulant. Also, the use of LMWH may affect a patient's eligibility for epidural anesthesia due to a longer half-life and concern for spinal hematoma. Administration of therapeutic doses of LMWH is not recommended within 24 h of epidural placement or 12 h after epidural removal. Current guidelines recommend therapeutic anticoagulation until 6 weeks postpartum with a minimum duration of therapy of 3 months [48, 49].

Thrombolytics are reserved as a life-saving intervention in pregnancy for the treatment of VTE. There are no data on thrombolytics from randomized controlled trials in pregnancy, but a small number of case reports have shown therapeutic success with massive PE in pregnancy [50–52] remote from delivery when bleeding risk is prohibitive. Inferior vena cava (IVC) filters are recommended in pregnancy if there is a contraindication to or need for interruption of anticoagulation; an acute thrombosis occurs close to delivery, or recurrent VTE occurs despite adequate anticoagulation. Temporary filters can be placed in the suprarenal IVC as the risk of complications for suprarenal is likely similar to infrarenal [53]. Failure to retrieve temporary filters in pregnancy has been reported [54].

In cases of a CVT, a multidisciplinary team including neurology and neurosurgery is recommended. The initial goal of therapy is to stabilize the patient to prevent or reverse cerebral herniation. Treatment should include anticoagulation once there is confirmation of the diagnosis and no evidence of hemorrhage. In severe cases, intravenous mannitol, neurosurgical intervention, or thrombolysis may be required. The majority of patients with CVT have a good outcome [24].

VTE Management Around Labor and Delivery and Postpartum

Issues to consider regarding VTE management at the time of labor and delivery include risk of bleeding, possibility of regional anesthesia [55], and the risk of recurrence of VTE. If a VTE occurs within 2 weeks of delivery, a retrievable IVC filter is preferable. Between 2 and 4 weeks of delivery, UFH is preferred. If it occurs

Table 6.5 Antepartum indications for thromboprophylaxis

Lower risk	Higher risk
Single prior VTE[a] without thrombophilia	Recent or recurrent thrombosis
Single prior VTE with the following thrombophilia: protein S deficiency, protein C deficiency, heterozygote for FVL or PGM	Single prior VTE with the following thrombophilia: homozygote for FVL or PGM, antiphospholipid antibodies
No prior VTE with the following thrombophilia: protein S deficiency, protein C deficiency, heterozygote for FVL or PGM	Antithrombin III deficiency
No prior VTE with obstetric complication and thrombophilia	Multiple thrombophilias/compound heterozygotes
Prolonged bed rest	Antiphospholipid antibody syndrome (low-dose aspirin (75–100 mg/day) also recommended)
	Single prior VTE with a first-degree relative with prior VTE or thrombophilia

Source: (ACOG Practice Bulletin No. 123 2011, Bates 2012, RCOG 2009)
[a]Risk increased if single VTE idiopathic or pregnancy or estrogen related

Table 6.6 Thromboembolism in pregnancy

Clinical scenario	Antepartum management	Postpartum management
Low risk thrombophilia without previous VTE	Surveillance without anticoagulation Therapy or prophylactic LMWH or UFH	Surveillance without anticoagulation therapy or postpartum anticoagulation therapy if the patient has additional risks factors
Low risk thrombophilia with a single previous episode of VTE—Not receiving long term anticoagulation therapy	Prophylactic or intermediate—dose LMWH/UFH or surveillance without anticoagulation therapy	Postpartum anticoagulation therapy or intermediate dose LMWH/UFH
High risk thrombophilia without previous VTE	Prophylactic LMWH or UFH	Postpartum anticoagulation therapy
High risk thrombophilia with a single previous Episode of VTE—Not receiving long term anticoagulation therapy	Prophylactic intermediate dose, or adjusted dose LMWH/UFH regimen	Postpartum anticoagulation therapy or intermediate or adjusted dose LMWH/UFH for 6 weeks (therapy level should be at least as high as antepartum treatment)
No thrombophilia with previous single episode of VTE associated with transient risk factor that is no longer present—Excludes pregnancy- or estrogen-related	Surveillance without anticoagulation therapy	Postpartum anticoagulation therapy
No thrombophilia with previous single episode of VTE without an associated risk factor (idiopathic)—Not receiving long-term anticoagulation therapy	Prophylactic dose LMWH or UFH	Postpartum anticoagulation therapy
Thrombophilia or no thrombophilia with two or more episodes of VTE—Not receiving long-term anticoagulation therapy	Prophylactic or therapeutic dose LMWH or Prophylactic or therapeutic dose UFH	Postpartum anticoagulation therapy or Therapeutic dose LNWH/UFH for 6 weeks

Source: Thromboembolism in Pregnancy. ACOG Practice Bulletin, Number 123, Table 2, September 2011

a month or more prior to delivery, then consider timing anticoagulant offset prior to induction of labor [56]. Following delivery, LMWH can typically be restarted within 4–6 h, once maternal bleeding risk has been minimized. If anticoagulation will be extended into the postpartum period, bridging from a heparin treatment to coumarin is a safe alternative, including with breastfeeding [48, 49].

VTE Prophylaxis

All pregnant women should be assessed for VTE risk, and when appropriate prophylactic anticoagulation should begin early in the pregnancy. Table 6.5 lists the antepartum indications for thromboprophylaxis. The lower-risk group may consider surveillance alone and withhold prophylactic anticoagulation but have a low threshold for treatment when added risk factors are present. In the postpartum, all women with one or more prior VTE should receive prophylaxis. Women without a prior history of VTE but with a high-risk thrombophilia should be considered for antepartum prophylaxis and receive postpartum thromboprophylaxis. Women with no history of VTE and with a lower-risk thrombophilia may undergo surveillance alone with anticoagulation added for additional risk factors (Table 6.6) [57]. Following a cesarean section, prophylaxis is indicated for women with risk factors beyond the surgery and pregnancy.

LMWH is the preferred preventive treatment. The dose and frequency of treatment is at the practitioner's discretion based on estimated risk level. For example, lower-risk patients can be treated with the LMWH enoxaparin 40 mg once a day and higher-risk patients twice a day. Postpartum thromboprophylaxis should be extended to 6 weeks or longer when indicated [48].

Conclusions

The incidence of VTE is higher in pregnancy compared to age-/sex-/time-matched controls. Risk assessment and identification of pregnancy-specific factors are important to reduce mortality. Thrombophilias and family and obstetric history are strong risk factors for VTE. Diagnosis and treatment of VTE in pregnancy is challenging. Ongoing research is needed to guide practitioners in an evidence-based approach to prevention and management of thrombosis in pregnancy.

References

1. James AH, Jamison MG, Brancazio LR, Myers ER. Venous thromboembolism during pregnancy and the postpartum period: incidence, risk factors, and mortality. Am J Obstet Gynecol. 2006;194(5):1311–5. Epub 2006/05/02.
2. James AH, Tapson VF, Goldhaber SZ. Thrombosis during pregnancy and the postpartum period. Am J Obstet Gynecol. 2005;193(1):216–9. Epub 2005/07/16.
3. Sultan AA, Tata LJ, West J, Fiaschi L, Fleming KM, Nelson-Piercy C, et al. Risk factors for first venous thromboembolism around pregnancy: a population-based cohort study from the United Kingdom. Blood. 2013;121(19):3953–61. Epub 2013/04/04.
4. Wijetilleka S, Scoble T, Khamashta M. Novel insights into pathogenesis, diagnosis and treatment of antiphospholipid syndrome. Curr Opin Rheumatol. 2012;24(5):473–81. Epub 2012/05/16.
5. Kauffmann RH, Veltkamp JJ, Van Tilburg NH, Van Es LA. Acquired antithrombin III deficiency and thrombosis in the nephrotic syndrome. Am J Med. 1978;65(4):607–13. Epub 1978/10/01.
6. Den Heijer M, Lewington S, Clarke R. Homocysteine, MTHFR and risk of venous thrombosis: a meta-analysis of published epidemiological studies. J Thromb Haemost. 2005;3(2):292–9. Epub 2005/01/27.

7. McColl MD, Ellison J, Reid F, Tait RC, Walker ID, Greer IA. Prothrombin 20210 G–>A, MTHFR C677T mutations in women with venous thromboembolism associated with pregnancy. BJOG. 2000;107(4):565–9. Epub 2000/04/12.
8. Lockwood C, Wendel G. Committee on practice bulletins O. Practice bulletin no. 124: inherited thrombophilias in pregnancy. Obstet Gynecol. 2011;118(3):730–40.
9. Nelson SM, Greer IA. Thrombophilia and the risk for venous thromboembolism during pregnancy, delivery, and puerperium. Obstet Gynecol Clin N Am. 2006;33(3):413–27. Epub 2006/09/12.
10. Marik PE, Plante LA. Venous thromboembolic disease and pregnancy. N Engl J Med. 2008;359(19):2025–33. Epub 2008/11/07.
11. Zotz RB, Gerhardt A, Scharf RE. Inherited thrombophilia and gestational venous thromboembolism. Best Pract Res Clin Haematol. 2003;16(2):243–59. Epub 2003/05/24.
12. Robertson L, Wu O, Langhorne P, Twaddle S, Clark P, Lowe GD, et al. Thrombophilia in pregnancy: a systematic review. Br J Haematol. 2006;132(2):171–96. Epub 2006/01/10.
13. Castoldi E, Rosing J. APC resistance: biological basis and acquired influences. J Thromb Haemost. 2010;8(3):445–53. Epub 2009/12/17.
14. Greer IA. Thrombosis in pregnancy: maternal and fetal issues. Lancet. 1999;353(9160):1258–65. Epub 1999/04/27.
15. Lockwood CJ. Heritable coagulopathies in pregnancy. Obstet Gynecol Surv. 1999;54(12):754–65. Epub 1999/12/22.
16. Alfirevic Z, Roberts D, Martlew V. How strong is the association between maternal thrombophilia and adverse pregnancy outcome? A systematic review. Eur J Obstet Gynecol Reprod Biol. 2002;101(1):6–14. Epub 2002/01/23.
17. Kupferminc MJ. Thrombophilia and pregnancy. Reprod Biol Endocrinol. 2003;1:111. Epub 2003/11/18.
18. Rodger MA, Betancourt MT, Clark P, Lindqvist PG, Dizon-Townson D, Said J, et al. The association of factor V leiden and prothrombin gene mutation and placenta-mediated pregnancy complications: a systematic review and meta-analysis of prospective cohort studies. PLoS Med. 2010;7(6):e1000292. Epub 2010/06/22.
19. Roque H, Paidas MJ, Funai EF, Kuczynski E, Lockwood CJ. Maternal thrombophilias are not associated with early pregnancy loss. Thromb Haemost. 2004;91(2):290–5. Epub 2004/02/13.
20. Committee on Practice Bulletins-Obstetrics ACoO, Gynecologists. Practice bulletin no. 132: Antiphospholipid syndrome. Obstet Gynecol. 2012;120(6):1514–21. Epub 2012/11/22.
21. Jacobsen AF, Sandset PM. Venous thromboembolism associated with pregnancy and hormonal therapy. Best Pract Res Clin Haematol. 2012;25(3):319–32. Epub 2012/09/11.
22. Ray JG, Chan WS. Deep vein thrombosis during pregnancy and the puerperium: a meta-analysis of the period of risk and the leg of presentation. Obstet Gynecol Surv. 1999;54(4):265–71. Epub 1999/04/13.
23. Goldhaber SZ, Tapson VF, Committee DFS. A prospective registry of 5,451 patients with ultrasound-confirmed deep vein thrombosis. Am J Cardiol. 2004;93(2):259–62. Epub 2004/01/13.
24. Stam J. Thrombosis of the cerebral veins and sinuses. N Engl J Med. 2005;352(17):1791–8. Epub 2005/04/29.
25. Heit JA, Kobbervig CE, James AH, Petterson TM, Bailey KR, Melton 3rd LJ. Trends in the incidence of venous thromboembolism during pregnancy or postpartum: a 30-year population-based study. Ann Intern Med. 2005;143(10):697–706. Epub 2005/11/17.
26. Andersen BS, Steffensen FH, Sorensen HT, Nielsen GL, Olsen J. The cumulative incidence of venous thromboembolism during pregnancy and puerperium–an 11 year Danish population-based study of 63,300 pregnancies. Acta Obstet Gynecol Scand. 1998;77(2):170–3. Epub 1998/03/25.
27. Simpson EL, Lawrenson RA, Nightingale AL, Farmer RD. Venous thromboembolism in pregnancy and the puerperium: incidence and additional risk factors from a London perinatal database. BJOG. 2001;108(1):56–60. Epub 2001/02/24.
28. Anderson Jr FA, Wheeler HB, Goldberg RJ, Hosmer DW, Patwardhan NA, Jovanovic B, et al. A population-based perspective of the hospital incidence and case-fatality rates of deep vein

thrombosis and pulmonary embolism. The Worcester DVT Study. Arch Intern Med. 1991; 151(5):933–8. Epub 1991/05/01.
29. Jacobsen AF, Skjeldestad FE, Sandset PM. Incidence and risk patterns of venous thromboembolism in pregnancy and puerperium–a register-based case-control study. Am J Obstet Gynecol. 2008;198(2):233 e1–7. Epub 2007/11/13.
30. Chang J, Elam-Evans LD, Berg CJ, Herndon J, Flowers L, Seed KA, et al. Pregnancy-related mortality surveillance–United States, 1991–1999. MMWR Surveill Sum (Washington, DC: 2002). 2003;52(2):1–8. Epub 2003/06/27.
31. Cantwell R, Clutton-Brock T, Cooper G, Dawson A, Drife J, Garrod D, et al. Saving mothers' lives: reviewing maternal deaths to make motherhood safer: 2006–2008. The Eighth report of the confidential enquiries into maternal deaths in the United Kingdom. BJOG. 2011;118 Suppl 1:1–203. Epub 2011/03/05.
32. Horlander KT, Mannino DM, Leeper KV. Pulmonary embolism mortality in the United States, 1979-1998: an analysis using multiple-cause mortality data. Arch Intern Med. 2003;163(14): 1711–7. Epub 2003/07/30.
33. Bergqvist A, Bergqvist D, Lindhagen A, Matzsch T. Late symptoms after pregnancy-related deep vein thrombosis. Br J Obstet Gynaecol. 1990;97(4):338–41. Epub 1990/04/01.
34. Wik HS, Jacobsen AF, Sandvik L, Sandset PM. Prevalence and predictors for post-thrombotic syndrome 3 to 16 years after pregnancy-related venous thrombosis: a population-based, cross-sectional, case-control study. J Thromb Haemost. 2012;10(5):840–7. Epub 2012/03/29.
35. Wells PS, Anderson DR, Rodger M, Stiell I, Dreyer JF, Barnes D, et al. Excluding pulmonary embolism at the bedside without diagnostic imaging: management of patients with suspected pulmonary embolism presenting to the emergency department by using a simple clinical model and d-dimer. Ann Intern Med. 2001;135(2):98–107. Epub 2001/07/17.
36. Kjellberg U, Andersson NE, Rosen S, Tengborn L, Hellgren M. APC resistance and other haemostatic variables during pregnancy and puerperium. Thromb Haemost. 1999;81(4):527–31. Epub 1999/05/11.
37. Powrie RO, Larson L, Rosene-Montella K, Abarca M, Barbour L, Trujillo N. Alveolar-arterial oxygen gradient in acute pulmonary embolism in pregnancy. Am J Obstet Gynecol. 1998;178(2):394–6. Epub 1998/03/21.
38. Rodger M, Makropoulos D, Turek M, Quevillon J, Raymond F, Rasuli P, et al. Diagnostic value of the electrocardiogram in suspected pulmonary embolism. Am J Cardiol. 2000; 86(7):807–9. A10. Epub 2000/10/06.
39. Turkstra F, Kuijer PM, van Beek EJ, Brandjes DP, ten Cate JW, Buller HR. Diagnostic utility of ultrasonography of leg veins in patients suspected of having pulmonary embolism. Ann Intern Med. 1997;126(10):775–81. Epub 1997/05/15.
40. Chan WS, Ray JG, Murray S, Coady GE, Coates G, Ginsberg JS. Suspected pulmonary embolism in pregnancy: clinical presentation, results of lung scanning, and subsequent maternal and pediatric outcomes. Arch Intern Med. 2002;162(10):1170–5. Epub 2002/05/22.
41. Bourjeily G, Paidas M, Khalil H, Rosene-Montella K, Rodger M. Pulmonary embolism in pregnancy. Lancet. 2010;375(9713):500–12. Epub 2009/11/06.
42. Shahir K, Goodman LR, Tali A, Thorsen KM, Hellman RS. Pulmonary embolism in pregnancy: CT pulmonary angiography versus perfusion scanning. AJR Am J Roentgenol. 2010;195(3):W214–20. Epub 2010/08/24.
43. Cogo A, Lensing AW, Koopman MM, Piovella F, Siragusa S, Wells PS, et al. Compression ultrasonography for diagnostic management of patients with clinically suspected deep vein thrombosis: prospective cohort study. BMJ. 1998;316(7124):17–20. Epub 1998/02/06.
44. Chan WS, Lee A, Spencer FA, Crowther M, Rodger M, Ramsay T, et al. Predicting deep venous thrombosis in pregnancy: out in "LEFt" field? Ann Intern Med. 2009;151(2):85–92. Epub 2009/07/22.
45. Greer IA, Nelson-Piercy C. Low-molecular-weight heparins for thromboprophylaxis and treatment of venous thromboembolism in pregnancy: a systematic review of safety and efficacy. Blood. 2005;106(2):401–7. Epub 2005/04/07.

46. Yang CJ, Chen TC, Liao LF, Ma L, Wang CS, Lu PL, et al. Nosocomial outbreak of two strains of Burkholderia cepacia caused by contaminated heparin. J Hosp Inf. 2008;69(4):398–400. Epub 2008/05/31.
47. Chunilal SD, Young E, Johnston MA, Robertson C, Naguit I, Stevens P, et al. The APTT response of pregnant plasma to unfractionated heparin. Thromb Haemost. 2002;87(1):92–7. Epub 2002/02/19.
48. Bates SM, Greer IA, Middeldorp S, Veenstra DL, Prabulos AM, Vandvik PO, et al. VTE, thrombophilia, antithrombotic therapy, and pregnancy: Antithrombotic Therapy and Prevention of Thrombosis, 9th ed: American College of Chest Physicians Evidence-Based Clinical Practice Guidelines. Chest. 2012;141(2 Suppl):e691S–736S. Epub 2012/02/15.
49. Gynaecologists. RCoOa. Acute management of thrombosis and embolism during pregnancy and the puerperium (Green-top Guidelines No. 37A). London, UK: Royal College of Obstetricians and Gynaecologists; 2009.
50. Ahearn GS, Hadjiliadis D, Govert JA, Tapson VF. Massive pulmonary embolism during pregnancy successfully treated with recombinant tissue plasminogen activator: a case report and review of treatment options. Arch Intern Med. 2002;162(11):1221–7. Epub 2002/06/01.
51. Holden EL, Ranu H, Sheth A, Shannon MS, Madden BP. Thrombolysis for massive pulmonary embolism in pregnancy–a report of three cases and follow up over a two year period. Thromb Res. 2011;127(1):58–9. Epub 2010/07/16.
52. Leonhardt G, Gaul C, Nietsch HH, Buerke M, Schleussner E. Thrombolytic therapy in pregnancy. J Thromb Thrombolysis. 2006;21(3):271–6. Epub 2006/05/10.
53. Kalva SP, Chlapoutaki C, Wicky S, Greenfield AJ, Waltman AC, Athanasoulis CA. Suprarenal inferior vena cava filters: a 20-year single-center experience. J Vasc Intervent Radiol. 2008;19(7):1041–7. Epub 2008/07/01.
54. McConville RM, Kennedy PT, Collins AJ, Ellis PK. Failed retrieval of an inferior vena cava filter during pregnancy because of filter tilt: report of two cases. Cardiovasc Intervent Radiol. 2009;32(1):174–7. Epub 2008/08/05.
55. Horlocker TT, Wedel DJ, Rowlingson JC, Enneking FK, Kopp SL, Benzon HT, et al. Regional anesthesia in the patient receiving antithrombotic or thrombolytic therapy: American Society of Regional Anesthesia and Pain Medicine Evidence-Based Guidelines (Third Edition). Reg Anesth Pain Med. 2010;35(1):64–101. Epub 2010/01/08.
56. Kearon C, Hirsh J. Management of anticoagulation before and after elective surgery. N Engl J Med. 1997;336(21):1506–11. Epub 1997/05/22.
57. James A. Committee on Practice B-O. Practice bulletin no. 123: thromboembolism in pregnancy. Obstet Gynecol. 2011;118(3):718–29.

Chapter 7
Special Hematologic Issues in the Pregnant Patient

Tina Rizack, Kimberly Perez, and Rochelle Strenger

An understanding of hematological disorders in pregnancy requires knowledge of the normal physiologic changes in pregnancy (Table 7.1) [1]. During pregnancy, plasma volume increases by about 50 %, initially rapidly by week 6 of gestation and then more gradually peaking by week 30. Erythrocyte mass increases by 18 to 30 % during typical pregnancy but at a slower rate than plasma volume resulting in a dilutional effect (hematocrit between 30 and 32 %) referred to as physiological or dilutional anemia of pregnancy [2, 3]. Other physiologic changes including an increase in clotting factors occur as the parturient accommodates a growing uterus and placenta and prepares for hemostasis needed for delivery.

This chapter is an updated version of previously published article: Rizack T, Rosene-Montella K. Special hematological issues in the pregnant patient. Hematology/Oncology Clinics of North America 2012;26(2):409-32.

T. Rizack, M.D., M.P.H. (✉)
Department of Medicine, Women and Infants Hospital, The Warren Alpert Medical School of Brown University, 101 Dudley Street, Providence, RI 02905, USA
e-mail: trizack@wihri.org

K. Perez, M.D.
Hematology/Oncology, Rhode Island Hospital, Providence, RI 02905, USA

Assistant Professor of Internal Medicine, Warren Alpert School of Medicine of Brown University, Providence, RI 02905, USA

R. Strenger, M.D.
Department of Hematology/Oncology, The Miriam Hospital, 164 Summit Avenue, Providence, RI 02906, USA

The Warren Alpert Medical School of Brown University, 164 Summit Avenue, Providence, RI 02906, USA

Table 7.1 Normal hematologic values and changes in pregnancy

Test	Reference intervals	Change in pregnancy
CBC		
WBC	3.00–10.5×10⁹/L	↑to 10–16x10⁹/L
Hb	115–155 g/L	↓to 100–130 g/L
Platelet count	100–400×10⁹/L	↓near term to as low as 100 x10 ⁹/L
PTT	24–36 s	↔
INR	0.9–1.2	↔
Fibrinogen	>2.0 g/L	↑↑
vWF	*Group O:* 0.40–1.75 Um/L	
	Nongroup 0: 0.70–2.10 U/mL	↑
Factor VIII	0.6–1.95 U/mL	↑
D-dimer	<300 μg/L	↑
Protein C	*Functional:* 0.75–1.60 U/mL	
	Antigen: 0.70–1.20 U/mL	↔
Protein S	*Functional:* 0.50–1.00 U/mL	
	Antigen: 0.57–1.20 U/mL	↓
AT	0.80–1.25 U/mL	↔
Homocysteine	<10 μmol/L	↓
Ferritin		↑
ESR		↑

Source: Rodger M. Normal Hematologic Changes in Pregnancy. 2nd ed. Rosene Montella K KE, Barbour LA, Lee RV., editors. Philadelphia, PA, USA: American College of Physicians; 2008, with permission

AT antithrombin, *CBC* complete blood count, *ESR* erythrocyte sedimentation rate, *Hb* hemoglobin, *INR* international normalized ratio, *PTT* partial thromboplastin time, *vWf* von Willebrand factor antigen, *WBC* leukocytes

Anemia

In pregnancy, anemia is generally well tolerated. The Centers for Disease Control and Prevention defines anemia in pregnancy as a hemoglobin of less than 11 g/dL in the first and third trimesters and less than 10.5 g/dL in the second trimester [4]. For women with adequate iron stores, the hemoglobin should return to normal around 1 to 6 weeks after delivery [5]. A hemoglobin of less than 10 g/dL should prompt a work-up for a pathological cause. Severe anemia, defined as a hemoglobin below 6 g/dL, has been associated with reduced amniotic fluid volume, fetal cerebral vasodilation, and nonreassuring fetal heart rate tracings [6]. There have also been reports of increased risk of prematurity, spontaneous abortion, low birth weight, and fetal death [7]. A hemoglobin of less than 7 g/dL increases the risk of maternal mortality as well [8]. Current recommendations are for all pregnant women to have a baseline complete blood count prior to pregnancy or at the first prenatal visit and again in the third trimester.

Iron Deficiency Anemia

Iron deficiency anemia accounts for the majority (>90 %) of nonphysiologic anemias. During a normal singleton pregnancy, a woman loses 1000 mg of iron to the fetus and placenta, expansion of red blood cells, and insensible losses [9]. Studies of the efficacy of iron supplementation on pregnancy outcomes are lacking. Transferrin is usually elevated with pregnancy. Serum ferritin is a useful screening test for iron deficiency in pregnancy with a sensitivity of 90 % and specificity of 85 % [10]. Iron repletion recommendations are generally the same for pregnant patients as nonpregnant patients and current recommendations suggest 15 to 30 mg daily of supplemental elemental iron for all pregnant women. Parental iron can be used for patients who do not absorb or are intolerant of oral iron. Iron sucrose in pregnancy has better safety data and is preferred over iron dextran. Recombinant erythropoietin has been shown to be of some benefit in patients with an inadequate response to iron but may cause a hypertensive effect [11]. However, in patients refractory to standard iron repletion, another cause of anemia should be investigated.

Macrocytic Anemias

Macrocytic anemias are most commonly due to folate deficiency and rarely vitamin B12 deficiency. Accurate diagnosis of both folate and B12 deficiency in pregnancy usually requires measuring plasma homocysteine and methylmalonic acid levels. Folate deficiency is caused by both increased demands of the fetus and erythropoiesis from the expansion of red cell mass. Hormonal changes of pregnancy can decrease folate absorption and increase urine losses [12]. Folate requirements increase from 50 µg/day in the nonpregnant patient to 150 µg/day in pregnant patients. Current recommendations are for pregnant women to take 1 mg daily of folate to prevent neural tube defects, which is also adequate for prevention and treatment of folic acid deficiency. Higher doses of folate are recommended in patients on antiepileptic drugs and in patients with a previously effected child with a neural tube defect. Repletion for both vitamin B12 and folate deficiency is the same as for nonpregnant patients. Other less common causes of macrocytic anemia include alcohol use, medications, hypothyroidism, and liver disease.

Hemoglobinopathies

For the majority of women with hemoglobinopathies, pregnancy is possible and successful with increased monitoring to avoid maternal and fetal complications.

Sickle Cell Disease

Sickle cell syndrome is caused by an inherited single nucleotide (GAG/GTG) mutation in the β-globin gene. Heterozygosity for Hb S (sickle cell trait) does not cause disease, but homozygous inheritance or compound heterozygous inheritance with another mutant β-globin gene does result in sickle cell disease. At least 17 hemoglobinopathies resulting in sickle cell disease variants exist. The more common types are listed in Table 7.2 [13]. Some risks to the mother and fetus are caused by pregnancy. Pregnancy-related increases in adhesion and coagulation proteins such as von Willebrand factor, fibrinogen, and factor VIII may exacerbate RBC adhesion and ultimately occlusion [14]. This results in occlusion of the vessels and a vaso-occlusive event, which may be more frequent during pregnancy. The frequency of obstetric complication in women with sickle cell disease can be found in Table 7.3 [13]. Sickle cell disease carries approximately a 6.5 % risk of spontaneous abortion

Table 7.2 Characteristics of common sickle cell diseases compared with sickle cell trait

Disease	Baseline Hb(g/dL)	MCV	Baseline reticulocyte (%)	Relative clinical severity
HbSS	6.0–9.0	Normal	5–30	++++
HbS-β⁰-thalassemia	6.0–9.0	Low	5–30	++++
HbSC	10.0–13.0	Normal	3–4	+++
HbS-β⁺-thalassemia	10.0–14.0	Low	3–4	++
HbAS	14.0–16.0	Normal	0–1	0

HBAS, sickle cell trait; HBSC, sickle hemoglobin C disease; HbSS, sickle cell anemia; MCV, mean corpuscular volume
Source: Hassell K. Hemoglobinopathies, Thalassemia, and Anemia: Hemoglobinopathies and Thalassemias. 2nd ed. Rosene-Montella K KE, Barbour LA, Lee RV., editor, Philadelphia, PA; American College of Physicians; 2008, with permission

Table 7.3 Frequency of obstetric complications in women with sickle cell disease

Transfusion study, 1978–1986 [22]					
	Control	SS	SC	Sβthal	Cooperative study, 1979–1986 [12]
Number of pregnancies	8981	100	66	23	225
Gestational age at delivery (week)	40	37.5	38.6	37.1	37.7
Preterm labor (%)	17	26	15	22	9
Placenta previa (%)	0.4	1	2	4	–
Abruptio placentae (%)	0.5	3	2	4	–
Toxemia (%)	4	18	9	13	11
Cesarean section (%)	14	29	30	26	–

Source: Hassell K. Hemoglobinopathies, Thalassemia, and Anemia: Hemoglobinopathies and Thalassemias. 2nd ed. Rosene-Montella K KE, Barbour LA, LeeRV.,editors. Philadelphia, PA: American College of Physicians; 2008, with permission
Sβthal sickle β thalassemia, *SS* sickle cell anemia, *SC* sickle hemoglobin C

according to the Cooperative Study of Sickle Disease [15]. Rates of intrauterine growth restriction may be increased in women with sickle cell disease especially those with acute complications of sickle cell disease during pregnancy [15, 16]. Preterm labor, placental abruption, and preeclampsia may be more common in patients with Hb SS disease compared to healthy African American females without sickle cell disease [15, 17].

Patients should be followed in a high-risk clinic in conjunction with a healthcare provider familiar with the care of patients with sickle cell disease, ideally at 2-week intervals. A complete blood count, reticulocyte count, urinalysis, and blood pressure check are recommended with each visit. A prenatal vitamin without iron and additional folate should be prescribed [18]. During the first trimester preventing nausea and dehydration may decrease sickle cell-related complications. Close monitoring for the development of sickle cell pain events such as acute chest syndrome, acute sequestration or splenic infarct, and acute multiorgan failure is recommended during pregnancy, labor, and postpartum period. Pain crises are treated similar to nonpregnant patients and are outlined in Table 7.4 [13]. Adequate hydration and oxygenation should be maintained during labor. Analgesia doses may exceed those usually required for obstetrical pain due to increased tolerance of pain medications used for pain crises [19]. Indications for cesarean section are obstetric and the same as for patients without sickle cell disease.

Chronic anemia associated with sickle cell disease is exacerbated by the usual dilution effect of pregnancy. Iron repletion will not correct the anemia and should be avoided, as many patients are already iron overloaded due to repeat transfusions. The use of prophylactic blood transfusions is not supported by the literature [20, 21]. Simple or exchange transfusions should be instituted for the same indications as nonpregnant patients: stroke, ocular events, severe acute chest syndrome, splenic sequestration, symptomatic aplastic crisis, and cerebrovascular accident [22].

Table 7.4 Management of acute sickle cell pain episodes in pregnant women

- IV fluids: correct dehydration, then maintain euvolemia
- Oxygen therapy: maintain normal oxygen saturation
- Investigation and treatment of infection
- Pain control: IV on a regular schedule (not prn)
- Monitor for complications of sickle cell disease:
    - Daily complete blood count and reticulocyte count
    - Baseline chemistry profile: repeat as needed for clinical deterioration
    - Frequent pulse oximetry

Narcotics (IV)	Nonnarcotic adjuncts (first–second trimester)
• Morphine sulfate	Nonsteroidal anti-inflammatory drugs
• Hydromorphone	Diphenhydramine
• Fentanyl	

Source: Hassell K. Hemoglobinopathies, Thalassemia, and Anemia: Hemoglobinopathies and Thalassemias. 2nd ed. Rosene- Montella K KE, Barbour LA, Lee RV., editor. Philadelphia, PA: American College of Physicians: 2008, with permission

Pregnant patients with sickle cell trait carry an increased risk of bacteriuria that may lead to urinary tract infections or pyelonephritis. Sickle cell trait should be confirmed, and even asymptomatic bacteriuria, as in all pregnant patients, should be treated (Table 7.5) [23].

Thalassemia

Thalassemias are a result of quantitative disorders of hemoglobin production. This is a result of decreased or imbalanced production of generally structurally normal globins. In β-thalassemia, a mutation in β-globin leads to decreased production and an excess of α-globins and the reverse for mutations in α-globins in α-thalassemias. These mutations result in membrane damage and red cell fragility causing microcytosis with target cell morphology and a chronic hemolytic anemia with compensatory reticulocytosis and splenomegaly. α-Thalassemias are more common in persons of Asian, African, or Mediterranean descent. β-Thalassemias occur more commonly in persons of Mediterranean and African descent. The more common types of thalassemias are described in [13].

In general, women with α- or β-thalassemia trait tolerate pregnancy well. These patients have a mild baseline microcytic anemia, and despite increased iron absorption characteristic of thalassemia, iron deficiency can develop and iron studies may need to be checked during pregnancy [13]. Patients with severe α- and β-thalassemia intermedia have compromised fertility and few pregnancies have been reported. Approximately 50 % of pregnancies result in stillbirth, intrauterine growth restriction, and/or preterm delivery [24]. However, successful pregnancies have been achieved in patients with severe thalassemia with adequate cardiac function, good chelation regimens, and transfusion support with a goal HB of 10 g/dL during pregnancy as well as careful maternal and fetal monitoring [25].

Table 7.5 Recommended indications for transfusion in pregnant women with sickle cell disease

Toxemia
• Severe anemia (drop of 30 % below or Hb ≤ 6.0 g/dL)
• Acute renal failure
• Septicemia/bacteremia
• Acute chest syndrome with hypoxia or other severe sickle cell complication
• Anticipated surgery
Source: Hassell K. Hemoglobinopathies, Thalassemia, and Anemia: Hemoglobinopathies and Thalassemias. 2nd ed. Rosene-Monella K KE, Barbour LA, Lee RV., editor. Philadelphia: American College of Physicians; 2008

Hb hemoglobin

Thrombocytopenia

Thrombocytopenia affects 10 % of pregnancies and can be isolated or part of a systemic disorder, and causes may be specific to or unrelated to pregnancy. The major causes of thrombocytopenia in pregnancy are presented in Table 7.6 (see attached table). A 10 % decrease in platelets can commonly be seen in pregnancy. For general management, most women can continue routine obstetrical care. The mode of delivery for patients with thrombocytopenia should be determined by obstetrical indications. No studies have been conducted to determine the optimal platelet count, but observational data indicate that a platelet count above 50 is adequate for epidural anesthesia, vaginal delivery, and cesarean section [26, 27]. Per current guidelines [28], vaginal deliveries are felt to be safe with a platelet count of 50,000. While the ASH guidelines also use a platelet count of 50,000 as appropriate for cesarean deliveries, concerns regarding bleeding from epidural anesthesia and possible neurologic complications led the The British Committee for Standards in Haematology (BCSH) [26] to recommend a platelet count of 80,000 for epidural anesthesia and for cesarean sections. Given that recommendations vary by institution, the treating team and the anesthesiologist should individualize each patient's care.

Gestational thrombocytopenia, a benign condition initially diagnosed in the second or third trimester, is usually mild and is often difficult to differentiate from idiopathic thrombocytopenia (ITP). The former is typically mild with platelet counts rarely below 70,000/uL. ITP is found in approximately 1 in 10,000 pregnancies and usually presents in the first trimester. Whereas gestational thrombocytopenia has no affect on the neonate, there have been isolated cases of ITP that appeared to cause thrombocytopenia in the neonate. No correlation has been found between maternal and fetal/neonatal platelet counts, and most cases of severe fetal or neonatal thrombocytopenia are related to alloimmune thrombocytopenia (see below). Antiplatelet antibody testing has not been shown to be of value in predicting the risk of a thrombocytopenic infant or complications related to delivery. Current guidelines from the American Society of Hematology (ASH) and the British Committee for Standards in Haematology (BCSH) do not recommend the use of antiplatelet antibody testing for ITP in pregnancy [28, 29].

There is no evidence to support the need for intrapartum fetal platelet counts in patients with ITP. Women with preexisting ITP are less likely to have complications during pregnancy or require treatment. A clinical presentation of bleeding rather than an absolute platelet count directs the need for treatment remote from term. ITP in pregnancy is generally treated with either corticosteroids or IVIG for similar indications as in nonpregnant patients, with an attempt to keep platelet counts above 50–75,000 u/L toward term (Table 7.7 and 7.8) [30]. Although rituximab use in pregnancy has not been formally evaluated, rituximab has been used successfully during pregnancy for non-Hodgkin lymphoma, Crohn's disease, and other indications in a limited number of patients and is pregnancy class C [31, 32]. Thrombopoietic

Table 7.6 Differential diagnosis of thrombocytopenia in pregnancy

	Incidence	Timing of incidence	Degree of thrombocytopenia	Microangiopathic hemolytic anemia	Hypertension	Coagulopathy	Liver disease	Renal disease	CNS disease
ITP	3–4 %	Most common in 1st trimester, anytime	Mild to severe	None	None	None	None	None	None
Gestational/incidental thrombocytopenia	75–80 %	Second–third trimester	Mild	None	None	None	None	None	None
Preeclampsia	15–20 %	Late 2nd to 3rd trimester	Mild to moderate	Mild	Moderate to severe	None to mild	None	Proteinuria	Seizures with preeclampsia
HELLP		Late 2nd to 3rd trimester	Moderate to severe	Moderate to severe	None to severe	Absent to mild	Moderate to severe	None to moderate	None to moderate
DIC	Rare	Anytime	Moderate to severe	Mild to moderate	None	Mild to severe	Variable	Variable	None
AFLP	Rare	3rd trimester	Mild	Mild	None to mild	Severe	Severe	None to mild	None to mild
TTP	Rare	2nd to 3rd trimester	Severe	Moderate to severe	None	None	None	None to moderate	None to severe
HUS	Rare	Postpartum	Moderate to severe	Moderate to severe	None to mild	None	None	Moderate to severe	None to mild

AFLP acute fatty liver of pregnancy, *DIC* disseminated intravascular coagulation, *HELLP* hemolysis, elevated liver function tests, low platelets, *HUS* hemolytic uremic syndrome, *ITP* immune thrombocytopenia, *TTP* thrombocytopenic purpura

Table 7.7 Medical management of immune thrombocytopenic purpura in pregnancy: American Society of Hematology guidelines

Treatment indications	Platelets < 10,000/µl in
	Platelets 10–30,000/µl in Second or third trimester
	Bleeding
Intravenous immunoglobulin	Initial treatment: third trimester Platelets < 10,000/µl
	Initial treatment: platelets 10–30,000 /µl and bleeding
	After steroid failure: platelets < 10,000/µl
	After steroid failure: platelets 10–30,000/µl
	After steroid failure: third trimester, platelets 10–30,000/µl, asymptomatic
Splenectomy	Second trimester, platelets < 10,000/µl, bleeding
Safe platelet count for delivery	50,000/µl

Source: Gernsheimer T, Mc Crae KR. Immune thrombocytopenic purpura in pregnancy Curr Opin Hematol 2007; 14:574-580, with permission

Table 7.8 Maternal management of immune thrombocytopenic purpura in pregnancy: British Committee for Standards in Haematology guidelines

Treatment indications	Platelets < 20,000/µl, unless delivery imminent
Intravenous immunoglobulin	Oral corticosteroids and IVIg have similar responses as in nonpregnant state
Splenectomy	If essential, in the second trimester, laparoscopic advantageous
Safe platelet count	50,000 /µl, vaginal
For delivery	80,000/µl cesarean section or epidural

Source: Gernsheimer T, McCrae KR. Immune thrombocytopenic purpura in pregnancy Curr Opin Hematol 2007; 14:574-580, with permission

agents' romiplostim and eltrombopag are pregnancy class C, and there are no data to recommend use in pregnancy.

Preeclampsia affects 6 % of first pregnancies and about 50 % of these patients will have thrombocytopenia. The pathophysiology is not well understood, but accelerated platelet consumption is felt to contribute. HELLP (hemolysis, elevated liver function tests, and low platelets) syndrome (see Liver chapter), which affects between 0.1 % and 0.89 % of pregnancies, shares many clinical features with preeclampsia and is often considered a variant of severe preeclampsia. HELLP has a higher rate of maternal and fetal mortality than preeclampsia making correct diagnosis and treatment imperative. Patients with HELLP typically have a microangiopathic hemolytic anemia (schistocytes on peripheral blood smear) and an elevated lactate dehydrogenase (LDH), serum levels of aspartate aminotransferase greater than 70 unit/L, and platelets less than 100,000/uL. HELLP is often difficult to differentiate from thrombotic thrombocytopenic purpura-hemolytic uremic syndrome (TTP-HUS). While TTP-HUS can occur throughout pregnancy and in the postpartum period, HELLP is most likely seen in the third trimester. Initial clinical symptoms appear nonspecific including gastrointestinal symptoms such as right upper quadrant or midepigastric tenderness, nausea and vomiting, and malaise. It is presumed that these symptoms are secondary to hepatic sinusoid blood flow obstruction. 75 % of patients have associated proteinuria: hypertension is seen in 50–60 % [33, 34]. In contrast to TTP, the presence of schistocytes on peripheral smear is seen to a minor degree and ADAMTS-13 deficiency is rarely seen.

Treatment of preeclampsia and HELLP consists of stabilization of the mother followed by expeditious delivery, which usually results in resolution of the disorder within 3 to 4 days in the majority of patients. However, occasionally both syndromes, especially HELLP, can worsen or develop postpartum. There is limited data from several, small randomized studies looking at the use of corticosteroids in the pre- or postnatal setting. Corticosteroids for HELLP are felt to hasten the resolution of thrombocytopenia and laboratory abnormalities and may be continued for 5 to 7 days after delivery for worsening thrombocytopenia or other signs of clinical decline, but the efficacy of corticosteroids for this indication has not been established [35].

The risk of TTP during pregnancy is increased and pregnant women comprise 10 % to 20 % of TTP patients. TTP typically develops in the second or third trimester. TTP-HUS may be confused with severe preeclampsia as common signs and symptoms may occur. Treatment is plasmapheresis. The risk of HUS also increases with pregnancy and the majority of cases develop 3 to 4 weeks postpartum. Atypical HUS with renal failure as the predominant manifestation is the most common. The prognosis of postpartum HUS is poor with more than 25 % of patients with persistent renal failure. Plasmapheresis is recommended despite low response rates due to the difficulty discerning HUS from TTP. Although in the past prompt delivery had been advocated, there is no level 1 data demonstrating that delivery alters the natural history of this disorder. It is likely that previous recommendations were confounded by mixing of cases of preeclampsia with TTP-HUS.

Disseminated intravascular dissemination (DIC) may accompany preeclampsia and may also result from retained fetal products, sepsis, placental abruption, or amniotic fluid embolization. In general, the thrombocytopenia is milder and the degree of microangiopathic hemolysis is less. DIC in pregnancy can be abrupt, severe, and fatal if not addressed appropriately. Treatment is aimed at treating the underlying condition that precipitated the DIC. BCSH has published guidelines for the management of DIC [36]. Transfusion support should be based on the presence of bleeding such as from low platelets or a prolonged prothrombin time. Cryoprecipitate may be used for severe hypofibrinogenemia (fibrinogen <100 g/dL) that persists after plasma therapy. Low doses of heparin may be indicated for patients with significant thrombosis.

Acute fatty liver of pregnancy, another pregnancy-specific cause of thrombocytopenia, usually occurs during the third trimester, and its incidence is increased in primiparas and twin gestations. Typical symptoms are usually nausea, vomiting, right upper quadrant pain, anorexia, jaundice, and elevated liver enzymes consistent with cholestasis with mild thrombocytopenia. Bleeding is common due to coagulopathy resulting from diminished hepatic synthesis of coagulation factors, as well as DIC and acquired antithrombin deficiency. The majority of patients have some degree of DIC, and diabetes insipidus and hypoglycemia are present in more than half of cases (see Liver chapter).

Additional causes of thrombocytopenia include spurious (due to EDTA-induced platelet aggregation); hypersplenism; congenital platelet disorders such as Bernard-Soulier syndrome, May-Hegglin anomaly, gray platelet syndrome, and Glanzmann thrombasthenia; bone marrow disease; drug-induced, HIV, and other autoimmune thrombocytopenias; congenital thrombocytopenias; and type 2b von Willebrand disease (vWD) which is discussed later.

Platelet Function Disorders

Treatment of platelet function disorders is based on the underlying disorder and personal bleeding history. Routine cesarean sections are not recommended. Episiotomy, instrumental vaginal delivery, and epidural anesthesia should be avoided. Platelet transfusions are often indicated to prevent or treat bleeding with prophylactic platelet transfusions reserved for patients with severe disorders [37]. DDAVP during labor has been used successfully in some patients with platelet function disorders [38]. Patients with Bernard-Soulier syndrome and Glanzmann thrombasthenia may be treated with recombinant factor VIIa to prevent alloimmunization or for patients with platelet antibodies [39]. These patients require monthly antiplatelet antibodies after 20 weeks and if identified care coordinated with maternal-fetal medicine to prevent neonatal alloimmune thrombocytopenia.

von Willebrand Disease and Other Bleeding Disorders

Pregnancy normally leads to a shift in the hemostatic balance toward coagulation. However, 10 % of maternal deaths are a result of bleeding disorders, and hemorrhage is the leading cause of maternal mortality in developing nations. Patients with known disorders are at higher risk and may require additional screening and therapy to prevent or stop bleeding complications. Pregnancy is often the first manifestation of an undiagnosed bleeding disorder. Bleeding disorders can be congenital or acquired (Table 7.9) [37] and due to either low levels of coagulation factors or platelet abnormalities. von Willebrand disease (vWD) and deficiencies of factor VIII, IX, and XI are the most common inherited coagulation factor deficiencies complicating pregnancy. General principles for management of congenital bleeding disorders in pregnancy can be found in Table 7.10 [37] and treatment options in Table 7.11 [40].

Table 7.9 Bleeding disorders in pregnancy

Congenital disorders
- von Willebrand disease
- Hemophilia A carrier
- Hemophilia B carrier
- Factor Xl deficiencies
- Other rare coagulation factor defects
- Hyperfibrinolytic disorders
- Platelet function disorders (e.g., Glanzmann thrombasthenia, Bernard-Soulier syndrome)

Acquired disorders
- ITP
- TTP
- HELLP syndrome
- Drug-related thrombocytopenia
- Acquired factor VIII deficiency
- DIC
- Anticoagulants (oral, intravenous, subcutaneous)
- Vitamin K deficiency
- Antiplatelet agents (e.g., acetylsalicylic acid, nonsteroidal anti-inflammatories)
- Renal failure

DIC disseminated intravascular coagulation, *HELLP* hemolysis, elevated liver enzymes, low platelets, *ITP* immune thrombocytopenia purpura, *TTP* thrombotic thrombocytopenic purpura
Source: Tinmouth AT RM. Bleeding Disorders: 2nd ed. Rosene- Montella K KE, Barbour LA, Lee RV., editors. Philadelphia PA: American College Of Physicians; 2008, with permission

Table 7.10 General principles for management of pregnancy in patients with congenital bleeding disorders

- Close liaison between a hematologist/hemophilia treatment center and the obstetrical service
- Prepregnancy counseling including determination of coagulation factor/vWF levels or carrier status
- Baseline coagulation factor/vWF levels early in pregnancy and at 28 to 32 weeks of gestation
- Fetal sex determination for hemophilia carriers
- Prenatal fetal diagnosis for hemophilia carriers
- Elective cesarean section not routinely indicated
- Prophylactic therapy for invasive procedures and delivery if coagulation factor levels decreased
- Fetal scalp electrodes and blood sampling should be avoided for any potentially affected fetuses
- Vacuum extraction and forceps delivery should be avoided for any potentially affected
- Cord blood sampling for clotting factor levels for any potentially affected fetuses
- Vitamin K by mouth for any potentially affected fetuses
- Circumcision should be delayed until coagulation factor level is known and appropriate management arranged

Source: Tinmouth AT RM. Bleeding Disorders. 2nd ed. Rosene-Montella K KE, Barbour LA, Lee RV., editor. Philadelphia, PA: American College of Physicians; 2008
vWF von Willebrand factor

7 Special Hematologic Issues in the Pregnant Patient

Table 7.11 Treatment options for factor deficiencies

Inherited bleeding disorder	Preferred therapeutic option	Secondary options
von Willebrand disease	DDAVP or vWF containing concentrates	Platelets (in type 2B vsd)
Hemophilia A carrier	DDAVP or rFVIII	FVIII concentrate
Hemophilia B carrier	rFIX	FIX concentrate
Fibrinogen abnormalities	Fibrinogen concentrate	Plasma
FII deficiency	Prothrombin complex concentrates (PCC)	Plasma
FV deficiency	Plasma	
FVII deficiency	rFVIIa	FVII concentrate
FV and FVII deficiency	Plasma or FVIII	FVIII concentrate
FX deficiency	PCC	Plasma
FXI deficiency	FXI concentrates, rFVIIa, or tranexamic acid	Plasma
FXIII deficiency	FXIII concentrates	Plasma

Modified from Huq F and Kadir R. Haemophilia. 2011; 17 (suppl1), 20–30.

von Willebrand Disease

von Willebrand disease (vWD) is the most common inherited bleeding disorder and found in approximately 1 % of the general population [41]. von Willebrand factor (vWF) is the primary plasma protein required for platelet adhesion and is important for platelet aggregation. Absence or reduced amounts of vWF or an abnormal vWF protein results in defective platelet adhesion and aggregation that leads to mucocutaneous bleeding. There are several variants. The majority (75 %) of patients have type 1 vWD, which is a result of a partial, quantitative deficiency of vWF. Type 2 vWD is less common. It is caused by a qualitative defect and has several subtypes: type 2a, type 2b, type 2 N, and type 2 M. Both types 1 and 2 are autosomal dominant modes of inheritance. Type 3 vWD is autosomal recessive with incomplete penetrance. It is characterized by severe deficiency in vWF resulting in a deficiency in factor VIII (FVIII) and is the most rare of the three [42].

The diagnosis of vWD is based on a clinical history of bruising or bleeding. Characteristics and laboratory findings of von Willebrand disease can be found in Table 7.12 [37]. Levels of vWF are also affected by ABO blood groups and levels do not always correspond with bleeding phenotype [43]. A healthcare provider experienced in bleeding disorders should follow patients.

There is no evidence that vWD affects fertility or the rate of miscarriage [44]. In two reviews, pregnant women with vWD demonstrated a higher rate of bleeding episodes in the form of threatened miscarriage or antepartum bleeding. Of 31 pregnant women with vWD in a UK study, first-trimester vaginal bleeding was reported in 33 % of pregnancies, compared to 7–19 % in the general population. This was further supported by a US study in which pregnant women with vWD were ten times more likely to present with antepartum bleeding [45].

Table 7.12 von Willebrand disease characteristics and laboratory findings

Type	Characteristic	Diagnostic laboratory findings
1	Partial quantitative deficiency	Factor VIII, vWF:Ag, vWF: RCoF proportionately decreased
		Normal multimer pattern
2A	Loss of high molecular weight multimers	vWF:RCoF disproportionately decreased
		Loss of high molecular weight multimers on electrophoresis gel
2B	Increased affinity of vWF multimers to platelet glycoprotein Ib/IX	vWF:RCoF disproportionately decreased
		Decrease in high molecular weight multimers on electrophoreses gel
		Increased ristocetin-induced platelet aggregation
		Decreased platelets
2M	Decreased platelet activity with preservation of high molecular weight multimers	vWF:RCoF disproportionately decreased
		Normal multimer pattern
		Factor VIII disproportionately decreased
2N	Decreased binding of factor VIII	Absent vWF:Ag, vWF:RCoF
3	Absence or near absence of detectable vWF	No multimers on electrophoresis gel

Source: Tinmouth AT RM. Bleeding Disorders. 2nd ed. Rosene-Montella K KE, Barbour LA, Lee RV., editors. Philadelphia, PA: American College of Physicians; 2008, with permission
RcoF ristocetin cofactor, *vWF* von Willebrand factor

Elevated estrogen levels in pregnancy result in an increase in vWF and FVIII beginning in the early second trimester and peaking between 29 and 35 weeks. The majority of patients with type 1 vWD normalize levels of vWF and FVIII during pregnancy, but patients with severe disease may not. The response rate of vWF and FVIII in individual pregnancies is unpredictable, and it is recommended that measurement of vWF levels be done between 32 and 34 weeks of pregnancy for delivery planning and both immediately postpartum and at 2 to 3 weeks after delivery when plasma levels may fall rapidly and bleeding may occur [46, 47]. Levels of vWF may increase in patients with type 2 vWD, but functional levels may not be changed because of the production of functionally deficient proteins. In type 3 vWD, levels generally do not increase with pregnancy.

For epidural anesthesia and delivery vWF and FVIII, levels should be at least 50 IU/dL. Prophylactic therapy should be considered for levels less than this, which is usually desmopressin acetate (DDAVP) for type 1 and some type 2 vWDs at the time of parturition, particularly with cesarean delivery, and for approximately 3 to 5 days afterward [48–50]. Both intravenous and intranasal formulations are safe in the second and third trimesters. However, intranasal DDAVP is generally reserved for less serious bleeding in an outpatient setting. Typical intravenous dosing is 0.3 mcg/kg IV every 8 to 12 hours. Judicious use of fluids is recommended with the use of DDAVP to avoid severe hyponatremia related to diabetes insipidus. Tachyphylaxis can occur with repeated doses of DDAVP. For type 3 vWD, levels remain low or unmeasurable during pregnancy and replacement therapy with vWF concentrates is needed during labor and postpartum [44]. In type 2B vWD, thrombocytopenia may develop or worsen during pregnancy. However, whether this thrombocytopenia exacerbates bleeding is unclear [51]. Some of these patients may require vWF concentrates.

Other Congenital Disorders of Coagulation

Other congenital disorders of coagulation are less common and include hemophilia A and B and factor XI deficiency. All of these can also be sporadic as well as inherited. Hemophilia A and B are X-linked disorders. Female carriers of hemophilia A and B may have decreased levels of factor VIII and IX, respectively, with associated bleeding risks. Normally, factor levels in female carriers are greater than 50 %, but levels can be quite variable. In 10 to 20 % of carriers, coagulation factors are less than 40 %. Diagnosis is made by family history of hemophilia and measuring individual coagulation factor levels with or without genetic analysis. Hematologists experienced in treating hemophilia and associated with an institution with a hemophilia or bleeding disorder comprehensive care clinic should follow these women [37]. Factor VIII levels discussed above in vWD tend to rise in the second and third trimester but can be variable. Factor IX levels tend to remain unchanged during pregnancy. Baseline coagulation factors should be established early in pregnancy and rechecked in the third trimester and prior to invasive procedures. No treatment is required for levels above 0.5 U/mL. For levels below 0.5 U/mL, factor should be given prior to delivery or invasive procedures. General recommendations are to keep the levels above 0.5U/mL for 3 to 4 days after vaginal delivery and 4 to 5 days for a cesarean section.

Factor XI deficiency is relatively rare affecting 5 % of all patients with bleeding disorders. Diagnosis is usually made by family history or investigation of a bleeding disorder. Although an aPTT can be elevated in patients with factor XI levels less than 30 %, factor XI assays are required for diagnosis. In general, patients who are homozygous or compound heterozygotes have low factor levels, less than 20 %, and bleeding problems with hemostatic challenge. Heterozygotes have factor XI levels between 20 and 60 % with variable bleeding complications [52]. Bleeding is less severe and less predictable than hemophilia A and B [53]. Levels of factor XI during pregnancy have been reported as both increased and decreased [54–57]. Treatment decisions are based on bleeding history and factor XI levels with a goal factor XI level of 0.7 U/mL during delivery and cesarean section or other procedures [37]. Treatment options include fresh frozen plasma (FFP), factor XI concentrate, and recombinant factor VIIa. Given the limited availability of factor XI concentrate and the small amount of factor XI in FFP, the use of recombinant factor VIIa is favored [58].

Acquired Disorders

Acquired factor VIII inhibitor (acquired hemophilia A) is a rare disorder caused when autoantibodies develop against factor VIII. It is often associated with pregnancy, malignancy, pemphigoid, rheumatoid arthritis, systemic lupus erythematosus, and other autoimmune diseases. However, in about half the patients, no clinical association is identified [59]. Approximately 10 to 15 % of cases are associated with pregnancy [60]. The majority of cases occur during the postpartum period, usually within 4 months of delivery. Bleeding symptoms can vary and are associated with the level of antibody activity and can be life threatening. Treatment consists of controlling bleeding and therapy to eradicate the inhibitor. For patient with low antibody titer levels (<10 Bethesda units), factor VIII concentrates can be used. Patients with high titer antibodies are treated with bypassing agents. Treatment aimed at eradicating the inhibitor consists of immunosuppressive therapy usually alone or with cyclophosphamide. Cyclophosphamide and other alkylating agents should be avoided in women who desire future fertility [61]. Rituximab is recommended for second line treatment. There is limited data on first-line use of rituximab, but large prospective trials are lacking [62].

Thrombophilia and Thromboembolism

Pregnancy and the puerperium are hypercoagulable states that prepare for the bleeding challenge of delivery. Pregnancy increases the risk of thromboembolism four to five times and cesarean section doubles that risk [63]. Venodilitation with venous stasis is a progesterone effect that begins early in pregnancy. The majority of pregnancy-related thrombotic events are venous thromboembolic (VTE): deep venous thrombi (DVT) with pulmonary emboli (PE) are less common. Most VTE occur during pregnancy, but more than one third occur postpartum [64]. Arterial thromboembolism risk is also increased during pregnancy.

Many coagulation factors (fibrinogen, factors V, VII, VIII, X, and vWF) increase during normal pregnancy by 20 % to 100 % from the first to the third trimester (Table 7.13) [1]. Plasminogen activator inhibitor types 1 and 2 are also increased. Factor XI and protein S decrease, while other coagulation factors, such as II and IX, remain the same [65]. Fibrinolysis is decreased. Thrombotic changes associated with pregnancy according to Virchow's triad are outlined in Fig. 7.1 [66]. The majority of DVTs (greater than 90 %) occur in the left leg likely due to compression of the iliac vein by the iliac artery and later from the compression of the pelvic vessels by the gravid uterus [67]. Pregnancy-associated VTE is associated not only with the acute morbidity from acute DVT and PE but also long-term morbidity including an 80 % risk of postthrombotic syndrome and a 65 % risk of deep venous insufficiency [68]. Pulmonary embolism continues to be the leading cause of maternal mortality in developed nations, so appropriate thromboprophylaxis and prompt diagnosis and treatment are needed.

Table 7.13 Changes in coagulation factor levels in pregnancy

Coagulation factor	Changes in pregnancy (percent)
Fibrinogen	↑(175-46)
Thrombin (factor ll)	↔
Factor V	↑ (0–30)
Factor Vlll	↑ (55–70)
Factor lX	↔
Factor X	↑(22–23)
Factor Xl	↓(10–40)
vWF antigen	↑(87–100)
vWF RCoF	↑ (100)
Protein C	↔
Protein S (total)	↓(7–16)
Protein S (free)	↓(30–54)
PA 1-1	↑(58)
PA 1-2	↑(385)

PA 1-1, plasminogen activator inhibitor 1; PA 1-2, plasminogen activator inhibitor 2; vWF von Willebrand facto; vWF RCoF, von Willebrand factor ristocetin cofactor
Source: Rodger M. Normal Hematologic Changes in Pregnancy, 2nd ed. Rosene – Montella K KE, Barbour LA, Lee RV., editors. Philadelphia, PA, USA: American College of Physicians; 2008, with permission

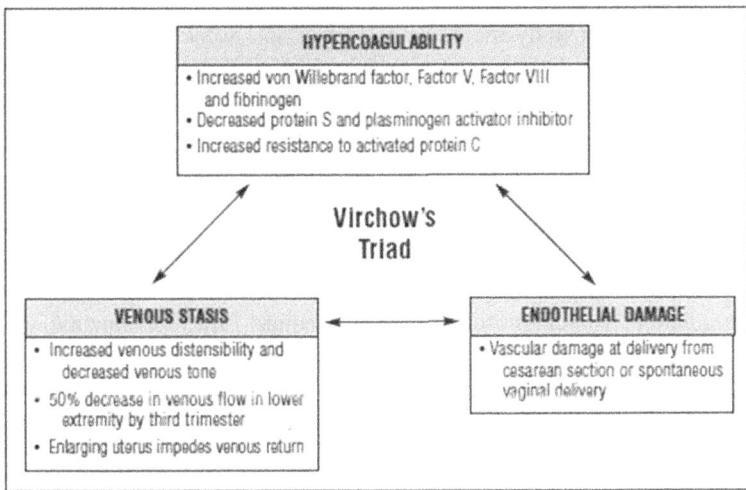

Fig. 7.1 Thrombotic changes associated with pregnancy according to Virchow's triad. Source: Rodger M R-MK, Barbour LA. Acute Thromboembolic Disease. 2nd ed. Rosene-Montella K KE, Barbour LA, Lee RV., editor. Philadelphia, PA, USA: American College of Physicians; 2008, with permission

Risk factors for VTE in pregnancy can be inherited or acquired. The most important individual risk factor for VTE in pregnancy is a personal history of thrombosis, followed by thrombophilia and family history. Approximately 20 to 50 % of pregnancy-associated thromboembolic events are associated with a thrombophilic disorder [69, 70], and 15–25 % of all cases are recurrent events. Factor V Leiden and prothrombin gene mutation are the most commonly inherited thrombophilias and antiphospholipid syndrome the most common acquired risk factor for VTE. Indications for a diagnostic evaluation of thrombophilia in pregnancy include previous VTE and family history of thrombophilia. Screening is no longer recommended by ACOG in all women with placenta-mediated pregnancy complications (i.e., pregnancy loss, IUGR, preeclampsia, and placenta abruptions), with the exception of antiphospholipid antibody screening for which there is data on efficacy of treatment. In women with a prior VTE and thrombophilia, the risk of a recurrent VTE in pregnancy is approximately 20 % [71]. The type of thrombophilia can aid in selection of treatment plans.

Diagnosis of VTE in pregnancy is made more difficult by a scarcity of literature on diagnostic management and a lack of validation of diagnostic imaging procedures. Guidelines are largely extrapolated from data in nonpregnant patients due to concern over radiation exposure to the fetus and mother. However, diagnostic evaluation for PE exposes the fetus to significantly less than the total pregnancy exposure of 5 rads recommended by the National Commission on Radiation Protection. Efforts to limit exposure should be attempted but must be weighed against the risk of an undiagnosed VTE. The diagnostic test of choice for DVT during pregnancy is compression ultrasonography. If the ultrasound is negative and clinically suspicion remains high, a repeat study should be performed in 1 week or earlier for progressive symptoms. Since iliofemoral and pelvic clot can arise de novo in pregnancy, MRV should be considered if repeat ultrasound fails to diagnose pelvic clot and symptoms persist. A proposed algorithm is found in Fig. 7.2 [66]. The diagnosis of PE in pregnancy, as in nonpregnant patients, can be a diagnostic challenge. The majority of pregnant patients with documented PE will have a normal A-a gradient so diagnostic testing is required for all patients suspected of having a PE. For suspected pulmonary embolus, initial work-up with a ventilation/perfusion (V/Q) scan is recommended or CT angiography with bismuth breast shields to reduce maternal breast irradiation. Nondiagnostic V/Q scans require further evaluation with CT angiography. D-dimers are unreliable in pregnancy as levels increase throughout normal pregnancy and remain elevated postpartum but have some clinical utility in patients with a high clinical suspicion of VTE in guiding diagnostic tests [72].

VTE in pregnancy warrants immediate anticoagulation. Warfarin is teratogenic and should be avoided in pregnancy for this indication. Therapeutic intravenous or subcutaneous unfractionated heparin (UFH) may be used as initial therapy. UFH carries a substantial risk of osteoporosis and a 2 to 3 % incidence of vertebral fractures when used throughout pregnancy [73]. Low molecular weight heparin (LMWH) is the preferred long-term anticoagulant in pregnancy. It has a better pharmacokinetic profile and a substantially lower risk of heparin-induced thrombocytopenia. Dose adjustments are required as pregnancy progresses and GFR and weight increase. LMWH is contraindicated in renal failure and has limited use in patients with high

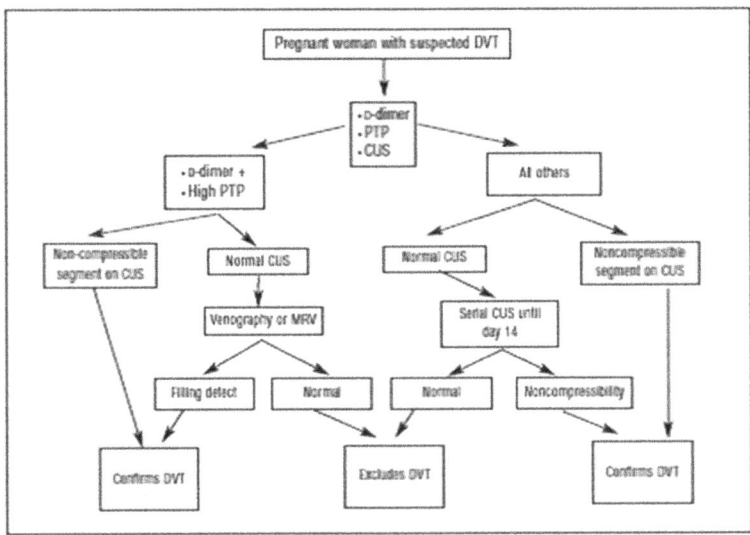

Fig. 7.2 Management of suspected DVT in pregnancy. *CUS* venous compression ultrasound imaging, *DVT* deep vein thrombosis, *PTP* pretest probability. Source: Rodger M R-MK, Barbour LA. Acute Thromboembolic Disease. 2nd ed. Rosene-Montella K KE, Barbour LA, Lee RV., editor. Philadelphia, PA, USA: American College of Physicians; 2008, with permission

bleeding risk or who need imminent surgery. When LMWH is used, anti-Xa levels should be closely monitored.

Patients who are on LMWH may be converted to unfractionated heparin at 34–36 weeks, due to its shorter half-life and reversibility to increase the likelihood that a patient can get epidural anesthesia and to decrease bleeding risk at delivery. Resumption of anticoagulation 4–6 hours after a vaginal delivery and 6–12 hours after cesarean section is recommended. In patients who have acute or high-risk thrombosis close to term, a temporary IVC filter may be used when anticoagulation is interrupted.

A paucity of trials regarding prevention and treatment of primary and recurrent thrombosis in pregnancy exists. Most guidelines recommend thromboprophylaxis in pregnant patients with prior thrombosis without a transient risk factor, or in whom the transient risk factor was estrogen containing oral contraceptives or pregnancy. The American College of Obstetricians and Gynecologists recommend prophylactic use of pneumatic compression devices before cesarean section for all women not already receiving anticoagulation due to the substantial risk of VTE in these patients [63].

Other Thromboses

Pregnancy is also associated with unusual thromboses. Ovarian vein thrombosis may occur in pregnant or postpartum patients, usually in the setting of infection, and may present as fever and flank pain. It predominantly occurs on the right side.

Due to reported cases of propagation into the inferior vena cava and embolization, treatment should be the same as for other DVT [74]. Pregnancy and the postpartum period are associated with an increased risk of cerebral venous thrombosis, which frequently presents as a severe headache that may or may not have neurological symptoms. MRI/MRV is recommended for diagnosis. Prothrombin gene mutation and factor V Leiden gene have been associated with an increased risk of cerebral venous thrombosis.

Hematological Malignancies

Hematological malignancies are a rare complication in pregnancy. However, in the United States, malignancy is the second leading cause of maternal death. Hematologic malignancies represent 25 % of malignancies diagnosed in pregnancy [75]. Hodgkin lymphoma is the most common, affecting 1 in 1000 to 6000 pregnancies [76] followed by non-Hodgkin lymphoma and acute and chronic leukemias. Management of hematological malignancies requires balancing the need for immediate therapy and its maternal and fetal effects with the effect of the natural progression of the disease on the fetus and the pregnancy. Treatment decisions must take into consideration gestational age, clinical stage of disease, and patient preferences. Within these limitations, treatment decisions should try and mimic that of nonpregnant patients, so that necessary treatment or diagnostic evaluation is not withheld due to pregnancy. A multi-specialty team including hematologists, high-risk obstetricians, obstetric internists, social workers, geneticists, and clergy is recommended.

Diagnosis and staging can be challenging in pregnancy. An excisional biopsy of a lymph node is preferred for lymphomas. Bone marrow aspiration and biopsy may safely be performed. X-rays and non-contrast MRIs both with abdominal shielding and ultrasound are preferred over CT scans. PET scans and bone scans should be used when their utility in guiding treatment outweighs the risk of exposure.

Whenever possible treatment should be deferred until the second trimester after organogenesis is completed. Chemotherapy in the first trimester has been associated with spontaneous abortion and carries a significant risk of congenital abnormalities. The risk of congenital malformations in the first trimester is estimated at 10 % for single-agent chemotherapy and 15–35 % with combination therapy [77, 78]. Vincristine has the lowest risk and alkylating agents and antimetabolites, the highest risk [78]. Therapeutic abortion is recommended if chemotherapy cannot be delayed. The risk of congenital malformations approaches that of the nonpregnant population for most chemotherapeutic agents after the first trimester. To date studies of offspring have not shown significant short- or long-term effects on the exposed fetus [79–81].

Treatment regimens should be tailored individually and based on the latest available data. Standard doses of drugs should be used adjusted to continuing weight gain. Melphalan and procarbazine, both alkylating agents, should not be used in pregnancy due to limited case series showing a significant risk of early and late spontaneous abortion and congenital malformations [82]. Thalidomide and lenalidomide are contraindicated in pregnancy as they are highly teratogenic. Most experts recommend avoidance of the antimetabolite methotrexate (which has both a dose- and trimester-dependent effect) during pregnancy, unless no alternative exists [83]. Many newer agents, including monoclonal antibodies and tyrosine kinase inhibitors, lack data. Interferon therapy appears to be safe in pregnancy with forty cases of successful use in the literature with only one case of fetal malformation with concurrent use of hydroxyurea but may adversely affect future fertility. The choice of chemotherapeutic agents must be weighed against the benefit and availability of alternative therapies. Recommendations should be based on the most recent published literature. Radiation therapy is generally avoided but can be used in certain limited situations with extreme precautions [82].

Delivery indications are usually the same as for nonpregnant patients. However, delivery should be planned at least 2 weeks after chemotherapy to allow for recovery of maternal and fetal blood counts. The placenta should be sent for pathology at delivery. The majority of pregnant women presenting with a hematological malignancy have prognoses similar to nonpregnant patients and normal pregnancy outcomes [82].

References

1. Rodger M. Normal hematologic changes in pregnancy. 2nd ed. In: In: Medical Care of the Pregnant Patient. Rosene-Montella KKE, Barbour LA, Lee RV, editors. Philadelphia, PA, American College of Physicians; 2008
2. Taylor DJ, Lind T. Red cell mass during and after normal pregnancy. Br J Obstet Gynaecol. 1979;86(5):364–70. Epub 1979/05/01.
3. Whittaker PG, Macphail S, Lind T. Serial hematologic changes and pregnancy outcome. Obstet Gynecol. 1996;88(1):33–9. Epub 1996/07/01.
4. Centers for Disease. CDC criteria for anemia in children and childbearing-aged women. MMWR. 1989;38(22):400–4. Epub 1989/06/09.
5. Messer RH. Pregnancy anemias. Clin Obstet Gynecol. 1974;17(4):163–84. Epub 1974/12/01.
6. Carles G, Tobal N, Raynal P, Herault S, Beucher G, Marret H, et al. Doppler assessment of the fetal cerebral hemodynamic response to moderate or severe maternal anemia. Am J Obstet Gynecol. 2003;188(3):794–9. Epub 2003/03/14.
7. Sifakis S, Pharmakides G. Anemia in pregnancy. Ann N Y Acad Sci. 2000;900:125–36. Epub 2000/05/20.
8. Brabin BJ, Hakimi M, Pelletier D. An analysis of anemia and pregnancy-related maternal mortality. J Nutr. 2001;131(2S-2):604S–14S. discussion 14S–15S. Epub 2001/02/13.
9. Mani S, Duffy TP. Anemia of pregnancy. Clin Perinatol. 1995;22(3):593–607. Epub 1995/09/01.
10. Bridges KR SP. Disorders of iron metabolism. RI H, editor1995.
11. Breymann C, Visca E, Huch R, Huch A. Efficacy and safety of intravenously administered iron sucrose with and without adjuvant recombinant human erythropoietin for the treatment of resistant iron-deficiency anemia during pregnancy. Am J Obstet Gynecol. 2001;184(4):662–7. Epub 2001/03/23.
12. Shojania AM. Folic acid and vitamin B12 deficiency in pregnancy and in the neonatal period. Clin Perinatol. 1984;11(2):433–59. Epub 1984/06/01.

13. Hassell K. Hemoglobinopathies, Thalassemias, and Anemia: Hemoglobinopathies and Thalassemias. 2nd ed. Rosene-Montella K KE, Barbour LA, Lee RV., editor. Philadelphia, PA: American College of Physicians; 2008
14. Cines DB, Pollak ES, Buck CA, Loscalzo J, Zimmerman GA, McEver RP, et al. Endothelial cells in physiology and in the pathophysiology of vascular disorders. Blood. 1998;91(10):3527–61. Epub 1998/06/20.
15. Smith JA, Espeland M, Bellevue R, Bonds D, Brown AK, Koshy M. Pregnancy in sickle cell disease: experience of the Cooperative Study of Sickle Cell Disease. Obstet Gynecol. 1996;87(2):199–204. Epub 1996/02/01.
16. Serjeant GR, Loy LL, Crowther M, Hambleton IR, Thame M. Outcome of pregnancy in homozygous sickle cell disease. Obstet Gynecol. 2004;103(6):1278–85. Epub 2004/06/03.
17. Hassell K. Pregnancy and sickle cell disease. Hematol Oncol Clin N Am. 2005;19(5):903–16. vii–viii. Epub 2005/10/11.
18. Rappaport VJ, Velazquez M, Williams K. Hemoglobinopathies in pregnancy. Obstet Gynecol Clin N Am. 2004;31(2):287–317. vi. Epub 2004/06/18.
19. Rathmell JP, Viscomi CM, Ashburn MA. Management of nonobstetric pain during pregnancy and lactation. Anesth Analg. 1997;85(5):1074–87. Epub 1997/11/14.
20. Koshy M, Burd L, Wallace D, Moawad A, Baron J. Prophylactic red-cell transfusions in pregnant patients with sickle cell disease. A randomized cooperative study. N Engl J Med. 1988;319(22):1447–52. Epub 1988/12/01.
21. Mahomed K. Prophylactic versus selective blood transfusion for sickle cell anaemia during pregnancy (Review). Cochrane Database Syst Rev. 2005;1, CD000040.
22. Wanko SO, Telen MJ. Transfusion management in sickle cell disease. Hematol Oncol Clin N Am. 2005;19(5):803–26. v–vi. Epub 2005/10/11.
23. Tuck SM, Studd JW, White JM. Pregnancy in women with sickle cell trait. Br J Obstet Gynaecol. 1983;90(2):108–11. Epub 1983/02/01.
24. Kilpatrick SJ, Laros RK. Thalassemia in pregnancy. Clin Obstet Gynecol. 1995;38(3):485–96. Epub 1995/09/01.
25. Mordel N, Birkenfeld A, Goldfarb AN, Rachmilewitz EA. Successful full-term pregnancy in homozygous beta-thalassemia major: case report and review of the literature. Obstet Gynecol. 1989;73(5 Pt 2):837–40. Epub 1989/05/01.
26. Neunert C, Lim W, Crowther M, Cohen A, Solberg Jr L, Crowther MA, et al. The American Society of Hematology 2011 evidence-based practice guideline for immune thrombocytopenia. Blood. 2011;117(16):4190–207. Epub 2011/02/18.
27. Karovitch A RM. Thrombocytopenia. 2nd ed. In: Medical Care of the Pregnant Patient. Rosene-Montella K KE, Barbour LA, Lee RL., editors. Philadelphia, PA: American College of Physicians; 2008
28. Provan D et al. British Journal of Haematology Guidelines. Br J Haematol. 2003(120): 574–96
29. George JN, Woolf SH, Raskob GE, Wasser JS, Aledort LM, Ballem PJ, et al. Idiopathic thrombocytopenic purpura: a practice guideline developed by explicit methods for the American Society of Hematology. Blood. 1996;88(1):3–40. Epub 1996/07/01.
30. Gernsheimer T, McCrae KR. Immune thrombocytopenic purpura in pregnancy. Curr Opin Hematol. 2007;14(5):574–80. Epub 2007/10/16.
31. Herold M, Schnohr S, Bittrich H. Efficacy and safety of a combined rituximab chemotherapy during pregnancy. J Clin Oncol. 2001;19(14):3439. Epub 2001/07/17.
32. Kimby E, Sverrisdottir A, Elinder G. Safety of rituximab therapy during the first trimester of pregnancy: a case history. Eur J Haematol. 2004;72(4):292–5. Epub 2004/04/20.
33. McCrae KR. Thrombocytopenia in pregnancy. Hematology Am Soc Hematol Am Soc Hematol Educ Progr. 2010;2010:397–402. Epub 2011/01/18.
34. Sibai BM. Diagnosis, controversies, and management of the syndrome of hemolysis, elevated liver enzymes, and low platelet count. Obstet Gynecol. 2004;103(5 Pt 1):981–91. Epub 2004/05/04.

35. Woudstra DM, Chandra S, Hofmeyr GJ, Dowswell T. Corticosteroids for HELLP (hemolysis, elevated liver enzymes, low platelets) syndrome in pregnancy. Cochrane Database Syst Rev. 2010;9, CD008148. Epub 2010/09/09.
36. Levi M, Toh CH, Thachil J, Watson HG. Guidelines for the diagnosis and management of disseminated intravascular coagulation. British Committee for Standards in Haematology. Br J Haematol. 2009;145(1):24–33. Epub 2009/02/19.
37. Tinmouth AT RM. Bleeding Disorders. 2nd ed. Rosene-Montella K KE, Barbour LA, Lee RV., editor. Philadelphia, PA: American College of Physicians; 2008
38. Schulman S, Johnsson H, Egberg N, Blomback M. DDAVP-induced correction of prolonged bleeding time in patients with congenital platelet function defects. Thromb Res. 1987;45(2):165–74. Epub 1987/01/15.
39. Poon MC, D'Oiron R, Von Depka M, Khair K, Negrier C, Karafoulidou A, et al. Prophylactic and therapeutic recombinant factor VIIa administration to patients with Glanzmann's thrombasthenia: results of an international survey. J Thromb Haemost. 2004;2(7):1096–103. Epub 2004/06/29.
40. Huq FY, Kadir RA. Management of pregnancy, labour and delivery in women with inherited bleeding disorders. Haemophilia. 2011;17 Suppl 1:20–30. Epub 2011/07/01.
41. Rodeghiero F, Castaman G, Dini E. Epidemiological investigation of the prevalence of von Willebrand's disease. Blood. 1987;69(2):454–9. Epub 1987/02/01.
42. Sadler JE. A revised classification of von Willebrand disease. For the Subcommittee on von Willebrand Factor of the Scientific and Standardization Committee of the International Society on Thrombosis and Haemostasis Thrombosis and haemostasis. Thromb Haemostat. 1994;71(4):520–5. Epub 1994/04/01.
43. Gill JC, Endres-Brooks J, Bauer PJ, Marks Jr WJ, Montgomery RR. The effect of ABO blood group on the diagnosis of von Willebrand disease. Blood. 1987;69(6):1691–5. Epub 1987/06/01.
44. Lak M, Peyvandi F, Mannucci PM. Clinical manifestations and complications of childbirth and replacement therapy in 385 Iranian patients with type 3 von Willebrand disease. Br J Haematol. 2000;111(4):1236–9. Epub 2001/02/13.
45. Chi C, Bapir M, Lee CA, Kadir RA. Puerperal loss (lochia) in women with or without inherited bleeding disorders. Am J Obstet Gynecol. 2010;203(1):56 e1–5. Epub 2010/04/27.
46. Conti M, Mari D, Conti E, Muggiasca ML, Mannucci PM. Pregnancy in women with different types of von Willebrand disease. Obstet Gynecol. 1986;68(2):282–5. Epub 1986/08/01.
47. Roque H, Funai E, Lockwood CJ. von Willebrand disease and pregnancy. J Mater Fetal Med. 2000;9(5):257–66. Epub 2001/01/02.
48. Mannucci PM. How I, treat patients with von Willebrand disease. Blood. 2001;97(7):1915–9. Epub 2001/03/27.
49. Pacheco LD, Costantine MM, Saade GR, Mucowski S, Hankins GD, Sciscione AC. von Willebrand disease and pregnancy: a practical approach for the diagnosis and treatment. Am J Obstet Gynecol. 2010;203(3):194–200. Epub 2010/04/27.
50. Lee CA, Chi C, Pavord SR, Bolton-Maggs PH, Pollard D, Hinchcliffe-Wood A, et al. The obstetric and gynaecological management of women with inherited bleeding disorders–review with guidelines produced by a taskforce of UK Haemophilia Centre Doctors' Organization. Haemophilia. 2006;12(4):301–36. Epub 2006/07/13.
51. Pareti FI, Federici AB, Cattaneo M, Mannucci PM. Spontaneous platelet aggregation during pregnancy in a patient with von Willebrand disease type IIB can be blocked by monoclonal antibodies to both platelet glycoproteins Ib and IIb/IIIa. Br J Haematol. 1990;75(1):86–91. Epub 1990/05/01.
52. Bolton-Maggs PH. Factor XI, deficiency and its management. Haemophilia. 2000;6 Suppl 1:100–9. Epub 2000/09/12.
53. Bolton-Maggs PH. Bleeding problems in factor XI deficient women. Haemophilia. 1999;5(3):155–9. Epub 1999/08/12.

54. Condie RG, Ogston D. Sequential studies on components of the haemostatic mechanism in pregnancy with particular reference to the development of pre-eclampsia. Br J Obstet Gynaecol. 1976;83(12):938–42. Epub 1976/12/01.
55. Bremme KA. Haemostatic changes in pregnancy. Best Pract Res Clin Haematol. 2003;16(2):153–68. Epub 2003/05/24.
56. Clark P, Brennand J, Conkie JA, McCall F, Greer IA, Walker ID. Activated protein C sensitivity, protein C, protein S and coagulation in normal pregnancy. Thromb Haemost. 1998;79(6):1166–70. Epub 1998/07/10.
57. Nossel HL, Lanzkowsky P, Levy S, Mibashan RS, Hansen JD. A study of coagulation factor levels in women during labour and in their newborn infants. Thrombosis et diathesis haemorrhagica. 1966;16(1):185–97. Epub 1966/07/31.
58. Myers B, Pavord S, Kean L, Hill M, Dolan G. Pregnancy outcome in Factor XI deficiency: incidence of miscarriage, antenatal and postnatal haemorrhage in 33 women with Factor XI deficiency. BJOG. 2007;114(5):643–6. Epub 2007/04/19.
59. Green D, Lechner K. A survey of 215 non-hemophilic patients with inhibitors to Factor VIII. Thromb Haemost. 1981;45(3):200–3. Epub 1981/06/30.
60. Delgado J, Jimenez-Yuste V, Hernandez-Navarro F, Villar A. Acquired haemophilia: review and meta-analysis focused on therapy and prognostic factors. Br J Haematol. 2003;121(1):21–35. Epub 2003/04/03.
61. Hay CR, Brown S, Collins PW, Keeling DM, Liesner R. The diagnosis and management of factor VIII and IX inhibitors: a guideline from the United Kingdom Haemophilia Centre Doctors Organisation. Br J Haematol. 2006;133(6):591–605. Epub 2006/05/18.
62. Franchini M, Lippi G. Acquired factor VIII inhibitors. Blood. 2008;112(2):250–5. Epub 2008/05/09.
63. Wright JD, Pawar N, Gonzalez JS, Lewin SN, Burke WM, Simpson LL, et al. Scientific evidence underlying the American College of Obstetricians and Gynecologists' practice bulletins. Obstet Gynecol. 2011;118(3):505–12. Epub 2011/08/10.
64. Gherman RB, Goodwin TM, Leung B, Byrne JD, Hethumumi R, Montoro M. Incidence, clinical characteristics, and timing of objectively diagnosed venous thromboembolism during pregnancy. Obstet Gynecol. 1999;94(5 Pt 1):730–4. Epub 1999/11/05.
65. Williams MD, Wheby MS. Anemia in pregnancy. Med Clin N Am. 1992;76(3):631–47. Epub 1992/05/01.
66. Rodger M R-MK, Barbour LA. Acute thromboembolic disease. 2nd ed. In: Rosene-Montella K KE, Barbour LA, Lee RV., editor. Philadelphia, PA: American College of Physicians; 2008.
67. Ray JG, Chan WS. Deep vein thrombosis during pregnancy and the puerperium: a meta-analysis of the period of risk and the leg of presentation. Obstet Gynecol Surv. 1999;54(4):265–71. Epub 1999/04/13.
68. Bergqvist A, Bergqvist D, Lindhagen A, Matzsch T. Late symptoms after pregnancy-related deep vein thrombosis. Br J Obstet Gynaecol. 1990;97(4):338–41. Epub 1990/04/01.
69. Robertson L, Wu O, Langhorne P, Twaddle S, Clark P, Lowe GD, et al. Thrombophilia in pregnancy: a systematic review. Br J Haematol. 2006;132(2):171–96. Epub 2006/01/10.
70. Gerhardt A, Scharf RE, Beckmann MW, Struve S, Bender HG, Pillny M, et al. Prothrombin and factor V mutations in women with a history of thrombosis during pregnancy and the puerperium. N Engl J Med. 2000;342(6):374–80. Epub 2000/02/10.
71. Brill-Edwards P, Ginsberg JS, Gent M, Hirsh J, Burrows R, Kearon C, et al. Safety of withholding heparin in pregnant women with a history of venous thromboembolism. Recurrence of Clot in This Pregnancy Study Group. N Engl J Med. 2000;343(20):1439–44. Epub 2000/11/18.
72. Kjellberg U, Andersson NE, Rosen S, Tengborn L, Hellgren M. APC resistance and other haemostatic variables during pregnancy and puerperium. Thromb Haemost. 1999;81(4):527–31. Epub 1999/05/11.
73. Ginsberg JS, Hirsh J. Use of antithrombotic agents during pregnancy. Chest. 1998;114(5 Suppl):524S–30S. Epub 1998/11/20.

74. DHSS. Report on confidential inquiries: maternal deaths in England and Wales 1986-1988. London: Office HMsS; 1991
75. Hurley TJ, McKinnell JV, Irani MS. Hematologic malignancies in pregnancy. Obstet Gynecol Clin N Am. 2005;32(4):595–614. Epub 2005/11/29.
76. Stewart Jr HL, Monto RW. Hodgkin's disease and pregnancy. Am J Obstet Gynecol. 1952;63(3):570–8. Epub 1952/03/01.
77. Doll DC, Ringenberg QS, Yarbro JW. Management of cancer during pregnancy. Arch Intern Med. 1988;148(9):2058–64. Epub 1988/09/01.
78. Doll DC, Ringenberg QS, Yarbro JW. Antineoplastic agents and pregnancy. Semin Oncol. 1989;16(5):337–46. Epub 1989/10/01.
79. Kalter H, Warkany J. Medical progress. Congenital malformations: etiologic factors and their role in prevention (first of two parts). N Engl J Med. 1983;308(8):424–31.
80. Shapira T, Pereg D, Lishner M. How I treat acute and chronic leukemia in pregnancy. Blood Rev. 2008;22(5):247–59. Epub 2008/05/13.
81. Aviles A, Neri N. Hematological malignancies and pregnancy: a final report of 84 children who received chemotherapy in utero. Clin Lymphoma. 2001;2(3):173–7. Epub 2002/01/10.
82. Rizack T, Rosene-Montella K. Special hematological issues in the pregnant patient. Hematology/Oncology Clinics of North America 2012;26(2):409–32.
83. Feldkamp M, Carey JC. Clinical teratology counseling and consultation case report: low dose methotrexate exposure in the early weeks of pregnancy. Teratology. 1993;47(6):533–9. Epub 1993/06/01.
84. Rizack T, Rosene-Montella K. Special hematological issues in the pregnant patient. Hematol Oncol Clin North Am. 2012;26(2):409–32.

Part VII
Hypertension/Preeclampsia

Chapter 8
Hypertensive Disorders of Pregnancy

Margaret A. Miller and Marshall Carpenter

Background

Hypertensive disorders in pregnancy are a major cause of both maternal and fetal morbidity and mortality and account for approximately one quarter of all antenatal admissions to the hospital [1]. The spectrum of hypertensive disorders in pregnancy includes preexisting hypertension, new-onset hypertension in pregnancy, as well as hypertension that may occur de novo in the postpartum period. Challenges in the management of hypertension in pregnancy include choosing when to use antihypertensive medication, goals of antihypertensive therapy, and which drugs to use. Recent data also show that hypertensive disorders of pregnancy are associated with long-term cardiovascular risks in women.

Definition

Hypertension in pregnancy is defined as systolic blood pressure >140 mmHg OR diastolic blood pressure >90 mmHg. Severe hypertension in pregnancy is defined as systolic blood pressure >160 mmHg OR diastolic blood pressure >110 mmHg [2].

M.A. Miller, M.D. (✉)
Obstetric Medicine, Women's Medicine Collaborative, The Miriam Hospital, Providence, RI, USA

The Warren Alpert Medical School of Brown University, Providence, RI, USA

M. Carpenter, M.D.
Women's Medicine Collaborative, The Miriam Hospital, Providence, RI, USA

Department of Obstetrics and Gynecology, Tufts University School of Medicine, Boston, MA, USA

Hypertensive disorders of pregnancy include four distinct clinical disorders including:

- Chronic hypertension
- Gestational hypertension
- Superimposed preeclampsia
- Preeclampsia

Table 8.1 outlines the common terminology used to describe the various clinical presentations of hypertensive disorders in pregnancy.

Table 8.1 Common terminology describing hypertensive disorders in pregnancy

Hypertensive disorders of pregnancy	
Chronic hypertension	Use of antihypertensive medication prior to pregnancy New-onset hypertension <20 weeks gestation Hypertension that presents initially in pregnancy, but does not resolve by 12 weeks postpartum is retrospectively diagnosed as chronic hypertension
Gestational hypertension	New-onset hypertension >20 weeks gestation without proteinuria or other evidence of preeclampsia Hypertension resolves by 12 weeks postpartum Also referred to as transient hypertension of pregnancy or pregnancy-induced hypertension

Preeclampsia	SBP>140 mmHg OR DBP>90 mmHg >20 weeks gestation with any of the following:
	• Proteinuria defined as:
	  • More than 300 mg protein in a 24-h urine
	  • Urine protein/creatinine ratio >0.3
	• Elevated transaminases to twice normal
	• Platelets <100,000/ml
	• Creatinine >1.1 mg/dl or doubling of baseline creatinine
	• Pulmonary edema
	• New-onset headache or visual disturbance

Superimposed preeclampsia	Underlying diagnosis of hypertension and >20 weeks gestation development of: • Worsening hypertension PLUS • New-onset proteinuria or increase in preexisting proteinuria OR • Other signs and symptoms of preeclampsia
Other clinical terms	
Severe preeclampsia	Preeclampsia with any of the following features SBP>160 mmHg OR DBP>110 mmHg >20 weeks gestation on at least 2 occasions, at least 1 h apart, while patient is on bed rest PLUS: • Platelets <100,000/ml • Transaminases elevated to twice normal, severe persistent RUQ or epigastric pain unresponsive to treatment no alternate diagnosis • Serum creatinine >1.1 or doubling of creatinine • Pulmonary edema • New-onset headache or visual disturbances
HELLP syndrome	Hemolysis, elevated liver enzymes, low platelets HELLP is considered a severe form of preeclampsia
Eclampsia	Preeclampsia with seizure

Overall hypertensive disorders affect up to 8 % of pregnancies in the USA [3], and up to 5 % of pregnancies are complicated by chronic hypertension [4–6]. Gestational hypertension is thought to occur in approximately 6 % of pregnancies, and 3–7 % of all pregnancies are complicated by preeclampsia [1, 7].

Pathophysiology

In normal pregnancy, blood pressure drops beginning in the first trimester and reaches a nadir by the end of the second trimester. The early drop in blood pressure is due to a significant reduction in peripheral vascular resistance mediated by endothelial production of vasodilating factors. During the third trimester, the blood pressure slowly rises back to the prepregnancy baseline. Because of this normal physiologic drop in blood pressure, chronic hypertension may be masked in the first half of pregnancy. It is important that blood pressure values in the first half of pregnancy are interpreted in the context of these known physiologic changes.

In the past 10 years, much has been learned about the pathophysiology of preeclampsia. Although the clinical manifestations of preeclampsia are not seen until after 20 weeks gestation, the underlying pathology begins much earlier in pregnancy. Research has now shown that preeclampsia likely starts at the time of placentation and is proposed to involve abnormal trophoblastic invasion of the maternal spiral arteries leading to decreased perfusion of the placenta [8, 9]. The ischemic placenta then triggers release of mediators that leads to endothelial dysfunction and altered angiogenesis leading to the clinical manifestations of the disorder. While hypertension and, previously, proteinuria are the hallmarks of the disease, preeclampsia is a multisystem disease that can affect all organ systems.

Chronic Hypertension

Risk of Chronic Hypertension in Pregnancy

Most women with chronic hypertension will have normal healthy pregnancies, especially if the hypertension is mild. Women with stage 1 hypertension (<160/100) who have no evidence of end-organ damage and are otherwise healthy have an excellent prognosis for pregnancy. The primary risk for women in this category is superimposed preeclampsia which occurs in approximately 20 % [5]. Women with severe hypertension (>160/100) have a risk of preeclampsia of 50 %, and women with the most severe disease including those who already have end-organ damage or have a secondary cause of hypertension, have been reported to have a risk of preeclampsia as high as 75 % [4, 10]. The incidence of both maternal and fetal adverse outcomes is related to the duration of disease, severity of disease, and whether or not the mother develops superimposed preeclampsia [11].

Maternal complications are primarily associated with preeclampsia and include a fivefold increase in maternal mortality, as well as an increased risk of maternal cerebrovascular event, pulmonary edema, seizure, and renal failure [12].

Fetal complications include an increased risk of premature birth, intrauterine growth restriction (IUGR), fetal demise, placental abruption, and cesarean delivery [13, 14]. Adverse fetal outcomes are also much more likely in women who develop superimposed preeclampsia [2].

Diagnosis

About 5–10 % of women enter pregnancy with a diagnosis of chronic hypertension [5]. In addition, the overwhelming majority of women who have new-onset hypertension prior to 20 weeks gestation will, ultimately, be diagnosed with chronic hypertension. Ideally a woman with chronic hypertension should have a comprehensive evaluation prior to pregnancy. The evaluation of chronic hypertension includes three components: (1) screening for secondary causes, (2) assessment for target organ damage, and (3) a review of cardiovascular risk factors.

Essential hypertension accounts for 90 % of chronic hypertension and is more common in African American women and women who have a family history of hypertension, are obese, or are over 35 years old. If a woman has none of these risk factors, then consideration of secondary causes is important. In addition, any woman with severe refractory hypertension, with sudden escalation of blood pressure, or with specific signs or symptoms should be evaluated for secondary causes (Table 8.2). Although secondary hypertension is rare, it may pose significant risk in pregnancy if undiagnosed.

Target organs that are most commonly affected by chronic hypertension include the heart, the brain, the kidneys, and the eye. Patients should be screened by symptoms, signs, or lab abnormalities (Table 8.3).

All women with hypertension should be screened for other cardiovascular risk factors. In addition to hypertension, independent risk factors for cardiovascular disease in women include obesity (BMI > 30), sedentary lifestyle, hyperlipidemia, diabetes, smoking, end-stage renal disease, a history of gestational hypertension or preeclampsia, and a family history of premature cardiovascular disease [15]. Although there is insufficient evidence to suggest that lifestyle changes will affect the outcome of the pregnancy, there is well-established long-term data showing that lifestyle changes can significantly reduce the likelihood of target organ damage. Pregnant women are often motivated to make behavior changes, and with the frequency of prenatal visits, pregnancy provides an opportunity to provide important education about healthy lifestyles.

The initial lab evaluation for a nonpregnant woman with new hypertension should include CBC, creatinine, electrolytes, urinalysis, TSH, calcium, EKG, and fasting blood sugar and fasting lipids. In pregnancy, the lipid panel may be deferred until 12 weeks postpartum as lipid levels may be affected by pregnancy, and an appropriate

Table 8.2 Evaluation for secondary causes of hypertension

	Symptoms	Signs other than HTN	Screening test
Primary renal disease (renal artery stenosis glomerular disease)	Usually none	Abdomen/flank bruit Hematuria, large palpable kidneys, edema	U/A, Cr
Pheochromocytoma	"5 Ps" palpitation, pallor, perspiration, pain (chest, head, abdomen), pressure (HBP)	Tremor, weight loss, anxiety	Urine or serum metanephrines
Primary hyperaldosteronism	Usually asymptomatic	Abnormalities on exam are rare	Electrolytes (may have low K+, high Na)
Hyperthyroidism	Anxiety, increased sweating, heat intolerance, palpitations, dyspnea, fatigue, weight loss	Tachycardia, weight loss, may have goiter, tremor, warm, moist skin, exophthalmos	TSH
Hyperparathyroidism	"bones, stones, groans, moans" = painful bones, renal stones, abdominal pain, and psychiatric symptoms	Nephrolithiasis, polyuria, weight loss, bone pain, muscle weakness, apathy	Calcium
Cushing	Emotional lability, muscle weakness, easy bruising,	Moon facies, central obesity, striae, osteoporosis, diabetes, hirsutism	Urinary 24-h cortisol
Sleep apnea	Excessive daytime sleepiness, snoring	Obesity, low-lying palate	Sleep study
Coarctation of the aorta	Usually asymptomatic, may have headaches, exertional leg fatigue and pain, epistaxis	Prominent neck pulsations, delayed peripheral pulses bruit over back	CXR (may have rib notching, "3 signs") Echo
Drugs (OCP, NSAIDs, pseudoephedrine)	Usually asymptomatic	None	Medication history

Table 8.3 Screening for target organ damage in chronic hypertension

Organ system	Screening test
Heart	EKG to r/o left ventricular hypertrophy or ischemic changes
Kidney	Urinalysis, urine protein/creatinine ratio, serum creatinine
Eyes	Fundoscopic exam to r/o retinopathy
Brain	Neurologic and mental status exam

screening test for diabetes in pregnancy should be done rather than the fasting blood sugar. Otherwise, this evaluation should be completed for all women with a new diagnosis of hypertension, whether pregnant or not. Many clinicians also find it helpful to document baseline preeclampsia labs in women at risk of preeclampsia.

Management

A careful review of both maternal and fetal risks and benefits must be considered in the decision to use pharmacologic therapy in the treatment of hypertensive disorders of pregnancy. In women with systolic blood pressure >160 or diastolic blood pressure >110, there is good evidence that medications should be initiated to prevent acute maternal end-organ damage, particularly stroke [16]. However, the benefit of antihypertensive therapy in mild to moderate hypertension (SBP 140–159 or DBP 90–109) has not been demonstrated in clinical trials. A 2007 meta-analysis showed a 50 % reduction in the risk of severe hypertension, but no reduction in preeclampsia, perinatal mortality, preterm birth, or SGA infant [17]. In fact aggressive lowering of blood pressure in pregnancy may be associated with harm. A 2002 study found that treatment of mild to moderate hypertension in pregnancy was associated with a significant reduction in birth weight. This effect was consistent regardless of etiology of hypertension or choice of medication [18]. International guidelines differ with respect to threshold for starting antihypertensive medications and blood pressure goals in the management of hypertension in pregnancy, but most agree that mild to moderate hypertension over the course of 9 months of pregnancy is unlikely to result in significant poor maternal or fetal outcomes [19–23].

Therefore, women with SBP < 160 **AND** DBP < 110 mmHg are candidates for non-pharmacologic management and should not be started on medications.

It is best to discuss plans for management of chronic hypertension before conception. Since 50 % of pregnancies are unplanned, women in their reproductive years are best treated with a medication whose safety in pregnancy has been established. For women with chronic hypertension, it is likely that blood pressure will drop in the first half of gestation due to physiologic vasodilation. In women with no target organ damage, it is reasonable to discontinue antihypertensive therapy in early gestation and monitor closely for rising BP. Medication should be restarted if BP rises >160/100.

There are no large, randomized controlled trials to help guide decisions about which antihypertensive medication to use in pregnant women. Head-to-head comparisons on specific medications are limited, and well-designed trials evaluating pregnancy outcome and fetal safety are inadequate. Drugs of first choice in pregnancy are those with an acceptable safety profile and include labetalol and methyldopa. Methyldopa has been used extensively in pregnancy and long-term safety has been demonstrated [24]. However, its side effect profile often limits dosing that is adequate to achieve blood pressure control. Labetalol is a nonselective beta-blocker with vascular alpha-blocking properties and has been postulated to preserve uteroplacental blood flow better than other beta-blockers. It has been found to be both safe and effective [25–28] with fewer side effects than methyldopa and has become the first choice for treatment of hypertension in pregnancy.

Alternative beta-blockers include pindolol and metoprolol. Other beta-blockers, especially propranolol and atenolol, are best avoided due to individual reports of adverse outcomes such as preterm labor, neonatal bradycardia, and fetal growth restriction [29]. Calcium channel blockers are considered a second-line drug for hypertension in pregnancy. Nifedipine is the most widely used calcium channel blocker in pregnancy and is not associated with teratogenic risk [30]. Data on efficacy and long-term safety are limited. Amlodipine, used widely in the nonpregnant population, has not been studied in pregnancy and is best avoided. Hydralazine is most commonly used as an intravenous treatment of acute severe hypertension in the setting of preeclampsia. A meta-analysis demonstrated a slightly increased rate of adverse events with hydralazine compared to labetalol, but the evidence was not sufficient to make a definitive recommendation for one drug over the other [31]. The use of thiazide diuretics in pregnancy is controversial. Blood volume in pregnancy increases by 50 %, and while studies have not shown an association between diuretic use and adverse pregnancy outcomes [3], there are data demonstrating that diuretic use counteracts this normal expansion of blood volume.

ACE inhibitor use in the first trimester is associated with an increased risk of congenital abnormalities [32]. In addition, fetal renal abnormalities have been reported with ACE inhibitor use in the latter half of pregnancy. ARBs, direct renin inhibitors, while not studied in pregnancy, have a similar mechanism of action, so may pose similar risk. These drugs are contraindicated in pregnant women and should be discontinued in women planning pregnancy [32]. Table 8.4 presents a summary of antihypertensive medications in pregnancy.

Table 8.4 Medications for the treatment of hypertension in pregnancy

Drug	Dose	Comments
Preferred agents		
Methyldopa	0.5–3 g/day in 2 divided doses	Long-term safety established Slow in onset Side effects may limit use
Labetalol	200–1,200 mg/day in 2–3 divided doses	Safe and effective Available both orally and parenterally Fewer side effect than methyldopa
Second-line agents		
Nifedipine	30–120 mg/day of slow release	Calcium channel blocker of choice in pregnancy
Hydralazine	50–300 mg/day in 2–4 divided doses	May cause reflex tachycardia Neonatal thrombocytopenia has been reported Most commonly used for acute severe hypertension in pregnancy
B-blockers	Metoprolol 0.5–3.0 mg/day in 2–3 divided doses	Avoid atenolol, propranolol
Hydrochlorothiazide	12.5–50 mg/day	May cause volume depletion Monitor electrolytes after
Contraindicated		
ACE-I/ARBs		

Preeclampsia

Preeclampsia occurs in about 5–8 % of all pregnancies and is thought to be the result of abnormal placentation, leading to poor placental perfusion and release of factors that cause widespread endothelial dysfunction. It occurs almost exclusively after 20 weeks gestation (although the underlying pathology likely starts earlier in pregnancy) and can be life-threatening for both the mother and the baby. Risk factors for preeclampsia are listed in Table 8.5.

Preeclampsia may affect multiple organ systems and is associated with both significant maternal and fetal morbidity and mortality (Table 8.6).

Diagnosis

The diagnosis of preeclampsia is made in a woman with new-onset hypertension and either proteinuria or other end-organ dysfunction after 20 weeks gestation.

Criteria for diagnosis include:

- Systolic blood pressure >140 mmHg OR diastolic blood pressure >90 mmHg.
PLUS
- Proteinuria >300 mg in 24-h urine OR protein/creatinine ratio >0.3 mg/dl or >30 mg/mmol.
OR
- Other end-organ dysfunction defined as platelet <100,000/ml, serum creatinine >1.1 mg/dl, or doubling of the baseline creatinine and serum transaminases twice the normal [7].

The diagnosis of preeclampsia in women with chronic hypertension or renal disease can be challenging but should be suspected if there is a worsening of blood pressure or proteinuria in the second half of pregnancy, especially if it occurs acutely.

Table 8.5 Risk factors for preeclampsia

Risk factor	Relative risk (95 % confidence interval)
Preeclampsia in previous pregnancy	RR 7.19 (95 % CI 5.85–8.83)
First pregnancy	RR 2.91 (95 % CI 1.28–6.61)
Family history of preeclampsia	RR 2.90 (95 % CI 1.70–4.93)
Pregestational diabetes	RR 3.56 (95 % CI 2.54–4.99)
BP >130/80 at 1st prenatal visit	RR 1.38–2.37
Antiphospholipid antibodies	RR 9.72 (95 % CI 4.34–21.75)
Overweight/obese BMI >26.1	RR 2.47 (95 % CI 1.66–3.67)
Chronic kidney disease	Risk depends on severity, Stage 3, 4, 5: risk as high as 40–60 % [2]
Twin pregnancy	RR 2.93 (95 % 2.04–4.21)
Advanced maternal age ≥40 years old	RR 1.96, (95 % CI 1.34–2.87 for multiparas and RR 1.68, 95 % CI 1.23–2.29 for primiparas)

Duckitt and Harrington [57], with permission

Table 8.6 Clinical manifestations of preeclampsia

Organ system	Clinical features
Maternal features	
Renal dysfunction	Elevated creatinine Proteinuria Oliguria
Hematologic involvement	Thrombocytopenia Hemolysis DIC
Liver	Elevated serum transaminases Epigastric or RUQ pain Hepatic infarct Hepatic rupture HELLP (hemolysis, elevated liver enzymes, low platelets)
Neurologic	Seizure (eclampsia) Hyperreflexia with clonus Severe headache Visual disturbance (photopsia, scotoma, cortical blindness, retinal vasospasm) Stroke
Pulmonary	Laryngeal edema Pulmonary edema
Eye	Retinal edema Retinal detachment
Fetal features	
Fetal growth restriction	Fetal growth <10 %
Placental abruption	Vaginal bleeding, abdominal and/or back pain, contractions

In many cases, a woman will meet some but not all of the criteria as outlined above. It is critically important that clinicians recognize that preeclampsia is a progressive and unpredictable disease. Women who present with some features of preeclampsia need to be frequently monitored to watch for evolving disease. Twice weekly blood pressure checks and once weekly labs are recommended.

Management of Preeclampsia

Since preeclampsia is a disease of the placenta, it is only with delivery of the placenta that the disorder will start to resolve. Timing of the delivery can be challenging as the clinician must weigh the risk of fetal morbidity from preterm delivery with the risk of both fetal and maternal morbidity in the face of worsening preeclampsia. The administration of steroids for fetal lung maturity has been associated with improved perinatal outcomes in women requiring delivery prior to 34 weeks gestation. In addition, treatment with intravenous magnesium is associated with a significant reduction in the risk of initial or recurrent eclamptic seizure and should be given to women with severe features of preeclampsia in the intrapartum period [33].

Once a woman has been diagnosed with preeclampsia, the next step is to determine the severity of disease. Severe features of preeclampsia include:

- SBP >160 mmHg OR DBP>110 mmHg >20 weeks gestation on at least two occasions, at least 1 h apart while patient is on bed rest.
- Platelets <100,000/ml.
- Transaminases elevated to twice the normal, severe persistent RUQ, or epigastric pain unresponsive to treatment and no alternate diagnosis.
- Serum creatinine > 1.1 or doubling of creatinine.
- Pulmonary edema.
- New-onset headache or visual disturbances.

Box 8.1 outlines an algorithm for the management of women with preeclampsia, but with none of these severe features. Box 8.2 presents an algorithm for the management of women with severe features of preeclampsia.

Acute, severe elevations of blood pressure in women with preeclampsia should be treated as a hypertensive emergency. Severe systolic hypertension is the most important predictor of cerebral hemorrhage and stroke which is the most common cause of maternal death in preeclampsia [16]. Systolic blood pressure greater than

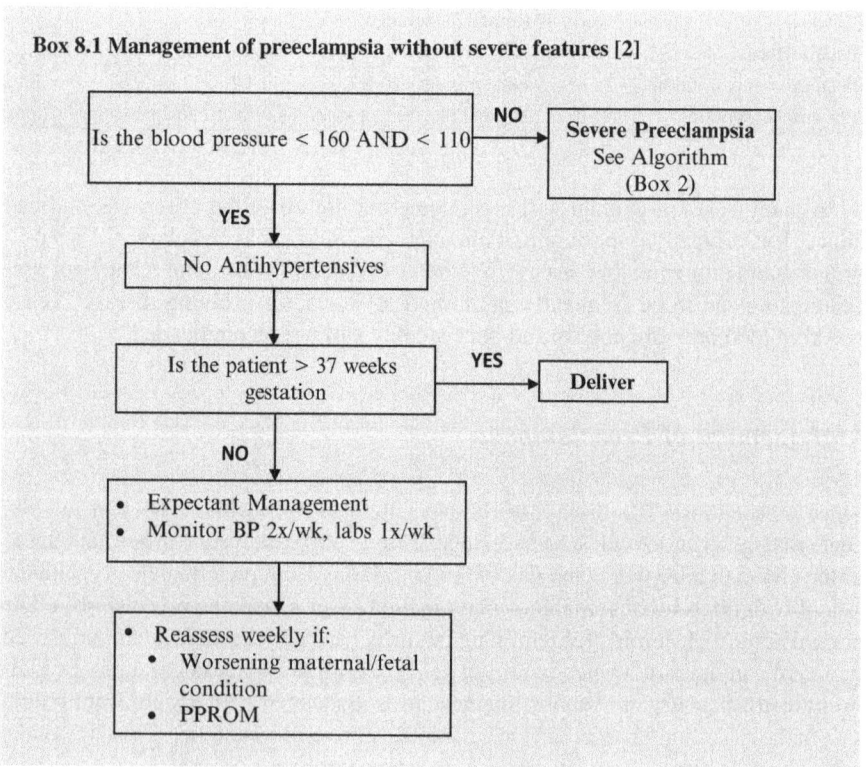

Box 8.1 Management of preeclampsia without severe features [2]

8 Hypertensive Disorders of Pregnancy

Box 8.2 Management of preeclampsia with severe features [2]

Features of Severe Preeclampsia:
- BP > 160/110
- Platelet < 100,000
- LFT > 2X normal
- Severe persistent RUQ or epigastric pain
- Cr > 1.1 or twice baseline
- Pulmonary edema
- New cerebral or visual disturbance

↓ YES

Treat BP to goal

↓

Previable Fetus or > 34 weeks gestation — YES →
- Deliver without delay once maternal condition stabilized
- Give MgSO4

↓ NO

Any of the following?
- Uncontrolled hypertension
- Eclampsia
- Pulmonary edema
- Abruptio placenta
- DIC
- Nonreassuring fetal status
- IUFD

YES ↓
- Deliver without delay once maternal condition stabilized
- Give MgSO4
- Give steroids for fetal lung maturity

NO ↓

Any of the following?
- PPROM
- Labor
- Platelet < 100,000
- Transaminases 2X normal
- IUGR < 5th%
- Severe oligo AFI < 5cm
- Reverse end diastolic flow on umbilibcal artery Doppler study
- New onset or worsening renal dysfunction

YES ↓
- Give steroids for fetal lung maturity
- Delay delivery 48 hours

NO →
- Expectant management should only be undertaken at facilities with adequate maternal and neonatal intensive care resources
- Give steroids for fetal lung

Table 8.7 Pharmacologic management of acute, severe hypertension in pregnancy

Drug	Dose	Onset of action	Duration	Comment
Labetalol	Initial: 20 mg IV Double dose every 10 min; if not at acceptable threshold up to max IV dose of 300 mg. Or use constant infusion of 1–2 mg/min	5–10 min	3–6 h	Avoid in women with active asthma or heart failure, bradycardia, or cocaine Inform pediatrician as labetalol may cause neonatal bradycardia Considered by most experts to be first-line agent
Hydralazine	Initial: 5 mg IV or IM Double dose (10 mg, 20 mg, 40 mg) every 20 min if not at goal BP	10–20 min	3–6 h	May be associated with increased risk of maternal hypotension
Nifedipine	10–30 mg po, repeat in 45 min if needed	<30 min	4–5 h	May cause headache

160 mmHg and/or diastolic blood pressure greater than 110 mmHg for more than 15 min requires urgent treatment. Severe hypertension should be stabilized prior to delivery and/or intubation. The goal of treatment is to achieve a systolic blood pressure between 140 and 160 and diastolic blood pressure between 90 and 100 mmHg. First-line medications for the treatment of acute severe hypertension to a maximum of 300 mg per day. YTC in pregnancy include intravenous labetalol and hydralazine (see Table 8.7). Rapid successive doses of either of these drugs should be administered followed by the second drug if BP goals are still not achieved. Labetalol is initiated at 20 mg IV over 2 min, and the dose should be doubled every 10 min up to 80 mg IV if BP goal is not achieved to a maximum of 300 mg per day. Hydralazine can be started at either 5 or 10 mg IV over 2 min with a second 10 mg dose given after 20 min if BP goals are still not achieved. If both of these medications fail to improve blood pressure, emergent consultation with obstetric medicine, maternal fetal medicine, or critical care specialist is recommended. Sodium nitroprusside is reserved for extreme emergencies as it may be associated with fetal thiocyanate toxicity. Magnesium sulfate is used for seizure prophylaxis, and is not an effective antihypertensive medication.

Postpartum

Postpartum hypertension may occur as a result of preexisting chronic hypertension, persistent gestational hypertension, or preeclampsia which can continue into or occur de novo in the postpartum period [34, 35]. For women with hypertension during pregnancy, blood pressure is expected to peak at about 3–6 days postpartum [36]. Resolution of hypertension is unpredictable and may occur in just a few days or may take as long as 6 months. Therefore, close monitoring of the postpartum woman is important.

Factors that may contribute to persistent or even new-onset hypertension in the postpartum period include fluids, NSAIDs, and other vasoconstricting medications such as ergots that may be given for uterine atony. Women presenting with new-onset hypertension should be screened for preeclampsia. If other symptoms are present such as tachycardia, shortness of breath, headache, or neurologic findings, secondary causes of hypertension such as pheochromocytoma, peripartum cardiomyopathy, or stroke should be ruled out. The approach to treatment of hypertension in the postpartum period is much the same as during pregnancy. Severe hypertension should be treated urgently and aggressively. Both labetalol and nifedipine are effective medications and may be used safely in breastfeeding. Nifedipine, compared to labetalol, has been shown to improve renal blood flow leading to improved diuresis and is the drug of choice in women with volume overload [35, 37]. ACE inhibitors are also safe in breastfeeding and may be used in postpartum women [36].

The risk of recurrence of preeclampsia in subsequent pregnancies varies with the severity and the time of onset of the initial episode. Women diagnosed with early-onset preeclampsia (prior to 32 weeks) have a risk as high as 25–65 % of recurrence in a subsequent pregnancy. Women who had non-severe preeclampsia have a much lower risk (5–7 %) [38, 39].

Prevention

The majority of women with chronic hypertension will have a normal, healthy pregnancy. Preconception evaluation is important to address blood pressure control and choice of antihypertensive medication prior to pregnancy. Much research has focused on the prevention of preeclampsia, but, to date, no effective interventions to prevent preeclampsia have been clearly established.

Smaller, older studies found that low-dose aspirin was associated with a reduced risk of preeclampsia, but a larger RCT did not find this same effect [40]. A recent meta-analysis concluded that low-dose aspirin is not beneficial in low-risk women but may be effective in high-risk women in reducing the risk of preeclampsia [41]. Therefore, it is reasonable to recommend low-dose aspirin (81–100 mg daily) to women with risk factors for preeclampsia (most commonly women <18 years old, with multiple pregnancy, preexisting hypertension, renal disease, diabetes, or previous preeclampsia).

Calcium supplementation of at least 1 g/day has been associated with a reduced risk of preeclampsia in women with poor dietary calcium intake [42].

Conclusive studies have found that antioxidants such as vitamin C and vitamin E do not reduce the risk of preeclampsia and should not be recommended [43–45]. Control of blood pressure is also not associated with a reduction in the risk of preeclampsia, so antihypertensive therapy cannot be recommended solely for preeclampsia prevention.

There is insufficient evidence to make a recommendation about the usefulness of a heart healthy diet and exercise to reduce the risk of preeclampsia, but since these interventions are associated with many other positive health outcomes, it is always worthwhile to recommend.

Early data suggests that exercise may be effective in preventing preeclampsia; however, further studies are needed to confirm these findings [46, 47]. Preeclampsia is more common in obese women, so it is certainly reasonable to recommend lifestyle changes to achieve a healthy weight prior to conception.

Long-Term Risk

Women who develop gestational hypertension or preeclampsia have an increased risk of hypertension, stroke, and cardiovascular disease later in life. Numerous epidemiologic studies have shown that women with a history of preeclampsia have approximately twice the risk of ischemic heart disease [48, 49]. In women with preeclampsia with premature delivery or low birth weight baby, the relative risk may be as high as eight to ninefold [50–52]. In their 2011 guidelines for the prevention of cardiovascular disease in women, the American Heart Association sites preeclampsia as an important risk factor for women [15]. Therefore, women with a history of preeclampsia should be counseled postpartum about the importance of lifestyle modifications, adequate BP control, and control of metabolic factors to prevent cardiovascular disease [53].

Even in the absence of gestational diabetes, both gestational hypertension and preeclampsia have been associated with a twofold increased risk of diabetes later in life. In women with GDM, the diagnosis of either gestational hypertension or preeclampsia increases the risk of future diabetes from a 13-fold increased risk to 16–18-fold [50, 54, 55]. Preeclampsia has been associated with an increased risk of end-stage renal disease in later life, but the absolute risk is small [56].

Summary

Chronic hypertension in pregnancy is associated with both acute and long-term adverse maternal and fetal outcomes. Women with severe hypertension or advanced disease with end-organ damage are at a higher risk. Poor outcomes are more common in women with severe hypertension or advanced disease with end-organ damage or those who develop superimposed preeclampsia. Preeclampsia is potentially life-threatening to both mother and baby, and early recognition is critical to improved outcomes.

References

1. Yoder SR, Thornburg LL, Bisognano JD. Hypertension in pregnancy and women of childbearing age. Am J Med. 2009;122(10):890–5.
2. Hypertension in pregnancy. Report of the American College of Obstetricians and Gynecologists' Task Force on Hypertension in Pregnancy. Obstet Gynecol. 2013;122(5):1122–31.

3. Roberts JM, Pearson G, Cutler J, Lindheimer M. Summary of the NHLBI working group on research on hypertension during pregnancy. Hypertension. 2003;41(3):437–45.
4. Sibai BM, Grossman RA, Grossman HG. Effects of diuretics on plasma volume in pregnancies with long-term hypertension. Am J Obstet Gynecol. 1984;150(7):831–5.
5. Sibai BM. Chronic hypertension in pregnancy. Obstet Gynecol. 2002;100(2):369–77.
6. Zetterstrom K, Lindeberg SN, Haglund B, Hanson U. Maternal complications in women with chronic hypertension: a population-based cohort study. Acta Obstet Gynecol Scand. 2005; 84(5):419–24.
7. Ananth CV, Keyes KM, Wapner RJ. Pre-eclampsia rates in the United States, 1980-2010: age-period-cohort analysis. BMJ. 2013;347:f6564.
8. Callaway LK, Lawlor DA, O'Callaghan M, Williams GM, Najman JM, McIntyre HD. Diabetes mellitus in the 21 years after a pregnancy that was complicated by hypertension: findings from a prospective cohort study. Am J Obstet Gynecol. 2007;197(5):492 e1–7.
9. Steegers EA, von Dadelszen P, Duvekot JJ, Pijnenborg R. Pre-eclampsia Lancet. 2010; 376(9741):631–44.
10. Berg CJ, An LC, Kirch M, Guo H, Thomas JL, Patten CA, et al. Failure to report attempts to quit smoking. Addict Behav. 2010;35(10):900–4.
11. Powe CE, Levine RJ, Karumanchi SA. Preeclampsia, a disease of the maternal endothelium: the role of antiangiogenic factors and implications for later cardiovascular disease. Circulation. 2011;123(24):2856–69.
12. Gilbert WM, Young AL, Danielsen B. Pregnancy outcomes in women with chronic hypertension: a population-based study. J Reprod Med. 2007;52(11):1046–51.
13. Poston L, Briley AL, Seed PT, Kelly FJ, Shennan AH. Vitamins in Pre-eclampsia Trial C. Vitamin C and vitamin E in pregnant women at risk for pre-eclampsia (VIP trial): randomised placebo-controlled trial. Lancet. 2006;367(9517):1145–54.
14. Engeland A, Bjorge T, Daltveit AK, Skurtveit S, Vangen S, Vollset SE, et al. Risk of diabetes after gestational diabetes and preeclampsia. A registry-based study of 230,000 women in Norway. Eur J Epidemiol. 2011;26(2):157–63.
15. Mosca L, Benjamin EJ, Berra K, Bezanson JL, Dolor RJ, Lloyd-Jones DM, et al. Effectiveness-based guidelines for the prevention of cardiovascular disease in women–2011 update: a guideline from the American heart association. Circulation. 2011;123(11):1243–62.
16. European Society of Gynecology (ESG), Association for European Paediatric Cardiology (AEPC), German Society for Gender Medicine (DGesGM), Regitz-Zagrosek V, Blomstrom Lundqvist C, Borghi C, et al. ESC Guidelines on the management of cardiovascular diseases during pregnancy: the Task Force on the Management of Cardiovascular Diseases during Pregnancy of the European Society of Cardiology (ESC). Eur Heart J. 2011;32(24):3147–97.
17. Abalos E, Duley L, Steyn DW, Henderson-Smart DJ. Antihypertensive drug therapy for mild to moderate hypertension during pregnancy. Cochrane Database Syst Rev. 2007;1, CD002252.
18. von Dadelszen P, Magee LA. Fall in mean arterial pressure and fetal growth restriction in pregnancy hypertension: an updated metaregression analysis. J Obstet Gynaecol Can. 2002; 24(12):941–5.
19. American College of Obstetricians and Gynecologists. ACOG Practice Bulletin No. 125: Chronic hypertension in pregnancy. Obstet Gynecol. 2012;119(2 Pt 1):396–407.
20. Vanek M, Sheiner E, Levy A, Mazor M. Chronic hypertension and the risk for adverse pregnancy outcome after superimposed pre-eclampsia. Int J Gynaecol Obstet. 2004;86(1):7–11.
21. Lowe SA, Brown MA, Dekker GA, Gatt S, McLintock CK, McMahon LP, et al. Guidelines for the management of hypertensive disorders of pregnancy 2008. Aust N Z J Obstet Gynaecol. 2009;49(3):242–6.
22. Magee LA, Helewa M, Moutquin JM, von Dadelszen P, Hypertension Guideline C. Strategic training initiative in research in the reproductive health sciences S. Diagnosis, evaluation, and management of the hypertensive disorders of pregnancy. J Obstet Gynaecol Can. 2008;30 (3 Suppl):S1–48.
23. National Collaborating Centre for Women's and Children's Health (UK). Hypertension in pregnancy: the management of hypertensive disorders during pregnancy. London: RCOG Press; 2010.

24. van Rijn BB, Hoeks LB, Bots ML, Franx A, Bruinse HW. Outcomes of subsequent pregnancy after first pregnancy with early-onset preeclampsia. Am J Obstet Gynecol. 2006;195(3): 723–8.
25. Sibai BM, Mabie WC, Shamsa F, Villar MA, Anderson GD. A comparison of no medication versus methyldopa or labetalol in chronic hypertension during pregnancy. Am J Obstet Gynecol. 1990;162(4):960–6. discussion 6-7.
26. Sibai BM, Gonzalez AR, Mabie WC, Moretti M. A comparison of labetalol plus hospitalization versus hospitalization alone in the management of preeclampsia remote from term. Obstet Gynecol. 1987;70(3 Pt 1):323–7.
27. Sibai BM. Etiology and management of postpartum hypertension-preeclampsia. Am J Obstet Gynecol. 2012;206(6):470–5.
28. Roberts JM, Myatt L, Spong CY, Thom EA, Hauth JC, Leveno KJ, et al. Vitamins C and E to prevent complications of pregnancy-associated hypertension. N Engl J Med. 2010;362(14): 1282–91.
29. Ray JG, Burrows RF, Burrows EA, Vermeulen MJMOSHIP. McMaster outcome study of hypertension in pregnancy. Early Hum Dev. 2001;64(2):129–43.
30. Podymow T, August P. Antihypertensive drugs in pregnancy. Semin Nephrol. 2011;31(1): 70–85.
31. Plouin PF, Breart G, Maillard F, Papiernik E, Relier JP. Comparison of antihypertensive efficacy and perinatal safety of labetalol and methyldopa in the treatment of hypertension in pregnancy: a randomized controlled trial. Br J Obstet Gynaecol. 1988;95(9):868–76.
32. Cooper WO, Hernandez-Diaz S, Arbogast PG, Dudley JA, Dyer S, Gideon PS, et al. Major congenital malformations after first-trimester exposure to ACE inhibitors. N Engl J Med. 2006;354(23):2443–51.
33. Pickles CJ, Symonds EM, Broughton PF. The fetal outcome in a randomized double-blind controlled trial of labetalol versus placebo in pregnancy-induced hypertension. Br J Obstet Gynaecol. 1989;96(1):38–43.
34. Pell JP, Smith GC, Walsh D. Pregnancy complications and subsequent maternal cerebrovascular events: a retrospective cohort study of 119,668 births. Am J Epidemiol. 2004;159(4): 336–42.
35. Matthys LA, Coppage KH, Lambers DS, Barton JR, Sibai BM. Delayed postpartum preeclampsia: an experience of 151 cases. Am J Obstet Gynecol. 2004;190(5):1464–6.
36. Mongraw-Chaffin ML, Cirillo PM, Cohn BA. Preeclampsia and cardiovascular disease death: prospective evidence from the child health and development studies cohort. Hypertension. 2010;56(1):166–71.
37. Martin Jr JN, Thigpen BD, Moore RC, Rose CH, Cushman J, May W. Stroke and severe preeclampsia and eclampsia: a paradigm shift focusing on systolic blood pressure. Obstet Gynecol. 2005;105(2):246–54.
38. Magee LA, Schick B, Donnenfeld AE, Sage SR, Conover B, Cook L, et al. The safety of calcium channel blockers in human pregnancy: a prospective, multicenter cohort study. Am J Obstet Gynecol. 1996;174(3):823–8.
39. Magee LA, Cham C, Waterman EJ, Ohlsson A, von Dadelszen P. Hydralazine for treatment of severe hypertension in pregnancy: meta-analysis. BMJ. 2003;327(7421):955–60.
40. CLASP: a randomised trial of low-dose aspirin for the prevention and treatment of preeclampsia among 9364 pregnant women. CLASP (Collaborative Low-dose Aspirin Study in Pregnancy) Collaborative Group. Lancet. 1994;343(8898):619–29.
41. Askie LM, Duley L, Henderson-Smart DJ, Stewart LA, Group PC. Antiplatelet agents for prevention of pre-eclampsia: a meta-analysis of individual patient data. Lancet. 2007;369(9575): 1791–8.
42. Hofmeyr GJ, Atallah AN, Duley L. Calcium supplementation during pregnancy for preventing hypertensive disorders and related problems. Cochrane Database Syst Rev. 2006;3, CD001059.
43. Lindheimer MD, Taler SJ, Cunningham FG. Hypertension in pregnancy. J Am Soc Hypertens. 2010;4(2):68–78.

44. Lawler J, Osman M, Shelton JA, Yeh J. Population-based analysis of hypertensive disorders in pregnancy. Hypertens Pregnancy. 2007;26(1):67–76.
45. Irgens HU, Reisaeter L, Irgens LM, Lie RT. Long term mortality of mothers and fathers after pre-eclampsia: population based cohort study. BMJ. 2001;323(7323):1213–7.
46. Saftlas AF, Logsden-Sackett N, Wang W, Woolson R, Bracken MB. Work, leisure-time physical activity, and risk of preeclampsia and gestational hypertension. Am J Epidemiol. 2004;160(8):758–65.
47. Sorensen TK, Williams MA, Lee IM, Dashow EE, Thompson ML, Luthy DA. Recreational physical activity during pregnancy and risk of preeclampsia. Hypertension. 2003;41(6):1273–80.
48. Ray JG, Vermeulen MJ, Schull MJ, Redelmeier DA. Cardiovascular health after maternal placental syndromes (CHAMPS): population-based retrospective cohort study. Lancet. 2005;366(9499):1797–803.
49. Bellamy L, Casas JP, Hingorani AD, Williams DJ. Pre-eclampsia and risk of cardiovascular disease and cancer in later life: systematic review and meta-analysis. BMJ. 2007;335(7627):974.
50. Lykke JA, Langhoff-Roos J, Sibai BM, Funai EF, Triche EW, Paidas MJ. Hypertensive pregnancy disorders and subsequent cardiovascular morbidity and type 2 diabetes mellitus in the mother. Hypertension. 2009;53(6):944–51.
51. Lydakis C, Lip GY, Beevers M, Beevers DG. Atenolol and fetal growth in pregnancies complicated by hypertension. Am J Hypertens. 1999;12(6):541–7.
52. Barton JR, Sibai BM. Prediction and prevention of recurrent preeclampsia. Obstet Gynecol. 2008;112(2 Pt 1):359–72.
53. Sattar N, Greer IA. Pregnancy complications and maternal cardiovascular risk: opportunities for intervention and screening? BMJ. 2002;325(7356):157–60.
54. Chappell LC, Enye S, Seed P, Briley AL, Poston L, Shennan AH. Adverse perinatal outcomes and risk factors for preeclampsia in women with chronic hypertension: a prospective study. Hypertension. 2008;51(4):1002–9.
55. Berks D, Steegers EA, Molas M, Visser W. Resolution of hypertension and proteinuria after preeclampsia. Obstet Gynecol. 2009;114(6):1307–14.
56. Vikse BE, Irgens LM, Leivestad T, Skjaerven R, Iversen BM. Preeclampsia and the risk of end-stage renal disease. N Engl J Med. 2008;359(8):800–9.
57. Duckitt K, Harrington D. Risk factors for pre-eclampsia at antenatal booking: systematic review of controlled studies. BMJ. 2005;330(7491):565.

Part VIII
Infectious Diseases

Chapter 9
Viral Infection in Pregnancy: HIV and Viral Hepatitis

Erica J. Hardy, Silvia Degli Esposti, and Judy Nee

HIV

Background/Definition

The human immunodeficiency virus (HIV) infection is a chronic infection caused by the retrovirus HIV infection of T cells that express CD4 receptors causing immunodeficiency. Once the CD4-positive cell count falls below a certain level, HIV infection causes increased susceptibility to infections, malignancies, and neurologic damage. The syndrome was first recognized in the United States in 1981.

Perinatal transmission of HIV was common before medical intervention and informed public health policy changes. With antenatal HIV testing to diagnose

---

E.J. Hardy, M.D., M.M.Sc. (✉)
Women's Infectious Diseases Consultation, Women and Infants Hospital, Providence, RI, USA

The Warren Alpert Medical School of Brown University, Providence, RI, USA
e-mail: ehardy@wihri.org

S.D. Esposti, M.D.
Center for Women's Gastrointestinal Medicine, Women's Medicine Collaborative, The Miriam Hospital, 146 West River Street, Ste 11C, Providence, RI 02904, USA

The Warren Alpert Medical School of Brown University, Providence, RI, USA
e-mail: silvia_degli_esposti@brown.edu

J. Nee, M.D.
Internal Medicine, Beth Israel Deaconess Medical Center, Boston, MA, USA

Harvard Medical School, Boston, MA, USA
e-mail: Judy_nee@brown.edu

unknown maternal HIV infection, antiretroviral medication administered antepartum and peripartum to the mother, infant treatment, scheduled operative delivery when indicated, and avoidance of breastfeeding when there is a safe alternative, the transmission rate from mother to child can be less than 1 % [1]. With these strategies, there has been a 90 % decline in the numbers of perinatally infected infants in the United States, and a vertical transmission rate of less than 1 % in the United States and Europe [2, 3].

Epidemiology

Women represent about 49 % of all adults living with HIV. In some areas such as sub-Saharan Africa and the Caribbean, 60 % of those living with HIV are women. The most common mode of infection among women is heterosexual transmission.

According to a data from 2009, women represented 24 % of all diagnoses of HIV infection among US adults and adolescents, and in that year, there were approximately 11,200 new HIV infections among US women. In 2008, an estimated 25 % of adults and adolescents living with HIV were women. HIV disproportionately affects black and Hispanic/Latina women with the rate of new HIV infection among black women 15 times that of the white women and over three times the rate among Hispanic/Latina women. The most common mode of transmission is heterosexual sex [3].

As women are living longer and well with HIV, the number of women with HIV giving birth in the United States has increased by about 30 %. Despite that fact, the number of perinatal infections has continued to decline, yet they still occur [3]. Challenges to eliminating perinatal transmission altogether are missed opportunities for prenatal HIV testing and therefore diagnosis of HIV infection during pregnancy (since approximately 18 % of those with HIV are not aware of their diagnosis). Lack of preconception counseling in women with HIV, unintended pregnancies, and lack of access to or poor adherence to antiretroviral medication during pregnancy (or late initiation of antiretroviral medications often due to late prenatal care) all contribute to persistence of vertical transmission. Among mothers of HIV-infected infants reported to the CDC between 2003 and 2007, only 62 % had at least one prenatal visit, 27 % were diagnosed with HIV after delivery, and only 29 % had received some kind of antiretroviral medication during pregnancy [3].

Pathobiology

Pregnancy does not generally affect the course of HIV disease. With good prenatal care and careful monitoring, HIV-infected women can have healthy pregnancies and deliver HIV-uninfected infants. The majority of the perinatal transmission occurs during labor and delivery, when there is the most exposure of the infant to maternal blood and secretions. HIV can be transmitted to the fetus at any gestation, but most transmission occurs at >28 weeks. In areas where there is not a safe alternative to breastfeeding such as in some areas of sub-Saharan Africa, there is significant HIV transmission from mother to child during breastfeeding.

Antiretroviral therapy is the mainstay of perinatal HIV prevention, and the mechanism is likely twofold. The largest benefit is probably from decreasing the maternal viral load and therefore limiting the exposure of the infant to high levels of circulating HIV in the blood and genital secretions. However, this is not the only mechanism of prevention because vertical transmission happens across all viral loads, even in women with undetectable virus [4–6]. The other mechanism of action is likely the provision of preexposure prophylaxis to the infant while in utero by utilizing antiretroviral drugs that cross the placenta and reach adequate levels in the fetal circulation [1]. The infant also receives antiretroviral medications for 6 weeks postpartum, and this is also effective in decreasing the risk of HIV transmission, even in the absence of maternal antiretroviral therapy [4, 5].

Diagnosis

Acute infection with HIV, or acute retroviral conversion syndrome, can present as a mononucleosis-like illness, and a high level of suspicion must be maintained if a pregnant woman presents with fever because acute seroconversion is associated with a very high risk of perinatal transmission due to the very high viral load [6]. It is important to know the performance characteristics of the HIV test in use at individual institutions because early in HIV infection, the HIV antibody (the basis of most HIV tests) can be negative. The viral load must be checked in order to diagnose acute infection during the early window period before the HIV antibody forms. The new fourth-generation HIV tests have shortened this window period between infection and positive antibody test to 1–2 weeks and may be particularly useful in pregnancy [7].

In newly diagnosed HIV infection during pregnancy, a CD4 with percentage and a quantitative HIV RNA (viral load) level should be obtained and an HIV genotype to evaluate for transmitted drug resistance. Testing should also be done for hepatitis B, C, and A infection past or present, in order to vaccinate for hepatitis A (if indicated) and B if not immune from prior infection or vaccination. Other sexually transmitted infections such as syphilis, Chlamydia, gonorrhea, as well as consideration of herpes serology, should be obtained. Serology for toxoplasmosis should be obtained, and if negative, the patient should be counseled to avoid exposure that can lead to infection. Screening for tuberculosis with a TST skin test or serum quantiF-ERON gold assay should be performed [8]. The newly diagnosed pregnant patient should be comanaged with a specialist in treating patients with HIV infection and ideally with experience in pregnancy.

Management/Treatment

HIV care in pregnancy begins with careful preconception counseling in all women of childbearing age independent of reproductive plans. Ideally, the goal of therapy is a stable, suppressed viral load prior to conception. This can be addressed prior to conception and will increase the chances of an HIV-uninfected infant. The importance of safe contraception methods in the case of a serodiscordant couple can also be addressed as part of preconception counseling, as well as the availability of effective contraception in order to prevent unintended pregnancy. In the United States, the Centers for Disease Control and Prevention, the American College of Obstetricians and Gynecologists, and other national organizations have formal recommendations for preconception care [2].

Antepartum management focuses on maintaining a suppressed viral load throughout pregnancy and especially later in gestation when the majority of perinatal transmission can occur [1]. The consensus guidelines for antiretroviral therapy in the nonpregnant patient in the United States now recommend treatment for everyone regardless of CD4 cell count, although the strength of that recommendation varies by CD4 count [9]. This means that many HIV-infected pregnant patients will already be on antiretroviral therapy. If that therapy is effective in maintaining a suppressed viral load, then the recommendation is not to change drugs, regardless of the regimen, as it is thought that switching regimens increases the risk of viral escape and therefore increases the risk of perinatal HIV transmission in that setting [2]. The drug efavirenz warrants mention since until recently, cessation of this drug was recommended upon pregnancy; however, data shows that the small increased risk of neural tube defects with this drug is isolated to very early pregnancy, 4–5 weeks gestation, prior to the usual recognition of pregnancy. Recently, the US Health and Human Services Panel on Prevention of Perinatal HIV Transmission updated their treatment guidelines to recommend continuing efavirenz in women who are on an efavirenz-containing regimen and present for antenatal care in the first trimester, as long as the regimen is effectively suppressing the viral load [2]. Additional fetal monitoring should be considered for efavirenz exposure in the first trimester.

Choice of antiretroviral medication for the pregnant woman should take into consideration her prior treatment history and resistance mutations and should be chosen with the assistance of a practitioner specializing in the HIV care of the pregnant woman. In general, a recommended regimen would consist of two nucleoside reverse transcriptase inhibitors (NRTIs) (and currently those recommended are zidovudine and lamivudine) with the addition of a protease inhibitor (currently recommended are lopinavir or atazanavir, each boosted with ritonavir) [2]. Because one mechanism of perinatal HIV transmission prevention is preexposure prophylaxis in the fetus, at least two agents that cross the placenta (such as the NRTIs) should be chosen [2]. Viral load should be monitored every 2–4 weeks until viral suppression and then every 3 months or at least once per trimester during pregnancy. A viral load should be checked close to delivery so that mode of delivery can be planned.

Women who are on an effective antiretroviral regimen during pregnancy with a suppressed viral load should continue this regimen throughout labor and delivery.

If the viral load is >1000 copies/ml, then intravenous zidovudine is recommended at the start of labor or 3–4 h prior to a cesarean section and continued until the cord is clamped [2]. If the viral load is <1000 copies/ml, then intravenous zidovudine is not necessary.

In terms of mode of delivery, if the HIV viral load is >1,000, then data have shown a reduction in the rate of perinatal transmission with a cesarean section [10, 11], and this is the current recommendation [2, 12].

The continuation of maternal antiretroviral therapy after delivery will largely be based on the indications for the nonpregnant adult. In general, antiretroviral medication is recommended for all HIV-infected adults regardless of CD4 count or viral load, although the strength of that recommendation varies based on CD4 count or other details such as HIV-negative partner, need for hepatitis B treatment, renal disease, and history of opportunistic infection [9]. Because there is significant risk of HIV transmission to the infant, breastfeeding is contraindicated in the developed world where there are safe and acceptable alternatives such as formula feeding. Avoidance of breastfeeding should be discussed with the patient over the course of her antepartum visits and again postpartum. The infant will receive 6 weeks of oral antiretroviral medication (usually zidovudine as a single agent), and the importance of adherence to the infant's medications should be stressed as well as the need for regular HIV testing of the infant over the course of the first year of life.

Adherence to antiretroviral medication in the postpartum period can be poor, and support should be provided if possible, as poor adherence can have lifelong implications for drug resistance, future options for antiretroviral therapy, and opportunistic infections [13, 14]. Comprehensive family planning including choices for effective contraception should be discussed in the antepartum as well as the postpartum period. There may be some pharmacologic interactions between antiretroviral medication and hormonal contraception so these should be taken into consideration when choosing a contraceptive method or methods [15–18].

Summary

With universal HIV testing prior to or early in pregnancy, early and effective antiretroviral therapy for all pregnant women, scheduled cesarean delivery if indicated, and antiretroviral therapy for the infant, as well as effective pre- and postconception counseling, HIV-infected women can have healthy and successful pregnancies. Their care requires a comprehensive, collaborative, and multidisciplinary approach.

Acute Hepatitis

Acute viral hepatitis is considered the most common cause of jaundice in pregnancy. Viral hepatitis E and herpes simplex hepatitis have a particular severe course and can progress to acute liver failure (ALF) in pregnant patients. Table 5.11 covers evaluation of abnormal LFT's (see GI, Chap. 5).

Hepatitis E

Hepatitis E is caused by an RNA virus of the family of *Herpesviridae* [19]. Infection is more common in nonindustrialized countries, and it is spread by orofecal route: person to person and through contaminated water sources. In rare cases, transmission has been described parenterally and vertically. It affects humans but similar viruses infect pigs, wild boars, and rats [20]. Globally, HEV is the most common cause of acute viral hepatitis and an important cause of maternal and perinatal death claiming 57,000 deaths worldwide yearly. In developing counties in Asia, the Middle East, Africa, and Central America, it occurs as an epidemic disease during the monsoon season but may also be endemic in these areas. Infection in industrialized countries is mainly a sporadic infection in patients returning from endemic areas. However, its prevalence is rising and might be an important cause of unexplained severe hepatitis.

Clinical Course and Management in Pregnancy

Acute hepatitis presents following 4–8 weeks of incubation, and it is characterized by malaise, fatigue, and jaundice. In children, it follows a mild course; in adults, it can be severe and in 7 % of cases leads to hepatic failure. Pregnant mothers infected with HEV have higher rates of fulminant hepatic failure and death than the general population. Acute infection is associated with 20–40 % maternal mortality and 26 % fetal mortality including intrauterine death and perinatal mortality. It is the most common cause of acute liver failure in pregnancy in countries such as Pakistan and India [21]. Diagnosis is made by serological testing for HEV IGG and IGM antibodies. PCR assay is not yet FDA approved, but it is available through the Centers of Disease Control and Prevention (CDC). HEV testing should be included in any workup of acute elevation of LFTs.

The therapy of the affected women is supportive. Two vaccines were developed and tested in small groups of risk individuals with good results. Unfortunately, China is the only country that pursued the commercialization and distribution of the vaccine to the population. Elsewhere, the production of the vaccine that would have saved many women's lives is stalling.

Hepatitis B

Epidemiology

The hepatitis B virus is a DNA virus of the *Hepadnavirus* family that is transmitted from infected individuals parenterally, sexually, and vertically. As a blood-borne pathogen, it is present in all major body fluids including saliva, semen, and maternal milk [22]. Hepatitis B virus infection is a serious global health problem, with two billion people infected worldwide and 350 million chronic carriers. In the United States, 0.1–0.2 % of the population is infected with HBV, but in certain areas of Southeast Asia, Africa, and East Europe, the infection rates are as high as 8 % of the total population [23]. In the United States, the prevalence of HBV infection varies widely in the population with the highest in individuals born in areas with high endemic prevalence.

Acute hepatitis occurs 6–12 weeks from contact, and resolution of illness with permanent immunity occurs in 90 % of adult cases. Infection acquired in children younger than age 5 years usually leads to chronic infection, as 90 % of infants infected at birth will remain chronically infected. Thus, nearly 50 % of the 350 million people chronically infected with hepatitis B acquired the infection through maternal vertical transmission.

All chronically infected individuals, defined as those with persistence of virus for longer than 6 months after an acute infection, are at risk of developing chronic active hepatitis, cirrhosis, and/or hepatocellular carcinoma (HCC). Recent therapeutic advances have modified the natural history of the disease. Appropriate antiviral therapy delays the onset of liver damage and might be protective against HCC development [24].

Due to safe and effective immunoprophylaxis, the epidemiology of the disease has changed radically. In the United States, vaccination for HBV was recommended for at-risk individuals in 1982 and then recommended for all newborns and children in 1991. In 1988, universal testing for hepatitis B early in pregnancy in all women and active and passive immunoprophylaxis of their newborn was recommended. The estimated number of infections in 2000 fell dramatically to 81,000, a 70 % decrease from the peak of the disease in the mid-1980s. However, according to the Institute of Medicine (IOM), 1,000 infants born to HBV-infected mothers are chronically infected with HBV per year, which has not declined further in the last decade. In 2010, the Institute of Medicine (IOM) renewed the efforts to eradicate HBV infection. It included enhanced immunoprophylaxis upon delivery, targeted testing of adults at risk, vaccination of adults, and public education in schools and local communities [25] (Table 9.1).

Table 9.1 2011 HHS action plan for the prevention, care, and treatment of viral hepatitis B

New cases of viral hepatitis are prevented
Persons who are already infected are tested
Informed about their infection
Provided with counseling, care, and treatment
Educate providers and communities to reduce health disparities
Improving testing and link to care to prevent HBV-related liver disease
Eliminate vertical transmission

Table 9.2 Prevalence of HBsAg positive among pregnant women

Mirrors the prevalence in the adult community	
In the United States, varies by race	
• 6 % Asian	
• 1 % Black	
• 0.6 % White	
• 0.14 % Hispanic	

Table 9.3 The HBsAg-positive patient: initial encounter key points

Education
• Natural history of chronic hepatitis B: discuss long-term complications and available therapies
• Discuss pregnancy outcomes
• Vertical transmission prevention: discuss immunoprophylaxis and immunoprophylaxis failure
• Household contacts: encourage vaccinations
Action
• Initial evaluation of chronic hepatitis B and referral to the specialist for consultation
• Report the patient to the Department of Health and to the DOH Perinatal Hepatitis Prevention Program

The Pregnant Patient with Hepatitis B

Screening and Diagnosis

The prevalence of HBsAg positivity in pregnant mothers mirrors the general population (Table 9.2) [26] and varies by race: 6 % Asian, 1 % Black, 0.6 % Caucasian, and 0.14 % Hispanic.

In American-born patients, the most likely source of infection is drug use or sexual transmission, whereas patients born in endemic areas have most likely acquired the infection at birth. Foreign-born individuals represent the majority of HBsAg-positive mothers. In the United States, there is universal screening for HBV infection in all pregnant women with an estimated 96 % of all pregnant women tested. Mothers who have not had antenatal testing are tested at delivery by the birthing hospital [27].

Counseling

For many patients, prenatal screening coincides with the time of initial diagnosis. The role of the physician in this instance is of increased importance given the emotional implications of the diagnosis (Table 9.3). Moreover, given the multicultural background of the patients, the counseling must be provided in a context that is sensitive to this diverse and vulnerable population.

Reassurance regarding the likelihood of good outcomes in pregnancy and education regarding transmission inside the household and to the unborn child must be provided. Moreover, pregnancy is a unique and in many cases the only opportunity for these patients to be educated about hepatitis B, its long-term effects, and the available therapies.

Pregnancy Outcomes

Effect of HBV Infection on Pregnancy

It is thought that hepatitis B virus infection does not adversely affect the course of pregnancy, nor does pregnancy adversely affect the natural history of the disease. Indeed large retrospective cohorts have shown no difference in maternal or fetal outcomes compared to healthy non-HBV-infected controls. However, acute HBV infection is associated with high vertical transmission rates when occurring in the third trimester and increased incidence of low birth weight and prematurity [28]. Moreover recent studies suggested an increased risk of preterm birth, antepartum hemorrhage, and gestational diabetes in mothers chronically infected with hepatitis B [29, 30]. However, it is possible that the underlying advanced liver disease itself contributed to the high complication rate rather than the HBV infection itself.

Effect of Pregnancy on Hepatitis B Virus-Related Liver Disease

HBV-related liver disease typically does not worsen during pregnancy. However, a small percentage of patients may develop cholestasis, chronic hepatitis B flare, or liver failure [28, 31]. During normal pregnancy, increased HBV viral load has been observed, leading to minor fluctuations in liver function tests and thought to be secondary to high levels of adrenal corticosteroids and estrogen hormones [32].

In one study, HBV virus levels remained stable, but ALT levels increased particularly in late pregnancy and postpartum periods. Further evidence supports the postpartum period as the most vulnerable time for HBV exacerbations. In a Japanese study, of 269 pregnant patients with chronic HBV infection, alteration of liver function was found in 43 % during the first month postpartum with some exacerbations leading to HBV seroconversion. Given the uncertainty of the natural history of HBV infection during and after pregnancy, patients should be monitored closely during pregnancy and postpartum.

Evaluation the Underlying Liver Disease

Although pregnancy is not contraindicated in HBV-infected individuals or for patients with severe liver disease, a comprehensive assessment of the underlying chronic hepatitis B is advised for all HBsAg-positive patients. This will serve two purposes: first to detect cirrhosis and potential liver insufficiency that will complicate the pregnancy, second to inform the patient about her disease and the available therapy, and third to set up appropriate follow-up care.

The recommendation endorsed by The American College of Obstetrics and Gynecology is that all HBsAg-positive mothers should be referred during pregnancy to a physician familiar with evaluation and treatment of viral hepatitis. Unfortunately, in a recent survey, only a third of patients were seen for consultation [33].

Table 9.4 Initial evaluation of the HBsAg-positive patient

History	Risk factors Previous history of HBsAg+ Treatment history	
Physical exam	Presence of signs and symptoms of chronic liver disease	
Laboratory tests	Viral studies	• HBc Ab IGM and total, HBeAg, HBeAb, HBV, DNA • HDV, HIV, HCV serology
	Liver function	• CBC with platlets, PT/INR, ALT, AST, total bilirubin
Imaging	Liver damage	Right upper quadrant U/S

Table 9.5 Serological markers of HBV infection

HBsAg	Component of viral envelope	Indicator of disease
Anti-HBs	Antibody response to HBsAg	Indicates recovery and acquired immunity
HBeAg	Antigen that correlates with replication and infectivity	High level of infectivity and replication
Anti-HBe	Antibody response to HBeAg	Decreasing level of replication Remission/resolution High replication in mutant strains
Anti-HBc IgM	Nonprotective antibody to the HBcAg Early marker of infection	Acute HBV infection
Anti-HBc IgG	As above	Previous or current HBV infection
HBV DNA	Replicative genetic material of HBV infectious agent	Viral replication and continues infection

HBsAg positivity is associated with advanced liver disease in 30 % of all patients. Assessing the extent of the liver disease is particularly challenging because it usually requires liver biopsy and histological analysis. Liver biopsy may be performed in this population, because the risks are same as in a nonpregnant patient; however, invasive testing is usually avoided during pregnancy unless absolutely necessary. The use of ultrasound and other newer noninvasive predictor of advanced liver damage such as MRI, FibroScan, and FibroSure have not been validated in pregnancy. The diagnosis thus relies on clinical and laboratory data (Table 9.4).

The immunoglobulin M class of hepatitis B core antibody (HBcAb) is the first to appear during acute infection, and its presence is used as the serologic marker of acute HBV infection. The presence of HBeAg positivity is associated with high infectivity and presence of high number of viral particles in the circulating blood (viral load). The presence of HBeAb positivity is associated with low infectivity, low replicative state, and low or undetectable viral load. Viral load is considered the most reliable indication of viral replication. HBV serological markers and their significance are reviewed in Table 9.5.

HBV viral load range is wide going from undetectable in inactive carriers to billions of viral copies in highly infective individuals. The definition of "high viral load" is not standardized. In general, a viral load exceeding 10 to the sixth copies/mL or >200,000 IU/ml is considered high, but several scientific publications and

Table 9.6 Immunoprophylaxis: current recommendations

- Mandatory testing for HBsAg in all pregnant patients (implementation in 19 states. Proof of test required in some states to obtain birth certificate)
- During pregnancy, vaccinate uninfected mother at risk. Retest them during the third trimester
- Postexposure immunoprophylaxis of infants born to HBsAg+ mothers with HBIg in 12 h from birth and HBV vaccine at birth, completion of subsequent doses (at least 2) within 6 months. Second dose in 10 weeks
- Infants retested for HBsAg and HBsAb at 9 months to exclude vertical transmission and ensure adequate antibody titer
- Perinatal Hepatitis Prevention Programs with "Case Managers" performing education and follow up

guideline use the terminology of "high viral load" for values from 10 to the fifth to 10 to the eighth.

HBsAg-positive patients with normal LFT's, platelets, and liver synthetic functions and low or undetectable viral load are inactive carriers. It is important to remember that they still need to be followed yearly since they are at risk for reactivation and hepatocellular carcinoma.

Vertical Transmission

Overall, the virus infects 75 % of all babies born from HBsAg-positive mothers in the absence of immunoprophylaxis. If the mother has a high viral load, as is the case in hepatitis B eAg-positive patients, this number is more than 90 %. However, newborns from mothers who are healthy carriers with minimal viral replication and hepatitis BeAb positivity are infected in less than 10 % of cases [34]. In the United States, the vertical transmission of hepatitis B has been reduced dramatically by the implementation of a nationally funded Perinatal Hepatitis Prevention Programs. Table 9.6 summarizes the steps.

Currently, available vaccines are safe in pregnancy, and mothers who are at risk for acquiring infection during pregnancy (injection drug users, patients with multiple sexual partners or who are infected with other sexually transmitted diseases] should be vaccinated and retested for HBsAg again in the third trimester close to the time of delivery [35]. Passive immunoprophylaxis with HBIG is also safe in pregnancy and should be given to women with documented exposure. Management of babies born from HBsAg+ mothers (including preterm infants) is outlined above. This schedule has achieved nearly a 97 % success rate in preventing overall vertical transmission [36].

Immunization Failure

Despite HBIG administration and vaccination, the rate of HBV infection in the newborn may still reach 8.5 % in mothers with high viral load [37]. CDC estimated that 1,000 newborns are infected vertically each year in the United States. In a recent study, all cases of immunoprophylaxis failure occurred in mothers with high viral load (defined as >10^6 copies/mL) [38]. The reason for immunoprophylaxis failure is that multifactorial prophylaxis regimens have been implemented in only 62 % [39] of cases. Vertical transmission of HBV occurs during delivery from blood-to-blood contact and occasionally in uteri by transplacental translocation of the virus [40]. Amniocentesis risk is controversial and not well established, but the test should be performed only if absolutely necessary [41].

Delivery and Breastfeeding

Elective cesarean session has been found in some studies to be protective from immunization failure, and it is advocated for mothers with high viral load and risk of vertical transmission [42]. However, this recommendation is not generally accepted, and conflicting data still exist in the literature. Specific guidelines do not exist regarding the mode of delivery [43, 44].

Breastfeeding has been a major concern for source of transmission; however, several studies have refuted this and shown that breastfeeding carries no additional risk to transmission of the virus in the setting of prompt newborn immunoprophylaxis and vaccination [45].

Antiviral Therapy in Pregnancy

Antiviral agents are used in pregnancy both to treat the expectant mother and to reduce vertical transmission.

Antiviral for Maternal Benefit

Decisions regarding therapy initiation, continuation, and termination should be the same for pregnant patients and general population. Antiviral therapy in pregnancy, however, is in general postponed until after birth unless necessary for treatment of acute flares or advanced liver disease. Successful treatment of liver failure in pregnancy has been described with antiviral therapy.

The discontinuation of treatment will result in rebound increasing viremia and subsequent disease flares. Continuation of the therapy in pregnancy is prudent especially in view of their relatively safe profile and the risk of fulminant hepatic failure associated with disease flares in pregnancy and postpartum [24] (Table 9.7).

Antiviral Therapy to Reduce Vertical Transmission

Immunization failure has been prevented by short courses of antiviral therapy during the second and third trimester of gestation in a few studies [46, 47]. In this patient population of high viral load mothers with otherwise limited underlying liver damage, therapy was initiated solely to prevent immunization failure.

Table 9.7 Algorithm for treatment of hepatitis B in pregnancy

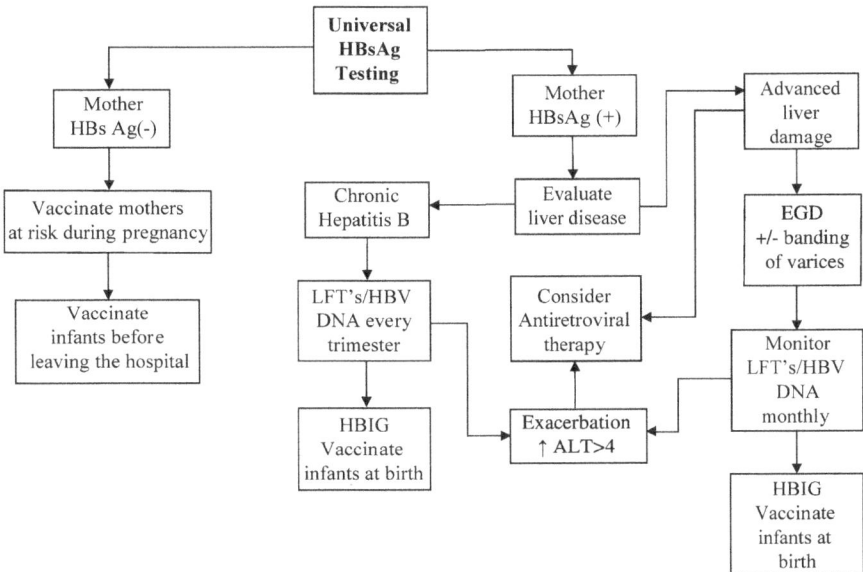

Current use of antiviral to decrease vertical transmission is endorsed by many experts and was incorporated in the 2012 EASL Guidelines. This strategy is not uniformly accepted. Substantial debate still exists regarding the patient population to treat, choice of drug, length of treatment, and appropriate follow-up [48].

Two meta-analyses concluded that lamivudine treatment from 24 to 32 weeks of gestation until 1 month postpartum in those mothers who had high viral loads ($>10^6$) was not only safe but more effective than HBIG and vaccination of the newborn alone [43, 49]. Most recently, a meta-analysis included four randomized controlled trials with a total of 306 mothers showing that telbivudine given late in pregnancy was safe as well as effective in reducing vertical transmission [50].

Safety of Antiviral Therapy

The safety data for antiviral therapy is derived from the antiretroviral pregnancy registry (APR) and the Development of Antiretroviral Therapy Study (DART). No significant differences in rates of adverse outcomes have been reported for HB antiviral drugs initiated throughout the three trimesters of pregnancy [51]. These rates were comparable to the defect rates in the general population (reported by the CDC).

Lamivudine and tenofovir have the largest data set because they have been used in HIV-infected patients. Tenofovir and entecavir are the most potent drugs with less likelihood of developing resistance and the ones recommended to treat nonpregnant patients. Tenofovir has been associated with skeletal abnormalities [52], and further studies assessing newborn bone density are planned. Limited data are available for entecavir and adefovir use in pregnancy Table 9.8.

Table 9.8 Birth defects associated with antiviral exposure (APR report, July 2013)

Antiviral agent	Pregnancy category	Live birth earliest exposure first trimester	Prevalence birth defects
Telbivudine	B	32	n/a
Lamivudine	C	4,360	3.1 % (CI 2.6–3.7 %)
Tenofovir	B	1,982	2.3 % (CI 1.7–3.1 %)
Adefovir	C	66	n/a

Adapted from: [53]

Hepatitis C in Pregnancy

Previously known as non-A, non-B hepatitis, hepatitis C was discovered only in 1989. Hepatitis C virus is an RNA single-stranded virus of the *Filoviridae* family. As a blood-borne pathogen, the main causes of infection are intravenous drug use and contaminated blood products. More than 80 % of drug users are positive for HCV. Sexual transmission is thought to occur, but so rarely that monogamous couples with only one partner infected are not advised to use barrier contraception. In 10 % to 20 % of patients, the source of infection is unknown. Interestingly, baby boomers (those born between 1945 and 1965) are five times more likely to have HCV infection. The CDC now recommends one time testing in this population given the increased risk.

Unfortunately, a vaccine is not available. Hepatitis C infection affects 3 % of the world population. In the United States 4 million people are infected. Although the number of new HCV infections is declining, the number of patients suffering from HCV-related chronic liver disease is still mounting. Prevalence of HCV infection in the pregnant population is 0.5 %. Despite its prevalence, the American College of Gynecology does not recommend routine screening for HCV infection.

Acute infection with HCV is usually asymptomatic, and clearance of virus occurs in 25–30 % of cases. In children and young women, this percentage is even higher. Chronic infection is common, with patients remaining asymptomatic for decades. Only 20–30 % of those chronically infected will develop significant liver damage, i.e., cirrhosis, and 30 % of those who develop cirrhosis will consequently develop HCC 20–30 years after the original infection. Alcohol consumption, male gender, and obesity are predisposing factors associated with development of liver damage. Hepatitis C is a systemic disease associated with the development of autoimmune diseases such as thyroiditis, autoimmune hepatitis, and rheumatoid arthritis. In addition, HCV infection may cause insulin resistance and depressive symptoms associated with mild cognitive impairment.

Effect of Pregnancy on Hepatitis C Virus Disease

Through unclear mechanisms, female gender has a positive effect on HCV disease course and response to therapy. After menopause, this benefit seems to disappear. Derivatives of estrogen, such as estradiol, are thought to have powerful antioxidant effects likely leading to decreased inflammatory by-products as well as decreased fibrosis [54]. In pregnancy, both exacerbation and improvement in liver histology and clinical parameters have been found. Normalization of liver function tests, decrease of the viral load, and even spontaneous viral clearance have been reported [54]. Pregnancy is generally well tolerated by patients without severe liver damage. Postpartum, however, may be a time of increased replication associated with fatigue, body aches, and elevation of liver function tests.

Effect of Hepatitis C Virus on Pregnancy

Complications of pregnancy caused by HCV infection are probably rare. However, retrospective studies suggest an increased incidence of fetal/maternal complications including low birth weight and requirement for assisted ventilation [55]. Prospective studies are lacking. Women with HCV are at increased risk of developing gestational diabetes as well as cholestasis of pregnancy [56].

Preconception Counseling

HCV identification during pregnancy is a time to discuss the normal progression of HCV infection as well as reduce future HCV transmission. Pregnancy is not discouraged in patients infected with HCV, but the potential for vertical transmission to the baby must be discussed as well as its effect on the course of pregnancy. Ribavirin, one of the mainstays of HCV therapy, should be avoided within 6 months of pregnancy, given its long half-life. Patients with stigmata of liver disease should be referred to obstetric medicine and gastroenterology specialists for careful monitoring during pregnancy.

Children born infected with HCV through vertical transmission may be at increased risk for low birth weight and small for gestational age. It has been observed, however, that these children generally have minimal progression of fibrosis.

Table 9.9 HCV screening

- Ever injected illegal drugs
- Received clotting factors made before 1987
- Received blood/organs before July 1992
- Ever on chronic hemodyalisis
- Evidence of liver disease/and any abnormal LFT's
  High risk birth cohort (Born between 1945 and 1965)
- Healthcare, emergency, public safety workers after needle stick/mucosal exposures to HCV-positive blood
- Sexual partners of HCV positive individuals

Risk Factors and Screening

Currently, universal screening for HCV is not recommended. Every effort should be made to identify risks factors in order to test high-risk patients with HCV antibody. Risk factors that should trigger HCV testing in pregnancy are given in Table 9.9.

Pregnancy is a time to provide counseling and is an important step in the control of the HCV epidemic.

To confirm HCV infection, it is necessary to check HCV PCR for direct viral particle detection in the blood, as well as genotype determination. Those individuals whose HCV PCR is undetectable are aviremic but still considered infectious because further characterization of their status is not possible. HCV antibodies develop up to 6 months from the initial infection, and HCV PCR should be used to diagnose HCV acute hepatitis.

Management

Exciting drug development is changing the landscape of HCV therapy. In addition to pegylated interferon and ribavirin, protease inhibitors such as boceprevir and telaprevir have been used for treatment of HCV genotype 1 in nonpregnant patients with evidence of liver damage. Treatment for 24–48 weeks is effective in up to 60–80 % of all patients in decreasing the viral load to undetectable levels (sustained viral response). New direct antivirals (DDA) Sofosbuvir and Simeprevir were approved in December 2013 including an interferon free therapy for genotype 2 and 3 [57]. Historically with ribavirin- and interferon-based treatment, women have a much better response rate than men to therapy. Ribavirin is teratogenic and should not be administered during pregnancy.

Immunoprophylaxis for Prevention of Vertical Transmission

Vertical transmission of HCV from mother to fetus occurs but much less frequently than for HBV virus [58]. As with HBV, amniocentesis should be performed only if absolutely necessary [41]. The rate of transmission varies widely from as low as 3 % to as high as 35 %. This rate depends in part on the viral load: high viral load leads to increased transmission to the child and is very unlikely in aviremic mothers. In mothers coinfected with HIV, HCV viral loads are higher, leading to an observed higher rate of transmission (nearly 30–35 %), yet it is unclear if HIV is an independent risk factor for vertical transmission [59]. Newborn girls are twice as likely to be infected as are males for unknown reasons.

There is no specific immunoprophylaxis for HCV. Recommendations from two recent prospective studies to reduce the risk of transmission include delivery within 6 h of membrane rupture and avoidance of invasive monitoring during delivery. Cesarean section does not decrease the rate of transmission. Although HCV virus may be found in breast milk, breastfeeding is safe in the absence of breast sores [60].

Children born from HCV-positive mothers should be tested for the infection. Hepatitis C virus and HCV maternal antibodies may be detected up to 12–18 months in the neonate. The AASLD recommends checking for HCV antibody after 18 months. However, in practice, most physicians perform two HCV tests by PCR between 2 and 6 months followed by HCV antibody testing at age 18 months. Infected children should be referred to a pediatric hepatologist for treatment.

References

1. Panel on Treatment of HIV-Infected Pregnant Women and Prevention of Perinatal Transmission. Recommendations for use of antiretroviral drugs in pregnant HIV-1-infected women for maternal health and interventions to reduce perinatal HIV transmission in the [internet]. 2012 (cited 4 Feb 2012).
2. Recommendations for use of antiretroviral drugs in pregnant HIV-1-infected women for maternal health and interventions to reduce perinatal HIV-1 transmission in the united states. 2012 (cited 28 Sept 2014).
3. HIV in women: Centers for disease control and prevention [internet]. Available from: http://www.cdc.gov/hiv/pdf/risk_women.pdf.
4. Nielsen-Saines K, Watts DH, Veloso VG, Bryson YJ, Joao EC, Pilotto IH, Gray G, Theron G, Santos B, Fonseca R, Kreitchmann R, Pinto J, Mussi-Pinhata MM, Ceriotto M, Machado D, Bethel J, Morgado MG, Dickover R, Camarca M, Mirochnick M, Siberry G, Grinsztejn B, Moreira RI, Bastos FI, Xu J, Moye J, Mofenson LM, Team NHPP. Three postpartum antiretroviral regimens to prevent intrapartum HIV infection. N Engl J Med. 2012;366:2368–79.
5. Gray GE, Urban M, Chersich MF, Bolton C, van Niekerk R, Violari A, Stevens W, McIntyre JA, Group PEPS. A randomized trial of two postexposure prophylaxis regimens to reduce mother-to-child HIV-1 transmission in infants of untreated mothers. AIDS. 2005;19:1289–97.
6. Morrison CS, Demers K, Kwok C, Bulime S, Rinaldi A, Munjoma M, Dunbar M, Chipato T, Byamugisha J, Van Der Pol B, Arts E, Salata RA. Plasma and cervical viral loads among Ugandan and Zimbabwean women during acute and early HIV-1 infection. AIDS. 2010;24: 573–82.

7. Chetty V, Moodley D, Chuturgoon A. Evaluation of a 4th generation rapid HIV test for earlier and reliable detection of HIV infection in pregnancy. J Clin Virol. 2012;54:180–4.
8. Aberg JA, Gallant JE, Ghanem KG, Emmanuel P, Zingman BS, Horberg MA. Primary care guidelines for the management of persons infected with HIV: 2013 update by the HIV medicine association of the infectious diseases society of America. Clin Infect Dis. 2014;58:e1–34.
9. Dybul M, Fauci AS, Bartlett JG, Kaplan JE, Pau AK. Panel on clinical practices for treatment of HIV. Guidelines for using antiretroviral agents among HIV-infected adults and adolescents. Ann Intern Med. 2002;137:381–433.
10. The International Perinatal HIV Group. The mode of delivery and the risk of vertical transmission of human immunodeficiency virus type 1–a meta-analysis of 15 prospective cohort studies. N Engl J Med. 1999;340:977–87.
11. European Mode of Delivery Collaboration. Elective caesarean-section versus vaginal delivery in prevention of vertical HIV-1 transmission: a randomised clinical trial. Lancet. 1999;353:1035–9.
12. Committee on Obstetric Practice. American College of Obstetricians and Gynecologists. Acog committee opinion scheduled cesarean delivery and the prevention of vertical transmission of HIV infection. Number 219, August 1999. Int J Gynaecol Obstet. 1999;66:305–6.
13. Kreitchmann R, Harris DR, Kakehasi F, Haberer JE, Cahn P, Losso M, Teles E, Pilotto JH, Hofer CB, Read JS, Team NLS. Antiretroviral adherence during pregnancy and postpartum in Latin America. AIDS Patient Care STDs. 2012;26:486–95.
14. Mellins CA, Chu C, Malee K, Allison S, Smith R, Harris L, Higgins A, Zorrilla C, Landesman S, Serchuck L, Larussa P. Adherence to antiretroviral treatment among pregnant and postpartum HIV-infected women. AIDS Care. 2008;20:958–68.
15. Cohn SE, Park JG, Watts DH, Stek A, Hitti J, Clax PA, Yu S, Lertora JJ, Team AAP. Depomedroxyprogesterone in women on antiretroviral therapy: effective contraception and lack of clinically significant interactions. Clin Pharmacol Ther. 2007;81:222–7.
16. Vogler MA, Patterson K, Kamemoto L, Park JG, Watts H, Aweeka F, Klingman KL, Cohn SE. Contraceptive efficacy of oral and transdermal hormones when co-administered with protease inhibitors in HIV-1-infected women: pharmacokinetic results of actg trial a5188. J Acquir Immune Defic Syndr. 2010;55:473–82.
17. Womack J, Williams A. Hormonal contraception in HIV-positive women. AIDS Read. 2008;18:372–7. 381.
18. World Health Organization. Review of priorities in research on hormonal contraception and IUDs and HIV infection. Geneve: WHO; 2010.
19. Reyes GR, Purdy MA, Kim JP, Luk KC, Young LM, Fry KE, Bradley DW. Isolation of a cdna from the virus responsible for enterically transmitted non-a, non-b hepatitis. Science. 1990;247:1335–9.
20. Scobie L, Dalton HR. Hepatitis e: source and route of infection, clinical manifestations and new developments. J Viral Hepat. 2013;20:1–11.
21. Aggarwal R. Hepatitis E: clinical presentation in disease-endemic areas and diagnosis. Semin Liver Dis. 2013;33:30–40.
22. Wright TL. Introduction to chronic hepatitis b infection. Am J Gastroenterol. 2006;101 Suppl 1:S1–6.
23. Goldstein ST, Zhou F, Hadler SC, Bell BP, Mast EE, Margolis HS. A mathematical model to estimate global hepatitis b disease burden and vaccination impact. Int J Epidemiol. 2005;34:1329–39.
24. Kim HY, Choi JY, Park CH, Jang JW, Kim CW, Bae SH, Yoon SK, Yang JM, Lee CD, Lee YS. Outcome after discontinuing antiviral agents during pregnancy in women infected with hepatitis b virus. J Clin Virol. 2013;56:299–305.
25. US Department of Health and Human Services. Combating the silent epidemic of viral hepatitis: action plan for the prevention, care, and treatment of viral hepatitis. Washington, DC: HHS; 2011:1–76.
26. Euler GL, Wooten KG, Baughman AL, Williams WW. Hepatitis b surface antigen prevalence among pregnant women in urban areas: implications for testing, reporting, and preventing perinatal transmission. Pediatrics. 2003;111:1192–7.

27. Fischer G, Wang S, Ahring S, Fowler K, Hainline S, Chinglong M, Jacques-Carroll L, Bell B, Williams I. An investigation of perinatal hepatitis b virus infections among a high risk population: the delivery hospital as a safety net. Pediatr Infect Dis J. 2009;28:593–7.
28. Nguyen G, Garcia RT, Nguyen N, Trinh H, Keeffe EB, Nguyen MH. Clinical course of hepatitis b virus infection during pregnancy. Aliment Pharmacol Ther. 2009;29:755–64.
29. Connell LE, Salihu HM, Salemi JL, August EM, Weldeselasse H, Mbah AK. Maternal hepatitis b and hepatitis c carrier status and perinatal outcomes. Liver Int. 2011;31:1163–70.
30. Safir A, Levy A, Sikuler E, Sheiner E. Maternal hepatitis b virus or hepatitis c virus carrier status as an independent risk factor for adverse perinatal outcome. Liver Int. 2010;30: 765–70.
31. Potthoff A, Berg T, Wedemeyer H, Group H-NBCCS. Late hepatitis b virus relapse in patients co-infected with hepatitis b virus and hepatitis c virus after antiviral treatment with pegylated interferon-a2b and ribavirin. Scand J Gastroenterol. 2009;44:1487–90.
32. Tan HH, Lui HF, Chow WC. Chronic hepatitis b virus (hbv) infection in pregnancy. Hepatol Int. 2008;2:370–5.
33. Godbole G, Irish D, Basarab M, Mahungu T, Fox-Lewis A, Thorne C, Jacobs M, Dusheiko G, Rosenberg WM, Suri D, Millar AD, Nastouli E. Management of hepatitis b in pregnant women and infants: a multicentre audit from four london hospitals. BMC Pregnancy Childbirth. 2013;13:222.
34. Okada K, Kamiyama I, Inomata M, Imai M, Miyakawa Y. E antigen and anti-e in the serum of asymptomatic carrier mothers as indicators of positive and negative transmission of hepatitis b virus to their infants. N Engl J Med. 1976;294:746–9.
35. CDC. General recommendations on immunization: recommendations of the advisory committee on immunization practices(acip). MMWR Morb Mortal Wkly Rep. 2011;60:26.
36. Centers for Disease Control and Prevention. Postvaccination serologic testing results for infants aged </=24 months exposed to hepatitis b virus at birth: United States, 2008–2011. MMWR Morb Mortal Wkly Rep. 2012;61:768–71.
37. Wiseman E, Fraser MA, Holden S, Glass A, Kidson BL, Heron LG, Maley MW, Ayres A, Locarnini SA, Levy MT. Perinatal transmission of hepatitis b virus: an Australian experience. Med J Aust. 2009;190:489–92.
38. Zou H, Chen Y, Duan Z, Zhang H, Pan C. Virologic factors associated with failure to passive-active immunoprophylaxis in infants born to hbsag-positive mothers. J Viral Hepat. 2012;19:e18–25.
39. Willis BC, Wortley P, Wang SA, Jacques-Carroll L, Zhang F. Gaps in hospital policies and practices to prevent perinatal transmission of hepatitis b virus. Pediatrics. 2010;125:704–11.
40. Zhang SL, Yue YF, Bai GQ, Shi L, Jiang H. Mechanism of intrauterine infection of hepatitis b virus. World J Gastroenterol. 2004;10:437–8.
41. Davies G, Wilson RD, Desilets V, Reid GJ, Shaw D, Summers A, Wyatt P, Young D, Society of Obstetricians and Gynaecologists of Canada. Amniocentesis and women with hepatitis b, hepatitis c, or human immunodeficiency virus. J Obstet Gynaecol Can. 2003;25(145–148): 149–52.
42. Yang J, Zeng XM, Men YL, Zhao LS. Elective caesarean section versus vaginal delivery for preventing mother to child transmission of hepatitis b virus–a systematic review. Virol J. 2008;5:100.
43. Xu H, Zeng T, Liu JY, Lei Y, Zhong S, Sheng YJ, Zhou Z, Ren H. Measures to reduce mother-to-child transmission of hepatitis b virus in china: a meta-analysis. Dig Dis Sci. 2014; 59:242–58.
44. Hu Y, Chen J, Wen J, Xu C, Zhang S, Xu B, Zhou YH. Effect of elective cesarean section on the risk of mother-to-child transmission of hepatitis b virus. BMC Pregnancy Childbirth. 2013;13:119.
45. Hill JB, Sheffield JS, Kim MJ, Alexander JM, Sercely B, Wendel GD. Risk of hepatitis b transmission in breast-fed infants of chronic hepatitis b carriers. Obstet Gynecol. 2002;99: 1049–52.

46. Xu WM, Cui YT, Wang L, Yang H, Liang ZQ, Li XM, Zhang SL, Qiao FY, Campbell F, Chang CN, Gardner S, Atkins M. Lamivudine in late pregnancy to prevent perinatal transmission of hepatitis b virus infection: a multicentre, randomized, double-blind, placebo-controlled study. J Viral Hepat. 2009;16:94–103.
47. Han GR, Cao MK, Zhao W, Jiang HX, Wang CM, Bai SF, Yue X, Wang GJ, Tang X, Fang ZX. A prospective and open-label study for the efficacy and safety of telbivudine in pregnancy for the prevention of perinatal transmission of hepatitis b virus infection. J Hepatol. 2011;55:1215–21.
48. Ayres A, Yuen L, Jackson KM, Manoharan S, Glass A, Maley M, Yoo W, Hong SP, Kim SO, Luciani F, Bowden DS, Bayliss J, Levy MT, Locarnini SA. Short duration of lamivudine for the prevention of hepatitis b virus transmission in pregnancy: lack of potency and selection of resistance mutations. J Viral Hepat. 2013;21(11):809–817.
49. Han L, Zhang HW, Xie JX, Zhang Q, Wang HY, Cao GW. A meta-analysis of lamivudine for interruption of mother-to-child transmission of hepatitis b virus. World J Gastroenterol. 2011;17:4321–33.
50. Deng M, Zhou X, Gao S, Yang SG, Wang B, Chen HZ, Ruan B. The effects of telbivudine in late pregnancy to prevent intrauterine transmission of the hepatitis b virus: a systematic review and meta-analysis. Virol J. 2012;9:185.
51. Brown Jr RS, Verna EC, Pereira MR, Tilson HH, Aguilar C, Leu CS, Buti M, Fagan EA. Hepatitis b virus and human immunodeficiency virus drugs in pregnancy: findings from the antiretroviral pregnancy registry. J Hepatol. 2012;57:953–9.
52. Gafni RI, Hazra R, Reynolds JC, Maldarelli F, Tullio AN, DeCarlo E, Worrell CJ, Flaherty JF, Yale K, Kearney BP, Zeichner SL. Tenofovir disoproxil fumarate and an optimized background regimen of antiretroviral agents as salvage therapy: impact on bone mineral density in HIV-infected children. Pediatrics. 2006;118:e711–718.
53. Antiretroviral Pregnancy Registry Steering Committee. Antiretroviral Pregnancy Registry International iterim report for 1 January 1989 through 31 January 2013. Wilmington, NC: Registry Coordinating Center; 2014. Available from http://www.apregistry.com.
54. Floreani A. Hepatitis c and pregnancy. World J Gastroenterol. 2013;19:6714–20.
55. Pergam SA, Wang CC, Gardella CM, Sandison TG, Phipps WT, Hawes SE. Pregnancy complications associated with hepatitis c: data from a 2003–2005 Washington state birth cohort. Am J Obstet Gynecol. 2008;199:38e31–39.
56. Locatelli A, Roncaglia N, Arreghini A, Bellini P, Vergani P, Ghidini A. Hepatitis c virus infection is associated with a higher incidence of cholestasis of pregnancy. Br J Obstet Gynaecol. 1999;106:498–500.
57. Thomas DL. Cure of hepatitis c virus infection without interferon alfa: scientific basis and current clinical evidence. Top Antivir Med. 2013;21:152–6.
58. Ohto H, Terazawa S, Sasaki N, Sasaki N, Hino K, Ishiwata C, Kako M, Ujiie N, Endo C, Matsui A, et al. Transmission of hepatitis c virus from mothers to infants. The vertical transmission of hepatitis c virus collaborative study group. N Engl J Med. 1994;330:744–50.
59. Mast EE, Hwang LY, Seto DS, Nolte FS, Nainan OV, Wurtzel H, Alter MJ. Risk factors for perinatal transmission of hepatitis c virus (hcv) and the natural history of hcv infection acquired in infancy. J Infect Dis. 2005;192:1880–9.
60. Tovo PA, Palomba E, Ferraris G, Principi N, Ruga E, Dallacasa P, Maccabruni A. Increased risk of maternal-infant hepatitis c virus transmission for women coinfected with human immunodeficiency virus type 1. Italian study group for hcv infection in children. Clin Infect Dis. 1997;25:1121–4.

Part IX
Neurology

Chapter 10
Headaches and Seizures

Julie L. Roth and Courtney Bilodeau

Abbreviations

AED	Antiepileptic drugs
CH	Cluster headache
CT	Computerized tomography
EEG	Electroencephalogram
MRI	Magnetic resonance imaging
TTH	Tension-type headache

Introduction

Disorders of the nervous system that occur in pregnant patients can be classified into those that predated the pregnancy—including those that may affect or be affected by pregnancy—and those that arise de novo during pregnancy or as a consequence of the pregnant state. Of these neurological disorders, some of the most commonly encountered by providers of obstetrical care include headaches and

---

J.L. Roth, M.D. (✉)
Department of Neurology, Comprehensive Epilepsy Program, Rhode Island Hospital,
110 Lockwood Street, Suite 342, Providence, RI 02903, USA

The Warren Alpert Medical School of Brown University, Providence, RI, USA
e-mail: Julie_Roth@brown.edu

C. Bilodeau, M.D.
Department of Obstetric Medicine, Women's Medicine Collaborative, Miriam Hospital,
146 West River Street, Ste 11C, Providence, RI 02904, USA

The Warren Alpert Medical School of Brown University, Providence, RI, USA
e-mail: cbilodeau1@lifespan.org

seizures. Headaches are defined as head pain, either of primary origin (migraines, cluster headaches, tension headaches) or secondary origin (cerebral venous sinus thrombosis, mass lesion, elevated intracranial pressure, and vascular, infectious, or metabolic conditions). Seizures are defined as the various clinical sequelae of a hypersynchronous, hyperexcitable state involving neurons in the brain; similarly, seizures can be of primary origin (epilepsy) or secondary (due to a structural cause, toxic-metabolic derangement, infection, inflammation, or vascular). Eclampsia involves both headaches and seizures and will be discussed elsewhere in this textbook. This chapter will focus on alterations in preexisting neurological conditions of primary origin (primary headache disorders, epilepsy), including diagnosis and management during pregnancy.

Primary Headaches in Pregnancy

Background/Definition

The International Headache Society (IHS) defines headache as pain in the head classified into three major groups and subdivided into types. The three major groups are (1) primary headaches, (2) secondary headaches, and (3) cranial neuralgias, including central and primary facial pain and other headaches [1]. Primary headaches are head pain not due to a causative disorder. The three major types of primary headaches are tension-type headache (TTH), cluster headache (CH), and migraine headache; these will be discussed in detail. Secondary headaches occur as a symptom of an identified medical disorder, such as tumor or infection. Examples of secondary headaches in pregnancy include headache associated with preeclampsia/eclampsia or post-dural puncture following regional anesthesia. Pseudotumor cerebri (also known as idiopathic intracranial hypertension) and headache due to cerebral venous sinus thrombosis are more common in pregnancy and should be explored appropriately. A treatable cranial neuralgia commonly diagnosed in pregnancy and postpartum is occipital neuralgia. In some cases, local nerve block can be used in pregnancy to treat neuralgia.

Epidemiology

Headaches are one of the most common complaints for which patients seek medical attention. Migraine occurs in 11–26 % of women of childbearing age, although the prevalence of migraine during pregnancy is unknown [2]. Women have a higher incidence than men for TTH and migraine headaches (3:1), with a high frequency during childbearing age. CH are more frequently diagnosed in men, but the number of female cases has risen [3]. One third or more of pregnancies are complicated by headache [4].

Pathobiology

While migraine, among other primary headache disorders, may have genetic implications, known triggers for individual headache attacks include factors that are common in pregnancy such as sleep disturbance, stress, and hormonal changes. Pregnant women who acutely cut down or discontinue medication (i.e., benzodiazepines, selective serotonin reuptake inhibitors, and tricyclic antidepressants), caffeine, nicotine, and illicit substances are also more prone to headaches. Other risk factors for headaches in pregnancy and postpartum include rebound headache from overuse of analgesics, including NSAIDs and acetaminophen, and the use of regional anesthesia during labor and delivery.

The etiology of TTH is unknown, but neurobiologic factors affecting central and peripheral pain mechanisms likely contribute to the episodic or chronic pain of a TTH [5]. There remains a paucity of data on the effect of pregnancy on TTH, but frequency of TTH appears to mostly improve or remain unchanged in pregnancy [6]. There are no known associations between TTH and adverse pregnancy outcomes.

Newer imaging modalities such as positron emission tomography and functional magnetic resonance imaging have helped to understand the pathophysiology of CHs. Defects in the posterior hypothalamic gray matter from circadian biological changes, and neuroendocrine disturbances disinhibit trigeminal nociceptive pathways [7]. There is no definitive evidence for a link between CH pathophysiology and sex hormone levels. Only a small percent of women suffer from cluster headaches in pregnancy and postpartum. CH do not appear to have any effect on pregnancy outcomes, although fewer pregnancies occur in women who suffer from cluster headaches, perhaps due to patient preference because of the limitations of CH pain management [4].

Migraine pathophysiology is believed to be due to primary neuronal dysfunction leading to activation in the trigeminovascular system [8]. The aura of migraine is caused by an electrical phenomenon known as cortical spreading depression of Leao—a slow spread of reduced electrical activity over the cortex of the brain, coupled with alterations in blood flow that may contribute to activation of the trigeminal vascular system, which is thought to trigger the pain of migraine. Hormonal fluctuations are known triggers for migraine headaches. More specifically, high levels of estrogen worsen migraines with aura, and low levels of estrogen trigger migraines without aura [6]. Therefore depending on whether or not a woman has migraines with aura, she may be more likely to experience increased migraine frequency during pregnancy (migraine with aura) or the postpartum (migraine without aura). However, in clinical practice, migraine during pregnancy can be less predictable—women can describe either worsening or improvement of migraines during pregnancy that may not correspond to the presence of an aura. Aura without

Table 10.1 Diagnosis and management of primary headaches in pregnancy

Cause of headache	Common features	Treatment in pregnancy	Treatment postpartum
Migraine	Frontal (often unilateral), prolonged, and pulsatile Other: nausea, vomiting, and aversion to loud noise, bright light, and physical activity	Acetaminophen, antiemetics, caffeine, corticosteroids (prednisone), intravenous hydration, and opioids	*Treatment in pregnancy* plus NSAIDS and triptans (sumatriptan)
Tension-type	Bifrontal, bitemporal, bioccipital, or neck with squeezing and aching Other: nausea, light, and sound sensitivity	Acetaminophen, caffeine, and opioids Alternative therapies: relaxation techniques, biofeedback, and physical therapy	*Treatment in pregnancy* plus NSAIDS
Cluster	Unilateral, orbitotemporal, non-throbbing, and penetrating Other: ptosis, conjunctival injection, or lacrimation	Oxygen, intranasal lidocaine	*Treatment in pregnancy* plus triptans (sumatriptan)

migraine can also occur de novo in pregnancy, in a migraineur. There is limited evidence for a biological effect of migraine on maternal and fetal complications of pregnancy. The disorder has been linked with low birth weight and hypertensive disorders of pregnancy [4, 6], with a purported mechanism of vasospasm, endothelial dysfunction, and platelet dysfunction. Migraine during pregnancy, particularly in second half of pregnancy, and with or without features of aura, has also been associated with increased risk of stroke in pregnancy or the postpartum period [2], but further study is needed.

Increasing body weight and circulating hormones in pregnancy are thought to be risk factors for the development of pseudotumor cerebri (idiopathic intracranial hypertension). Estrogen also contributes to a thrombophilic state, and therefore pregnancy is a risk factor for the development of cerebral venous sinus thrombosis—which can be life-threatening.

Diagnosis and Management

In the diagnosis of peripartum headaches, the clinician must first rule out potentially life-threatening etiologies including preeclampsia, infection, tumor, or thrombosis. New onset headaches during pregnancy warrant a thorough workup—bedside exam must include fundoscopy—to evaluate for signs of elevated intracranial pressure, and based on characteristics of the headache, evaluation with laboratory studies, radiologic studies (such as magnetic resonance imaging with venous phase or MRV), and possibly a lumbar puncture to evaluate opening pressure may be needed. Following the workup for secondary causes of headache, clinical signs and

Table 10.2 Prevention therapy for headaches in pregnancy

Drug class	Example
Antidepressants	Amitriptyline, nortriptyline
Beta-blockers	Propranolol, metoprolol
Calcium channel blockers	Nifedipine, verapamil
NSAIDS	Low-dose aspirin
Supplements	Magnesium, riboflavin

symptoms are used for the diagnosis of primary headache. Table 10.1 provides a summary of primary headache diagnosis and management.

Prophylactic medication may be needed in the management of headache in pregnancy based on frequency, severity, and duration of headaches. Below is a list of common prophylactic medications used in pregnancy (Table 10.2). A headache diary is often helpful to monitor the clinical course, triggers, and management. The clinical benefit of prophylaxis is variable and requires a clinical trial of daily use for at least 6 weeks to determine efficacy. Consideration of coexisting conditions and potential for medication interactions should be used to guide choice of prophylactic medication. For example, the use of a beta-blocker is typically contraindicated in a pregnant woman with low blood pressure especially with symptomatic dizziness. Reevaluation of therapy is important to monitor medication efficacy, side effects, and clinical course and to rule out development of a new headache etiology, such as preeclampsia. Nonpharmacologic therapies for headache prevention include relaxation, biofeedback, and stress management [9]. Lifestyle modification including avoidance of skipped meals, sleep deprivation, and dehydration should also be stressed. Women who are treated with anticonvulsant (also known as antiepileptic drug or AED) class medications for migraine prophylaxis prior to pregnancy (such as topiramate and valproic acid) should be counseled on the risk of birth defects associated with these drugs, and whenever possible, these drugs should be discontinued. Anticonvulsants are discussed later in this chapter.

Seizures in Pregnancy

Background/Definition

Seizures represent the clinical manifestation of paroxysmal, synchronous firing of neurons within the cortex of the brain—generally thought of as "electrical storms" of the brain. Seizures can have provoking factors—irritation of the cortex by blood, infection, inflammation, an abnormal structure or mass, exposure to toxins, or derangements of glucose or electrolytes, among many other causes (see Table 10.3). Seizures also occur in eclampsia, among other vascular disorders of pregnancy. When seizures occur de novo in a pregnant patient, a thorough workup is

Table 10.3 Possible causes of seizure in pregnancy

Vascular causes – Eclampsia – Stroke, including hemorrhagic stroke, ischemic stroke due to arterial or venous occlusion, and cerebral venous sinus thrombosis – Hypertensive encephalopathy – Reversible posterior leukoencephalopathy syndrome – Primary central nervous system vasculitis
Thrombotic thrombocytopenic purpura (TTP)
Mass lesions (neoplasm, abscess)
Infection (meningitis and encephalitis)
Metabolic disorders (hypoglycemia, hyperglycemia, hyponatremia, hypocalcemia, hypomagnesemia, uremia, hyperammonemia, and liver failure, pyridoxine deficiency, thyrotoxicosis, and porphyria)
Hypoxic-ischemic cerebral injury
Drug exposure (amphetamines, cocaine, tricyclic antidepressants, theophylline, and lidocaine)
Withdrawal syndromes (including withdrawal from antiepileptic drugs, benzodiazepine, alcohol, and barbiturates)
Idiopathic epilepsy

necessary to rule out these conditions. When no provoking factors are identified, seizures may be a manifestation of epilepsy, which is defined as "two or more unprovoked seizures." An alternative definition of epilepsy is "a tendency toward unprovoked seizures"; this second definition presupposes an abnormality detected on an electroencephalogram (EEG), which may be characteristic of an underlying idiopathic epilepsy syndrome.

Preexisting epilepsy is the most common reason for seizures during pregnancy. Among patients known to have a seizure tendency—or epilepsy—prior to the pregnancy, special challenges arise. Seizures themselves can be harmful to the developing fetus, but all antiepileptic drugs (AEDs) used to treat the disorder are felt to be teratogenic to varying degrees. Seizures can change during pregnancy, in part due to circulating hormones and in part due to fluctuating levels of AEDs in response to physiologic changes of pregnancy. These changes will be discussed below.

Epidemiology

Epilepsy affects an estimated one in one hundred people, half of whom are female. About 0.5–1.3 million women with epilepsy in the United States are of childbearing age [10], and the prevalence of epilepsy in pregnant women is 0.3–0.7 % [11]. Approximately 1 % of pregnancies are thought to be complicated by seizures.

Pathobiology

The pathophysiology of seizures during pregnancy is strongly based on the etiology of the seizures. For example, eclamptic seizures are thought to result from neuronal irritation in the context of cerebral vascular dysregulation and resultant cerebral edema—although the specific cause of this process is yet unknown. Similar, hypoxic, or ischemic damage to cerebral tissue, acute blood products, cerebral edema of other etiologies—structural and otherwise—and exposure to toxic-metabolic or infectious processes (Table 10.3) can cause neuronal misfiring and resultant seizures. Epilepsy, in contrast, is considered idiopathic by nature and may be attributed to any number of causes of abnormal neuronal signaling. Some epilepsy syndromes are genetic, while for the vast majority, the cause is unidentified.

Normal Physiologic Changes

The importance of hormones in epilepsy and seizure control is well known; approximately one third of nonpregnant women with epilepsy commonly note an increase in seizures during a predictable point in their menstrual cycles, and up to 40 % of women with epilepsy note worsening seizures around menopause. Both estrogen and progesterone receptors are present in structures of the brain; experimentally, estrogen has pro-convulsant properties, while progesterone (experimentally and clinically) has anticonvulsant properties.

Effect of Pregnancy on the Disease

As both estrogen and progesterone rise during pregnancy, the clinical effect on epileptic seizures can vary among women. Among epileptic women, approximately 20–33 % experience an increase in seizures, 7–25 % experience a decrease in seizures, and 50–83 % experience no significant change [12]. While the majority of women with epilepsy maintain seizure control during pregnancy, the strongest predictor of a seizure-free pregnancy is a 9-month period of seizure freedom prior to conception [10].

Normal physiologic changes of pregnancy can also influence the metabolism of the drugs used to treat epilepsy. These changes include increases in total body water and extracellular fluid, fat stores, cardiac output, renal blood flow and glomerular filtration rate, hormone-dependent metabolic pathways such as glucuronidation, sex hormone binding, and decreases in maternal albumin. The result for many antiepileptic drugs—whether renally excreted or hepatically metabolized—is a net reduction in blood levels of the drugs through the pregnancy; this can potentially lead to breakthrough seizures for the patient. Drugs that are extensively metabolized through glucuronidation include lamotrigine and oxcarbazepine. Consequently, levels of these AEDs may fall by approximately 50 % in the first trimester, and early blood monitoring for patients taking these two drugs can be helpful. Levetiracetam, in contrast, is renally excreted, and a marked drop (over twofold) can occur in the third trimester due to increased plasma clearance. In the postpartum period, the levels of drugs can be even less predictable. Close monitoring of drug levels during pregnancy and during the postpartum period is warranted.

Effect of Disease on the Pregnancy

Some of the biggest concerns for women with epilepsy who are pregnant or contemplating pregnancy are the potential teratogenic effect of AEDs on the developing fetus and the long-term effects of these drugs on neurocognitive development. These concerns are well-founded. Major congenital malformations such as orofacial clefts, congenital heart disease, neural tube defects, microcephaly, other facial deformities, and skeletal and fingernail abnormalities have been associated with anticonvulsants, since first described in the 1960s; these diverse findings, often seen in isolation from one another, comprise the "fetal anticonvulsant syndrome." Originally hypothesized the result of AEDs acting as folate antagonists, the true mechanism of these malformations is debatable and likely varied, according to the specific anticonvulsant. Nonetheless, folic acid supplementation is recommended for all women with epilepsy preconception and during pregnancy—particularly to reduce neural tube defects, one of the most devastating consequences of fetal anticonvulsant exposure—despite its lack of strong evidence for improved fetal outcomes [10]. The teratogenic effect of AEDs is confounded by the observation that seizures themselves are associated with an increased rate of congenital malformations among exposed infants; a 1992 study suggested that seizures in the first trimester were associated with a 12.3 % rate of malformations versus 4.0 % rate among those not exposed to maternal seizures [13]. However, maternal epilepsy and lifestyle issues may have played a role in this and other studies of seizure risk. Nonetheless, seizures during pregnancy are in fact thought to be potentially more harmful to maternal and fetal health than the medications themselves, justifying their use in pregnancy. Seizures—often characterized by uncontrolled movements and loss of awareness—can result in falls and other forms of trauma. Several other risks of seizures described in the literature include placental hypoperfusion resulting in fetal hypoxia and acidemia, alterations in fetal heart rate, and fetal intracranial hemorrhage—sometimes resulting in antenatal death. A large study in Taiwan in 2009 found an association between maternal seizure and an increased risk of low birth weight and small for gestational age infants (1.36-fold and 1.37-fold, respectively) as well as a 1.63-fold increased risk of preterm delivery—adjusting for lifestyle and socioeconomic differences [14].

Whether women with epilepsy have higher rates of obstetrical complications is controversial. A large meta-analysis was performed by the American Academy of Neurology in 2009, resulting in guidelines regarding the antenatal and postnatal care of women with epilepsy and the associated risks during pregnancy [10]. The guidelines demonstrated good evidence (Level B) that there was no substantially increased risk of late pregnancy bleeding or for preterm contractions, labor and delivery for most women with epilepsy taking AEDs; however, women with epilepsy who smoked were at greater risk for preterm labor compared to smokers without epilepsy (Level C). Weak evidence (Level C) suggested moderately increased risk (over 1.5-fold) of cesarean delivery for women with epilepsy taking AEDs, though a "substantially" increased risk (defined as over twofold) was not demonstrated (Level B). Increased risk of pregnancy-induced hypertension, preeclampsia, and spontaneous abortion could not be consistently demonstrated at the time of the guidelines [10]. However, some studies and consensus statements published since these guidelines have suggested contrary evidence—an increased risk of preeclampsia, pregnancy-induced hypertension, preterm labor, and bleeding complications—despite (and possibly even due to) anticonvulsant use [11].

Diagnosis

Seizures are most often a clinical diagnosis; a neurological change in a patient—many times characterized by repetitive or stereotyped signs and or symptoms—may prompt further workup. When occurring de novo in pregnancy, the workup can include neuroimaging and electroencephalogram (EEG). An EEG during the ictal (seizure) state cannot differentiate an epileptic from a "provoked" seizure of other etiology. A search for provoking factors or a cause of the seizures (Table 10.3) is most important and may help determine whether the use of an AED during pregnancy is necessary. For toxic-metabolic causes, for example, treatment or reversal of the underlying cause may be sufficient to stop the seizures.

Among women with suspected underlying idiopathic epilepsy and among women whose seizures are felt to relate to an underlying neurological condition (stroke, cerebral neoplasm, venous sinus thrombosis, or other structural cerebral abnormality), an early referral to a neurologist is important, and AEDs are most often used. A neurologist can also be helpful in differentiating epilepsy or seizures from a variety of seizure mimics—among them syncope (including convulsive syncope), movement disorders, parasomnias, and psychogenic nonepileptic spells, to name a few. Treatment of women with known epilepsy during pregnancy requires a partnership with a neurologist who may attend to the frequent clinical and blood monitoring of the patient to prevent seizures as a consequence of the disorder and to minimize maternal-fetal risk.

Toxic-metabolic factors or systemic infections are more commonly associated with generalized seizures than partial (focal) seizures. However, exceptions can include herpes simplex virus (HSV) meningoencephalitis, hypo- or hyperglycemia, and exposure to specific medications (e.g., carbapenem antibiotics), which can cause partial seizures. Fever with seizure warrants infectious workup. Seizures accompanied by a fixed neurological deficit on exam imply a likely cerebral structural abnormality.

Differential Diagnosis

Epilepsy is considered by most to be a clinical diagnosis, because 50 % of patients with epilepsy may have a normal routine EEG and because mild abnormalities on EEG can be seen among the general population. The diagnosis of epilepsy should be distinguished by history and workup from mimics, including syncope (including convulsive syncope), migraine, stroke or transient ischemic attack, episodic movement disorder (including tics), parasomnias, systemic disorders of the heart, gastrointestinal tract, psychiatric episodes such as panic attacks, and psychogenic nonepileptic spells.

Diagnostic Evaluation

Antiepileptic treatment following a first-time generalized seizure in pregnancy is based on whether provoking factors were present and based furthermore on a careful history, exam, and workup including EEG and neuroimaging—to look for a focus and possibly identify an epilepsy syndrome. An EEG poses no risk to pregnant patients. A routine EEG can be used as a screening test; however, if spells in question are frequent enough and the etiology of the spells is not clear, a prolonged EEG (over 24–72 h) can be useful either in the outpatient or inpatient setting to assess the spells themselves and solidify a diagnosis. Magnetic resonance imaging (MRI) of the brain is more sensitive in detecting cerebral abnormalities than computerized tomography (CT); because it does not use radiation, it is the neuroimaging modality of choice in the pregnant patient with seizures. MR venogram or arteriogram can also be used if a vascular etiology to seizures is suspected; these tests do not require gadolinium contrast agent, which is generally avoided during pregnancy. Routine lumbar puncture for first-time seizures—including those in pregnancy—is indicated *only* if systemic or CNS infection is suspected.

Management/Treatment

Prevention of seizures in epileptic women is paramount in antepartum management. Women should be counseled that a seizure-free interval of at least 9 months prior to pregnancy is correlated highly (84–92 %) with a seizure-free pregnancy [10]. For some women, it may be possible to reduce the dosage or wean off AEDs prior to pregnancy; however, for most women with epilepsy, AEDs should be continued. Pregnancy registries for women with epilepsy have appeared worldwide to determine risk of major congenital malformation rate among specific AEDs; consequently, some drugs have been found to be safer in pregnancy than others [15]. While rates of major congenital malformations appear lowest in exposures to lamotrigine and levetiracetam (2–3 %), rates are highest in exposures to valproic acid (10 %). Furthermore, neurocognitive delay has been associated with antenatal exposure to valproic acid in a number of recent longitudinal studies in the United States and abroad. Women taking valproic acid are advised to switch to a safer agent if contemplating pregnancy.

Levels of AEDs can be checked during pregnancy and in the postpartum period to help guide therapeutic dosage changes that may be necessary to maintain a seizure-free pregnancy. At least one level per trimester, as well as a postpartum level, is common practice, with dosage adjusted accordingly to maintain a baseline level. External effects such as sleep deprivation after delivery can also be a trigger for seizures in epileptic women.

A theoretical risk of hemorrhagic complications of infants born to mothers taking certain AEDs (phenobarbital, phenytoin, primidone, carbamazepine) is based on their properties as hepatic enzyme inducers of vitamin K; consequently, many providers recommend maternal supplementation of vitamin K during the 9th month of pregnancy (10 mg/day). While high-level evidence for this common practice is lacking, newborns routinely receive vitamin K at delivery in any case [10]. There are several second-generation AEDs felt to be "weak" hepatic enzyme inducers—among them are oxcarbazepine and topiramate—and the importance of vitamin K supplementation for women or newborns exposed to these drugs is unknown.

While evidence for folic acid supplementation during pregnancy among women taking AEDs is weak, it is overall recommended by the American Academy of Neurology (at least 0.4 mg/day) given the lack of harmful effects (AAN 2009). Dose of folic acid has been studied less, but many neurologists recommend 4 mg/day for women taking phenytoin, phenobarbital, carbamazepine, and valproic acid, or for those requiring polytherapy. All seizures and auras should be reported to the treating neurologist, as this may prompt a medication adjustment. Seizure safety precautions for pregnant women include avoiding swimming or taking baths alone and avoiding heights (or any situation in which a seizure with loss of consciousness could have catastrophic results). Driving laws for women with epilepsy vary by state, though driving safety is always advised.

Peripartum management of seizures during labor and delivery are similar to that of nonpregnant patients—intravenous benzodiazepines are considered "first line," and loading longer-acting anticonvulsants (phenytoin or phenobarbital for status epilepticus) may be appropriate for longer seizures to prevent maternal morbidity and mortality. Intravenous magnesium, used acutely for eclamptic seizures, does not appear to influence epileptic seizures.

In the postpartum period, new mothers with epilepsy should be counseled on the risks of sleep deprivation as contributing to seizure frequency and severity, as well as the importance for self-monitoring for medication toxicity, as postpartum levels may rise—dizziness, blurred vision, slurred speech, and gait imbalance. Furthermore, seizure safety precautions include avoiding bathing the infant alone, avoiding diaper changes on raised surfaces (such as a changing table), and avoiding carrying the infant up and down stairs whenever possible. Comorbid depression is prevalent among women with epilepsy, and while the risk of postpartum depression is unknown in this particular population, providers are encouraged to counsel patients on the risks and warning signs and to screen with a validated tool such as the Edinburgh Postnatal Depression Scale. Regarding breastfeeding, most AEDs are excreted in breast milk, through to varying degrees, based on protein binding and free levels of the drugs. The benefits of breastfeeding should be weighed against the risks of further AED exposure. For example, some of the medications that appear most highly concentrated in breast milk (e.g., levetiracetam) do not demonstrate the level of risk of neurocognitive delay among infants who were exposed in utero, compared to medications like valproic acid and phenobarbital—which demonstrate a lower breast milk to maternal concentration ratio, but are known to be harmful to neurocognitive development. There are no guidelines as of yet regarding breastfeeding recommendations for women with epilepsy taking AEDs.

Conclusions

While both seizures and headaches can improve and worsen during pregnancy in individual patients, the most salient point for the outpatient provider of medical care for patients suffering from these conditions is the assessment of risk versus benefit of the treatments versus the risks associated with the underlying disorder. A number of medications for headaches taken prior to the pregnancy may be known by the patient to help with the symptoms, but particularly those medications in the antiepileptic class may be harmful to the fetus; for other medications, the risk is unknown. Headaches can be debilitating, but primary headache disorders are not life-threatening. The patient should be enlisted as a partner in medical decision-making, taking into account the severity of symptoms, general trajectory of worsening or improvement through the pregnancy, and risks of the medications. For those patients with seizures, the risk of the seizures during pregnancy (particularly if convulsive in nature) is generally thought to outweigh the risk of maternal and fetal exposure to medications, and frequent adjustments to the dosages of these medications during the pregnancy are common, given fluctuating levels. Again, a partnership with the patient to minimize risk, promote medication compliance, and share up to date information is important in keeping the mother and fetus healthy.

References

1. Headache Classification Subcommittee of the International Headache Society (IHS). The International Classification of Headache Disorders. 2nd ed. 1st revision, (ICHD-IIRI), May 2005, http://www.ihs-classification.org.
2. Bushnell CD, Jamison M, James AH. Migraines during pregnancy linked to stroke and vascular diseases: US population based case-control study. BMJ. 2009;338:b664.
3. Giraud P, Chauvet S. Cluster headache during pregnancy: case report and literature review. Headache. 2009;49(1):136–9.

4. Pearce CF, Hansen WF. Headache and neurological disease in pregnancy. Clin Obstet Gynecol. 2012;55:810–28.
5. Fumal A, Schoenen J. Tension-type headache: current research and clinical management. Lancet Neurol. 2008;7:70–83.
6. MacGregor EA. Headache in pregnancy. Neurol Clin. 2012;30:835–66.
7. Goadsby PJ. Pathophysiology of cluster headache: a trigeminal autonomic cephalgia. Lancet Neurol. 2002;1:251–7.
8. Cutrer FM. Pathophysiology of migraine. Semin Neurol. 2006;26(2):171.
9. Menon R, Bushnell CD. Headache and pregnancy. The Neurologist. 2008;14:108–19.
10. Harden CL, et al. Practice parameter update: management issues for women with epilepsy. Report of the Quality Standards Subcommittee and Therapeutics and Technology Assessment Subcommittee of the American Academy of Neurology and American Epilepsy Society. Neurology. 2009; 73:126–32, 133–41, and 142–9.
11. Borthen I, Gilhus NE. Pregnancy complications in patients with epilepsy. Curr Opin Obstet Gynecol. 2012;24:78–83.
12. Pennell PB. Antiepileptic Drugs during pregnancy: what is known and which AEDs seem to be safest? Epilepsia. 2008;49 Suppl 9:43–55.
13. Lindhout D, Omtzigt JG, Cornel MC. Spectrum of neural-tube defects in 34 infants prenatally exposed to antiepileptic drugs. Neurology. 1992;42(4 Suppl 5):111–8.
14. Chen YH, Chiou HY, Lin HC, Lin HL. Affect of seizures during gestation on pregnancy outcomes in women with epilepsy. Arch Neurol. 2009;66(8):979–84.
15. The North American Antiepileptic Drug Pregnancy Registry. http://www.aedpregnancyregistry.org

Part X
Pulmonary

Chapter 11
Pulmonary Disorders in Pregnancy

Mariam Louis, D. Onentia Oyiengo, and Ghada Bourjeily

Pulmonary Disorders in Pregnancy

Pregnancy is associated with some profound changes in the cardiovascular, respiratory, immune, and hematologic systems that impact the clinical presentation of respiratory disorders, their implications in pregnancy, and the decisions to treat. In addition, concerns for fetal well-being and safety of various interventions complicate the management of these disorders. In many circumstances, especially life-threatening ones, decisions are based upon a careful assessment of the risk benefit ratio rather than absolute safety of drugs and interventions. In this chapter, we review some of the common respiratory disorders that internists or obstetricians may be called upon to manage.

M. Louis, M.D. (✉)
Division of Pulmonary, Critical Care and Sleep Medicine, College of Medicine, University of Florida, 655 West 8th Street, Jacksonville, FL 32209, USA
e-mail: mariam.louis@jax.ufl.edu

D.O. Oyiengo, M.B.Ch.B.
Pulmonary and Critical Care Fellowship, Brown University/Rhode Island Hospital,
593 Eddy Street, Providence, RI 02903, USA

G. Bourjeily, M.D.
Pulmonary, Critical Care and Medicine, Women's Medicine Collaborative,
The Miriam Hospital, 146 West River Street, Suite 11C, Providence, RI 02904, USA

The Warren Alpert, Medical School of Brown University, Providence, RI, USA
e-mail: Ghada_Bourjeily@brown.edu

Asthma

Asthma is the most common respiratory disease during pregnancy. Asthma affects 4–8 % of pregnancies in the United States and up to 12 % in the United Kingdom and Australia. Difference in prevalence around the world may be related to reporting methods, diagnostic methods, or possibly some environmental or genetic influences.

Pregnancy is a state of important physiological changes in the respiratory system. These physiological changes vary across the course of the pregnancy and are summarized in Table 11.1.

Table 11.1 Respiratory physiological changes during pregnancy

	Changes Seen
Upper respiratory tract	• Hyperemia and edema of naso- and oropharynx resulting in rhinitis of pregnancy
Thorax/diaphragm	• Diaphragm rises by 4 cm • Chest diameter increases by 2 cm • Subcostal angle widens from 68° to 104°
Minute ventilation	• ↑↑↑(40–50 %)
Tidal volume	• ↑↑↑(40 %)
Respiratory rate	• ↔ to ↑(10 %)
O_2 consumption	• ↑(20–30 %)
Lung Volumes (ml)	
TLC	• ↔to ↓(5 %)
ERV	• ↓(15–20 %)
RV	• ↓(20–25 %)
FRC	• ↓(20–30 %)
VC	• ↔
IC	• ↑(5–10 %)
IRV	• ↔
Spirometry	
FEV1 (L/min)	• ↔
FVC	• ↔
Diffusion capacity	• ↔
Arterial Blood Gases	
PaO_2 (mm Hg)	• 105–106 in first trimester and 101–106 by third trimester
$PaCO_2$ (mmHg)	• 28–29 in first trimester and 26–30 by third trimester
pH	• 7.43
HCO_3 (mEq/L)	• 17–18

TLC total lung capacity, *ERV* expiratory reserve volume, *RV* residual volume, *FRC* functional residual capacity, *VC* vital capacity, *IC* inspiratory capacity, *IRV* inspiratory reserve volume, *FEV1* forced expiratory volume in 1 s, *FVC* forced vital capacity, *PaO₂* partial arterial pressure of oxygen, *PaCO₂* partial arterial pressure of carbon dioxide

Effect of Pregnancy on Asthma

The course of asthma during pregnancy is variable. The majority of patients who improve in pregnancy tend to worsen in the postpartum period and vice versa [1]. In general, asthma improves toward the end of the pregnancy, including labor and delivery. However, the rate of asthma *exacerbations* is increased between gestational weeks 17 and 32 [1, 2]. This may in part be due to medication noncompliance during the earlier part of the pregnancy upon discovery of the pregnancy but may also have to do with other pregnancy-related factors such as esophageal reflux, nasal congestion, hormonal factors, and alterations in immunity that may result in increased susceptibility to infections. The major predictor of disease course is the severity of asthma prior to the pregnancy, but race and obesity may also play a role. African American and Hispanic women are more likely to have asthma exacerbations. Poor compliance with medications and difficulties with access to medical services may be important confounders. Additionally, obese women tend to have more severe asthma as both asthma and obesity share a common inflammatory pathway at the cellular level. Asthma also tends to behave in a similar fashion in subsequent pregnancies.

Effect of Asthma on Pregnancy

While well-controlled asthma does not appear to have adverse consequences during pregnancy, poorly controlled asthma may negatively impact some maternal and fetal outcomes.

In the largest study performed to date on over 37,000 women with asthma and over 280,000 controls, asthmatic women were more likely to have pregnancies complicated by miscarriage, antepartum and postpartum hemorrhage, anemia, and depression [3]. However, the risk of other negative outcomes such as gestational hypertensive disorders and stillbirths was not significant in this study. In other large studies, a small, but statistically significant risk of perinatal mortality, preeclampsia, and preterm deliveries have been reported [4, 5]. A more recent retrospective cohort study performed in 12 clinical centers in the United States has shown increased risk of preeclampsia, gestational diabetes, and all preterm births [6]. Secondary analysis of a recent randomized controlled trial showed that women with perception of good asthma control had a reduced risk of planned cesarean deliveries, asthma exacerbations, and preterm birth [7]. In the same study, women with increased anxiety had a higher risk of exacerbations. There is some evidence suggesting that poorly controlled asthma also confers an increased risk of small for gestational age, and low birth weight [8]. Growth restriction may, however, be confounded by smoking. Babies born to severe asthmatics are possibly more likely to have congenital anomalies [5].

Management/Treatment

General Principles and Management

The treatment of asthma involves assessment and management from preconception to the postpartum period. Please refer to Table 11.3 and Figure 11.1 for a general overview of the classification and management of chronic asthma.

There are four general components of asthma care, irrespective of gestational age. These are (1) monitoring of respiratory status, (2) avoidance of possible triggers, (3) patient education, and (4) pharmacological treatment. Patients should get a baseline spirometry and be instructed in how to follow their peak expiratory flow rate (PEFR) at home. Ideally, this should be done twice a day in patients with persistent disease. Since pregnancy does not affect flow rates, reductions in these numbers usually indicate a worsening degree of airflow obstruction and should prompt quick medical evaluation. Second, it is critical that patients avoid their known triggers to asthma including tobacco, dust, extreme temperatures, and allergens such as pollen and pet dander. Third, patients need to be educated about their disease. Pregnancy constitutes a perfect window to educate women given the multiple contacts with providers increased motivation due to concerns for fetal well-being. Trigger control from washing bed sheets to vacuuming to rodent control are important strategies to review, especially since in most circumstances, women are more likely to be exposed to these triggers. Important topics that need to be reviewed also include inhaler technique, early recognition of symptoms of worsening asthma, an action plan for acute asthma exacerbations, as well as an overview of how poorly

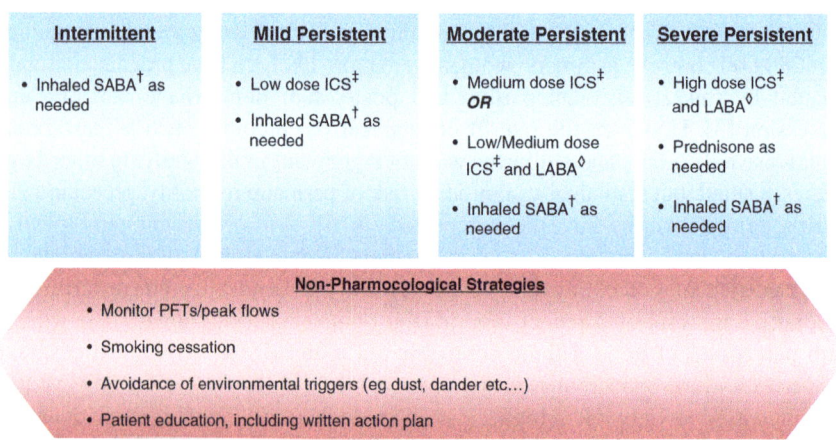

† Short Acting Beta-2 Agonist. Albuterol is the most studied during pregnancy

‡ Inhaled Corticosteroids. Budesonide is the most studied during pregnancy

◊ Long Acting Beta-2 Agonist. Salmeterol is the most studies during pregnancy

Fig. 11.1 Management of chronic asthma during pregnancy

controlled asthma can affect the pregnancy. Patients should also be provided with the opportunity to express their concerns and ask questions. In a multi-institutional prospective study, lower forced expiratory volume in 1 s (FEV1), but not asthma symptom frequency, was shown to be associated with adverse perinatal outcomes [9]. These data may be a reflection of the effect of asthma severity or poor asthma control on perinatal outcomes and emphasize the possibility of discrepancies between symptom-based assessment and more objective measurement of lung function in pregnant women with asthma. Finally, women with asthma need to receive the appropriate pharmacological treatment to achieve disease control. Population-based data do show that well-controlled asthmatics without exacerbations have better outcomes than women with exacerbations, but for obvious reasons, there are no randomized controlled trials evaluating this particular question. Although most clinical practices use symptom-based, guideline-directed assessments to decide on medication use, recent data from a randomized controlled trial suggest lower rates of exacerbation, improved quality of life, and reduced neonatal hospitalization when management decisions were based on measurements of exhaled nitric oxide in pregnancy [10]. It is likely that this improvement in outcomes is due to improved control, rather than the method of assessment itself.

Table 11.2 provides an overview of the asthma medications that are used in pregnancy. As in the nonpregnant population, the choice of pharmacological agent depends on disease severity. A frank discussion with the expectant mother and her partner should occur to encourage them to voice their concerns regarding asthma treatment in pregnancy. Most women are told to stop their inhalers at the time of pregnancy diagnosis because of FDA category listing. For that reason, a good amount of time should be spent on counseling about the use of asthma drugs in pregnancy. Explaining to women that asthma control is key to the health of the pregnancy and their baby is an important part of counseling and may have to be done repeatedly during the course of pregnancy. In general, most asthma medications are justifiable in pregnancy, and some have adequate safety data. As noted in Table 11.2, many of the drug choices are category C according to the FDA classification; however, these drugs are used routinely in the care of pregnant women with asthma. In addition, although leukotriene inhibitors are listed as category B, safety data are less reassuring than other drugs classified as category C. Omalizumab is classified as category B by the FDA despite the fact that all of the initial trials have excluded pregnant women. These safety data are based on animal studies which are limited by the fact that teratogenicity may be species specific. In addition, although prednisone may be associated with a small risk of cleft palate when administered in early pregnancy, the benefit of this drug in an acute exacerbation of asthma by far outweighs the small risk of malformation. Table 11.3 reviews the classification of asthma severity, which includes not only symptoms but also peak flow meter measurements.

Other coexisting diseases may worsen asthma and may have to be treated in order to achieve optimal control. The most common of these disorders are allergic rhinitis, gastroesophageal reflux disease (GERD), sleep apnea, and psychiatric illnesses. Allergic rhinitis occurs in 80–90 % of nonpregnant asthmatics and worsens asthma symptoms.

Table 11.2 Overview of medications used in the treatment of asthma during pregnancy

Category	Best studied example	Risk category	Comment
Short-acting ßeta 2-agonist	Albuterol	C	No clear risk of teratogenic effect on fetus. Specific birth defects have been reported but are not the same. These findings may be due to chance. Benefit outweighs risk
Long-acting ßeta 2-agonist	Salmeterol	C	No clear risk of teratogenic effect on fetus. Benefit outweighs risk. Slightly more data available in salmeterol than formoterol
Inhaled corticosteroids	Budesonide	B	Human experience reassuring. Infants should be monitored for hypoaldosteronism. Some recent data suggestive of increased risk of metabolic dysfunction in the offspring
Anticholinergics	Ipratropium	B	Typically not used as primary agent but helpful in the treatment of acute exacerbations. Not expected to increase the risk of congenital malformations
Methylxanthines	Theophylline	C	No human reports of teratogenicity. Requires monitoring levels due to increased clearance in the third trimester and significant drug interactions
Cromoglycates	Cromolyn sodium	B	Not expected to increase the risk of congenital malformations. Human data reassuring
Leukotriene modifiers	Montelukast	B	Safety data are limited in pregnancy. However, although congenital limb defects, no syndrome of malformations has been identified in relation to montelukast
Systemic steroids	Prednisone/methylprednisolone	C/D	Increased risk of growth abnormalities in animals, likely increased risk of cleft palates during first trimester exposures. Risk outweighs the risk in severe asthma
Epinephrine	Terbutaline	B	Unlikely to increase the risk of birth defects
Immunotherapies	Omalizumab	B	Limited human data. Risk benefit ratio needs to be considered. Pregnancy registry available

Management of the allergic rhinitis with drugs such as steroidal nasal sprays often improves asthma symptoms. Women who are pregnant can also develop a different form of rhinitis, called rhinitis of pregnancy. This typically occurs in the latter part of pregnancy and resolves completely within 2 weeks after delivery.

The prevalence of GERD among nonpregnant asthmatics varies between 30 and 90 %. In pregnant women with asthma, this number is likely higher given that

Table 11.3 Classification of asthma severity[a]

	Intermittent	Persistent		
		Mild	Moderate	Severe
Symptoms	≤2 days/week	>2 days/week but not daily	Daily	Throughout the day
Nighttime awakenings	≤2×/month	3–4×/month	>1×/week but not nightly	Often 7×/week
Short-acting beta$_2$-agonist use	≤2 days/week	>2 days/week but not daily and not more than 1× on any day	Daily	Several times per day
Interference with normal activity	None	Minor limitation	Some limitation	Significant limitation
Peak Flow/ Pulmonary function tests	• Normal FEV$_1$ • FEV$_1$ > 80 % predicted • FEV$_1$/FVC normal	• FEV$_1$ ≥ 80 % predicted • FEV$_1$/FVC normal	• FEV$_1$ > 60 but < 80 % predicted • FEV$_1$/FVC decreased by 5 %	• FEV$_1$ < 60 % predicted • FEV$_1$/FVC decreased by > 5 %

FEV1 forced expiratory volume in 1 s, *FVC* forced vital capacity
[a]http://www.nhlbi.nih.gov

GERD has been reported to be present in nearly 75 % of all pregnant women [11]. GERD can worsen bronchoconstriction via increased vagal tone, heightened bronchial reactivity, and microaspiration of gastric contents into the upper airway. Patients who have symptoms of GERD benefit from treatment. Although proton pump inhibitors are not expected to increase the risk of congenital malformation in experimental animal studies and limited human pregnancy exposures, ranitidine constitutes a safer first choice. Finally, asthma and psychiatric comorbidities may coexist. Stress and mental illness can worsen asthma in the pregnant women and may also complicate compliance.

During labor, the general management of asthma is not significantly different than above. Most patients with asthma do not require a labor and delivery plan. However, patients with more severe disease or those who suffered an exacerbation close to term would require a detailed plan. Stress dosing with steroids during labor can be considered in patients who have been on prolonged periods of systemic steroids during the pregnancy. Patients with active symptoms or more severe asthma may benefit from regional anesthesia. Epidural anesthesia reduces minute volume and oxygen consumption and may help prevent hyperinflation in patients with active symptoms and reduce oxygen consumption. If general anesthesia is to be considered, then ketamine and halogenated anesthetics are preferred. It is safe to use oxytocin and prostaglandin E2. However, ergotamine and ergot derivatives, 15-methyl prostaglandin F2 alpha, morphine, and meperidine should be avoided in pregnant women with asthma as they may be associated with an increased risk of bronchospasm.

Treatment of Acute Asthma Exacerbations

An overview of the management of acute asthma exacerbations in the pregnant woman is detailed in Fig. 11.2. More detailed information can be found in National Heart Lung and Blood Institute guidelines on asthma and pregnancy published in 2004. The treatment is similar to nonpregnant women with a few key differences that need to be highlighted. The first is to remember that during pregnancy, the normal $PaCO_2$ is lower than in the nonpregnant state. Therefore, a normal or high $PaCO_2$ heralds worsening respiratory failure and should be acted upon quickly. Second, hypoxia during asthma exacerbations can lead to fetal distress and decelerations. Therefore, immediate bronchodilators and supplemental oxygen should be administered. Finally, it should be noted that while the indications for airway intubation are the same in the pregnant asthmatic as the nonpregnant asthmatic, intubation during pregnancy, especially in the third trimester, can be more difficult. This is due to increased airway edema, low FRC and oxygen reserve, and a more profound response to sedatives from decreased venous return. Hence, the most experienced member of the team should perform the intubation and be familiar with difficult airway management procedures. Airway intubation is discussed in more detail in the critical care Chap. 2.

Pneumonia in Pregnancy

Bacterial Pneumonia

Pneumonia is one of the leading causes of non-obstetric maternal deaths in the United States [12]. There are several categories of pneumonia based on the likely spectrum of pathogens: community-acquired pneumonia (CAP), healthcare-associated pneumonia, hospital-acquired pneumonia, and ventilator-associated pneumonia as well as pneumonia in the immune-compromised host. As pregnant women are usually young and healthy, CAP predominates.

Microbiology and Epidemiology

The overall rate of CAP in pregnant women is 0.5–1/1,000 pregnancies depending on the population being studied [13–15]. The risk of pneumonia is notably increased in gravidas with comorbid conditions such as asthma, anemia, and human immunodeficiency virus [16]. Tobacco and substance abuse have also been independently associated with an increased risk for pneumonia. Influenza increases the risk for development of bacterial pneumonia by denuding the respiratory epithelium and predisposing the host to infection.

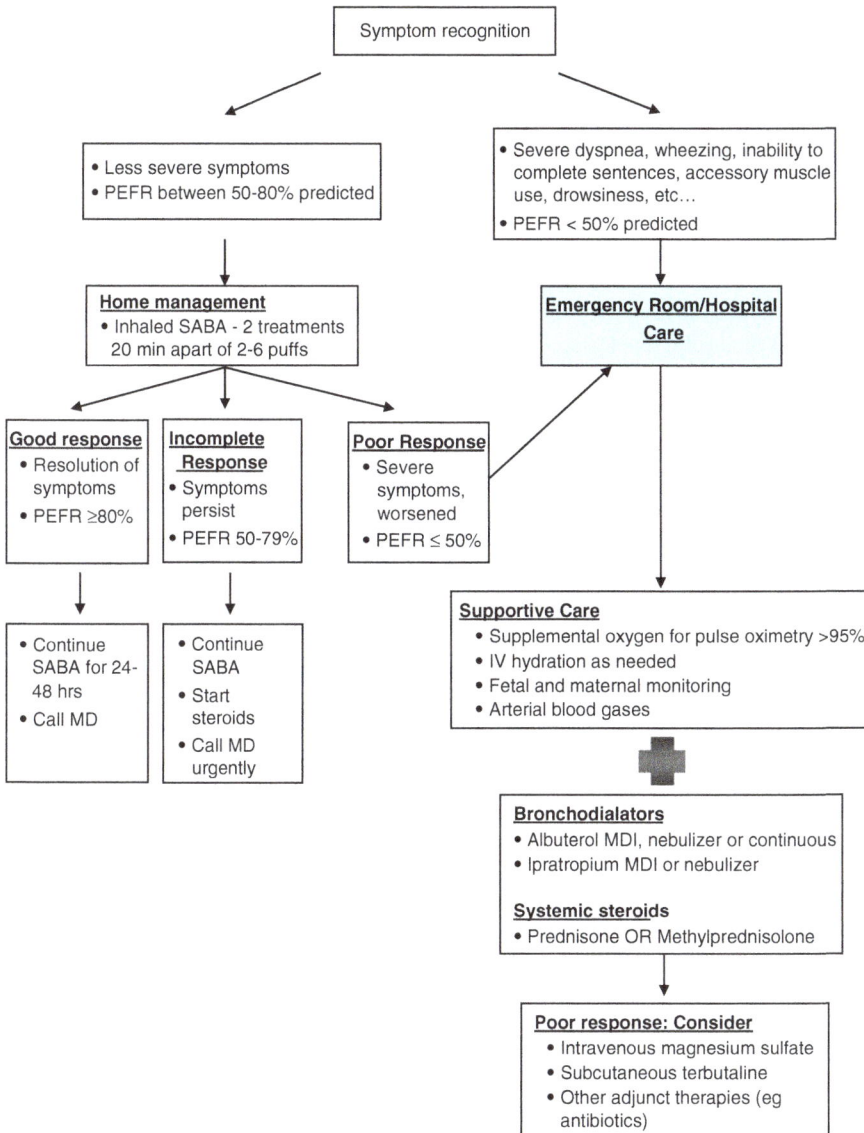

Fig. 11.2 Management of acute asthma exacerbation during pregnancy. Simplified from http://www.nhlbi.nih.gov/health/prof/lung/asthma/astpreg/astpreg_qr.pdf

In adults, the causative agents for CAP are identified in 40–60 % of cases when advanced testing techniques are utilized [17, 18]. The yield is much lower, in the range of 10–25 %, with regular testing. Though specific studies in pregnant women are lacking, the likely pathogens are not considered to be significantly different from those in the general population. *Streptococcus pneumoniae* is the most common single pathogen isolated in 30–50 % followed by *Haemophilus influenzae* and *Mycoplasma pneumonia* [19]. Pregnant women may be more likely to contract viral infections and tend to have more severe disease than the nonpregnant population. Therefore, the estimates above may be somewhat different in pregnancy.

Effect of Pregnancy on the Disease

Gingival hyperplasia in pregnancy may promote changes in oral flora and promote growth of anaerobic bacteria. Aspiration risk and heartburn [11] may be increased in pregnancy, especially when undergoing sedative procedures or general anesthesia. Whether these changes and increased gastroesophageal reflux disorders are associated with increased risk of pneumonia is not clear. Immune alterations in pregnancy that promote maternal tolerance to the fetus may impair optimal function of host defense mechanisms and increase the risk of infections. Pregnant women have decreased lung capacity and decreased ERV and RV resulting in a reduction in functional residual capacity. A state of compensated respiratory alkalosis is established by increasing minute ventilation. This is largely secondary to an increase in tidal volume and to a lesser extent an increase in respiratory rate. Healthy gravid subjects have increased cardiac output and decreased oncotic pressure which peaks in the third trimester that promotes transudation of fluid into the pulmonary interstitium. These changes diminish oxygen reserve, increase the risk of development of pulmonary edema with fluid resuscitation, and predispose to respiratory failure and predispose women to more severe disease.

Effect of Disease on the Pregnancy

Pneumonia may be complicated by hypoxia, respiratory failure, or death, and preterm delivery appears to be the most common obstetric complication associated with maternal pneumonia. While intrauterine infection is known to cause preterm delivery, a causal relationship between pneumonia in pregnancy and preterm delivery is not well established. It is possible that higher levels of cytokines and other mediators such as TNF-α and prostaglandin F2 reported in bacterial infections may lead to preterm delivery and low birth weight. Other reported complications include placental abruption, preeclampsia and eclampsia, and low Apgar scores [20–22]. It is unclear, however, whether these complications are related to the actual infection or to other host factors.

Differential Diagnosis

Common causes for respiratory distress in pregnancy include infection such as urinary tract infection, pulmonary edema, asthma, aspiration, and pulmonary embolus.

Diagnostic Evaluation

The clinical spectra of pneumonia caused by different pathogens overlap considerably. Thorough history and examination along with microscopic examination of respiratory secretions may narrow the differential diagnosis and identify the offending pathogen. Urine pneumococcal and legionella antigen may also aid in guiding antibiotic therapy and should be considered for patients requiring admission. During influenza seasons, respiratory viral panel should be sent. Though blood cultures are usually negative and of low yield, they may add value in the patient requiring admission to the intensive care unit (ICU). Arterial blood gas should be done for all patients with hypoxia or those requiring admission to the ICU and interpreted according to pregnant status.

Chest X-ray should be performed in patients suspected of having pneumonia and helps confirm the diagnosis or show evidence of a complicated pneumonia such as lung abscess or pleural effusion. Computed tomography scan is unlikely to add value in the management of pneumonia, unless empyema is suspected. Ultrasound guidance likely reduces the risk of complications with thoracentesis in pregnancy given the cranial displacement of the diaphragm in pregnancy. Bronchoscopy though rarely needed can be performed safely in pregnancy and should not be withheld when indicated.

Management/Treatment

Supportive Treatment

General supportive measures are similar in patients with various types of pneumonia. For patients with a viable fetus who require admission, the obstetric team should be consulted for fetal monitoring as well as timing of delivery in the event of fetal distress. Hypoxia, acidosis, and fever should not be tolerated as they are independently associated with poor fetal outcomes. Oxygen should be supplemented for goal saturations > 95 % or PaO_2 above 70. Fever should be treated aggressively for a goal temp of less than 38 °C.

In cases of severe pneumonia associated with respiratory failure, early intubation should be considered. Intubations in pregnancy have a higher failure rate than the general surgical population (see Chap. 2 on airway intubation). Attempts to maintain CO_2 within an acceptable range may be challenging in the event of acute respiratory distress syndrome (ARDS) and the use of lung protective strategies. Low tidal volume ventilation strategy with a target tidal volume of 6 ml/kg is recommended for ARDS [23]. Though pregnant women were excluded in the acute respiratory distress network studies on lung protective strategies, low tidal volume ventilation should be attempted, initially with a higher respiratory rate to maintain ventilation given the survival benefit observed in the nonpregnant population. However, higher tidal volumes may be required to correct acidosis that may compromise the fetus, in such instances attempts should still be made to keep the plateau pressure below 30 cm of water as barotrauma is thought to contribute significantly to lung injury. $PaCO_2$ levels need to be watched closely, and given the 10 mmHg gradient between fetal and maternal, maternal $PaCO_2$ should be kept at 55 mmHg or lower. Use of bicarbonate to correct the PH has been suggested in the nonpregnant population though clinical studies to support this approach are limited. It is thought that the transfer of bicarbonate across the placenta is slow and may not be adequate to correct fetal acidosis. While the decision to admit patients to the ICU is complex and should be individualized, clinicians should have a lower threshold when evaluating pregnant mothers.

Antibiotic Therapy

Antibiotic therapy should be initiated empirically while awaiting confirmatory tests that may aid in narrowing the antimicrobial coverage. In influenza season, antiviral (usually oseltamivir) should be started empirically as well. Decisions about antibiotic choice should address the most likely pathogen, adverse effect on the mother, and should also weigh the risk of the specific drug to the fetus against the risk of inappropriately treated disease. An optimal drug would be one with maximal efficacy against the known pathogen and no risk to the fetus. However, such drugs are scarce, and in most circumstances, a drug with more benefit than risk can be selected. Other than concern for fetal safety, preferred antibiotics are not different from those in nonpregnant women, but dosing should take into account increased hepatic and renal clearance and increased volume of distribution. There is a theoretical concern that aminoglycosides and vancomycin may be associated with hearing and kidney dysfunction in the offspring, but this possibility has not been confirmed clinically. Penicillins, clindamycins, and most macrolides except clarithromycin have a good safety profile. Fluoroquinolones are usually avoided in pregnancy due to a theoretical risk of arthropathy in the offspring. However, some experts argue that this issue is not clinically significant in humans. Tetracyclines should be avoided as they may cause permanent dental discoloration.

Varicella Pneumonia

Varicella (chicken pox) is caused by *Varicella zoster* virus (VZV). Varicella is predominantly a childhood illness that is usually self-limited and rarely results in severe disease. In adults, however, it is much more likely to be severe. VZV is not only likely to have increased morbidity and mortality in pregnancy but may also be associated with congenital abnormalities and poor fetal outcomes. Varicella pneumonia is among the most severe maternal complication of VZV infection [24–27].

Viral particles are shed from varicella-associated vesicles and get airborne. Inhalation or contact with the conjunctiva results into contraction of the infection with entry of the virus through the respiratory mucosa. Crusting over of the last crop of vesicles usually marks the end of the contagious period. Patients are known to be infectious 2–3 days prior to development of the vesicular rash; for this reason, an alternative viral shedding site such as the respiratory tract is believed to exist [28].

Epidemiology

Varicella is highly contagious with seasonal variation in incidence, being most prevalent in the winter and spring. It has a very high clinical attack rate of 65–86 % following exposure to susceptible individuals [29]. Following a primary infection with varicella, lifelong immunity is usually established in the majority of subjects; in a few people, however, second attacks of varicella may occur [30].

While varicella follows a benign course in children, adults have up to 25 times increased risk of severe disease [31]. Pregnant women are at a uniquely increased risk for infection. In the United States, the incidence of primary varicella averages 0.7–3 cases/1,000 pregnancies. Varicella pneumonia complicates 10–20 % of all cases, and 40 % of mothers with pneumonia require mechanical ventilation [32, 33]. Maternal mortality from Varicella pneumonia used to be high at 20–45 % before the introduction of antiviral therapy but is currently estimated at less than 3–14 % [34, 35].

Effect of Pregnancy on the Disease

Changes in physiology and immunity associated with pregnancy may increase the risk of infection and severe outcomes in the pregnant women. In an effort to promote maternal tolerance to fetal antigens, pregnancy is associated with a shift from Th1 to Th2 lymphocyte responses and associated cytokines at the maternal fetal interface. Macrophage and lymphocyte-secreted Th2 cytokines stimulate B lymphocytes promoting a humoral response while suppressing cytotoxic lymphocytes. While pregnancy may not necessarily be an immune-suppressed state in the real sense, immunity against VZV infection is primarily cell mediated, and a systemic shift away from cell-mediated immunity may increase susceptibility to intracellular viral pathogens, parasites, and bacteria.

Effect of Disease on the Pregnancy

Primary varicella (chicken pox) is associated with several adverse effects in pregnancy such as preterm delivery and low birth weight. In one study involving 106 pregnant women with varicella compared to a similar number of noninfected controls, 14.3 % of pregnant women with chicken pox had a preterm delivery as compared to 5.6 % of controls [36]. Low birth weight and intrauterine growth restriction have been described. Nearly 1–2 % of cases of maternal primary VZV infection result in congenital varicella syndrome (CVS), which is associated with a mortality of up to 30 % in the first few months of life and severe disability in survivors. Primary VZV infection prior to the 20th week of pregnancy is associated with the highest risk for CVS [24, 36].

Clinical features of CVS include skin lesions in a dermatomal distribution that may lead to eventual scarring in up to 70 % of cases, muscle and limb hypoplasia in up to 72 % of cases, chorioretinitis and cataracts in up to 52 % of cases, and abnormalities of gastrointestinal, genitourinary, and cardiovascular system in 7–24 % of cases [37, 38]. Neurological abnormalities such as mental retardation, microcephaly, and hydrocephalus occur in 48–62 % of cases resulting in learning difficulties and developmental delays [39]. The pathobiology of CVS is thought to be in utero reactivation similar to that of herpes zoster with a shortened latency period that is likely due to immature fetal cell-mediated immunity.

While up to 25 % of babies born to mothers with primary VZV infection have serologic evidence of infection, there is no serologic evidence of infection in babies born to mothers with herpes zoster. Similarly, infants do not appear to be at risk of infection if maternal zoster occurs near delivery [40]. Unless disseminated, herpes zoster is thus not associated with a significant increase in adverse fetal outcomes [37, 41]. Peripartum varicella infection places the infant at risk for neonatal varicella, which is associated with mortality rate as high as 20 %.

Diagnosis

Following a 2- to 3-week incubation period, fever, headache, malaise, anorexia, and other constitutional symptoms precede the occurrence of the rash by 2–3 days. The rash is typically vesicular, generalized, and intensely pruritic. Varicella pneumonia can develop anywhere from day 1 to day 6 after the onset of the rash.

Late onset of respiratory symptoms with recurrence of fevers is suggestive of bacterial coinfection rather than primary viral pneumonia. Skin superinfection with staphylococcal bacteremia and neurological involvement with encephalitis may occur. A thorough history and skin exam may strongly suggest the diagnosis of varicella. Chest radiograph pattern in varicella pneumonia is nonspecific and may be normal or show unilateral or patchy areas of consolidation or nodular opacities. CT findings include multicentric hemorrhage and necrosis centered around the airways and small nodular opacities surrounded by ground glass which may coalesce to form consolidations. Healed and calcified pulmonary nodules may persist [42]. Skin lesion (rather than bronchoscopic) sampling offers a high yield and should be attempted first. The base of newly erupted vesicles has the highest yield and should be sampled. Specimens can then be sent for viral culture, polymerase chain reaction (PCR), and immunofluorescence (DFA). Direct fluorescent antibody test is rapidly available in most institutions. Though bronchoscopy in most cases is not necessary, varicella may be recovered from bronchial washings by viral PCR and viral culture techniques.

Management/Treatment

Pregnant women suspected of having varicella should be admitted for initiation of antivirals and other supportive treatment. Chest imaging should be performed on admission to evaluate for pulmonary involvement. Antiviral therapy is associated with a reduction in the duration of symptoms when initiated within the first 24 h of onset of the varicella rash. Due to the high risk of varicella pneumonia in pregnancy, empiric antiviral therapy should be initiated while awaiting confirmatory results.

Acyclovir or valacyclovir are the antivirals of choice. Oral acyclovir has low bioavailability that requires it to be administered in frequent doses to achieve therapeutic levels. Valacyclovir has high oral bioavailability and less frequent dosing intervals and is an alternative oral formulation. There is however less experience with valacyclovir compared to acyclovir. Presence of pulmonary symptoms should prompt admission to the ICU and initiation of intravenous acyclovir which has a guaranteed and higher bioavailability. Antiviral therapy is associated with significantly less morbidity and mortality when initiated prior to 72 h. Late presentation with varicella pneumonia should not obviate the initiation of antiviral therapy. A dose of 10–15 mg/kg intravenously every 8 h for 5–10 days is recommended for VZV pneumonia.

Pulmonary bacterial superinfection may occur. Studies characterizing bacterial pathogens likely to cause superinfection are lacking. Thus, empiric broad-spectrum antibiotic coverage should be initiated in pregnant women with pneumonia. Despite acyclovir crossing the placenta in significant amounts, there appears to be no reduction in congenital varicella syndrome with treatment. The neonate should be isolated from the mother in the peripartum period until the mother is deemed noncontagious. Consultation with high-risk obstetrics and neonatology would be useful given the risk of preterm labor and growth restriction.

Passive Immunization

Immunity to varicella consists of both VZV-specific neutralizing antibodies and cell-mediated immunity. Immunity against VZV can be assessed by the use of antibody serologic assays.

Though there are no adequate controlled trials examining the effectiveness of VZIG prophylaxis, VZIG is associated with more than 40–50 % reduction in risk of contracting varicella and a significant reduction in risk of severe disease [40]. VZV can be prevented by vaccination. VZV vaccine is a live attenuated vaccine and is generally not recommended in pregnancy and in immune-suppressed individuals. Varicella can be contracted from herpes zoster lesions as well. Family members with such lesions should minimize contact and cover their lesions to decrease the risk of transmission. Healthcare workers who deal with pregnant women should be screened and vaccinated, and similarly pregnant healthcare workers should avoid contact or exposure to patients with varicella.

Influenza Pneumonia

Infection with influenza virus can result in an acute respiratory illness of varying severity. The majority of healthy individuals infected with influenza is asymptomatic or has minimal symptoms. However, adults with comorbidities, elderly subjects, and healthy pregnant women are at increased risk of severe disease and death. In addition, influenza infection during pregnancy increases the risk of adverse fetal outcomes.

Epidemiology

In a regular endemic season, influenza is estimated to result in 200,000 hospitalizations and 36,000 deaths in the United States. Pregnant women are at increased risk for morbidity (including cardiorespiratory complications) and mortality from influenza compared with nonpregnant controls [43–46] that is more pronounced in the second and third trimester of pregnancy [47]. In 2010, the Pandemic H1N1 Influenza in Pregnancy Working Group reported on 788 pregnant women in the United States with 2009 influenza A(H1N1). Among those, 30 died (5 % of all reported 2009 influenza A (H1N1) influenza deaths in this period). Most hospitalizations and deaths occurred in the third trimester [47]. Pregnant women with comorbidities or those who smoke have an increased risk for severe disease requiring hospital admission compared to those without comorbidities [48, 49].

Effect of Pregnancy on the Disease

As discussed above, these physiological changes make pregnant women more susceptible to acquiring viral infections and subsequent development of severe disease.

Effect of Disease on the Pregnancy

Apart from direct effects to the mother, influenza has been associated with undesirable effects to the fetus. Risks of adverse fetal outcomes vary with the severity of maternal disease. Preterm delivery appears to be the most common and consistent complication associated with influenza pandemics. In the pandemic of 1918 and 1957, higher rates of pregnancy loss, premature delivery, preterm deliveries, as well as other adverse effects were reported. In several reports during the pandemic influenza of 2009 among pregnant women requiring admission, preterm delivery was close to 30 % and was even higher among mothers who were admitted to the ICU

[48, 50, 51]. Several other adverse fetal outcomes of maternal influenza have been reported especially during pandemics, including abortion, fetal distress, and placenta abruption [50, 52].

Diagnosis

Symptoms of influenza in pregnancy are similar to symptoms outside of pregnancy. Influenza virus-mediated leukopenia may make the host more susceptible to bacterial infections. Secondary bacterial pneumonia is characterized by the appearance of a new fever and productive cough during early convalescence.

Radiologic findings are generally similar to other viral pneumonias, and more extensive findings are associated with more severe complications. Tree in bud opacities may also be seen. Laboratory findings may include an elevated or low white count, lymphopenia, and hyponatremia. Myoglobinuria and renal failure can occur rarely. Cardiac muscle damage with associated electrocardiographic changes, disturbances of rhythm, and high levels of cardiac enzymes have been reported after influenza virus infection.

Sputum cultures may be revealing in the event of bacterial superinfection. *Streptococcus pneumoniae*, *Staphylococcus aureus*, *Haemophilus influenzae*, and group A hemolytic streptococci are the bacterial pathogens most commonly isolated in adults with influenza.

A definitive diagnosis of influenza requires laboratory confirmation. Diagnostic tests for influenza fall into four broad categories: virus isolation [culture], detection of viral proteins, detection of viral nucleic acid, and serological diagnosis. Detection of viral nucleic acid allows for typing and subtyping of the specific virus strain.

Management/Treatment

Supportive Management

Treatment of influenza consists of supportive management and specific antiviral therapy. Optimizing supportive treatment is central to the management of influenza and probably of more benefit than specific antiviral therapy. Supportive therapy is similar to other types of pneumonia as discussed above.

Pharmacotherapy

As with most drugs, information about safety and effectiveness of anti-influenza drugs during pregnancy is scarce. In view of potential severe maternal disease from influenza and adverse fetal outcomes, benefits of treatment with antivirals likely outweigh the potential risks to the fetus. There are two classes of antiviral drugs currently in general clinical use: adamantanes, (examples of which include amantadine and rimantadine) and neuraminidase inhibitors such as oseltamivir, zanamivir, and peramivir. Adamantanes are active against influenza A only, increase influenza A resistance to adamantanes, and are associated with embryotoxicity in animal studies. As such they are not recommended in pregnancy.

Neuraminidase inhibitors are active against influenza A and B viruses. They are preferred in all adults and in pregnancy. Though studies in pregnancy are inadequate, extensive use of oseltamivir in pregnancy during the 2009 HlN1 pandemic was not associated with adverse effects specific to the drug. Neuraminidase inhibitors reduce the duration and severity of symptoms and duration of viral shedding when initiated within 48 h of symptom onset [43, 48, 53, 54]. There is also evidence to support reduction in complication rate, duration of hospitalization, and mortality in adults. Observational studies published during the 2009 pandemic demonstrated that, among pregnant women hospitalized with pandemic H1N1 infection, treatment with oseltamivir was associated with fewer intensive care unit admissions, less use of mechanical ventilation, and decreased mortality [43, 48]. Empiric treatment should always be initiated in the gravid woman when influenza is suspected while awaiting confirmatory results as delay in initiation of treatment is associated with an increased risk of severe outcomes, ICU admission, and death [48, 49, 55]. Pregnant mothers presenting after 48 h of symptom onset should still be initiated on therapy as there is evidence of benefit even when initiated after 2 days of symptom onset. Initiation of antiviral therapy within the first 48 h is associated with the most benefit [43, 48, 49, 53, 56]. There is less experience with zanamivir which is administered by inhalation route. Zanamivir is also contraindicated in patients with asthma as it has a potential of worsening respiratory symptoms [57]. For patients requiring admission to ICU for influenza pneumonia or in cases of suspected secondary bacterial infection, empiric antibiotic therapy should be initiated. Sputum culture may be helpful in the case of isolation of resistant bacteria that may warrant changes or broadening of antibiotic coverage.

Prevention and Vaccination

In pregnant women, influenza vaccination induces an antibody response similar to that in nonpregnant women. CDC and WHO recommend pregnant women or women who will be pregnant during the winter or peak influenza season to be prioritized for vaccination. In addition to protection to the mothers, influenza vaccination may offer protection to the neonate as well as contribute to herd immunity in other family members. Pregnant mothers who have not been vaccinated or those with comorbidities such as asthma who have been exposed to influenza may benefit from antiviral prophylaxis. Oseltamivir is preferred for prophylaxis due to its ease of administration.

Sleep-Disordered Breathing

Sleep-disordered breathing (SDB) is a spectrum of disorders that encompasses snoring and upper airway resistance, obstructive sleep apnea (OSA), and other disorders. OSA is a disorder characterized by periodic and recurrent collapse of the upper airway during sleep. Obesity, age, and upper airway and facial abnormalities are the most recognized risk factors for the disorder. OSA is prevalent in patients with chronic hypertension, cardiovascular disease, and metabolic disorders such as diabetes mellitus. The pregnant population appears to be at risk for the disorder given anatomic upper airway changes that occur in pregnancy as well as physiological changes and hormones. Snoring occurs in close to 35 % of pregnant women [58]. The prevalence of OSA in pregnancy is not well known, but preliminary data suggest that close to 60 % of loud snorers in pregnancy have at least mild OSA. The natural history of snoring around pregnancy is, however, unclear. There are some data suggesting that OSA actually improves in untreated postpartum women around 3 months after delivery. Data on OSA predating pregnancy is missing and pregestational and gestational OSA may have different clinical consequences.

Screening

There is a significant lack in screening for the disorder by obstetric providers according to a recent study, even in obese patients [59]. Notably, the Berlin questionnaire, a widely used screening tool in the nonpregnant population, appears to have poor positive and negative predictive values in pregnancy [60]. Snoring and excessive daytime sleepiness may be important predictors [61]. Chronic hypertension, age, obesity, and snoring appear to have a good predictive value for OSA in high-risk populations [62]. Further validation of this potential predictive model in different pregnant populations is needed.

Pregnancy, Fetal, and Neonatal Outcomes

Snoring and OSA have been shown to be associated with a variety of adverse pregnancy outcomes including gestational hypertension, gestational diabetes, and cesarean deliveries. Gestational hypertension is the most studied link with numerous studies on snoring as well as OSA showing a two- to threefold increased risk of gestational hypertension in snorers, even after adjusting for confounders such as body mass index [63]. Mechanistic studies are lacking and the directionality of the association not well clarified, but it is possible that intermittent hypoxia, flow limitation, poor sleep, and arousals may play a role in causing endothelial dysfunction, inflammation, and hypercoagulability that are common to the two disorders.

A few studies to date have also shown worse abnormalities in glucose metabolism and a higher prevalence of gestational diabetes in women complaining of loud snoring and poor sleep [58, 64]. Gestational diabetes has been associated with a fivefold increase in the risk of type II diabetes at 5 years and a ninefold risk at 9 years [65]. Snoring, poor sleep, and OSA have all been associated with a higher risk of unplanned cesarean deliveries. This association may be harder to explain and may depend on the actual reason leading to unplanned cesarean delivery such as obstetric, fetal, or medical causes.

The impact of SDB on fetal and neonatal outcomes has also been studied, but the results of such studies have been more conflicting. Growth restriction has been reported to be associated with snoring in some studies but not in others. The effect on Apgar scores also appears to be controversial. There are some case reports and case series suggesting fetal decelerations secondary to sleep apnea, but a recent study evaluating synchronized limited sleep studies and fetal monitors have failed to show a significantly higher prevalence of late decelerations [60].

Management/Treatment

Once diagnosed, treatment of OSA is approved in patients with an apnea hypopnea index AHI >15 or those with AHI >5 who have symptoms that are known to respond to therapy such as daytime sleepiness. There are no specific guidelines on therapy initiation in pregnancy yet for various reasons. As stated above, the natural history of the disorder around the perinatal period is not well known. Thus, it is possible that, with weight loss and reversal of pregnancy physiology, the disorder may resolve or at least improve in the postpartum period. In addition, there have been no trials to date that have shown that treatment of OSA in pregnancy would improve pregnancy or fetal outcomes. This reason likely contributes to the fact that the disorder remains underscreened and underdiagnosed [59]. Based on current data, weight loss is unlikely to be an option in pregnancy because of concern that it may affect the nutritional status of the mother and therefore fetal well-being. Alcohol and cigarette smoking avoidance is another therapeutic strategy in pregnancy that carries additional pregnancy-specific benefits. Outside of pregnancy, CPAP therapy has been shown to improve quality of life and daytime sleepiness with some data suggesting improvement in cardiovascular outcomes such as hypertension. It is likely that these effects of CPAP are also true in pregnancy. Observational studies have shown improvement in daytime fatigue and daytime somnolence in pregnant women with OSA treated with CPAP and re-titrated around midpregnancy [66]. In women with preeclampsia, small, randomized trials have shown that in-laboratory positive airway pressure therapy improves hemodynamics, uric acid, and cardiac output compared to untreated women [67, 68]. Until future studies of CPAP therapy are available in pregnancy, indications for therapy are likely the same as in the nonpregnant population. We are awaiting trials evaluating the effect of PAP therapy on pregnancy-specific outcomes to be able to determine the "urgency" of starting PAP therapy in pregnancy. The type of PAP therapy that is most beneficial in pregnancy is unknown. However, auto-titrating PAP therapy has the advantage of avoiding repeat re-titration of pressure requirements.

In summary, pregnant women with the above disorders need to be managed with pregnancy physiology and fetal effects of the disease and the therapy in mind.

References

1. Schatz M, Harden K, Forsythe A, et al. The course of asthma during pregnancy, post partum, and with successive pregnancies: a prospective analysis. J Allergy Clin Immunol. 1988;81:509–17.
2. Stenius-Aarniala BS, Hedman J, Teramo KA. Acute asthma during pregnancy. Thorax. 1996;51:411–4.
3. Tata LJ, Lewis SA, McKeever TM, et al. A comprehensive analysis of adverse obstetric and pediatric complications in women with asthma. Am J Respir Crit Care Med. 2007;175:991–7.
4. Kallen B, Rydhstroem H, Aberg A. Asthma during pregnancy–a population based study. Eur J Epidemiol. 2000;16:167–71.
5. Demissie K, Breckenridge MB, Rhoads GG. Infant and maternal outcomes in the pregnancies of asthmatic women. Am J Respir Crit Care Med. 1998;158:1091–5.
6. Mendola P, Laughon SK, Mannisto TI, et al. Obstetric complications among US women with asthma. Am J Obstet Gynecol. 2013;208:127e1–8.
7. Powell H, McCaffery K, Murphy VE, et al. Psychosocial variables are related to future exacerbation risk and perinatal outcomes in pregnant women with asthma. J Asthma. 2013;50(4):383–9.
8. Namazy JA, Murphy VE, Powell H, Gibson PG, Chambers C, Schatz M. Effects of asthma severity, exacerbations and oral corticosteroids on perinatal outcomes. Eur Respir J. 2013;41(5):1082–90.
9. Schatz M, Dombrowski MP, Wise R, et al. Spirometry is related to perinatal outcomes in pregnant women with asthma. Am J Obstet Gynecol. 2006;194:120–6.
10. Powell H, Murphy VE, Taylor DR, et al. Management of asthma in pregnancy guided by measurement of fraction of exhaled nitric oxide: a double-blind, randomised controlled trial. Lancet. 2011;378:983–90.
11. Habr F, Raker C, Lin CL, Zouein E, Bourjeily G. Predictors of gastroesophageal reflux symptoms in pregnant women screened for sleep disordered breathing: a secondary analysis. Clin Res Hepatol Gastroenterol. 2012;37:93–9.
12. Kaunitz AM, Hughes JM, Grimes DA, Smith JC, Rochat RW, Kafrissen ME. Causes of maternal mortality in the United States. Obstet Gynecol. 1985;65:605–12.
13. Shariatzadeh MR, Marrie TJ. Pneumonia during pregnancy. Am J Med. 2006;119:872–6.
14. Yost NP, Bloom SL, Richey SD, Ramin SM, Cunningham FG. An appraisal of treatment guidelines for antepartum community-acquired pneumonia. Am J Obstet Gynecol. 2000;183:131–5.
15. Marrie TJ, Huang JQ. Epidemiology of community-acquired pneumonia in Edmonton, Alberta: an emergency department-based study. Can Respir J. 2005;12:139–42.
16. Munn MB, Groome LJ, Atterbury JL, Baker SL, Hoff C. Pneumonia as a complication of pregnancy. J Matern Fetal Med. 1999;8:151–4.
17. Cilloniz C, Ewig S, Polverino E, et al. Microbial aetiology of community-acquired pneumonia and its relation to severity. Thorax. 2011;66:340–6.
18. Johansson N, Kalin M, Tiveljung-Lindell A, Giske CG, Hedlund J. Etiology of community-acquired pneumonia: increased microbiological yield with new diagnostic methods. Clin Infect Dis. 2010;50:202–9.
19. Goodnight WH, Soper DE. Pneumonia in pregnancy. Crit Care Med. 2005;33:S390–7.

20. Chen YH, Keller J, Wang IT, Lin CC, Lin HC. Pneumonia and pregnancy outcomes: a nationwide population-based study. Am J Obstet Gynecol. 2012;207:288e1–7.
21. Romanyuk V, Raichel L, Sergienko R, Sheiner E. Pneumonia during pregnancy: radiological characteristics, predisposing factors and pregnancy outcomes. J Matern Fetal Neonatal Med. 2011;24:113–7.
22. Getahun D, Ananth CV, Peltier MR, Smulian JC, Vintzileos AM. Acute and chronic respiratory diseases in pregnancy: associations with placental abruption. Am J Obstet Gynecol. 2006;195:1180–4.
23. The Acute Respiratory Distress Syndrome Network. Ventilation with lower tidal volumes as compared with traditional tidal volumes for acute lung injury and the acute respiratory distress syndrome. N Engl J Med. 2000;342:1301–8.
24. Lamont RF, Sobel JD, Carrington D, et al. Varicella-zoster virus (chickenpox) infection in pregnancy. BJOG. 2011;118:1155–62.
25. Mohsen AH, McKendrick M. Varicella pneumonia in adults. Eur Respir J. 2003;21:886–91.
26. Sauerbrei A, Wutzler P. Neonatal varicella. J Perinatol. 2001;21:545–9.
27. Enders G, Miller E, Cradock-Watson J, Bolley I, Ridehalgh M. Consequences of varicella and herpes zoster in pregnancy: prospective study of 1739 cases. Lancet. 1994;343:1548–51.
28. Heininger U, Seward JF. Varicella. Lancet. 2006;368:1365–76.
29. Ross AH. Modification of chicken pox in family contacts by administration of gamma globulin. N Engl J Med. 1962;267:369–76.
30. Hall S, Maupin T, Seward J, et al. Second varicella infections: are they more common than previously thought? Pediatrics. 2002;109:1068–73.
31. Guess HA, Broughton DD, Melton 3rd LJ, Kurland LT. Epidemiology of herpes zoster in children and adolescents: a population-based study. Pediatrics. 1985;76:512–7.
32. Centers for Disease Control and Prevention (CDC). Varicella-related deaths among adult--nited States, 1997. MMWR Morb Mortal Wkly Rep. 1997;46:409–12.
33. Gardella C, Brown ZA. Managing varicella zoster infection in pregnancy. Cleve Clin J Med. 2007;74:290–6.
34. Broussard RC, Payne DK, George RB. Treatment with acyclovir of varicella pneumonia in pregnancy. Chest. 1991;99:1045–7.
35. Smego Jr RA, Asperilla MO. Use of acyclovir for varicella pneumonia during pregnancy. Obstet Gynecol. 1991;78:1112–6.
36. Pastuszak AL, Levy M, Schick B, et al. Outcome after maternal varicella infection in the first 20 weeks of pregnancy. N Engl J Med. 1994;330:901–5.
37. Enders G, Miller E. Varicella and herpes zoster in pregnancy and the newborn. In: Arvin AM, Gershon AA, editors. Varicella-Zoster virus virology and clinical management. Cambridge, MA: Cambridge University Press; 2000. p. 317–47.
38. Sauerbrei A, Wutzler P. Fetales Varizellensyndrom. Monatsschr Kinderheilkd. 2003; 151:209–13.
39. Mattson SN, Jones KL, Gramling LJ, et al. Neurodevelopmental follow-up of children of women infected with varicella during pregnancy: a prospective study. Pediatr Infect Dis J. 2003;22:819–23.
40. Cohen A, Moschopoulos P, Stiehm RE, Koren G. Congenital varicella syndrome: the evidence for secondary prevention with varicella-zoster immune globulin. CMAJ. 2011;183:204–8.
41. Paryani SG, Arvin AM. Intrauterine infection with varicella-zoster virus after maternal varicella. N Engl J Med. 1986;314:1542–6.
42. Kim JS, Ryu CW, Lee SI, Sung DW, Park CK. High-resolution CT findings of varicella-zoster pneumonia. AJR Am J Roentgenol. 1999;172:113–6.
43. Yu H, Feng Z, Uyeki TM, et al. Risk factors for severe illness with 2009 pandemic influenza A (H1N1) virus infection in China. Clin Infect Dis. 2011;52:457–65.
44. Louie JK, Jamieson DJ, Rasmussen SA. 2009 pandemic influenza A (H1N1) virus infection in postpartum women in California. Am J Obstet Gynecol. 2011;204:144e1–6.
45. Hartert TV, Neuzil KM, Shintani AK, et al. Maternal morbidity and perinatal outcomes among pregnant women with respiratory hospitalizations during influenza season. Am J Obstet Gynecol. 2003;189:1705–12.

46. Freeman DW, Barno A. Deaths from Asian influenza associated with pregnancy. Am J Obstet Gynecol. 1959;78:1172–5.
47. Siston AM, Rasmussen SA, Honein MA, et al. Pandemic 2009 influenza A(H1N1) virus illness among pregnant women in the United States. JAMA. 2010;303:1517–25.
48. Jamieson DJ, Honein MA, Rasmussen SA, et al. H1N1 2009 influenza virus infection during pregnancy in the USA. Lancet. 2009;374:451–8.
49. Mosby LG, Rasmussen SA, Jamieson DJ. 2009 pandemic influenza A (H1N1) in pregnancy: a systematic review of the literature. Am J Obstet Gynecol. 2011;205:10–8.
50. Ellington SR, Hartman LK, Acosta M, et al. Pandemic 2009 influenza A (H1N1) in 71 critically ill pregnant women in California. Am J Obstet Gynecol. 2011;204:S21–30.
51. Yates L, Pierce M, Stephens S, et al. Influenza A/H1N1v in pregnancy: an investigation of the characteristics and management of affected women and the relationship to pregnancy outcomes for mother and infant. Health Technol Assess. 2010;14:109–82.
52. Miller AC, Safi F, Hussain S, Subramanian RA, Elamin EM, Sinert R. Novel influenza A(H1N1) virus among gravid admissions. Arch Intern Med. 2010;170:868–73.
53. Louie JK, Acosta M, Jamieson DJ, Honein MA. California Pandemic Working G. Severe 2009 H1N1 influenza in pregnant and postpartum women in California. N Engl J Med. 2010;362: 27–35.
54. Fiore AE, Fry A, Shay D, et al. Antiviral agents for the treatment and chemoprophylaxis of influenza -- recommendations of the Advisory Committee on Immunization Practices (ACIP). MMWR Recomm Rep. 2011;60:1–24.
55. Yang P, Deng Y, Pang X, et al. Severe, critical and fatal cases of 2009 H1N1 influenza in China. J Infect. 2010;61:277–83.
56. Creanga AA, Johnson TF, Graitcer SB, et al. Severity of 2009 pandemic influenza A (H1N1) virus infection in pregnant women. Obstet Gynecol. 2010;115:717–26.
57. Product Information: RELENZA(R) oral inhalation powder, zanamivir oral inhalation powder. GlaxoSmithKline (per FDA). Research Triangle Park, NC; 2011.
58. Bourjeily G, Raker CA, Chalhoub M, Miller MA. Pregnancy and fetal outcomes of symptoms of sleep-disordered breathing. Eur Respir J. 2010;36:849–55.
59. Bourjeily G, Raker C, Paglia MJ, Ankner G, O'Connor K. Patient and provider perceptions of sleep disordered breathing assessment during prenatal care: a survey-based observational study. Ther Adv Respir Dis. 2012;6:211–9.
60. Olivarez SA, Maheshwari B, McCarthy M, et al. Prospective trial on obstructive sleep apnea in pregnancy and fetal heart rate monitoring. Am J Obstet Gynecol. 2010;202:552.e1–7.
61. Bourjeily G, Raker C, Chalhoub M, Miller M. Excessive daytime sleepiness in late pregnancy may not always be normal: Results from a cross sectional study. Sleep Breath. 2013;17(2): 735–40.
62. Facco FL, Ouyang DW, Zee PC, Grobman WA. Development of a pregnancy-specific screening tool for sleep apnea. J Clin Sleep Med. 2012;8:389–94.
63. Bourjeily G, Ankner G, Mohsenin V. Sleep-disordered breathing in pregnancy. Clin Chest Med. 2011;32:175–89.
64. Qiu C, Enquobahrie D, Frederick IO, Abetew D, Williams MA. Glucose intolerance and gestational diabetes risk in relation to sleep duration and snoring during pregnancy: a pilot study. BMC Womens Health. 2010;10:17.
65. Bellamy L, Casas JP, Hingorani AD, Williams D. Type 2 diabetes mellitus after gestational diabetes: a systematic review and meta-analysis. Lancet. 2009;373:1773–9.
66. Guilleminault C, Kreutzer M, Chang JL. Pregnancy, sleep disordered breathing and treatment with nasal continuous positive airway pressure. Sleep Med. 2004;5:43–51.
67. Blyton D, Sullivan C, Edwards N. Reduced nocturnal cardiac output associated with preeclampsia is minimized with the use of nocturnal nasal CPAP. Sleep. 2004;27:79–84.
68. Edwards N, Blyton DM, Kirjavainen T, Kesby GJ, Sullivan CE. Nasal continuous positive airway pressure reduces sleep-induced blood pressure increments in preeclampsia. Am J Respir Crit Care Med. 2000;162:252–7.

Part XI
Renal

Chapter 12
Renal Disease in Pregnancy

Lucia Larson

Introduction

The renal system undergoes significant adaptations in pregnancy to meet the needs of both the pregnant woman and her growing fetus. These changes have important implications in the evaluation and management of gravidas with kidney disorders. Renal disease in pregnancy falls into several categories. It may be chronic and diagnosed prior to pregnancy, chronic but first recognized during pregnancy, or it may present for the first time as an acute disorder in pregnancy. While the majority of women with underlying renal disease in pregnancy will have good pregnancy outcomes, there is an increased risk for adverse maternal and fetal outcomes especially in pregnant women with moderate to severe renal disease. These risks include worsening renal function, increase of baseline proteinuria, worsening hypertension, and the development of superimposed preeclampsia. From the fetal perspective, there is an increased risk of fetal growth restriction, preterm delivery, and the complications of superimposed preeclampsia. Other common disorders during pregnancy include pyelonephritis and renal stones. This chapter will outline renal changes during pregnancy, discuss the impact of pregnancy on renal disease and the impact of renal disease on pregnancy in general, and review several common kidney disorders occurring in pregnancy.

L. Larson, M.D. (✉)
Obstetric Medicine, Women's Medicine Collaborative, The Miriam Hospital,
Providence, RI 02904, USA

The Warren Alpert Medical School of Brown University, 146 West River Street, Ste 11C,
Providence, RI 02904, USA
e-mail: Lucia_larson@brown.edu

Table 12.1 Renal physiologic changes in pregnancy

Renal change	Mechanisms for change	Clinical implications
80 % increase in renal blood flow (RBF) 40–60 % increase in glomerular filtration rate (GFR) Less efficient tubular resorption Increased solute excretion	Increased relaxin of pregnancy causes decrease in both efferent and afferent resistance Increased cardiac output	Creatinine decreases by ~0.4 mg/dL with average creatinine = 0.5. Creatinine of 0.9 mg/dL considered abnormal BUN decreases to 8–10 mg/dL with 14 considered abnormal Serum uric acid decreased with abnormal >4.5 mg/dL Increased urinary protein excretion with abnormal >300 mg in a 24-h urine collection, >1+ on urine dipstick, or urine protein creatinine ratio (UPCR) ≥0.4 (urine PCR <0.1 is normal and urine PCR 0.1 to <0.4 is indeterminate) Increased glucosuria and calcium excretion
Increase in total body water of 6–8 l (4–6 l of which is extracellular)	Increased activation of renin-aldosterone-angiotensin system with sodium retention	Edema
Increased excretion of bicarbonate	Renal compensation for respiratory alkalosis	Decreased serum bicarbonate
Increased vasopressinase	Placental production	Decreased effectiveness of vasopressin rarely leads to diabetes insipidus (responsive to DDAVP)
Decrease in threshold for thirst and ADH secretion	Possibly related to vasodilatation	Lower serum osmolality and sodium

Pathobiology

The kidney undergoes marked structural and physiologic changes in pregnancy that begin early in the first trimester by 3–4 weeks after conception [1] (Table 12.1). Renal blood flow increases by 80 % and glomerular filtration rate (GFR) increases by approximately 40–60 % due to pregnancy-induced increases in plasma volume, cardiac output, and renal blood flow. This change has important clinical implications for medication use and laboratory interpretation. Renally excreted drugs may require higher doses and more frequent administration for therapeutic blood levels during pregnancy. Due to the increased GFR, the average creatinine in pregnancy is decreased to 0.5 mg/dL and a creatinine of 0.9 mg/dL or greater is abnormal. Blood urea nitrogen (BUN) averages 8–10 and a BUN of 14 mg/dL or greater is abnormal. The normal creatinine clearance in pregnancy is increased to 150–200 ml/min. Along with the increased GFR, protein excretion doubles and a normal pregnant woman may have up to 300 mg of protein in a 24-h urine collection. Other changes include increased excretion of amino acids, glucose, and calcium in the urine. Bicarbonate excretion increases to compensate for the increased minute ventilation resulting in an average decrease in serum bicarbonate of 4 meq/L. A downward reset of the osmotic threshold for vasopressin results in a decrease in serum osmolality of approximately 10 mosm/L and a decrease in serum sodium of approximately 5 meq/L. The kidney increases in size by 1–1.5 cm due to increased blood flow and dilatation of the renal collecting system. The dilatation occurs because of the effects of progesterone and relaxin as well as the mechanical changes of the enlarging uterus causing compression. Dilatation is typically greater on the right than left and is thought to be due to the anatomic differences in the course of the right ureter as it crosses the pelvic brim, right iliac artery, and right ovarian vein. Renal ultrasound reveals hydronephrosis, but true obstruction can be distinguished by the presence of bilateral ureteral jets. Erythropoietin and active vitamin D production also increase.

Urinary Tract Infection

Pregnant women are predisposed to urinary tract infections (UTIs) due to the stasis of urine in the dilated collecting system and changes in urinary composition with glucosuria and aminoaciduria. Approximately 2–10 % of pregnancies develop asymptomatic bacteriuria, and if untreated, up to 30 % of these women will develop pyelonephritis. Low birth weight and preterm delivery are associated with asymptomatic bacteriuria, but treatment with antibiotics decreases both the incidence of pyelonephritis (OR 0.23, 95 % CI 0.13–0.41) and low birth weight [2]. Asymptomatic bacteriuria and UTI have similar associated complications. Organisms infecting the urinary tract in pregnancy are the same as in nonpregnant patients with the most common organism being *E. coli*. Other pathogens include *Klebsiella*, *Enterobacter*, *Proteus*, and gram-positive organisms. Treatment is best guided by local microbiology data and susceptibilities and consists of 3–7 days of antibiotics with a follow-up test of cure 1 week after antibiotic completion. Monthly urine cultures are indicated for the remainder of the pregnancy due to the high likelihood of recurrence of asymptomatic bacteriuria and UTI. See Table 12.2 for suggested antibiotic regimens for treatment, but the fluoroquinolones should be avoided in pregnancy and breast-feeding. If a recurrent episode of asymptomatic bacteriuria or UTI occurs, suppressive or prophylactic therapy is recommended to prevent recurrence. See Table 12.3.

Table 12.2 Suggested treatment regimen of asymptomatic bacteriuria and UTI in pregnant women

Antibiotics	Oral regimen
Amoxicillin	500 mg three times a day
Amoxicillin–clavulanate	500 mg twice daily
Cephalexin	250 mg four times a day
Nitrofurantoin	100 mg twice a day
Trimethoprim–sulfamethoxazole	One DS twice daily (avoid in first trimester and near term)

Adapted from [24]

Table 12.3 Antibiotic prophylaxis in pregnancy

Antibiotic	Oral regimen
Nitrofurantoin	50–100 mg once daily
Cephalexin	250–500 mg once daily
Amoxicillin	250 mg once daily

Adapted from [24]

Table 12.4 Suggested intravenous antibiotic regimens for pyelonephritis in pregnancy

Antibiotic	Dose
Ceftriaxone	1 g every 24 h
Ampicillin–sulbactam	3 g every 6 h
Aztreonam	1 g every 8–12 h
Ampicillin plus gentamicin	1–2 g every 6 h 1.5 mg/kg every 8 h[a]
Ticarcillin–clavulanate	3.1 g every 6 h
Piperacillin–tazobactam	3.375 g every 6 h

[a]Once daily dosing in the treatment of pyelonephritis in pregnancy has not been adequately studied
Adapted from [24]

Pyelonephritis in pregnancy is associated with significant maternal and fetal morbidity including bacteremia and sepsis, acute respiratory distress syndrome (ARDS), and preterm labor and delivery. Approximately 8 % of pyelonephritis is associated with pulmonary edema [3, 4] suggesting that close monitoring of oxygen saturation and fluid status is prudent. Given these potential complications, pyelonephritis should be treated as an inpatient in pregnant women. Suggested intravenous regimens can be found in Table 12.4. After clinical improvement, gravidas with pyelonephritis can be changed to an oral regimen based on culture and sensitivity results to complete a 10–14-day course. Recurrence of pyelonephritis in the same pregnancy occurs in 6–8 % of women but can be prevented with prophylactic antibiotics [5, 6]. See Table 12.3.

Renal Calculi

Renal stones occur in approximately 1 in 200 to 1 in 1,500 pregnancies [7]. The physiologic changes predisposing women to UTI in pregnancy also predispose women to the development of renal calculi. In addition to stasis and an increase in excretion of calcium, uric acid, and oxalate, there is a decrease in pH favoring stone formation. The most common stones in pregnancy are calcium phosphate in distinction to calcium oxalate stones which are more common in nonpregnant patients. Flank pain and hematuria are a typical presentation. Though spiral CT to diagnose renal stones involves a radiation dose within an acceptable range for pregnant women, this is ideally avoided. Renal ultrasound can be done initially but may only identify 60 % of stones. A transvaginal ultrasound may be useful to identify distal stones. Magnetic resonance urography (MRU) can be used as a second-line test if it is available. Women may be initially treated for pain with narcotics while awaiting spontaneous passage of the stone. Whether medical expulsive therapy would be useful in pregnancy when there already is a dilated renal collecting system is unclear, but if considered, calcium channel blockers such as nifedipine can be used. On the other hand, there is no data on the use of tamsulosin in pregnant women. If intervention is indicated such as with the presence of renal insufficiency or failure of conservative treatment, ureteroscopy with stone removal can be done safely during pregnancy. Other temporizing procedures that may be considered include placement of ureteral stents or nephrostomy tubes. Lithotripsy is not recommended in pregnancy, however. Suggested laboratory evaluation includes electrolytes with calcium, BUN, creatinine, and complete blood count, as well as straining of urine and chemical analysis of any collected stones.

Acute Renal Failure

The etiologies of acute renal failure in pregnancy are the same as those in nonpregnant patients with additional causes specific to pregnancy. The more common pregnancy-related causes include obstetric hemorrhage; placental abruption; severe preeclampsia or hemolysis, elevated liver enzymes, low platelet (HELLP) syndrome; and septic abortion. A more complete differential diagnosis is outlined in Table 12.5. Preeclampsia must be strongly considered in any pregnant women after 20 weeks gestation either as a primary cause of renal dysfunction or as a cause superimposed on another underlying renal disease. Forty percent of acute renal insufficiency in pregnancy is caused by preeclampsia in developed countries [8]. The thrombotic microangiopathies (TMA) such as thrombotic thrombocytopenic purpura–hemolytic uremic syndrome (TTP–HUS) appear to be associated with pregnancy and can often be difficult to distinguish from preeclampsia/HELLP syndrome and acute fatty liver of pregnancy (AFLP). Approximately 10 % of women who develop TTP–HUS do so in association with pregnancy or the postpartum period [9, 10]. When the distinction is unclear, treatment should be targeted at both preeclampsia/HELLP and TTP HUS with delivery and plasma exchange.

The workup of acute renal insufficiency in pregnancy is the same as in nonpregnant patients. History often offers significant clues especially if there are signs and symptoms of obvious disorder such as bleeding, sources of infection or sepsis, or collagen vascular disease. The urine sediment should be examined for evidence of nephritis or acute tubular necrosis (ATN). Renal ultrasound can rule out obstruction which has been reported in rare cases and may also identify evidence for underlying renal disorders. In some cases serologic studies such as ANA, ANCA, antiGBM, and complement levels will be helpful. Because it is difficult to rule out whether preeclampsia is contributing, it is in both maternal and fetal interests to deliver

Table 12.5 Some causes of acute renal insufficiency/failure in pregnancy

1. Pregnancy related
   a. Hyperemesis gravidarum
   b. Preeclampsia/eclampsia/HELLP
   c Acute fatty liver of pregnancy
   d. Septic abortion
   e. Obstetric hemorrhage
   f. Placental abruption
   g. Amniotic fluid embolism

2. Causes coincidental to pregnancy (can be influenced by pregnancy)
   a. Thrombotic microangiopathy (TMA) may be difficult to differentiate from preeclampsia/HELLP and AFLP
      i. TTP–HUS
      ii. DIC
      iii. Catastrophic antiphospholipid antibody syndrome
   b. Infection, including sepsis
      i. Pyelonephritis
   c. Acute tubular necrosis
   d. Acute cortical necrosis
   e. Interstitial nephritis
   f. Glomerular disease
   g. Acute obstruction
      i. Renal obstruction due to mechanical effects of the gravid uterus (rare)
      ii. Surgical injury to ureters or bladder during C-section (typically emergent)
   h. Nephrotoxic drugs
      i. NSAID use (especially with postpartum use)

women with worsening creatinine at or near term. In women remote from term, the decision to deliver a premature infant is more complicated. If a clinical diagnosis cannot be made, renal biopsy can be considered when it will provide guidance for possible treatment that will allow pregnancy to be prolonged while a primary maternal disorder is treated. Renal biopsy can be done safely in pregnancy [11] though there are conflicting reports about whether the risk for bleeding is increased [12].

Chronic Kidney Disease

It has been estimated that approximately 3 % of women of childbearing age have chronic kidney disease (CKD) [13]. In those who become pregnant, diabetes and hypertension are the most common etiologies for CKD in pregnancy. The risk for complications during pregnancy is more strongly associated with the degree of renal dysfunction and the presence of hypertension prior to pregnancy than it is with the specific cause for CKD. Risks include worsening of renal function with the potential for progression to end-stage renal disease (ESRD) requiring dialysis, worsening

Table 12.6 Prepregnancy creatinine and pregnancy outcome[a]

Creatinine (mg/dL)	% Pregnancy-related long-term renal function decline	% Preeclampsia	% Preterm birth	% Fetal growth restriction
<1.4	<3	22	30	25
1.4–2.0	<30	40	60	40
>2.0	53	60	>90	65
Dialysis	–	75	>90	>90

[a]Adapted from [26]

hypertension, and superimposed preeclampsia. Stability of renal disease prior to pregnancy is important as disorders that are worsening prior to conception are more likely to continue to worsen as gestation proceeds. ACE inhibitors and angiotensin receptor blockers (ARBs) should be discontinued in pregnancy. Women with pre-pregnancy creatinine <1.4 mg/dL generally have good maternal and fetal outcomes. Approximately 40 % of gravidas with creatinine between 1.4 and 2.0 mg/dL will experience at least a 25 % decline in renal function during pregnancy of which 20 % will not improve after delivery. Two percent of these gravidas will have ESRD at 1 year postpartum. Women with the poorest prognosis in pregnancy are those with creatinine >2.0 mg/dL as 70 % will have decline in renal function of at least 25 % in pregnancy and in 50 % the decline persists. Thirty-five percent of these women will have ESRD at 1 year postpartum [14–16]. Urinary tract infection increases this risk. Obstetric complications associated with renal insufficiency include intrauterine growth restriction, preterm delivery, and superimposed preeclampsia. See Table 12.6. Proteinuria increases with pregnancy, and even women who had non-nephrotic range proteinuria before becoming pregnant can develop nephrotic levels of proteinuria as pregnancy progresses. Massive proteinuria severe enough to cause vulvar edema precluding vaginal delivery has been reported. Treatment with prophylactic doses of low-molecular-weight heparin (LMWH) is prudent in women with antithrombin III loss given the known increased risk of thrombosis in pregnancy and in nephrotic syndrome. See Chart 12.1 for an overview of the initial management of CKD in pregnancy.

Pregnant women with chronic renal disease require close follow-up during pregnancy to monitor for worsening renal function and to ensure adequate blood pressure control. Because UTI is associated with worsening renal function, urine should be cultured monthly and infection treated aggressively. It is reasonable to treat with low-dose aspirin for preeclampsia prophylaxis [17, 18], and there should be a low threshold to obtain preeclampsia labs. The obstetrician will follow closely for appropriate fetal growth and fetal well-being with ultrasound, nonstress tests, and biophysical profiles.

1. Obtain baseline assessment of renal function and obtain baseline preeclampsia labs: electrolytes, BUN/ creatinine, 24 urine for creatinine clearance and total protein, uric acid, AST, ALT, CBC with platelets
2. Assess for asymptomatic bacteriuria or UTI: urinalysis, urine culture
3. Avoid ace-inhibitors and ARBs in pregnancy (See Hypertension Chapter) (In women with diabetic nephropathy, diltiazem or verapamil may be used for antiproteinuric effects)(25)
4. Monitor and treat BP for goal <140/90
5. Educate patient on signs and symptoms of preeclampsia
6. Consider 81mg ASA for preeclampsia prophylaxis(17, 18)
7. Consider LMWH for thrombosis prophylaxis in women with nephrotic range proteinuria who may develop antithrombin III deficiency (See Chapter on Thrombophilia and Thrombosis)

Chart 12.1 Initial management of patient with CKD in pregnancy

Dialysis

Fertility is impaired in women on chronic dialysis, but pregnancy can occur when birth control is not used. The chances of successful pregnancy outcome may be improved with more frequent dialysis though there remains an increased risk for adverse outcomes. In 1980, only 23 % of pregnancies in women on dialysis ended with infants who survived, but more recently survival has been reported in more than 70 % of pregnancies [19]. Significant obstetric complications associated with these pregnancies include increased risk of spontaneous abortion, intrauterine fetal demise, intrauterine growth restriction, polyhydramnios, and preterm delivery. Reported maternal complications consist of anemia, requiring aggressive treatment with erythropoietin, intravenous iron, and blood transfusions as well as severe hypertension. For fetal well-being, the goal of dialysis is to keep BUN <50 mg/dL. Other adjustments in dialysis for pregnancy include lowering bicarbonate, monitoring phosphate and vitamin D needs, and allowing for the increased plasma volume in pregnancy. The most recent reports of pregnancy outcome of women on dialysis suggest that frequent and intense dialysis may be associated with improved fertility and pregnancy outcome. In a small retrospective study of five women treated with nocturnal hemodialysis who had 7 pregnancies, the estimated fertility rate was 15.6 % [20]. Of the 6 live infants, 2 had intrauterine growth restriction or a small for gestational age baby, 1 had preterm delivery at 30 weeks gestation, and 1 had threatened preterm delivery with shortened cervix. Interestingly, none had difficult to control hypertension and none had polyhydramnios. While pregnancy can be successful in women on dialysis, the risk for adverse outcome is increased, and some women may benefit from deferring pregnancy until after renal transplant.

Renal Transplant

Women with renal transplants experience return in fertility within 6 months. In those who have stable renal transplants and creatinine <1.4 mg/dL, pregnancy does not appear to have a long-term effect on renal function [21]. However, though outcome is better than in women with ESRD, there is an increased risk for fetal loss, preeclampsia, intrauterine growth restriction, and preterm delivery in the pregnancies of women with renal transplants [22, 23]. In a recent cohort study, predictive factors for adverse outcome were greater than the 2 previous renal transplants, first trimester creatinine >1.4 mg/dL, and diastolic BP >90 mmHg in the 2nd or 3rd trimester [23]. Ideally women should plan to enter pregnancy with a stable functioning graft. This requires a delay in pregnancy for 1–2 years after receiving a graft to allow for adjustment in immunotherapy and to ensure graft stability. Once pregnant, women should continue to take antirejection medication. Of note, mycophenolate mofetil (MMF) and sirolimus are not recommended for use in pregnancy, but azathioprine, cyclosporine, tacrolimus, and prednisone can be used. Drug levels and renal function should be followed during pregnancy as doses generally require adjustments upward because of pharmacokinetic changes in pregnancy. Blood pressure should be controlled and urine infection should be aggressively sought and treated as these can contribute to worsening renal function. Vaginal delivery is generally possible in renal transplant patients, but if there is a question, either surgical records or an ultrasound may clarify anatomy.

Labor and Delivery and the Postpartum Period

Obstetric indications should determine whether a woman with renal disease undergoes a vaginal or cesarean delivery. As with nonpregnant patients with CKD, dose adjustments for renally excreted drugs are necessary, and nephrotoxic agents should be avoided to prevent further renal impairment. In particular, magnesium sulfate which is used for prevention of seizures in preeclampsia is excreted by the kidneys and should only be used with close monitoring for signs and symptoms of magnesium toxicity and frequent magnesium levels if it is required. Nonsteroidal anti-inflammatory medications are often routinely prescribed for postpartum pain relief in many postpartum wards, and special care may be necessary to prevent inadvertent administration. ACE inhibitors and ARBs should be restarted after delivery. Breastfeeding ought to be encouraged for its many maternal and neonatal benefits. Tables 12.7 and 12.8 show the data on breastfeeding for ACE inhibitors and ARBs as well as drugs used in renal transplant patients.

Table 12.7 Breastfeeding and ACE inhibitors and angiotensin receptor blockers (ARBs)

Medication	Breastfeeding data
Captopril	Hale Lactation Risk Category L2[a] American Academy of Pediatrics recommendation: usually compatible with breastfeeding
Enalapril	Hale Lactation Risk Category L2[a] American Academy of Pediatrics recommendation: usually compatible with breastfeeding
Losartan	Hale Lactation Risk Category L3[a] American Academy of Pediatrics recommendation: not reviewed
Valsartan	Hale Lactation Risk Category L3[a] American Academy of Pediatrics recommendation: not reviewed
Candesartan	Hale Lactation Risk Category L3[a] American Academy of Pediatrics recommendation: not reviewed

[a]Hale Lactation Risk Categories: L1 safest, L2 safer, L3 moderately safe (comment: new medications that have absolutely no published data are automatically categorized in this category regardless of how safe they may be), L4 possibly hazardous, L5 contraindicated [27]

Table 12.8 Breastfeeding and renal transplant medications

Medication	Breastfeeding data
Mycophenolate mofetil (MMF)	Hale Lactation Risk Category L4[a] American Academy of Pediatrics recommendation: not reviewed
Azathioprine	Hale Lactation Risk Category L3[a] American Academy of Pediatrics recommendation: not reviewed
Cyclosporine	Hale Lactation Risk Category L3[a] American Academy of Pediatrics recommendation: cytotoxic drug that may interfere with the cellular metabolism of the nursing infant
Sirolimus	Hale Lactation Risk Category L4[a] American Academy of Pediatrics recommendation: not reviewed
Tacrolimus	Hale Lactation Risk Category L3[a] American Academy of Pediatrics recommendation: not reviewed
Prednisone	Hale Lactation Risk Category L2[a] American Academy of Pediatrics recommendation: usually compatible with breastfeeding

[a]Hale Lactation Risk Categories: L1 safest, L2 safer, L3 moderately safe (comment: new medications that have absolutely no published data are automatically categorized in this category regardless of how safe they may be), L4 possibly hazardous, L5 contraindicated [27]

References

1. Davison JM, Noble MC. Serial changes in 24 hour creatinine clearance during normal menstrual cycles and the first trimester of pregnancy. Br J Obstet Gynaecol. 1981;88(1):10–7. Epub 1981/01/01.
2. Smaill F, Vazquez JC. Antibiotics for asymptomatic bacteriuria in pregnancy. Cochrane Database Syst Rev. 2007;2, CD000490. Epub 2007/04/20.

3. Wing DA. Pyelonephritis. Clin Obstet Gynecol. 1998;41(3):515–26. Epub 1998/09/22.
 4. Gilstrap 3rd LC, Ramin SM. Urinary tract infections during pregnancy. Obstet Gynecol Clin N Am. 2001;28(3):581–91. Epub 2001/08/22.
 5. Wing DA, Hendershott CM, Debuque L, Millar LK. A randomized trial of three antibiotic regimens for the treatment of pyelonephritis in pregnancy. Obstet Gynecol. 1998;92(2):249–53. Epub 1998/08/12.
 6. Lenke RR, VanDorsten JP, Schifrin BS. Pyelonephritis in pregnancy: a prospective randomized trial to prevent recurrent disease evaluating suppressive therapy with nitrofurantoin and close surveillance. Am J Obstet Gynecol. 1983;146(8):953–7. Epub 1983/08/15.
 7. Semins MJ, Matlaga BR. Management of urolithiasis in pregnancy. Int J Women's Health. 2013;5:599–604. Epub 2013/10/11.
 8. Kuklina EV, Ayala C, Callaghan WM. Hypertensive disorders and severe obstetric morbidity in the United States. Obstet Gynecol. 2009;113(6):1299–306. Epub 2009/05/23.
 9. Fakhouri F, Roumenina L, Provot F, Sallee M, Caillard S, Couzi L, et al. Pregnancy-associated hemolytic uremic syndrome revisited in the era of complement gene mutations. J Am Soc Nephrol. 2010;21(5):859–67. Epub 2010/03/06.
10. George JN. The association of pregnancy with thrombotic thrombocytopenic purpura-hemolytic uremic syndrome. Curr Opin Hematol. 2003;10(5):339–44. Epub 2003/08/13.
11. Lindheimer MD, Davison JM. Renal biopsy during pregnancy: 'to b … or not to b …?'. Br J Obstet Gynaecol. 1987;94(10):932–4.
12. Piccoli GB, Daidola G, Attini R, Parisi S, Fassio F, Naretto C, et al. Kidney biopsy in pregnancy: evidence for counselling? A systematic narrative review. BJOG. 2013;120(4):412–27. Epub 2013/01/17.
13. Piccoli GB, Attini R, Vasario E, Conijn A, Biolcati M, D'Amico F, et al. Pregnancy and chronic kidney disease: a challenge in all CKD stages. Clin J Am Soc Nephrol. 2010;5(5):844–55. Epub 2010/04/24.
14. Williams D, Davison J. Chronic kidney disease in pregnancy. BMJ. 2008;336(7637):211–5. Epub 2008/01/26.
15. Bramham K, Lightstone L. Pre-pregnancy counseling for women with chronic kidney disease. J Nephrol. 2012;25(4):450–9. Epub 2012/05/30.
16. Davison JM, Lindheimer MD. Pregnancy and chronic kidney disease. Semin Nephrol. 2011;31(1):86–99. Epub 2011/01/27.
17. Coomarasamy A, Honest H, Papaioannou S, Gee H, Khan KS. Aspirin for prevention of pre-eclampsia in women with historical risk factors: a systematic review. Obstet Gynecol. 2003;101(6):1319–32. Epub 2003/06/12.
18. Duley L, Henderson-Smart DJ, Meher S, King JF. Antiplatelet agents for preventing pre-eclampsia and its complications. Cochrane Database Syst Rev. 2007;2, CD004659. Epub 2007/04/20.
19. Piccoli GB, Conijn A, Consiglio V, Vasario E, Attini R, Deagostini MC, et al. Pregnancy in dialysis patients: is the evidence strong enough to lead us to change our counseling policy? Clin J Am Soc Nephrol. 2010;5(1):62–71. Epub 2009/12/08.
20. Barua M, Hladunewich M, Keunen J, Pierratos A, McFarlane P, Sood M, et al. Successful pregnancies on nocturnal home hemodialysis. Clin J Am Soc Nephrol. 2008;3(2):392–6. Epub 2008/03/01.
21. Rahamimov R, Ben-Haroush A, Wittenberg C, Mor E, Lustig S, Gafter U, et al. Pregnancy in renal transplant recipients: long-term effect on patient and graft survival. A single-center experience. Transplantation. 2006;81(5):660–4. Epub 2006/03/15.
22. Deshpande NA, James NT, Kucirka LM, Boyarsky BJ, Garonzik-Wang JM, Montgomery RA, et al. Pregnancy outcomes in kidney transplant recipients: a systematic review and meta-analysis. Am J Transplant. 2011;11(11):2388–404. Epub 2011/07/29.
23. Bramham K, Nelson-Piercy C, Gao H, Pierce M, Bush N, Spark P, et al. Pregnancy in renal transplant recipients: a UK national cohort study. Clin J Am Soc Nephrol. 2013;8(2):290–8. Epub 2012/10/23.

24. Rosene-Montella K, Keely E, Barbour LA, Lee R, editors. Medical care of the pregnant patient. Philadelphia, PA: American College of Physicians; 2008.
25. Khandelwal M, Kumanova M, Gaughan JP, Reece EA. Role of diltiazem in pregnant women with chronic renal disease. J Matern Fetal Neonatal Med. 2002;12(6):408–12. Epub 2003/04/10.
26. Palma-Reis I, Vais A, Nelson-Piercy C, Banerjee A. Renal disease and hypertension in pregnancy. Clin Med. 2013;13(1):57–62. Epub 2013/03/12.
27. Hale T. Medication and mothers' milk. Amarillo, Texas: Hale Publishing; 2008.

Part XII
Rheumatology

Chapter 13
The Care and Management of Rheumatologic Disease in Pregnancy

Candice Yuvienco and Kerri Batra

Overview of Rheumatologic Disease in Pregnancy

Rheumatic diseases affect up to 6 % of the US population and encompass autoimmune inflammatory conditions such as systemic lupus erythematosus (SLE), rheumatoid arthritis (RA), systemic sclerosis (SSc), and Behcet's disease. Normal pregnancy results in a complex interplay of immunologic mechanisms with a goal of maintaining a balance between maternal and fetal health. The immunodynamics of pregnancy in rheumatic diseases are inherently more intricate, aiming to attain homeostasis between maternal autoimmune disease activity and acceptance of the fetoplacental unit.

Advances in understanding of the immunologic and endocrine interactions of normal pregnancy have led to deeper insight into the potential mechanisms of autoimmune disease during the pregnant state. On one hand, pregnancy can affect the status of inflammatory disease; on the other hand, active inflammation can impact the course and outcome of the pregnancy. In fact, increased disease activity provokes poor pregnancy outcomes such as stillbirth, prematurity, and preeclampsia in several autoimmune diseases. Thus, control of maternal disease is paramount to a successful pregnancy. This control can potentially be achieved with the use of

---

C. Yuvienco, M.D. (✉)
Division of Rheumatology, Department of Internal Medicine, UCSF Fresno,
2335 East Kashian Lane, Suite 301, Fresno, CA 93701, USA

University Rheumatology Associates, 2335 East Kashian Lane,
East Medical Plaza Suite 301, Fresno, CA 93701, USA
e-mail: cyuvienco@fresno.ucsf.edu

K. Batra, M.D.
Obstetric Medicine, Rheumatology, Women's Medicine Collaborative, The Miriam Hospital, Providence, RI 02904, USA

The Warren Alpert Medical School of Brown University, Providence, RI 02904, USA
e-mail: kbatra@lifespan.org

immunosuppressive medications. Physician comfort with use of these medications can be problematic due to the uncertain safety data of most medications during pregnancy and lactation.

It has been established that rheumatoid arthritis frequently improves or remits during pregnancy. In contrast, flares of SLE disease activity are common during pregnancy. These are likely reflective of the cytokine shifts induced by the extensive hormonal changes during pregnancy. Flares of autoimmune diseases can occur at any trimester of pregnancy or in the puerperium. In this chapter, we review the most common rheumatic diseases encountered in pregnancy, their impact upon pregnancy, and data and recommendations for their management during pregnancy.

Lupus in Pregnancy

Epidemiology

Systemic lupus erythematosus (SLE), or lupus, is the prototypic autoimmune disease. It is marked by excessive autoantibody production, impaired clearance of autoantibody-antigen complexes, and subsequent deposition and buildup of these complexes in tissues, which leads to tissue damage. The prevalence of SLE is approximately 1 in 2000 in the Caucasian population and around 1 in 500 in Latino, African-American, and Asian populations. It affects predominantly women of childbearing age and affects approximately 1 in 2000 births.

Clinical Manifestations

Clinical manifestations of lupus include photosensitive rashes, oral ulcers, arthritis, serositis (pleuritis, pericarditis), and renal disease. Hematologic manifestations include cytopenias (leukopenia, thrombocytopenia, hemolytic anemia), thrombosis due to underlying antiphospholipid antibodies, and presence of autoantibodies including ANA, anti-dsDNA, anti-Smith, anti-RNP, anti-Ro, and anti-La. SLE is a heterogeneous disease; many women have only mild skin and musculoskeletal manifestations. Other women have life-threatening renal and thrombotic disease.

Clinical Manifestations During Pregnancy

There is a lack of consensus regarding whether lupus flares are more frequent in pregnancy and if so, in which trimester. Some centers have demonstrated an increase in lupus flares and lupus activity during pregnancy [1, 2], while others have not [3, 4]. Lupus is a heterogeneous disease and affects various ethnic groups and individuals differently; thus, study centers with different population mixtures may (and do) observe wildly different manifestations and outcomes. Fortunately, for the majority of patients, lupus activity during pregnancy is mild and manifests mainly in the form of rashes, arthralgias, and mild cytopenias [4]. Patients most likely to do well are those in whom disease has been quiescent for 6 months prior to conception.

The risk of lupus flare during pregnancy is highest in women with heightened disease activity at conception and a history of lupus nephritis (LN). Lupus nephritis occurs in anywhere from 4 to 30 % of lupus pregnancies. However, in women with preexisting LN, recurrences can occur in 20–30 % women, with up to one quarter developing permanent renal damage during and after pregnancy [5]. Risk of lupus nephritis flare is highest in women who have a baseline creatinine of ≥ 1.2 or urine protein >500 mg in a 24-h collection at the time of conception [6].

Besides disease flare, an important adverse maternal outcome of pregnancy is preeclampsia (PEC). PEC is most common in women with lupus nephritis and renal insufficiency at the time of conception. Other risk factors include presence of antiphospholipid antibodies, maternal age >40, previous personal or family history of PEC, preexisting hypertension or diabetes mellitus, and obesity (BMI >35 kg/m^2).

A recent analysis of data from PROMISSE, a prospective study of 250 pregnant patients with SLE and/or APS, suggests that an impaired capacity to limit complement activation predisposes to PEC. Heterozygous mutations were found in genes encoding three complement regulatory proteins in 18 % of women who developed preeclampsia [7].

Other identified maternal complications associated with SLE include preeclampsia (PEC), cesarean section, postpartum hemorrhage, postpartum infection, and increased risk for rehospitalization in the first year postpartum [8–10].

Impact of Disease on Pregnancy Outcomes

The rate of all pregnancy loss in SLE has significantly decreased over the past 50 years, from levels as high as 43 % in the 1960s to approximately 17 % in 2000–2003, which is close to that of the general US population [11]. However, the rate of stillbirth (pregnancy loss >20 weeks' gestation) remains elevated, especially in women with high disease activity, active nephritis, and antiphospholipid syndrome (APS). One study out of Turkey demonstrated a stillbirth rate of 4.6 % [12], with most studies demonstrating rates of between 2 and 12 % [13].

The most common complication of SLE in pregnancy is preterm labor (PTL), which has rates of 15–40 % [8, 14]. Rates of intrauterine growth restriction are approximately 30 % [14].

Worse outcomes occur in women with antiphospholipid antibodies who are at higher risk for intrauterine growth restriction, spontaneous abortion, fetal demise, and early severe preeclampsia. The highest maternal risk is in patients with pulmonary hypertension, severe restrictive lung disease, active renal disease, cardiac disease, or stroke in the 6 months prior to conception.

Patients with anti-Ro (SSA) or anti-La (SSB) antibodies are at risk for neonatal lupus. Neonatal lupus presents as a skin rash in about 5 %, but in 2 %, congenital complete heart block occurs with up to a 30 % neonatal mortality. Presentation begins at 16–34 weeks with an inflammatory myocarditis manifesting as intermittent heart block or a prolonged PR or may first be detected when fibrosis in the conduction system and congenital complete heart block are already present.

For the neonate, an increase in preterm delivery means an increase in low birth weight (LBW), intensive care unit utilization and intubations, and stillbirths [10]. Babies born to mothers with SLE tend to be small for gestational age (SGA), although there does not seem to be an increased risk for hospitalization.

High clinical disease activity and serologic activity (high dsDNA, low C4, low C3) are risk factors for the development of PTL [15]. About 30 % of women with low to negligible SLE activity during pregnancy will also develop PTL; however; in those, C4 levels seem to be the best predictor of PTL [16].

Management of Disease During Pregnancy

A multidisciplinary approach to the management of SLE during pregnancy is recommended. A lupus flare during pregnancy may mimic symptoms of normal pregnancy.

Risk assessment during pregnancy should include a careful assessment of disease activity and evaluation of organ involvement.

We recommend baseline preconception or 1st trimester laboratory tests including complement levels (C3 and C4), anti-dsDNA antibodies, antiphospholipid antibodies, complete blood count with differential, creatinine, eGFR, urine sediment, and protein/creatinine ratio in addition to preeclampsia laboratory tests. Complement levels rise in normal pregnancy, so it is important to know the baseline complement level in individual pregnant patients. These labs should be repeated at least each trimester or with symptoms, with CBC and renal function assessed monthly.

If not already known, SSA (Ro) and SSB (La) antibodies should be checked; if positive, fetal M-mode echocardiography is recommended due to the risk of myocarditis and heart block in the fetus from 16 to 34 weeks' gestation. Most treatment algorithms recommend a trial of dexamethasone 4 mg daily for 6 weeks if prolonged PR and intermittent or complete heart block are found. Dexamethasone is continued if findings are stable or improved. There are currently trials under way of IVIg and/ or plasmapheresis for the most severe cases, particularly if there is fetal hydrops.

Additional fetal monitoring should include umbilical artery Doppler ultrasound for assessment of end-diastolic flow in all patients with intrauterine growth restriction, preeclampsia, renal or hypertensive disease, or decreased amniotic fluid volume.

Women with SLE who have antiphospholipid antibodies, but NO prior history of thrombosis or adverse pregnancy outcome, should receive prophylactic treatment with aspirin to prevent fetal loss. Women with SLE who have a history of thrombosis but are not on lifelong anticoagulation and women with a history of pregnancy loss should be managed with low-dose aspirin and prophylactic LMWH (see Chap. 6 Thrombosis and Thrombophilia).

Many women with SLE take hydroxychloroquine, which appears to decrease the risk of SLE flare and thrombosis and improves outcomes in lupus nephritis. This medication is safe to continue during pregnancy. Furthermore, its discontinuation during pregnancy is associated with an increase in SLE disease activity, poor outcomes, and the use of higher doses of prednisone [17].

Azathioprine is another safe immunosuppressant medication that can be used during pregnancy, as the fetal liver does not have the enzyme required to metabolize azathioprine to its active form. However, women with SLE on mycophenolate or methotrexate should discontinue these medications at least 3 months before conception to reduce teratogenic risk to the fetus (see medication discussion below).

SLE flares during pregnancy can be treated with corticosteroids, starting with a prednisone dose (<20 mg/day). The risks of prednisone use in pregnancy include hypertension and diabetes. High-dose prednisone use is associated with a slight increased risk of cleft palate, but the absolute risk is still very low, and frequently the risks are far outweighed by the benefits.

High-dose prednisone, cyclophosphamide, and rituximab are reserved for severe lupus complications, as they are associated with poor obstetric outcomes.

Preconception Counseling

The best pregnancy outcomes in SLE occur in those women who have had quiescent disease for 6–12 months prior to conception. Unfortunately, half of all pregnancies are unplanned; thus, we advocate pregnancy counseling in ALL women of childbearing age with SLE. This should include measurement of anti-Ro, anti-La, and antiphospholipid antibodies and a discussion of medications. ACE inhibitors should be discontinued prior to or immediately at conception.

During pregnancy, a multidisciplinary approach including the input of rheumatology, obstetrics, obstetric medicine, and, if needed, nephrology, hematology, and cardiology for systemic disease is ideal. Issues to be discussed include the risks of disease flare during pregnancy and the postpartum period, how they will be managed, as well as potential complications to the fetus. Early consultation with a high-risk obstetrician to discuss a fetal monitoring plan should be done in all patients with active disease and who are anti-Ro, anti-La, or antiphospholipid antibody positive.

Rheumatoid Arthritis in Pregnancy

Epidemiology

Rheumatoid arthritis (RA) is a systemic autoimmune disease characterized by inflammatory polyarthritis, which effects peripheral joints, especially the small joints of the hands and feet. Chronic untreated inflammation may lead to joint erosions and joint destruction. The prevalence is approximately 1 % worldwide, with a

2:1 female predominance. While the peak incidence steadily increases with age until the mid-8th decade, it can affect women of any age. Besides female sex, risk factors for development include age, tobacco use, exposure to silica, and obesity. Although the etiology is unknown, there is a heritable predisposition with rates of concordance up to 50 % in monozygotic twins and a 16-fold increased risk in first-degree relatives of patients with RA.

Clinical Manifestations

The initial presentation of rheumatoid arthritis frequently involves greater than 6 weeks of pain, swelling, warmth in one or more peripheral joints, with symmetric involvement of wrists, hands, and/or feet, and often associated with over one hour of morning stiffness. The small joints of the hands and feet are the most common joints involved, sparing the distal interphalangeal joints. Other joints involved are elbows, shoulders, hips, knees, and ankles, as well as the atlantoaxial joint (C1–C2) of the spine. Chronic long-standing poorly controlled disease can lead to erosive joint changes, leading to swan neck and boutonniere deformities of the hands, as well as "ulnar drift," where the finger dislocates medially. C1–C2 inflammation can lead to odontoid erosion and transverse ligament laxity, resulting in atlantoaxial subluxation and cord compression. Joint damage of wrists, elbows, shoulders, hips, and knees can lead to severe osteoarthritis, necessitating joint surgery and/or replacement.

There are various extra-articular manifestations of RA, including:

- Secondary Sjogren's syndrome (~35 %): Immune-mediated inflammation of lacrimal and salivary glands resulting in dry mouth and eyes (sicca syndrome).
- Rheumatoid nodules (25 %): On extensor surfaces and pressure points, in RF+disease. Histopathology demonstrates palisading histiocytes surrounding fibrinoid necrosis.
- Normocytic normochromic anemia.
- Felty's syndrome: RA with splenomegaly and leukopenia.
- Pulmonary disease:
  - Pleural disease (effusions, pleuritis)
  - Interstitial lung disease (up to 10 % clinically significant)
- Vasculitis.
- Cardiac disease:
  - Pericarditis
  - ↑ risk of cardiovascular disease
- Ocular disease:
  - Keratoconjunctivitis sicca (dry eye, without dry mouth/secondary Sjogren's) (10 %)
  - Episcleritis, scleritis

- Amyloidosis: Seen in long-standing RA. Can affect the heart, kidney, liver, spleen, intestines, and skin.

Clinical Manifestations During Pregnancy

It has been estimated that between 800 and 2100 pregnancies occur each year in women with rheumatoid arthritis [18]. For over 75 years, it has been observed that the symptoms of rheumatoid arthritis abate during pregnancy; improvement of disease activity occurs in nearly 75 % of pregnancies, and complete remission has been documented in up to 16 % [19]. It is unclear the exact mechanism of this improvement in disease, but it is likely related to T-cell changes that occur during pregnancy that favor acceptance of the fetal placental unit and thus suppress cell-mediated immunity. In up to 25 % of pregnancies, disease activity can worsen in the puerperium.

In the postpartum period, many women will note a worsening of their symptoms relative to pregnancy; that is, "reactivation" of RA seems to happen in nearly 100 % of women by the fifth month postpartum [20]. Furthermore, the postpartum period seems to be associated with an increased risk of developing new-onset rheumatoid arthritis [21].

Impact of Disease on Pregnancy Outcomes

Fertility

Population studies have demonstrated decreased parity in women with RA compared with population-based controls [22]. According to a recent Danish study, there is an association between RA and delayed time to pregnancy (>12 months), which was still borderline significant after adjusting for maternal age, parity, pre-pregnancy height and weight, maternal occupation, smoking, and alcohol consumption [23]. Furthermore, structured interviews with women with RA have demonstrated that one in five reports that their childbearing decisions have been affected by the disease, and they are much more likely to decide to have only one child [24].

Pregnancy Outcomes

Data regarding pregnancy outcomes in RA has been conflicting, but does seem to suggest an association between rheumatoid arthritis and adverse pregnancy outcomes. A retrospective of 38 pregnancies in women with RA in Calgary between 1998 and 2009 did NOT demonstrate a significantly increased odds ratio of preeclampsia (PEC), preterm labor (PTL), or small for gestational age (SGA) babies, albeit numbers were low [10]. A Washington State review of pregnancies in 243 women with RA, between 1987 and 2001, demonstrated increased risks of cesarean delivery, PTL, and longer birth hospitalization [25]. A US national database survey from 2002 demonstrated that among 1,425 births to women with RA, the rate of hypertensive disorders was significantly elevated (11.1 % compared to 7.8 % in the general obstetric population), as well as the length of hospital stay and frequency of cesarean section [26].

Treatment During Pregnancy

As noted above, many women will have attenuation of symptoms during pregnancy, but only ~16 % will go into full remission. Since chronic inflammation itself is likely detrimental to maternal fetal health, we advocate for continuation of disease-modifying antirheumatic drug (DMARD) therapy when possible during pregnancy. Some DMARDs are contraindicated in pregnancy due to risks of teratogenicity, whether clear-cut or theoretical, such as methotrexate (MTX) and leflunomide (LEF). However, many medications, such as sulfasalazine and anti-tumor necrosis factor agents (anti-TNFs), do not appear to contribute to teratogenicity and are likely safe to continue during pregnancy. Prednisone is the preferred corticosteroid for maternal treatment during pregnancy since very little gets to the fetus in the active form, although there has been some concern that first trimester exposure is related to an increase in oral clefts [133]. A recent population-based study with 51,973 corticosteroid-exposed pregnancies did not find an increase in orofacial clefts regardless of type of corticosteroid administered (oral, inhalation, nasal spray, topical) [134]. Corticosteroids are classified as category B medications.

Prolonged corticosteroid use during pregnancy is associated with an increased risk of pregnancy-induced hypertension, preeclampsia, gestational diabetes, osteopenia, and infections, especially at doses of above 20 mg/day.

Corticosteroids are secreted in the breast milk at low concentrations and are considered safe to use during breastfeeding, especially at doses less than 20 mg prednisone daily (or the equivalent) [135].

A more complete review of these medications is found at the end of this chapter.

Preconception Counseling

Women of childbearing age with rheumatoid arthritis should ALL be counseled regarding pregnancy, as up to 50 % of pregnancies are unplanned. Women on MTX should discontinue their treatment at least three to 6 months prior to conception, and leflunomide, given its very long half-life, should be discontinued 1–2 years prior to conception (see section on medications). Women on anti-TNFs should be aware of the known risks and benefits of staying on their therapy versus discontinuation. The importance of informed participation of the patient with rheumatoid arthritis is crucial.

Pregnancy in Scleroderma

Introduction

Systemic sclerosis (SSc) or scleroderma is a chronic, systemic, inflammatory, autoimmune disease characterized by progressive fibrosis of the skin and visceral tissues. Noninflammatory vasculopathy is also a prominent feature of scleroderma and could manifest as Raynaud phenomenon, pulmonary arterial hypertension, digital ulcers, and scleroderma renal crisis. The vascular disease is a major cause of morbidity and mortality in general, but is an even bigger concern in pregnancy, as the vasculopathy may preclude the hemodynamic adaptations necessary to support the maternal and fetoplacental unit.

Most women with SSc can be expected to have successful pregnancies, in the absence of severe vascular or extensive visceral disease. The composite effects of inflammation, ischemia from vasculopathy, and connective tissue fibrosis on pregnancy and puerperium will be discussed.

Epidemiology

Systemic sclerosis has a strong female predominance, affecting females five times more commonly than males [27]. Incidence estimates range from 9 to 19 cases/1 million/year, with prevalence rates ranging from 28 to 253 cases/1 million/year in the United States [28, 29].

The mean age of symptom onset of SSc is usually in the fifth decade, approximately 10 years prior to the mean age of menopause. Until the recent decades, most women would have completed their childbearing plans before their 40s. However there has been a trend for increasing maternal age as many women have postponed pregnancy until their 30s or 40s due to career or social change. Thus, there is an increased likelihood of concurrent pregnancy and scleroderma.

Clinical Manifestations

The term *scleroderma* is used to describe the presence of thickened, hardened skin. When this characteristic skin finding is associated with internal organ involvement, the disease is termed systemic sclerosis (SSc). The diverse range of manifestations of SSc is mainly centered on the dysregulated mechanisms of fibrosis, autoimmunity, and vasculopathy. Almost all patients have skin thickening in the fingers or toes (sclerodactyly). The musculoskeletal, renal, pulmonary, cardiac, neurologic, and gastrointestinal systems can be affected.

There are two main subsets of SSc: diffuse cutaneous systemic sclerosis and limited cutaneous systemic sclerosis. In diffuse cutaneous SSc (dcSSc) there is widespread skin thickening extending proximal to the elbows and knees and often involving the chest or abdominal wall. This subset is associated with higher incidence of pulmonary fibrosis and scleroderma renal crisis. Limited cutaneous SSc (lcSSc) has skin thickening limited to the distal extremities and face and is associated with higher prevalence of digital ulcers and pulmonary arterial hypertension. The lcSSc subtype is commonly associated with the CREST syndrome (CREST: calcinosis, Raynaud phenomenon, esophageal dysmotility, sclerodactyly, and telangiectasia) [30].

Vascular dysfunction is a prominent noninflammatory component of the pathophysiology of SSc. Raynaud phenomenon is the most notable vascular manifestation in SSc; it occurs as sequential color changes in the digits precipitated by cold exposure or stress. The color changes of pallor ("white"), cyanosis ("blue"), and reperfusion hyperemia ("red") characterize the classic Raynaud phenomenon. It is due to reversible vasospasm brought about by functional changes in the digital arteries of the hands and feet. However, structural changes may progressively develop in the small blood vessels with resultant permanent impairment in blood flow. When this occurs, episodes of arterial vasospasm may become prolonged and severe and can result in ischemic digital ulcerations or infarction.

Vascular damage and consequent chronic tissue ischemia underlie other serious systemic complications of SSc, including gastric antral vascular ectasia (which may lead to severe gastrointestinal bleeding), pulmonary artery hypertension, scleroderma renal crisis, and myocardial infarction.

Most patients with SSc (>95 %) have serum antinuclear autoantibodies (ANA), including hallmark autoantibodies specifically associated with SSc. The autoantibodies are almost always mutually exclusive and may have prognostic implications: centromere antibodies are associated with limited cutaneous systemic sclerosis, severe Raynaud phenomenon, digital ischemia, and pulmonary hypertension. Anti-DNA topoisomerase I (Scl-70) antibodies are associated with diffuse cutaneous SSc (dcSSc) and a higher risk of severe interstitial lung disease.

Clinical Manifestations: Interactions Between Scleroderma and Pregnancy

Normal Changes of Pregnancy

The pregnant woman's body must make multiple physiologic hemodynamic and vascular changes in order to accommodate and support the growing fetus. A decrease in systemic vascular resistance leads to some of the well-established vascular and hemodynamic changes of pregnancy. The degree of reduction of systemic vascular resistance is due in part to an increase in prostacyclin which plays a clear role in systemic vasodilation.

Nitric oxide (NO) is an additional mediator that is proposed to play a significant role as well in the maintenance of low peripheral vascular resistance. There seems to be a permanent basal activity of NO in the uterine and fetoplacental vasculature, with the trophoblast as a significant source. Some studies demonstrated a deficiency of NO in pregnancies complicated by preeclampsia and intrauterine growth restriction, which are manifestations of defective placental perfusion [31]. In addition, the maternal vasculature seems resistant to the effects of angiotensin II.

A 7–8 l increase in total body fluid during pregnancy is mediated by the renin-angiotensin-aldosterone system. Cardiac output increases by 50 % over the course of gestation, being preferentially distributed to the uterus, kidneys, skin, breast tissue, and away from skeletal muscle. Pulmonary vascular resistance decreases, basal oxygen consumption increases, and alveolar ventilation increases [32–34].

Effects of Pregnancy on Scleroderma

The changes in vascular blood flow and reduced vascular resistance may lead to improvement of some manifestations of SSc. Raynaud phenomenon tends to improve during pregnancy due to the peripheral vasodilation and decrease in systemic vascular resistance. On the other hand, an intrinsic inability to adapt to the necessary hemodynamic and vascular changes may contribute to adverse pregnancy outcomes, particularly due to the underlying vasculopathy in SSc [35].

Studies of disease activity of scleroderma during pregnancy have found no significant changes in the disease status during pregnancy. In a prospective series, maternal disease was stable in 60 % of pregnancies, improved in 20 %, and worsened in another 20 % [36].

The enlarging uterus may worsen the heartburn symptoms of gastro-esophageal reflux disease which are common in scleroderma, regardless of pregnancy. Limitation of diaphragmatic breathing may exacerbate dyspnea. Although pregnancy is not generally associated with worsening skin disease in SSc, skin thickening postpartum has been observed in diffuse disease [36].

As a whole, women with diffuse scleroderma are at greater risk for developing cardiopulmonary and renal problems early in the disease course. Problems may arise if pregnancy occurs in this subset of patients with early diffuse disease.

Scleroderma Renal Crisis in Pregnancy

Scleroderma renal crisis (SRC) is an acutely developing syndrome of malignant hypertension, proteinuria, acute renal failure, microangiopathic changes, and the pathognomonic "onion skin" appearance of renal arteries due to endothelial proliferation [37]. SRC affects 5–10 % of SSc patients overall. Renal crisis is the most serious complication of scleroderma and the cause of the most maternal deaths in scleroderma pregnancies [38].

Particularly at risk for SRC in general are those who have recent-onset, rapidly progressing diffuse skin disease [35, 38]. Treatment with high-dose prednisolone may be an additional risk factor [39]. Pregnancy itself has been hypothesized to be a precipitant of SRC [40]. Angiotensin-converting enzyme (ACE) inhibitors have brought about a dramatic change in the management and prognosis of SRC. Whereas renal crisis was almost uniformly fatal prior to the widespread use of ACE inhibitors, their use has reduced death rates from SRC to less than 10 % [41]. Nonetheless, perinatal deaths reported among SSc patients involved SRC [40].

Steen et al. reported two cases of SRC in a retrospective study of 86 pregnancies occurring after the diagnosis of SSc [42]. Both women developed SRC abruptly in the third trimester, and both resulted in preterm delivery; one mother developed end-stage renal disease, and the other died from status epilepticus. In a prospective study of 91 pregnancies, two additional cases of renal crisis were reported [36]. Both women required hemodialysis after delivery. All these cases occurred in women with early, rapidly progressive diffuse disease. It remains unclear if rates of renal crisis are increased in pregnant women compared to nonpregnant women with severe diffuse disease.

The severity of scleroderma renal crisis during pregnancy, with very high risks of maternal and fetal morbidity, and the profound benefits of treatment with ACE inhibitors to both mother and fetus if renal crisis is suspected would outweigh the risks of fetotoxicity associated with its use [43].

During the second half of pregnancy, differentiation between SRC and preeclampsia may be difficult. Both conditions carry a high risk of severe maternal and fetal complications if not treated aggressively. Seizures, elevated transaminases, or urate may assist in the diagnosis although, if the situation remains unclear, measurement of plasma renin may prove useful. In preeclampsia, the serum renin is low to normal, while, in the renal crisis of systemic sclerosis, plasma renin is elevated as a result of renocortical ischemia.

Pulmonary Arterial Hypertension

In contrast to SRC, pulmonary arterial hypertension (PAH) can occur with both limited and diffuse cutaneous disease. It can be more prevalent with limited cutaneous disease. PAH in SSc is due to the long-standing vasculopathy involving the pulmonary arterial vasculature. Pulmonary arterioles exhibit the same "onion skin" appearance as seen in renal crisis. The total prevalence of PAH in SSc was estimated to be 26.7 % in one study [44].

Women with PAH are at extremely high risk for severe hemodynamic compromise during pregnancy. This is because there is significantly less reserve in the pulmonary arterioles to reduce the vascular resistance which would have otherwise accommodated the increased blood volume and cardiac output that occurs during pregnancy.

Reports estimate a 36–50 % maternal death rate in women with PAH, with the most vulnerable period occurring during delivery and the first 2 weeks postpartum [45, 46]. A more recent study found a slightly lower maternal death rate of 17–33 %, but this is unacceptably high [47]. Death is usually due to acute cardiovascular collapse. Rates of preterm delivery with resultant neonatal morbidity and mortality are similarly high in the PAH population.

Raynaud Phenomenon and Digital Ulceration

Raynaud phenomenon and digital ulcers are the vascular complications of SSc that are most likely to improve during pregnancy, but tend to worsen postpartum [38]. The mechanism of vascular hyperreactivity and vasospasm causes the color changes of Raynaud phenomenon, but when the vasculopathy becomes more fixed as SSc advances, the chronically impaired perfusion can lead to digital ulceration.

Improvements in these vascular manifestations may be due to the normal hemodynamic changes in pregnancy of increased blood volume, generalized peripheral vasodilation, and reduced systemic vascular resistance. After delivery, reversal of hemodynamics leads to return of baseline peripheral circulatory complications, explaining the worsening of Raynaud symptoms postpartum.

Impact of Scleroderma on Pregnancy Outcomes

General Trends in Outcomes

There is concern for an increased risk of adverse pregnancy outcomes in SSc given the prominent vasculopathy known to this disease, which is associated with vascular derangements or inability to make appropriate hemodynamic adaptations to support a pregnancy.

Early reports suggested very high rates of maternal death during pregnancy. Case reports of pregnancy outcomes in SSc published before 1990 reported maternal and/or fetal death in 50 % of 42 pregnancies [48]. It is likely for these reasons that women with SSc in past decades had been strongly advised against pregnancy and often counseled to terminate pregnancies [40, 49]. However, case–control series have found much lower risks of 1–4 % [42]. A 10-year prospective study, summarizing the outcome of 91 pregnancies in fifty-nine scleroderma patients between 1987 and 1996, corroborated these rather optimistic findings [36].

More recently, a series of retrospective and prospective studies have provided more detailed analysis of pregnancy outcomes and have demonstrated that, for most women with SSc, pregnancy outcomes are reasonably good [38, 42, 50]. Overall, maternal flares of disease during pregnancy were generally mild. The majority of patients with SSc appear to have reasonable obstetric outcomes although women with rapidly progressive diffuse disease may be at higher risk for complications.

Conception

A large survey performed by Steen et al. compared 214 scleroderma patients to 167 rheumatoid arthritis (RA) patients and 105 normal controls [50]. This study found similar rates of conception and pregnancy among the three groups. While only 2–5 % of patients who had attempted to become pregnant were unsuccessful,

12–15 % of the women had at least a 1-year delay in conception. The overall rate of a successful pregnancy following a period of infertility was 37 % in the scleroderma patients, similar to the 40 % rate in RA patients and 43 % in normal controls.

Pregnancy Loss

Reported rates of early pregnancy loss of 14–15 % [42, 51] are somewhat increased from the estimated 10 % in the general population. Late pregnancy losses were few and generally occurred in women with severe diffuse SSc [51, 52]. The rate of miscarriage in patients with long-standing diffuse disease is double the rate experienced by patients with limited skin involvement (24 % vs. 12 %) [36]. Fetal loss complicated two pregnancies in women with severe diffuse SSc and the antiphospholipid antibody syndrome. The two most recent studies focusing on this subject matter showed higher rates for miscarriage but a lower incidence of premature deliveries and small term babies [53, 54].

Preterm Delivery

Preterm delivery rates have ranged from 8 % to 40 % [42, 51, 52]. The majority of preterm deliveries were on or after gestational age 34 [40]. Small for gestational age infants (<10th% tile for gestational age) [45] ranged from 0 % to 50 % [28, 40, 42]. Preterm births, with generally good neonatal outcomes, were common, occurring in 26 % of pregnancies [36]. Despite increased prematurity, the overall rate of a successful live birth was 84 % in limited and 77 % in diffuse scleroderma, compared with 84 % in historical controls [55].

Decidual and Placental Vasculopathy and Related Complications/Outcomes

With the diffuse vasculopathy complicating SSc, the same pathophysiologic changes are likely in the placental vasculature. Similar to SLE, it is likely that the higher rates of prematurity and small for gestation age pregnancies may be a direct result of placental vascular insufficiency.

Histopathologic examination of placentas reported normal placenta weight for gestational age [56–58]. One study of three placentas from SSc patients (gestational age at delivery between 34 and 38 weeks) found evidence of decidual vasculopathy with stromal fibrosis and infarcts in chorionic villi despite an absence of reported adverse pregnancy outcomes [59]. Another case of a pregnant SSc patient with intrauterine growth restriction was found to have increased resistance in the umbilical artery by Doppler examination at 31-week gestational age. Examination of the placenta after delivery at 37 weeks found numerous placental infarcts, placental mesenchymal dysplasia, decreased vascularity, and stromal fibrosis all consistent with decidual vasculopathy [57].

In the largest study to date, 13 placentas from SSc patients were examined and correlated with perinatal outcomes [58]. Five of 13 placentas demonstrated marked decidual vasculopathy, four of which were associated with intrauterine fetal demise between weeks 16 and 30. Chorioamnionitis and accelerated placental maturation complicated the majority of other placentas. These findings are similar to what is seen in pregnancies complicated by pregnancy-induced hypertension, SLE, and other vascular diseases.

In a nationwide study of pregnancy outcomes of SSc patients, 23 % carried a diagnosis of pregnancy-induced hypertension [54]. Cases of preeclampsia were isolated [51, 52]. A study [54] found a 22.9 % rate of hypertensive disorders including preeclampsia, a fourfold increased odds compared to the general population (85 % CI, 2.4–6.6). Similarly, a nearly fourfold increased rate of intrauterine growth restriction was found.

Thus, placental abnormalities may be present in SSc pregnancies, even in the absence of clinical perinatal complications, and these abnormalities may be more severe correlating with perinatal growth restriction and death.

Management During Pregnancy

Risk Assessment

Pregnancy in scleroderma patients should be considered high risk, in the setting of clinical effects of excess fibrosis and vascular damage. It should be managed in specialized obstetric clinics along with multidisciplinary coordinated care, in the light of the increased risk of premature delivery and potential for severe maternal complications such as renal crisis or pulmonary arterial hypertension.

Risk assessment during pregnancy should include categorization of disease and evaluation of organ involvement (see section below, on preconception planning, for summary of recommended evaluation and actions). Additionally, the presence of pulmonary fibrosis and cardiac disease such as myocardial fibrosis, pericarditis, arrhythmias, and conduction defects should be sought. Chest wall skin involvement may be underappreciated. If needed, pulmonary function tests could be done during the first trimester and repeated in later stages of pregnancy, to assess for severe restrictive lung disease [60]. Evaluation of autoantibody profile is helpful for risk association and prognostication.

Women who have less than 4 years of SSc symptoms, those who have diffuse cutaneous scleroderma, or those with anti-topoisomerase (Scl-70) or anti-RNA polymerase III are at greater risk for having more active, aggressive disease than those who have long-standing disease with anti-centromere antibodies [61].

Mode of Delivery

There are no data regarding the preferred or ideal mode of delivery in scleroderma patients. Vaginal delivery could be the optimal choice if there is no fetal distress and in the absence of severe musculoskeletal restriction.

Anesthesia Considerations

Thickened skin and chronic vasoconstriction could preclude venous access and hence may create great challenges for the anesthesiologist [62]. Flexion contractures and vasoconstriction could make even blood pressure monitoring difficult. Noninvasive blood pressure monitoring is preferred to arterial cannulation which may induce distal necrosis. Prolonged application of pulse oximeter probe to one digit should also be avoided, as there is usually already impaired distal circulation from vasculopathy and which could otherwise lead to digital ulcers or infarction.

Microstomia may make tracheal intubation very challenging. Bleeding from mucosal telangiectasia could occur if traumatized, such as in intubation attempts. Esophageal dysmotility and incompetence of the lower esophageal sphincter leading to reflux disease can increase the risk for aspiration.

Regional anesthesia is preferred if possible. This avoids the risks of aspiration and difficult/failed intubation. Particularly, epidural block is ideal as it provides adequate anesthesia and also provides peripheral vasodilatation and increased skin perfusion of the lower extremities. When regional anesthesia is contraindicated, awake tracheal intubation for general anesthesia should be considered for scleroderma patients who are planned for cesarean section. This is to ensure maintenance of spontaneous respirations if difficulties arise, and the cough reflex will be preserved if regurgitation occurs.

Other Special Management Considerations

- Discontinue use of disease-remitting drugs before pregnancy, particularly those with known teratogenicity (e.g., methotrexate, mycophenolate mofetil).
- Minimal use of proton pump inhibitors, histamine blockers, and calcium channel blockers for gastrointestinal and vascular problems.
- Avoidance of corticosteroids particularly in avoidance of risk of renal crisis.
- More frequent monitoring of fetal size and uterine activity.
- Frequent blood pressure monitoring.
- Aggressive treatment of hypertension.
- Close observation and treatment of premature labor (avoid beta-adrenergic agonists).
- Epidural anesthesia is preferred.
- Special warming of delivery room, intravenous fluids, and patient themselves (blankets, thermal socks, gloves) to prevent problems related to Raynaud phenomenon.

- Venous access before delivery.
- Careful attention to the episiotomy and cesarean section incisions, which generally heal without difficulty.
- No significant concern for hereditary neonatal scleroderma.

Management of Severe Systemic Complications

Management of Scleroderma Renal Crisis

Scleroderma renal crisis (SRC) is the most serious complication of scleroderma and has caused the most maternal deaths in scleroderma pregnancies. Again, it should be emphasized that SRC occurred in women early in the course of SSc and with rapidly progressive, diffuse skin disease. This is thus a subgroup at high risk for SRC independent of pregnancy and which should best postpone or refrain from pregnancy until the disease is controlled and stable. Fortunately, more recent pregnancy studies found fewer episodes of renal crises than were previously reported.

There have been several case reports of renal crisis occurring during pregnancy that have been successfully treated with ACE inhibitors. These drugs have dramatically changed the outcome of renal crisis, and despite their contraindications in pregnancy, they must be used if renal crisis occurs during pregnancy.

Close monitoring of blood pressure must be done. Even a slight elevation in blood pressure compared with previous levels should be considered potentially serious. A search for elevated creatinine, proteinuria, or microangiopathic hemolytic anemia should be done promptly. If there is even a slight question of whether the blood pressure elevation represents SRC, then an ACE inhibitor should be started immediately; their early use could make the difference between life and death of the mother and fetus. Before the availability of ACE inhibitors in the management of renal crisis, almost all patients died within the first year [38].

ACE inhibitors can cause significant fetal abnormalities including anhydramnios, renal atresia, and pulmonary hypoplasia and fetal death, particularly when used in the latter half of pregnancy [63]. If the pregnant patient has scleroderma renal crisis, however, there is no question that management of the hypertension without ACE inhibitors would have an unacceptably high risk for maternal problems that would outweigh the risk for toxicity to the fetus [38].

On the premise that ACE inhibitors lead to persistent improvement in renal function, it is recommended that therapy be continued even after onset of dialysis [64]. After an episode of renal crisis, ACE inhibitors are required to maintain blood pressure control and renal function indefinitely. Routine use of ACE inhibitors is not recommended at this time for fear of masking promontory manifestations of SRC without reducing its incidence. This controversial issue has an additional perspective in pregnancy, as first trimester use of ACE inhibitors has been associated with congenital malformations [43]. However, patients have had successful pregnancy outcomes while on ACE inhibitors [36].

At times when SRC is indistinguishable from preeclampsia, an immediate trial of ACE inhibitors may be instituted, or, in cases of profound maternal or fetal distress, emergent delivery, which curtails the eclampsia, should be performed, followed by ACE inhibitor therapy. In this situation, the definitive therapy for preeclampsia has been completed (delivery), and ACE inhibitors can be instituted without concern of risk of fetotoxicity of antenatal ACE inhibitor exposure [43]. Renal biopsy may be indicated in cases where the distinction between renal crisis and preeclampsia is necessary for management [65].

Management of Pulmonary Arterial Hypertension

Pre-pregnancy and During Pregnancy

Pulmonary arterial hypertension (PAH) is a major cause of morbidity and mortality in SSc. Women with known PAH should be strongly discouraged from becoming pregnant as they would be at extremely high risk for severe hemodynamic compromise. Scleroderma patients (diffuse or limited cutaneous disease) should undergo careful screening for subclinical PAH during pregnancy or when considering a future pregnancy. Noninvasive evaluation for PAH includes an echocardiogram looking for a pulmonary arterial pressure of >30 mmHg at rest or an isolated reduced diffusion capacity (DLCO) in the absence of restrictive lung disease on standard pulmonary function testing [44]. Furthermore, all complaints of dyspnea in pregnant SSc patients should prompt an immediate evaluation for development or worsening of PAH. Assessing diffusion capacity using carbon monoxide is considered safe during pregnancy [66].

If a woman with moderate to severe PAH discovers a pregnancy and wishes to continue with the pregnancy, or if PAH is diagnosed during an established pregnancy, careful hemodynamic monitoring and comanagement with pulmonologists experienced with PAH is essential. Case reports have described successful use of epoprostenol and sildenafil during pregnancy [44–47, 67–69]. Anticoagulation with low-molecular-weight heparin is recommended to reduce risk of thromboembolism [45], and some have suggested use of supplemental oxygen to maintain a PO2 greater than 70 mmHg [45]. Inhaled NO has been used in extreme circumstances during labor and delivery [45, 46].

During Labor and Delivery

Delivery is a period of extremely high risk in the woman with PAH. Acute hemodynamic changes occur including increase in cardiac output of 25–50 % during the second stage of labor through delivery with the return of blood volume from the uterus to the main circulation [45, 46].

Increased maternal mortality has been described with general anesthesia [47].

The preferred mode of delivery remains controversial: vaginal delivery is associated with less shifts in blood volume but has a prolonged second stage of labor and issues regarding increased pressure with contractions. Cesarean delivery reduces the second stage of labor and may be necessary in cases of extreme maternal or fetal distress but increases risks of infection and thrombosis [47].

Preconception Counseling and Planning

Women with SSc who are contemplating pregnancy or who discover an inadvertent pregnancy should undergo a thorough evaluation for systemic and organ-specific vasculopathy. Those with a history or high risk of scleroderma renal crisis or pulmonary arterial hypertension are at highest risk for maternal and fetal death and other severe morbidities of pregnancy. Thus, those with renal or pulmonary arterial vasculopathy should be strongly advised against becoming pregnant and to consider termination if a pregnancy occurs.

However, if after thorough evaluation a woman with SSc does not appear to have vasculopathy of the internal organs, pregnancy may be considered. Raynaud phenomenon should not be considered a contraindication to pregnancy in the absence of renal disease or PAH.

Organ evaluation (E) and recommendations (R) prior to conception are summarized as follows:

1. Lungs

    1.1. Pulmonary arterial hypertension (PAH)

    E = Cardiac echocardiogram and right heart catheterization if further indicated.
    R = Avoid pregnancy if severe PAH; allow with caution if mild.

    1.2. Interstitial lung disease (ILD)

    E = Pulmonary function tests including diffusion capacity for carbon monoxide and high-resolution CT scan of the chest if required.
    R = Avoid pregnancy if severe ILD, and allow with caution if mild.

2. Heart

    2.1. Congestive heart failure (CHF)

    E = Cardiac echocardiogram.
    R = Avoid pregnancy if severe CHF, and allow with caution in milder cases.

    2.2. Conduction blocks

    E = ECG
    R = Rarely require intervention

3. Kidney

    3.1. Scleroderma renal crisis (SRC)

E = Serum creatinine, evidence of microangiopathic hemolytic anemia, systemic blood pressure, and proteinuria.
R = Avoid pregnancy and treat aggressively with ACE inhibitors. Reconsider plans for pregnancy when stabilized.

4. Skin

   4.1. Diffuse cutaneous systemic sclerosis (dcSSc)

   E = Modified Rodnan skin score, evaluate for associated ILD, but PAH can also occur.
   R = Consider delaying pregnancy if early in the course, rapidly progressive, diffuse skin disease.

   4.2. Limited cutaneous systemic sclerosis (lcSSc)

   E = Modified Rodnan skin score, evaluate for associated PAH, but ILD can also occur.
   R = Avoid pregnancy if moderate to severe PAH is found.

5. Esophagus

   5.1. Gastroesophageal reflux disease

   E = Endoscopy in cases of long-standing disease or refractory iron-deficiency anemia.
   R = Optimize anti-acid therapy.

6. Digits

   6.1. Digital ulcers

   E = Assess for superinfection.
   R = These are a marker for decreased survival; reconsider pregnancy plans. Nonetheless, ulcers tend to improve during pregnancy.

   6.2. Raynaud phenomenon

   E = Clinical assessment and nailfold capillaroscopy.
   R = Counsel that it tends to improve during pregnancy, but may worsen postpartum.

7. Serologies

   7.1. Anti-topoisomerase (Scl-70) antibodies

   E = If + there is risk/association with diffuse skin disease, particularly with rapidly progressive disease, which has high risk of renal crisis, and with ILD
   R = Evaluation and recommendations as above with dcSSc and ILD

   7.2. Anti-centromere antibodies

E = If + there is risk/association with PAH and lcSSc and with CREST syndrome.

R = Evaluation and recommendations as above in PAH and lcSSc

7.3. Anti-RNA polymerase III

E = Associated with scleroderma renal crisis

R = Evaluation and recommendations as above in the kidney

7.4. Anti-Ro/SSA and anti-La/SSB

E = Associated with fetal heart block. Present in 12–37 % and 4 % of scleroderma pregnancies, respectively.

R = If found during pregnancy, monitor fetal heart function with fetal echo every 1–2 weeks from 16 weeks onward.

7.5. Antiphospholipid antibodies

E = Associated with macrovascular complications, PAH, and recurrent fetal loss. Thus assess for PAH and digital ulcers as above, and monitor for thromboembolic phenomena.

R = Anticoagulation with heparin may be required if with antiphospholipid syndrome.

Postpartum Management

The period after delivery remains a particularly vulnerable period. Patients may require extended observation following delivery to monitor for acute cardiovascular collapse in cases of PAH.

Continued careful monitoring for disease activity during the postpartum period should ensue. Particularly, progressive skin changes or new hypertension should be aggressively addressed immediately. Anticipate potential worsening of Raynaud symptoms during this period.

There is no data that postpartum depression is increased in scleroderma, but close observation and early therapeutic intervention are indicated if this occurs.

Early reinstitution of medications that had been disrupted specifically because of pregnancy should be planned.

Summary

Scleroderma is a multisystem disease with potential for severe complications during pregnancy. With close coordinated care, women with scleroderma have a high likelihood of successful pregnancies. Few manifestations may improve in the pregnant state. But due to the underlying vasculopathy or organ fibrosis, serious complications or adverse pregnancy outcomes may occur.

Renal crisis is the only unique risk in scleroderma pregnancies, the malignant hypertension of which must be treated aggressively with ACE inhibitors. Those with history of renal crisis or pulmonary arterial hypertension, or those at high risk for these conditions, are at the highest risk of maternal and fetal death and other highly morbid complications of pregnancy. Medications such as ACE inhibitors and prostaglandins, which may carry risks of congenital malformations or fetal toxicity, need to be considered as the benefits to both mother and fetus may outweigh known risks of its exposure.

Other pregnancy problems may not be unique to scleroderma, but could cause significant difficulties throughout the pregnancy, in labor and delivery including anesthesia concerns.

There is a high risk for premature and small infants, but can be minimized with specialized obstetric and neonatal care. With careful planning, close monitoring, and aggressive intervention, pregnancy in systemic sclerosis may be uneventful with good maternal and fetal outcomes.

Behcet's Disease and Pregnancy

Epidemiology

Behcet's disease (BD) is an inflammatory disorder of unknown etiology with oral ulceration as its hallmark. Other manifestations include genital ulcers; ocular disease; cutaneous, gastrointestinal, and neurologic involvement; and arthritis. BD is considered to be a systemic vasculitis condition which involves blood vessels of all sizes and can affect both arteries and veins.

For unknown reasons, BD has a unique geographic distribution, being more common along the ancient "Silk Road" which extends from eastern Asia to the Mediterranean [70]. It is most common in Turkey, but has been reported worldwide. The prevalence is similar in men and women in areas where BD is more common, but in the United States and northern Europe, women are affected more commonly. Young adults 20–40 years of age are typically affected, but can be seen in children [71]. BD is more severe in young, male, Middle Eastern or Far Eastern patients [72, 73].

Clinical Manifestations

The classic triad of BD consists of recurrent oral and genital ulcerations with uveitis. At onset it may present with vascular involvement instead of the classic triad. Recurrent, usually painful, mucocutaneous ulcers is the most common clinical feature in BD. The greatest morbidity and mortality occur with the following manifestations: ocular disease (affecting up to 2/3 of patients), vascular disease (affecting up to 1/3 of patients), and central nervous system disease (affecting 10–20 % of patients).

Cutaneous and articular manifestations are common. Renal disease and peripheral nervous system involvement are rare compared with other vasculitides [74].

A. Most patients initially manifest with recurrent, painful oral aphthous ulcerations or "canker sores." Oral ulcers typically heal spontaneously within 1–3 weeks.
B. Genital ulceration occurs in 75 % or more patients with BD. The ulcers are painful, and similar in appearance to the oral aphthae, but usually recur less frequently than oral ulcers. These are most commonly found on the scrotum in men and the vulva in women, although ulcers may occur on any mucous membrane. Scarring is frequent for genital lesions. Epididymitis, salpingitis, varicocele, and other genitourinary inflammatory conditions may also occur, but urethritis is unusual.
C. A wide variety of cutaneous lesions occur in more than 75 % of patients with BD. Acneiform lesions, papulovesicular-pustular eruptions, pseudofolliculitis, nodules, erythema nodosum, superficial thrombophlebitis, pyoderma gangrenosum-like lesions, erythema multiforme-like lesions, and palpable purpura. The acne lesions characteristic of Behcet's syndrome are not sterile and are commonly observed in combination with arthritis [71].

 Pathergy is a phenomenon observed in BD as a response to local skin injury. It is defined as an erythematous pustular or papular response that appears 48 h after a skin prick by a 20 gauge needle. Pathergy is less common in North American and North European patients with BD than in patients from endemic areas.
D. Ocular disease occurs in 25–75 % depending on the population studied. Repeated attacks of uveitis can cause blindness. Panuveitis, typically bilateral, is the most common ocular feature of BD. Hypopyon, which is a severe anterior uveitis, may be associated with retinal vasculitis. Posterior uveitis and optic neuritis may also occur.
E. Neurologic manifestations occur in less than 1/5 of patients with BD. The most common abnormalities include focal parenchymal lesions and complications of arterial or venous thrombosis in the central nervous system. Seizures, aseptic meningitis, encephalitis, and arterial vasculitis can also occur.
F. Vascular disease is one of the major sources of morbidity in BD. Most clinical manifestations of BD are believed to be due to vasculitis. It is unique among the systemic vasculitides in that all sizes of blood vessels (small, medium, and large) can be affected and can involve both the arterial and venous circulation. Vascular disease in BD is more common in men.

 1. Arterial: Arterial disease is most commonly a small vessel vasculitis. Medium and large vessel disease may also occur. Large vessel vascular involvement occurs in 1/3 of BD [75]. Perivascular and endovascular inflammation may lead to hemorrhage, stenosis, aneurysm formation, and thrombus formation in both arteries and veins. A number of factors may contribute to thrombosis, but the primary reason for clot seems to reside in the inflammatory process in the arterial wall, still incompletely understood [76].

   Carotid, pulmonary, aortic, iliac, femoral, and popliteal arteries are most commonly involved; cerebral and renal arteries are uncommonly involved [77].

Pulmonary artery aneurysms are the most common pulmonary vascular lesion in BD and are uncommonly seen in diseases other than BD. Hemoptysis is the most common presenting symptom of pulmonary arterial involvement. Pulmonary artery thrombosis may occur with pulmonary artery aneurysms [78].
2. Venous: Venous disease is more common than arterial disease. Superior and inferior vena cava occlusion, Budd-Chiari syndrome, dural sinus thrombosis, and other venous obstructive lesions can occur in addition to the more common superficial and deep vein thrombosis. Venous thrombosis is often an early feature of Behcet's [77].

G. A nonerosive, asymmetric, nondeforming arthritis can occur in about 50 % of BD, usually during exacerbations of disease. The medium and large joints (e.g., knee, ankle, wrist) are most commonly affected with an intermittent inflammatory arthritis [79].
H. Renal disease is less frequent and often less severe than in other vasculitis types. Proteinuria, hematuria, and mild renal insufficiency may occur, but can progress to renal failure. Amyloidosis (AA type), glomerulonephritis, renal arterial aneurysms, and interstitial nephritis are part of the spectrum of renal disease in BD [80].
I. Symptomatic cardiac disease is uncommon in Behcet's disease. Abnormalities that can occur include pericarditis, myocarditis, coronary artery aneurysms, atrial septal aneurysm, conduction system disturbances, ventricular arrhythmias, endocarditis, endomyocardial fibrosis, mitral valve prolapse, intracardiac thrombosis, and valvular insufficiency [81]. Acute myocardial infarction can occur due to coronary artery vasculitis but is uncommon. Atherosclerosis does not appear to occur at an accelerated rate in Behcet's disease [72].
J. Gastrointestinal ulcerations occur in some patients with Behcet's disease, and intestinal perforation can occur. Discrete ulcerations are most often seen in the terminal ileum, cecum, and ascending colon.
K. Other features: Patients with Behcet's disease may experience constitutional symptoms including fever and malaise. Problems with urinary and erectile function may be due to neural or vascular disease [82]. Inner ear involvement may cause tinnitus, deafness, or dizziness [83]. Fibromyalgia co-occurs in many patients with Behcet's disease.

Diagnosis: There are no pathognomonic laboratory tests in Behcet's disease. Thus, the diagnosis is made on the basis of the clinical findings. Markers of inflammation such as circulating immune complexes, C-reactive protein, and the erythrocyte sedimentation rate may be elevated in patients with active disease; however, these findings are nonspecific and are elevated in normal pregnancy.

The International Study Group (ISG) criteria published in 1990 [84] remain the most widely used and well-accepted criteria among experts in Behcet's disease. They require the presence of recurrent oral aphthae (at least three times in 1 year) plus two of the following in the absence of other systemic diseases:

- Recurrent genital aphthae (aphthous ulceration or scarring)
- Eye lesions (including anterior or posterior uveitis, cells in vitreous on slit lamp examination, or retinal vasculitis observed by an ophthalmologist)

- Skin lesions (including erythema nodosum, pseudo-vasculitis, papulopustular lesions, or acneiform nodules consistent with Behcet's disease)
- A positive pathergy test

Clinical Manifestations of Behcet's Disease During Pregnancy

Limited data are available concerning the influence of pregnancy on the course of BD, with existing reports conflicting. Behcet's disease during pregnancy has only been evaluated in a few studies [85–87]. These studies suggest that disease activity is somewhat reduced during pregnancy; however, the risk of complications may be higher in Behcet's patients than in matched controls without Behcet's disease.

In a retrospective analysis of 76 pregnancies in 46 patients with Behcet's disease [87], 35.5 % percent of pregnancies were associated with flares during gestation or postpartum period (within 3 months of delivery). Oral and genital ulcerations and ocular involvement were the most common flare symptoms during these pregnancies. The ocular lesions were observed threefold more frequently during the postpartum period than during pregnancy (P=0.038). Neurologic or vascular disease flares have also been reported [88, 89].

The annual incidence of flares per patient was approximately threefold lower during pregnancy than before or after pregnancy [87]. Progesterone may be the major hormone influencing the course of Behcet's disease as there have been associations of BD exacerbations related to menstruation or postpartum period [90].

There is no validated disease activity score to monitor BD activity; there are no reports on whether the activity of BD was improved overall during pregnancy. The maternal age at the time of conception did not impact the risk of BD flares during pregnancy [87]. Medications used during pregnancy did not influence disease flares, except that colchicine appeared to be protective [87].

Impact of Disease on Pregnancy Outcomes

Observational studies of pregnant women with BD are sparse and are comprised mainly by case reports and small series. The influence of BD on pregnancy varied among patients and even during different pregnancies in the same patient.

In 76 pregnancies in BD [87], the overall rate of pregnancy complications was 15.8 % percent, which included miscarriages, cesarean section, medical termination of pregnancy, HELLP syndrome, and immune thrombocytopenia. Maternal age at pregnancy and duration of BD did not influence pregnancy outcomes. In this study, the use of colchicine or corticosteroid treatment was not associated with an increased rate of pregnancy complications. Neither gestational age at the time of delivery nor neonatal outcome was influenced by the occurrence of pregnancy complications. No congenital abnormalities, fetal malformations, or neonatal BD was observed.

The aforementioned pregnancy complications were more common in patients with history of deep venous thrombosis, alone or in association with dural sinus thrombosis, pulmonary embolism, and/or renal vein thrombosis [87]. This association between a history of DVT in BD and the risk of obstetric complications is statistically significant (OR 7.25, 95 % confidence interval [95 % CI] 1.21-43-46, p=0.029). Complications such as miscarriages could be related to the existence of decidual vasculitis in BD [91].

A case–control study of 31 patients during 135 pregnancies demonstrated higher rates of miscarriage, pregnancy complications, and cesarean sections in Behcet's patients compared to controls [85]. Pregnancy in patients with BD did not appear to be associated with an increased rate of pregnancy-related complications [87].

Treatment During Pregnancy

The management of Behcet's disease is largely directed toward suppression of the individual symptoms with the goal to prevent organ damage. The number of controlled trials for BD treatment is lacking. Treatment of various manifestations, especially those involving the vascular, neurologic, and gastrointestinal systems, relies largely on uncontrolled studies. During pregnancy, the risks and benefits of immunosuppressive treatment should be discussed in detail, with options limited to medications that do not have clear teratogenic or fetotoxic potential.

Colchicine use during pregnancy may possibly reduce the risk of severe BD flares; the proportion of disease flares was twofold lower in BD patients treated with colchicine [87]. Because colchicine crosses the human placenta, the safety of colchicine treatment during pregnancy has been questioned. The safety of this drug during pregnancy was assessed in a prospective comparative cohort study in which 238 colchicine-exposed pregnancies were followed up [92]. This study suggests that colchicine does not appear to be a major human teratogen and probably has no cytogenetic effect. Despite the antimitotic effects of colchicine, no increase in teratogenicity or congenital abnormalities was observed. This finding is consistent with previous reports [93] and underscores the probable safety of colchicine during pregnancy, although adequate numbers for a definitive conclusion are not available.

Other medications such as azathioprine and glucocorticoids can also be used during pregnancy, without an apparent increased risk of complications. Early treatment with azathioprine improves the ocular and extraocular outcome at the long term [94]. A European League Against Rheumatism task force developed nine recommendations for the management of Behcet's syndrome, but have been developed for treatment in the nonpregnant state [95].

- Mucocutaneous lesions could be treated with local corticosteroid creams either alone or as an additive to systemic medications to provide symptomatic relief. Colchicine (1–2 mg/day) is recommended especially when the predominating symptom is erythema nodosum, but it is also effective for genital ulcers among

women [96]. Azathioprine is also effective in suppressing the mucocutaneous manifestations [97]. Its daily dose is 2.5 mg/kg, and a minimum of 3 months is required for its effect. In the only randomized controlled trial of TNF-α inhibitors, etanercept significantly suppressed oral ulcers and papulopustular lesions of Behcet's syndrome [98].
- Ocular disease: azathioprine, with or without systemic corticosteroids, is the first-line agent [95, 97]. The combination of azathioprine and corticosteroids is recommended for severe uveitis involving the retina or if with decreasing the visual acuity. In such refractory eye disease, addition of cyclosporine or infliximab could be considered. Cyclosporine, with its rapid onset of action, is effective in reducing the frequency and severity of ocular attacks while improving the visual acuity [99]. According to some case–control studies, cyclosporine may potentiate central nervous system involvement in BD and thus should not be used in patients with central nervous system involvement [95]. Successful use of infliximab in pregnancy has been reported [100]. Tacrolimus may be considered as another alternative [101].
- Arthritis can be often managed with colchicine. In refractory cases, sulfasalazine, brief courses of corticosteroids, azathioprine, and TNF-α antagonists may be considered.
- Deep vein thrombosis is treated with immunosuppressive agents such as azathioprine and cyclosporine with or without corticosteroids [95]. There are no data supporting the efficacy of anticoagulation in the management of venous involvement. No data, even uncontrolled, support the use of anticoagulant, antiplatelet, or fibrinolytic agents in the management of deep vein thrombosis or arterial lesions.

    Cyclophosphamide combined with high-dose corticosteroids seems to be effective for pulmonary artery aneurysms [102]; however, cyclophosphamide is known to be teratogenic and thus must not be used during pregnancy. Pulmonary aneurysms are usually bilateral and multiple and they recur; thus, surgery should be the last choice. Endovascular embolization can be lifesaving in emergent cases, but the high coexistence of venous thrombosis may render this intervention technically difficult. Peripheral aneurysms are managed surgically, but this should be supported with immunosuppressive agents to prevent relapses.
- Gastrointestinal involvement not infrequently necessitates emergency surgery, which requires large resections of bowel segments to prevent recurrences. Anecdotal reports suggest the use of sulfasalazine, azathioprine, and TNF-α antagonists for gastrointestinal involvement [95].
- There is no evidence-based treatment for central nervous system (CNS) disease. Parenchymal CNS involvement is usually treated with pulsed corticosteroids. TNF-α antagonists and azathioprine can be other alternatives. Dural sinus involvement usually responds to treatment with corticosteroids.

The abovementioned medications can be considered for use during pregnancy, as the reported experiences with these medications during pregnancy have been reassuring. Use of these medications during lactation requires reevaluation. A risk-benefit discussion with the mother and treatment team should always ensue, with the goal of optimizing both maternal and fetal outcomes.

Other medications that play a major immunosuppressive role in BD treatment are clearly known to have risks of teratogenicity or embryopathy, or abortifacient effects, thus are contraindicated during pregnancy: thalidomide, cyclophosphamide, methotrexate, and interferon-α.

Preconception Counseling

Behcet's disease is an inflammatory systemic illness that has protean manifestations with a broad range of disease severity. Minor disease manifestations, such as mucocutaneous disease and arthritis, can interfere significantly with quality of life but do not threaten vital organ function. Major disease manifestations may lead to the dysfunction of major organs and even to death. These include certain ocular and neurologic manifestations, as well as complications of arterial vasculitis and/or venous thrombotic disease.

Treatment goals should be decided upon prior to pregnancy, dictated by the severity of disease manifestations. This would entail decisions on continuation or withdrawal of immunosuppressive or immune-modulating medications. Consideration should also be made to the timing of pregnancy planning, as certain immunosuppressive medications have long half-lives and its effects may remain for a prolonged period after its withdrawal.

Postpartum Management

The postpartum stage remains a period of vulnerability. Flares of BD may occur, particularly ocular disease [87]. Treatments outlined during the pregnancy period may be used more liberally (glucocorticoids, azathioprine, cyclosporine, TNF antagonists, colchicine, surgery), directed by the severity of disease activity and its effect on quality of life. This period may allow use of a broader range of immunosuppressive medications (including thalidomide, cyclophosphamide, methotrexate, interferon-alpha, rituximab). However, consideration still has to be made with breastfeeding, as not all of these medications are compatible with lactation.

Treatment of Rheumatologic Disease During Pregnancy

For many of the rheumatologic diseases noted above, the treatment has advanced significantly over the past 50 years, making it more possible than ever for women of childbearing age with rheumatoid arthritis, lupus, and ankylosing spondylitis to consider childbearing. Unfortunately, there is uncertain safety data for many of the disease-modifying immune-modulating medications during pregnancy and lactation. Pregnant women are excluded from all drug clinical trials and safety studies for ethical reasons. The FDA categorization of medications (Table 13.1) is almost exclusively

13 The Care and Management of Rheumatologic Disease in Pregnancy

Table 13.1 Autoimmune diseases, their behavior during pregnancy, pregnancy outcomes, and medications

Autoimmune disease	Behavior during pregnancy	Risk of active maternal disease on pregnancy	Drugs used during the nonpregnant state	Drugs that can be used during pregnancy
Rheumatoid arthritis	Improves in 50–75 % of pregnancies, 10–25 % remain active	Rare—limited to very active RA or to therapy	Hydroxychloroquine, methotrexate, prednisone, sulfasalazine, leflunomide, intra-articular corticosteroids, TNF inhibitors, abatacept, tocilizumab, rituximab, tofacitinib, NSAIDs	Hydroxychloroquine, sulfasalazine, prednisone intra-articular corticosteroids
Systemic lupus erythematosus	50 % of patients have mild to moderate activity, severe flares occur in about 25 % of pregnancies	Miscarriage, IUGR, prematurity, preeclampsia, congenital heart block (SSa/Ro or SSb/La antibody-positive mothers), antiphospholipid syndrome	Hydroxychloroquine, prednisone, azathioprine, cyclosporine, tacrolimus, mycophenolate mofetil, cyclophosphamide, rituximab, belimumab	Hydroxychloroquine, prednisone, azathioprine cyclosporine, tacrolimus
Systemic sclerosis	No major effect of pregnancy on disease activity	Intrauterine growth restriction, prematurity	ACE inhibitors, endothelin receptor antagonists, prostaglandin analogs Phosphodiesterase inhibitors	Prostaglandin analogs Phosphodiesterase inhibitors, ACE inhibitor for scleroderma renal crisis
Vasculitis	No major effect of pregnancy on disease activity	Miscarriage, intrauterine growth restriction, prematurity	Methotrexate, cyclophosphamide, prednisone, azathioprine, rituximab	Prednisone, azathioprine

based on animal reproductive data and thus is limited in its ability to predict the human risk. This dilemma presents unique challenges to internists, rheumatologists, and obstetricians caring for the pregnant patient with autoimmune disease.

In this section, we will first discuss the medications that should be avoided during pregnancy, due to known teratogenicity. We will then review the medications for which the data is not so clear. Some of these have extensive case series and registry data, as well as decades of use, suggesting their safety in pregnancy. Some immune-modulating therapies, on the other hand, have just a handful of case reports to support their safety.

Medications Contraindicated During Pregnancy and Lactation

Methotrexate

Methotrexate (MTX) is the first-line disease-modifying antirheumatic drug (DMARD) for RA. MTX inhibits dihydrofolate reductase, thus interfering with folic acid metabolism and purine synthesis. Closure of the neural tube occurs during the fifth week of pregnancy; the embryo is therefore probably most vulnerable to antifolate drugs at this time. Thus, early folic acid supplementation is essential and should be continued during the preconception period, even after methotrexate is stopped, and should be continued throughout pregnancy. High-dose MTX crosses the placenta, is teratogenic, and is classified as a category X drug in pregnancy. Exposure to low doses (20 mg or less weekly, as used in the rheumatology setting) has been associated with a high rate (20 %) of spontaneous abortions [103].

Oral methotrexate has a half-life of 3–10 h, but can persist in the liver for several months after discontinuation. We recommend stopping MTX 3–4 months before conception to allow adequate time for elimination of the drug.

MTX is excreted into breast milk in low concentrations [104]. The significance of this small amount for the nursing child is unknown, but should be avoided due to theoretical risks.

Leflunomide

Leflunomide is used to treat patients with moderate to severe RA. It is an inhibitor of dihydroorotate dehydrogenase and pyrimidine synthesis. It was shown to be teratogenic in rats, rabbits, and mice and therefore labeled as a category X drug. Leflunomide has a half-life of 14 days, but its active metabolite undergoes enterohepatic circulation and may persist in the body for up to 2 years. A dosing regimen of cholestyramine has been described to reduce levels rapidly in less than 14 days [105].

The Organization of Teratology Information Specialists (OTIS) published the results of a prospective study of birth outcomes in women exposed before or during pregnancy to leflunomide. Compared with unexposed RA pregnancies, there was neither increase in birth defects nor any recognizable malformation pattern [106].

This result was confirmed in additional 45 pregnancies of patients who were exposed to leflunomide either within 2 years before conception or during the first trimester [107]. These data indicate that leflunomide is not a strong human teratogen. Nevertheless, due to the limited number of exposed pregnancies in these studies, safe and effective contraception is recommended while taking leflunomide, and a cholestyramine washout procedure should be done in the setting of a planned or unintended pregnancy.

No data exist on excretion into breast milk; breastfeeding is therefore not recommended.

Cyclophosphamide

Cyclophosphamide (CYC) is an alkylating agent commonly used for the treatment of malignancies, lupus nephritis, and vasculitis. It inhibits cell division and is teratogenic. Exposure to CYC early in pregnancy in several animal species and humans is associated with a severe embryopathy that includes craniosynostosis, facial anomalies, distal limb defects, and developmental delay [108]. Clowse et al. reported unfavorable outcomes on four lupus patients who were treated with CYC during pregnancy. Two patients who were inadvertently exposed to CYC at conception for the treatment of lupus nephritis experienced spontaneous abortions in the first trimester. Two additional patients, treated with CYC at gestational weeks 20 and 22 for severe lupus flare, both suffered fetal demise within 7 days of introduction of cyclophosphamide, despite normal ultrasounds prior to treatment [109].

Cyclophosphamide should thus be avoided in early pregnancy. It should only be considered in severely ill women during the second half of pregnancy when all other options have been exhausted and the risk of pregnancy loss has been frankly discussed with the mother, although outcomes may still be poor for both the mother and fetus. Lactation is contraindicated during CYC use.

Mycophenolate Mofetil

Mycophenolate mofetil (MMF) is a reversible inhibitor of inosine monophosphate that is being increasingly used for autoimmune conditions including lupus nephritis. MMF readily crosses the placenta. Exposure to MMF during embryogenesis leads to an increased rate of spontaneous abortions and an estimated 22–26 % rate of congenital malformations [110, 111]. A distinctive MMF embryopathy has been identified as the "EMFO tetrad: Ear (microtia and auditory canal atresia); Mouth (cleft lip and palate); Fingers (brachydactyly fifth fingers and hypoplastic toenails); and Organs (cardiac, renal, CNS, diaphragmatic and ocular)" [110]. Use of reliable contraception is mandatory for women of childbearing potential while taking MMF.

Women taking MMF who are planning pregnancy should discontinue the drug at a minimum of 6 weeks prior to conception [112]. In conditions where ongoing immunosuppression is required, azathioprine is a safer alternative. There are no data regarding the excretion of MMF into breast milk or its effect on the nursing infants. Therefore, lactation is also not recommended while using MMF.

Medications that Can Be Used During Pregnancy

Hydroxychloroquine

Hydroxychloroquine (HCQ) is an antimalarial agent used for treatment of SLE and mild to moderate RA. The exact mechanism of action of HCQ is unknown; it is thought to interfere with antigen presentation and processing, thereby modulating the immune response. Its half-life is about 8 weeks; complete elimination of HCQ may take 6 months after discontinuation.

Hydroxychloroquine does cross the placenta. Over the years, data have accumulated in support of the safe use of HCQ (up to 400 mg daily) during human pregnancy [113]. Data from the Johns Hopkins Lupus Cohort showed no fetal or maternal risks associated with the continuation of HCQ throughout pregnancy [17]. No congenital malformations were demonstrated in a single placebo-controlled, randomized, double-blind study assessing the role of HCQ during pregnancy in SLE [114].

Furthermore, use of HCQ is associated with reduced development of congenital heart block (CHB) in children of mothers positive for anti-Ro/La antibodies [115]. Clowse et al. reported that among pregnant SLE patients, the risk for flare increases when HCQ use is discontinued, and higher doses of corticosteroids are needed to keep disease activity under control [17].

Hydroxychloroquine is secreted in breast milk at very low concentrations. No adverse effects have been observed in breastfed infants [116]. HCQ thus appears to be a safe option for use during conception, pregnancy, and lactation.

Sulfasalazine

Sulfasalazine (SSZ) is a folic acid antagonist used for the treatment of rheumatoid arthritis (RA) and inflammatory bowel disease (IBD). The half-life of SSZ is between 5 and 10 h.

A meta-analysis of 2200 pregnant women with IBD, of which 642 women received sulfasalazine or related agents, found no statistically significant differences in congenital anomalies or other adverse pregnancy outcomes [117]. No increase in congenital malformations was found in exposed children in a registry-based Norwegian study [118].

A case was reported of congenital severe neutropenia in an infant whose mother was taking 3 g of SSZ daily throughout the pregnancy [119]. Thus, doses exceeding 2 g daily in pregnancy should be used cautiously.

There is a theoretical risk that sulfasalazine may cause folate deficiency since it inhibits dihydrofolate reductase and cellular uptake of folate [120]. As such, folate supplementation should probably be initiated before and throughout pregnancy. Furthermore, both SSZ and its metabolite sulfapyridine cross the placenta. A concern in late pregnancy is that sulfapyridine can displace bilirubin from albumin and lead to neonatal jaundice [121]. However, there are no reports of kernicterus occurring after in utero exposure to sulfasalazine.

Sulfapyridine is found in breast milk, at levels of approximately 30–60 % of the mother's serum [122]. Exposure to sulfonamides through breast milk apparently does not pose a significant risk for the healthy, full-term newborn infant, but this risk should be considered in ill, stressed, jaundiced, or premature infants [116].

Azathioprine

Azathioprine (AZA) has been used during pregnancy for management of solid organ transplantation, IBD, and rheumatic diseases. It is a prodrug that undergoes hepatic metabolism to 6-mercaptopurine (6-MP), its active metabolite. AZA and its metabolites are known to cross the placenta. The fetal liver lacks the enzyme inosinatopyrophosphorylase, which converts azathioprine to its active form. Therefore theoretically, the fetus is protected.

Azathioprine has a long track record of use in pregnancy with an acceptable safety profile. There was no significant increase in pregnancy complications or congenital malformations found in studies of pregnancies exposed to azathioprine for IBD or renal transplants [123–126], although there may be an increased risk of preterm labor and IUGR. These findings may reflect the severity of the underlying disease.

The AAP does not recommend breastfeeding while taking azathioprine because of the theoretical risk of immunosuppression. However, in women on azathioprine during lactation, mercaptopurine levels are undetectable, and no adverse events have been reported in breast-fed infants exposed to maternal azathioprine [127, 128].

Calcineurin Inhibitors: Cyclosporine and Tacrolimus

The calcineurin inhibitors cyclosporine and tacrolimus prevent activation of T and B cells. More than 800 pregnancies exposed to cyclosporine and tacrolimus have been reported, mainly in transplant recipients, but also more sporadically in autoimmune disease [129]. Most of the studies of pregnancies exposed to the calcineurin inhibitors have found an increase in premature delivery and low birth weight, but no increase in congenital malformations [127, 130, 131]. It is not clarified whether the findings of prematurity and low birth weight are attributable to cyclosporine or to the underlying maternal disease.

Small amounts of cyclosporine are excreted in the breast milk. The AAP does not recommend breastfeeding while taking cyclosporine because of theoretical risks, but successful breastfeeding without adverse effects was reported in 15 children [132].

Corticosteroids

Corticosteroids are potent anti-inflammatory medications. These are considered safe during pregnancy, although there has been some concern that first trimester exposure is related to an increase in oral clefts [133]. A recent population-based study with 51,973 corticosteroid-exposed pregnancies did not find an increase in orofacial clefts regardless of type of corticosteroid administered (oral, inhalation, nasal spray, topical) [134]. Corticosteroids are classified as category B medications.

Betamethasone and dexamethasone are fluorinated steroids that are considerably less well metabolized by the placenta; they cross the placenta and have direct effects on the fetus. Most other corticosteroids (e.g., prednisone, prednisolone, and methylprednisolone) are metabolized in the placenta to inactivated forms. If the goal is to treat the mother, prednisone is the most ideal glucocorticoid because only a very small amount of active drug will enter the fetal circulation. Conversely, if the goal is to treat the fetus (such as for respiratory distress), betamethasone and dexamethasone are better options.

Prolonged corticosteroid use during pregnancy is associated with an increased risk of pregnancy-induced hypertension, preeclampsia, gestational diabetes, osteopenia, and infections, especially at doses of above 20 mg/day.

Corticosteroids are secreted in the breast milk at low concentrations and are considered safe to use during breastfeeding, especially at doses less than 20 mg prednisone daily (or the equivalent) [135].

The "Biologics"

The "Biologics," or biologic DMARDs, are biologically engineered molecules designed to target and inhibit specific molecules associated with the initiation and maintenance of inflammation. Biologics have been designed to target a variety of pro-inflammatory cytokines (e.g., tumor necrosis factor [TNF]), as well as B-cell receptors and T-cell co-stimulatory molecules. Many of these are effective in controlling inflammation and in preventing joint damage and destruction. Some, like the TNF inhibitors, are consistently accumulating data to support their safety in pregnancy. Others, like abatacept and tocilizumab, have too little data at this point to recommend their use during most pregnancies.

Tumor Necrosis Factor Inhibitors

TNF inhibitors (TNFIs) are large molecules designed to inhibit the activity of TNF-a, a pro-inflammatory cytokine. There are five FDA-approved TNFIs in the United States: infliximab (IFX), etanercept (ETA), adalimumab (ADA), golimumab (GOL), and certolizumab pegol (CZP). They are used to treat rheumatoid arthritis, ankylosing spondylitis, and psoriatic arthritis. Infliximab, adalimumab, and certolizumab pegol are FDA approved for the treatment of Crohn's disease, and infliximab, adalimumab, and golimumab are FDA approved for the treatment of ulcerative colitis. All the TNFIs are listed as category B drugs in pregnancy.

IFX is a chimeric IgG1 monoclonal antibody, and ADA and GOL are human IgG1 monoclonal antibodies. Because of the human IgG1 constant region, IFX, ADA, and GOL are not thought to cross the placenta during the first trimester, a time of fetal development and organogenesis. However, they do cross the placenta in the late second and third trimesters. Multiple case reports, series, and registries have *not* demonstrated an increase in fetal anomalies, miscarriage, or fetal complication rates in women exposed to these medications during pregnancy [136]. However, IFX levels are seen in newborns of exposed mothers, and the drug remains in the system for up to 6 months after delivery. For this reason, live vaccines should be avoided in the newborn exposed to these medications, for at least the first 6 months of its life.

CZP is a pegylated Fab fragment of a human IgG4 isotype monoclonal antibody. Compared with IFX and ADA, there appears to be minimal placental transfer of CZP in the third trimester [137]. On the other hand, as CZP does not include the IgG1 constant region, but rather a pegylated Fab fragment, it may cross the placenta in the first trimester. Data on safety in pregnancy is limited, but several case reports and series do not demonstrate any increased risk of adverse pregnancy outcomes or congenital malformations compared with that of the general population.

Etanercept (ETA) is a soluble TNF receptor fusion protein linked to the Fc portion of IgG1. Case reports and series have not demonstrated an increase in fetal anomalies or pregnancy complications with ETA. The concentration of ETA in cord blood was found to be 1/30th of that in maternal blood, and while low levels of ETA were detected in breast milk, the drug was not detectable in the serum of a 3-month-old exclusively breast-fed baby [138].

Abatacept

Abatacept is a recombinant fusion protein combining the human Fc region of IgG1 and CTLA4. It is a potent inhibitor of T-cell costimulation and is FDA approved for the treatment of moderate to severe RA. Abatacept crosses the placenta, but animal studies have not demonstrated teratogenicity.

There is only one case report of a patient with abatacept exposure during the first trimester of pregnancy, resulting in delivery of a healthy newborn [139]. It is not known if abatacept is excreted in human breast milk or is absorbed systemically after ingestion.

Anakinra

Anakinra is an IL-1 receptor antagonist used to treat RA, as well as adult-onset Still's disease (AOSD). A case report describes two patients on anakinra during pregnancy for AOSD, with successful pregnancies [140]. It is not known if anakinra is excreted in human breast milk, or is absorbed systemically after ingestion.

Tocilizumab

Tocilizumab is an IL-6 inhibitor used to treat moderate to severe RA. There are currently no case reports on tocilizumab exposure during pregnancy. It is not known if tocilizumab is excreted in human breast milk or is absorbed systemically after ingestion.

Rituximab

Rituximab is a chimeric monoclonal antibody against the protein CD20 on B cells, which leads to B-cell depletion. It is FDA approved for the treatment of moderate to severe rheumatoid arthritis after TNFI failure, in combination with methotrexate. However, it has also been used off label for the treatment of severe SLE, autoimmune cytopenias, vasculitis, and Sjogren's syndrome.

There are no animal studies of the effects of rituximab on pregnancy. Human IgG is known to cross the placenta and therefore can possibly cause fetal B-cell depletion. Thus, it should only be used in pregnancy when potential risks are far outweighed by the benefits of the medication.

A case series describing six pregnancies following treatment with rituximab for SLE or vasculitis reports one case of esophageal atresia, born to a mother with lupus nephritis who was exposed to rituximab 12 months prior to conception [141]. Another recent case report describes two patients exposed to rituximab during their first trimester, both of which delivered healthy babies [139].

Human IgG is excreted into human milk, but it is unknown how much, if any, rituximab would be excreted, nor the effects on the nursing infant.

Conclusion

Pregnancy itself can prove to be a disease-modifying state, revealed by the behavior of autoimmune conditions such as RA. However, this and other autoimmune conditions can flare during pregnancy, which can become a disastrous experience for both mother and fetus. Active autoimmune disease is an independent risk factor for adverse pregnancy outcome. Thus, close monitoring and control of maternal disease activity is necessary to ensure a successful pregnancy outcome.

Preconception planning should be initiated in all women of childbearing potential with rheumatologic disease. Many pregnancies are unplanned, and it is important to educate women with inflammatory diseases about their options early. Care of the pregnant woman with rheumatologic disease requires adjustment of immune-modulating therapy to ensure that the underlying maternal disease remains quiescent, while using medications that are compatible with embryonic and fetal development.

Withdrawal of all maintenance immunosuppressive drugs prior to conception, as has frequently been done in the past, often results in disease flare, which increases risks of preterm labor, preeclampsia, and intrauterine growth restriction. Unless there is a clear risk of teratogenicity, the potential for embryotoxic effects of immunosuppressive medications must be weighed against the need for control of autoimmune disease activity during pregnancy. In conclusion, treatment choices always require careful consideration and discussion with the patient about the risks and benefits to the fetus, and decisions should be made with the coordinated care of internists, specialists, and obstetricians.

References

1. Petri M, Howard D, Repke J. Frequency of lupus flare in pregnancy. The Hopkins lupus pregnancy center experience. Arthritis Rheum. 1991;34(12):1538–45. Epub 1991/12/01.
2. Ruiz-Irastorza G, Lima F, Alves J, Khamashta MA, Simpson J, Hughes GR, et al. Increased rate of lupus flare during pregnancy and the puerperium: a prospective study of 78 pregnancies. Br J Rheumatol. 1996;35(2):133–8. Epub 1996/02/01.
3. Lockshin MD. Pregnancy does not cause systemic lupus erythematosus to worsen. Arthritis Rheum. 1989;32(6):665–70. Epub 1989/06/01.
4. Georgiou PE, Politi EN, Katsimbri P, Sakka V, Drosos AA. Outcome of lupus pregnancy: a controlled study. Rheumatology (Oxford, England). 2000;39(9):1014–9. Epub 2000/09/15.
5. Clowse ME. Lupus activity in pregnancy. Rheumatic diseases clinics of North America. 2007;33(2):237–52, v.
6. Moroni G, Quaglini S, Banfi G, Caloni M, Finazzi S, Ambroso G, et al. Pregnancy in lupus nephritis. Am J Kidney Dis. 2002;40(4):713–20.
7. Salmon JE, Heuser C, Triebwasser M, Liszewski MK, Kavanagh D, Roumenina L, et al. Mutations in complement regulatory proteins predispose to preeclampsia: a genetic analysis of the PROMISSE cohort. PLoS Med. 2011;8(3):e1001013.
8. Chen CY, Chen YH, Lin HC, Chen SF, Lin HC. Increased risk of adverse pregnancy outcomes for hospitalisation of women with lupus during pregnancy: a nationwide population-based study. Clin Exp Rheumatol. 2010;28(1):49–55.
9. Nili F, McLeod L, O'Connell C, Sutton E, McMillan D. Maternal and neonatal outcomes in pregnancies complicated by systemic lupus erythematosus: a population-based study. J Obstet Gynaecol Can. 2013;35(4):323–8.
10. Barnabe C, Faris PD, Quan H. Canadian pregnancy outcomes in rheumatoid arthritis and systemic lupus erythematosus. Int J Rheumatol. 2011;2011:345727.
11. Clark CA, Spitzer KA, Laskin CA. Decrease in pregnancy loss rates in patients with systemic lupus erythematosus over a 40-year period. J Rheumatol. 2005;32(9):1709–12.
12. Madazli R, Yuksel MA, Oncul M, Imamoglu M, Yilmaz H. Obstetric outcomes and prognostic factors of lupus pregnancies. Arch Gynecol Obstet. 2013.
13. Stojan G, Baer AN. Flares of systemic lupus erythematosus during pregnancy and the puerperium: prevention, diagnosis and management. Expert Rev Clin Immunol. 2012;8(5):439–53. Epub 2012/08/14.
14. Phadungkiatwattana P, Sirivatanapa P, Tongsong T. Outcomes of pregnancies complicated by systemic lupus erythematosus (SLE)=. J Med Assoc Thail. 2007;90(10):1981–5.
15. Clowse ME, Magder LS, Witter F, Petri M. The impact of increased lupus activity on obstetric outcomes. Arthritis Rheum. 2005;52(2):514–21.
16. Clowse ME, Wallace DJ, Weisman M, James A, Criscione-Schreiber LG, Pisetsky DS. Predictors of preterm birth in patients with mild systemic lupus erythematosus. Ann Rheum Dis. 2013;72(9):1536–9. Epub 2013/01/31.
17. Clowse ME, Magder L, Witter F, Petri M. Hydroxychloroquine in lupus pregnancy. Arthritis Rheum. 2006;54(11):3640–7.
18. Golding A, Haque UJ, Giles JT. Rheumatoid arthritis and reproduction. Rheum Dis Clin N Am. 2007;33(2):319–43, vi–vii.
19. Barrett JH, Brennan P, Fiddler M, Silman AJ. Does rheumatoid arthritis remit during pregnancy and relapse postpartum? Results from a nationwide study in the United Kingdom performed prospectively from late pregnancy. Arthritis Rheum. 1999;42(6):1219–27.
20. Oka M. Effect of pregnancy on the onset and course of rheumatoid arthritis. Ann Rheum Dis. 1953;12(3):227–9.
21. Peschken CA, Robinson DB, Hitchon CA, Smolik I, Hart D, Bernstein CN, et al. Pregnancy and the risk of rheumatoid arthritis in a highly predisposed North American native population. J Rheumatol. 2012;39(12):2253–60.

22. Kay A, Bach F. Subfertility before and after the development of rheumatoid arthritis in women. Ann Rheum Dis. 1965;24:169–73.
23. Jawaheer D, Zhu JL, Nohr EA, Olsen J. Time to pregnancy among women with rheumatoid arthritis. Arthritis Rheum. 2011;63(6):1517–21.
24. Katz PP. Childbearing decisions and family size among women with rheumatoid arthritis. Arthritis Rheum. 2006;55(2):217–23.
25. Reed SD, Vollan TA, Svec MA. Pregnancy outcomes in women with rheumatoid arthritis in Washington State. Matern Child Health J. 2006;10(4):361–6.
26. Chakravarty EF, Nelson L, Krishnan E. Obstetric hospitalizations in the United States for women with systemic lupus erythematosus and rheumatoid arthritis. Arthritis Rheum. 2006; 54(3):899–907.
27. Bernatsky S, Joseph L, Pineau CA, Belisle P, Hudson M, Clarke AE. Scleroderma prevalence: demographic variations in a population-based sample. Arthritis Rheum. 2009;61(3): 400–4. Epub 2009/02/28.
28. Mayes MD, Lacey Jr JV, Beebe-Dimmer J, Gillespie BW, Cooper B, Laing TJ, et al. Prevalence, incidence, survival, and disease characteristics of systemic sclerosis in a large US population. Arthritis Rheum. 2003;48(8):2246–55.
29. Steen VD, Oddis CV, Conte CG, Janoski J, Casterline GZ, Medsger TA, Jr. Incidence of systemic sclerosis in Allegheny County, Pennsylvania. A twenty-year study of hospital-diagnosed cases, 1963–1982. Arthritis Rheum. 1997;40(3):441–5. Epub 1997/03/01.
30. LeRoy EC, Black C, Fleischmajer R, Jablonska S, Krieg T, Medsger Jr TA, et al. Scleroderma (systemic sclerosis): classification, subsets and pathogenesis. J Rheumatol. 1988;15(2):202–5. Epub 1988/02/01.
31. Carbillon L, Uzan M, Uzan S. Pregnancy, vascular tone, and maternal hemodynamics: a crucial adaptation. Obstet Gynecol Surv. 2000;55(9):574–81. Epub 2000/09/07.
32. Ganzevoort W, Rep A, Bonsel GJ, de Vries JI, Wolf H. Plasma volume and blood pressure regulation in hypertensive pregnancy. J Hypertens. 2004;22(7):1235–42. Epub 2004/06/18.
33. Thornburg KL, Jacobson SL, Giraud GD, Morton MJ. Hemodynamic changes in pregnancy. Semin Perinatol. 2000;24(1):11–4. Epub 2000/03/10.
34. Frederiksen MC. Physiologic changes in pregnancy and their effect on drug disposition. Semin Perinatol. 2001;25(3):120–3. Epub 2001/07/17.
35. Chakravarty EF. Vascular complications of systemic sclerosis during pregnancy. Int J Rheumatol. 2010;2010. Epub 2010/09/04.
36. Steen VD. Pregnancy in women with systemic sclerosis. Obstet Gynecol. 1999;94(1):15–20. Epub 1999/07/02.
37. Batal I, Domsic RT, Shafer A, Medsger Jr TA, Kiss LP, Randhawa P, et al. Renal biopsy findings predicting outcome in scleroderma renal crisis. Hum Pathol. 2009;40(3):332–40. Epub 2008/11/01.
38. Steen VD. Pregnancy in scleroderma. Rheum Dis Clin N Am. 2007;33(2):345–58, vii. Epub 2007/05/15.
39. Steen VD, Conte, C, Medsger, TA, Jr. Case control study of corticosteroid use prior to scleroderma renal crisis. Arthritis Rheum. 1994;37:S360.
40. Karlen JR, Cook WA. Renal scleroderma and pregnancy. Obstet Gynecol. 1974;44(3):349–54. Epub 1974/09/01.
41. Steen VD, Costantino JP, Shapiro AP, Medsger Jr TA. Outcome of renal crisis in systemic sclerosis: relation to availability of angiotensin converting enzyme (ACE) inhibitors. Ann Intern Med. 1990;113(5):352–7. Epub 1990/09/01.
42. Steen VD, Conte C, Day N, Ramsey-Goldman R, Medsger Jr TA. Pregnancy in women with systemic sclerosis. Arthritis Rheum. 1989;32(2):151–7. Epub 1989/02/01.
43. Cooper WO, Hernandez-Diaz S, Arbogast PG, Dudley JA, Dyer S, Gideon PS, et al. Major congenital malformations after first-trimester exposure to ACE inhibitors. N Engl J Med. 2006;354(23):2443–51. Epub 2006/06/09.
44. Wigley FM, Lima JA, Mayes M, McLain D, Chapin JL, Ward-Able C. The prevalence of undiagnosed pulmonary arterial hypertension in subjects with connective tissue disease at the

secondary health care level of community-based rheumatologists (the UNCOVER study). Arthritis Rheum. 2005;52(7):2125–32. Epub 2005/06/30.
45. Madden BP. Pulmonary hypertension and pregnancy. Int J Obstet Anesth. 2009;18(2):156–64. Epub 2009/02/19.
46. Huang S, DeSantis ER. Treatment of pulmonary arterial hypertension in pregnancy. Am J Health Syst Pharm. 2007;64(18):1922–6. Epub 2007/09/08.
47. Bedard E, Dimopoulos K, Gatzoulis MA. Has there been any progress made on pregnancy outcomes among women with pulmonary arterial hypertension? Eur Heart J. 2009;30(3):256–65. Epub 2009/01/17.
48. Steen VD. Scleroderma and pregnancy. Rheum Dis Clin N Am. 1997;23(1):133–47. Epub 1997/02/01.
49. Ostensen M. Scleroderma pregnancy: can the price be too high to pay? Clin Exp Rheumatol. 2008;26(6):979–81. Epub 2009/02/13.
50. Steen VCC, Day, N, et al. Fertility and pregnancy outcome in systemic sclerosis. Arthritis Rheum. 1989;32:S92.
51. Steen VD, Medsger Jr TA. Fertility and pregnancy outcome in women with systemic sclerosis. Arthritis Rheum. 1999;42(4):763–8. Epub 1999/04/22.
52. Chung L, Flyckt RL, Colon I, Shah AA, Druzin M, Chakravarty EF. Outcome of pregnancies complicated by systemic sclerosis and mixed connective tissue disease. Lupus. 2006;15(9):595–9. Epub 2006/11/04.
53. van Wyk L, van der Marel J, Schuerwegh AJ, Schouffoer AA, Voskuyl AE, Huizinga TW, et al. Increased incidence of pregnancy complications in women who later develop scleroderma: a case control study. Arthritis Res Therapy. 2011;13(6):R183. Epub 2011/11/08.
54. Chakravarty EF, Khanna D, Chung L. Pregnancy outcomes in systemic sclerosis, primary pulmonary hypertension, and sickle cell disease. Obstet Gynecol. 2008;111(4):927–34. Epub 2008/04/02.
55. Steen VBM, Conte, C. Prospective pregnancy study in women with systemic sclerosis. Arthritis Rheum. 1996;39:51.
56. Ibba-Manneschi L, Manetti M, Milia AF, Miniati I, Benelli G, Guiducci S, et al. Severe fibrotic changes and altered expression of angiogenic factors in maternal scleroderma: placental findings. Ann Rheum Dis. 2010;69(2):458–61. Epub 2009/04/02.
57. Papakonstantinou K, Hasiakos D, Kondi-Paphiti A. Clinicopathology of maternal scleroderma. Int J Gynaecol Obstet. 2007;99(3):248–9. Epub 2007/09/25.
58. Doss BJ, Jacques SM, Mayes MD, Qureshi F. Maternal scleroderma: placental findings and perinatal outcome. Hum Pathol. 1998;29(12):1524–30. Epub 1998/12/29.
59. Kahl LE, Blair C, Ramsey-Goldman R, Steen VD. Pregnancy outcomes in women with primary Raynaud's phenomenon. Arthritis Rheum. 1990;33(8):1249–55. Epub 1990/08/01.
60. Lidar M, Langevitz P. Pregnancy issues in scleroderma. Autoimmun Rev. 2012;11(6–7):A515–9. Epub 2011/12/14.
61. Steen VD. Autoantibodies in systemic sclerosis. Bull Rheum Dis. 1996;45(6):6–8. Epub 1996/10/01.
62. Bailey AR, Wolmarans M, Rhodes S. Spinal anaesthesia for caesarean section in a patient with systemic sclerosis. Anaesthesia. 1999;54(4):355–8. Epub 1999/08/24.
63. Mehta N, Modi N. ACE inhibitors in pregnancy. Lancet. 1989;2(8654):96–7. Epub 1989/07/08.
64. Guiducci S, Giacomelli R, Cerinic MM. Vascular complications of scleroderma. Autoimmun Rev. 2007;6(8):520–3. Epub 2007/09/15.
65. Mok CC, Kwan TH, Chow L. Scleroderma renal crisis sine scleroderma during pregnancy. Scand J Rheumatol. 2003;32(1):55–7. Epub 2003/03/15.
66. Zavorsky GS, Blood AB, Power GG, Longo LD, Artal R, Vlastos EJ. CO and NO pulmonary diffusing capacity during pregnancy: safety and diagnostic potential. Respir Physiol Neurobiol. 2010;170(3):215–25. Epub 2010/02/13.
67. Higton AM, Whale C, Musk M, Gabbay E. Pulmonary hypertension in pregnancy: two cases and review of the literature. Intern Med J. 2009;39(11):766–70. Epub 2009/11/17.

68. Goland S, Tsai F, Habib M, Janmohamed M, Goodwin TM, Elkayam U. Favorable outcome of pregnancy with an elective use of epoprostenol and sildenafil in women with severe pulmonary hypertension. Cardiology. 2010;115(3):205–8. Epub 2010/02/23.
69. Leuchte HH, Schwaiblmair M, Baumgartner RA, Neurohr CF, Kolbe T, Behr J. Hemodynamic response to sildenafil, nitric oxide, and iloprost in primary pulmonary hypertension. Chest. 2004;125(2):580–6. Epub 2004/02/11.
70. Yurdakul S, Hamuryudan V, Yazici H. Behcet syndrome. Curr Opin Rheumatol. 2004;16(1):38–42. Epub 2003/12/16.
71. Karincaoglu Y, Borlu M, Toker SC, Akman A, Onder M, Gunasti S, et al. Demographic and clinical properties of juvenile-onset Behcet's disease: a controlled multicenter study. J Am Acad Dermatol. 2008;58(4):579–84. Epub 2007/11/30.
72. Kural-Seyahi E, Fresko I, Seyahi N, Ozyazgan Y, Mat C, Hamuryudan V, et al. The long-term mortality and morbidity of Behcet syndrome: a 2-decade outcome survey of 387 patients followed at a dedicated center. Medicine. 2003;82(1):60–76. Epub 2003/01/25.
73. Sakane T, Takeno M, Suzuki N, Inaba G. Behcet's disease. N Engl J Med. 1999;341(17):1284–91. Epub 1999/10/21.
74. Zouboulis CC, Vaiopoulos G, Marcomichelakis N, Palimeris G, Markidou I, Thouas B, et al. Onset signs, clinical course, prognosis, treatment and outcome of adult patients with Adamantiades-Behcet's disease in Greece. Clin Exp Rheumatol. 2003;21(4 Suppl 30):S19–26. Epub 2004/01/20.
75. Koc Y, Gullu I, Akpek G, Akpolat T, Kansu E, Kiraz S, et al. Vascular involvement in Behcet's disease. J Rheumatol. 1992;19(3):402–10. Epub 1992/03/01.
76. Calamia KT, Schirmer M, Melikoglu M. Major vessel involvement in Behcet disease. Curr Opin Rheumatol. 2005;17(1):1–8. Epub 2004/12/18.
77. Seyahi E, Melikoglu M, Yazici H. Clinical features and diagnosis of Behcet's syndrome. Int J Adv Rheumatol. 2007;5:8.
78. Seyahi E, Melikoglu M, Akman C, Hamuryudan V, Ozer H, Hatemi G, et al. Pulmonary artery involvement and associated lung disease in Behcet disease: a series of 47 patients. Medicine. 2012;91(1):35–48. Epub 2012/01/03.
79. Kim HA, Choi KW, Song YW. Arthropathy in Behcet's disease. Scand J Rheumatol. 1997;26(2):125–9. Epub 1997/01/01.
80. Akpolat T, Akkoyunlu M, Akpolat I, Dilek M, Odabas AR, Ozen S. Renal Behcet's disease: a cumulative analysis. Semin Arthritis Rheum. 2002;31(5):317–37. Epub 2002/04/20.
81. Geri G, Wechsler B, Thi Huong du L, Isnard R, Piette JC, Amoura Z, et al. Spectrum of cardiac lesions in Behcet disease: a series of 52 patients and review of the literature. Medicine. 2012;91(1):25–34. Epub 2011/12/27.
82. Erdogru T, Kocak T, Serdaroglu P, Kadioglu A, Tellaloglu S. Evaluation and therapeutic approaches of voiding and erectile dysfunction in neurological Behcet's syndrome. J Urol. 1999;162(1):147–53. Epub 1999/06/24.
83. Choung YH, Cho MJ, Park K, Choi SJ, Shin YR, Lee ES. Audio-vestibular disturbance in patients with Behcet's disease. Laryngoscope. 2006;116(11):1987–90. Epub 2006/11/01.
84. Disease ISGfBs. Criteria for diagnosis of Behcet's disease. International Study Group for Behcet's Disease. Lancet. 1990;335(8697):1078–80. Epub 1990/05/05.
85. Jadaon J, Shushan A, Ezra Y, Sela HY, Ozcan C, Rojansky N. Behcet's disease and pregnancy. Acta Obstet Gynecol Scand. 2005;84(10):939–44. Epub 2005/09/20.
86. Uzun S, Alpsoy E, Durdu M, Akman A. The clinical course of Behcet's disease in pregnancy: a retrospective analysis and review of the literature. J Dermatol. 2003;30(7):499–502. Epub 2003/08/21.
87. Noel N, Wechsler B, Nizard J, Costedoat-Chalumeau N, du Boutin LT, Dommergues M, et al. Behcet's disease and pregnancy. Arthritis Rheum. 2013;65(9):2450–6. Epub 2013/06/20.
88. Wechsler B, Genereau T, Biousse V, Vauthier-Brouzes D, Seebacher J, Dormont D, et al. Pregnancy complicated by cerebral venous thrombosis in Behcet's disease. Am J Obstet Gynecol. 1995;173(5):1627–9. Epub 1995/11/01.

89. Kale A, Akyildiz L, Akdeniz N, Kale E. Pregnancy complicated by superior vena cava thrombosis and pulmonary embolism in a patient with Behcet disease and the use of heparin for treatment. Saudi Med J. 2006;27(1):95–7. Epub 2006/01/25.
90. Bang D, Chun YS, Haam IB, Lee ES, Lee S. The influence of pregnancy on Behcet's disease. Yonsei Med J. 1997;38(6):437–43. Epub 1998/03/24.
91. Hwang I, Lee CK, Yoo B, Lee I. Necrotizing villitis and decidual vasculitis in the placentas of mothers with Behcet disease. Hum Pathol. 2009;40(1):135–8. Epub 2008/08/22.
92. Diav-Citrin O, Shechtman S, Schwartz V, Avgil-Tsadok M, Finkel-Pekarsky V, Wajnberg R, et al. Pregnancy outcome after in utero exposure to colchicine. Am J Obstet Gynecol. 2010;203(2):144 e1–6. Epub 2010/06/29.
93. Berkenstadt M, Weisz B, Cuckle H, Di-Castro M, Guetta E, Barkai G. Chromosomal abnormalities and birth defects among couples with colchicine treated familial Mediterranean fever. Am J Obstet Gynecol. 2005;193(4):1513–6. Epub 2005/10/06.
94. Hamuryudan V, Ozyazgan Y, Hizli N, Mat C, Yurdakul S, Tuzun Y, et al. Azathioprine in Behcet's syndrome: effects on long-term prognosis. Arthritis Rheum. 1997;40(4):769–74. Epub 1997/04/01.
95. Hatemi G, Silman A, Bang D, Bodaghi B, Chamberlain AM, Gul A, et al. EULAR recommendations for the management of Behcet disease. Ann Rheum Dis. 2008;67(12):1656–62. Epub 2008/02/05.
96. Yurdakul S, Mat C, Tuzun Y, Ozyazgan Y, Hamuryudan V, Uysal O, et al. A double-blind trial of colchicine in Behcet's syndrome. Arthritis Rheum. 2001;44(11):2686–92. Epub 2001/11/17.
97. Yazici H, Pazarli H, Barnes CG, Tuzun Y, Ozyazgan Y, Silman A, et al. A controlled trial of azathioprine in Behcet's syndrome. N Engl J Med. 1990;322(5):281–5. Epub 1990/02/01.
98. Melikoglu M, Fresko I, Mat C, Ozyazgan Y, Gogus F, Yurdakul S, et al. Short-term trial of etanercept in Behcet's disease: a double blind, placebo controlled study. J Rheumatol. 2005;32(1):98–105. Epub 2005/01/05.
99. Takayama K, Ishikawa S, Enoki T, Kojima T, Takeuchi M. Successful treatment with infliximab for Behcet disease during pregnancy. Ocul Immunol Inflamm. 2013;21(4):321–3. Epub 2013/04/27.
100. Masuda K, Nakajima A, Urayama A, Nakae K, Kogure M, Inaba G. Double-masked trial of cyclosporin versus colchicine and long-term open study of cyclosporin in Behcet's disease. Lancet. 1989;1(8647):1093–6. Epub 1989/05/20.
101. Mochizuki M, Masuda K, Sakane T, Inaba G, Ito K, Kogure M, et al. A multicenter clinical open trial of FK 506 in refractory uveitis, including Behcet's disease. Japanese FK 506 Study Group on Refractory Uveitis. Transplant Proc. 1991;23(6):3343–6.
102. Hamuryudan V, Er T, Seyahi E, Akman C, Tuzun H, Fresko I, et al. Pulmonary artery aneurysms in Behcet syndrome. Am J Med. 2004;117(11):867–70. Epub 2004/12/14.
103. Ostensen M, Hartmann H, Salvesen K. Low dose weekly methotrexate in early pregnancy. A case series and review of the literature. J Rheumatol. 2000;27(8):1872–5.
104. Johns DG, Rutherford LD, Leighton PC, Vogel CL. Secretion of methotrexate into human milk. Am J Obstet Gynecol. 1972;112(7):978–80.
105. Brent RL. Teratogen update: reproductive risks of leflunomide (Arava); a pyrimidine synthesis inhibitor: counseling women taking leflunomide before or during pregnancy and men taking leflunomide who are contemplating fathering a child. Teratology. 2001;63(2):106–12.
106. Chambers CD, Johnson DL, Robinson LK, Braddock SR, Xu R, Lopez-Jimenez J, et al. Birth outcomes in women who have taken leflunomide during pregnancy. Arthritis Rheum. 2010;62(5):1494–503.
107. Cassina M, Johnson DL, Robinson LK, Braddock SR, Xu R, Jimenez JL, et al. Pregnancy outcome in women exposed to leflunomide before or during pregnancy. Arthritis Rheum. 2012;64(7):2085–94.
108. Enns GM, Roeder E, Chan RT, Ali-Khan Catts Z, Cox VA, Golabi M. Apparent cyclophosphamide (cytoxan) embryopathy: a distinct phenotype? Am J Med Genet. 1999;86(3):237–41.

109. Clowse ME, Magder L, Petri M. Cyclophosphamide for lupus during pregnancy. Lupus. 2005;14(8):593–7.
110. Merlob P, Stahl B, Klinger G. Tetrada of the possible mycophenolate mofetil embryopathy: a review. Reprod Toxicol. 2009;28(1):105–8.
111. Sifontis NM, Coscia LA, Constantinescu S, Lavelanet AF, Moritz MJ, Armenti VT. Pregnancy outcomes in solid organ transplant recipients with exposure to mycophenolate mofetil or sirolimus. Transplantation. 2006;82(12):1698–702.
112. Elliott AB, Chakravarty EF. Immunosuppressive medications during pregnancy and lactation in women with autoimmune diseases. Women's Health. 2010;6(3):431–40. quiz 41-2.
113. Ostensen M, Khamashta M, Lockshin M, Parke A, Brucato A, Carp H, et al. Anti-inflammatory and immunosuppressive drugs and reproduction. Arthritis Res Therapy. 2006;8(3):209.
114. Levy RA, Vilela VS, Cataldo MJ, Ramos RC, Duarte JL, Tura BR, et al. Hydroxychloroquine (HCQ) in lupus pregnancy: double-blind and placebo-controlled study. Lupus. 2001;10(6):401–4.
115. Izmirly PM, Kim MY, Llanos C, Le PU, Guerra MM, Askanase AD, et al. Evaluation of the risk of anti-SSA/Ro-SSB/La antibody-associated cardiac manifestations of neonatal lupus in fetuses of mothers with systemic lupus erythematosus exposed to hydroxychloroquine. Ann Rheum Dis. 2010;69(10):1827–30.
116. American Academy of Pediatrics Committee on D. Transfer of drugs and other chemicals into human milk. Pediatrics. 2001;108(3):776–89.
117. Rahimi R, Nikfar S, Rezaie A, Abdollahi M. Pregnancy outcome in women with inflammatory bowel disease following exposure to 5-aminosalicylic acid drugs: a meta-analysis. Reprod Toxicol. 2008;25(2):271–5.
118. Viktil KK, Engeland A, Furu K. Outcomes after anti-rheumatic drug use before and during pregnancy: a cohort study among 150,000 pregnant women and expectant fathers. Scand J Rheumatol. 2012;41(3):196–201.
119. Levi S, Liberman M, Levi AJ, Bjarnason I. Reversible congenital neutropenia associated with maternal sulphasalazine therapy. Eur J Pediatr. 1988;148(2):174–5.
120. Hernandez-Diaz S, Werler MM, Walker AM, Mitchell AA. Folic acid antagonists during pregnancy and the risk of birth defects. N Engl J Med. 2000;343(22):1608–14.
121. Jarnerot G, Andersen S, Esbjorner E, Sandstrom B, Brodersen R. Albumin reserve for binding of bilirubin in maternal and cord serum under treatment with sulphasalazine. Scand J Gastroenterol. 1981;16(8):1049–55.
122. Esbjorner E, Jarnerot G, Wranne L. Sulphasalazine and sulphapyridine serum levels in children to mothers treated with sulphasalazine during pregnancy and lactation. Acta Paediatr Scand. 1987;76(1):137–42.
123. Successful pregnancies in women treated by dialysis and kidney transplantation. Report from the Registration Committee of the European Dialysis and Transplant Association. Br J Obstet Gynaecol. 1980;87(10):839–45.
124. Alstead EM, Ritchie JK, Lennard-Jones JE, Farthing MJ, Clark ML. Safety of azathioprine in pregnancy in inflammatory bowel disease. Gastroenterology. 1990;99(2):443–6.
125. Cleary BJ, Kallen B. Early pregnancy azathioprine use and pregnancy outcomes. Birth Defects Res A Clin Mol Teratol. 2009;85(7):647–54.
126. Moskovitz DN, Bodian C, Chapman ML, Marion JF, Rubin PH, Scherl E, et al. The effect on the fetus of medications used to treat pregnant inflammatory bowel-disease patients. Am J Gastroenterol. 2004;99(4):656–61.
127. Gisbert JP. Safety of immunomodulators and biologics for the treatment of inflammatory bowel disease during pregnancy and breast-feeding. Inflamm Bowel Dis. 2010;16(5):881–95.
128. Moretti ME, Verjee Z, Ito S, Koren G. Breast-feeding during maternal use of azathioprine. Ann Pharmacother. 2006;40(12):2269–72.
129. Hussein MM, Mooij JM, Roujouleh H. Cyclosporine in the treatment of lupus nephritis including two patients treated during pregnancy. Clin Nephrol. 1993;40(3):160–3.

130. Miniero R, Tardivo I, Curtoni ES, Segoloni GP, La Rocca E, Nino A, et al. Pregnancy after renal transplantation in Italian patients: focus on fetal outcome. J Nephrol. 2002;15(6): 626–32.
131. Perales-Puchalt A, Vila Vives JM, Lopez Montes J, Diago Almela VJ, Perales A. Pregnancy outcomes after kidney transplantation-immunosuppressive therapy comparison. J Matern Fetal Neonatal Med. 2012;25(8):1363–6.
132. Moretti ME, Sgro M, Johnson DW, Sauve RS, Woolgar MJ, Taddio A, et al. Cyclosporine excretion into breast milk. Transplantation. 2003;75(12):2144–6.
133. Park-Wyllie L, Mazzotta P, Pastuszak A, Moretti ME, Beique L, Hunnisett L, et al. Birth defects after maternal exposure to corticosteroids: prospective cohort study and meta-analysis of epidemiological studies. Teratology. 2000;62(6):385–92.
134. Hviid A, Molgaard-Nielsen D. Corticosteroid use during pregnancy and risk of orofacial clefts. CMAJ. 2011;183(7):796–804.
135. Ost L, Wettrell G, Bjorkhem I, Rane A. Prednisolone excretion in human milk. J Pediatr. 1985;106(6):1008–11.
136. Nielsen OH, Loftus Jr EV, Jess T. Safety of TNF-alpha inhibitors during IBD pregnancy: a systematic review. BMC Med. 2013;11:174.
137. Mahadevan U, Wolf DC, Dubinsky M, Cortot A, Lee SD, Siegel CA, et al. Placental transfer of anti-tumor necrosis factor agents in pregnant patients with inflammatory bowel disease. Clin Gastroenterol Hepatol. 2013;11(3):286–92; quiz e24. Epub 2012/12/04.
138. Murashima A, Watanabe N, Ozawa N, Saito H, Yamaguchi K. Etanercept during pregnancy and lactation in a patient with rheumatoid arthritis: drug levels in maternal serum, cord blood, breast milk and the infant's serum. Ann Rheum Dis. 2009;68(11):1793–4.
139. Ojeda-Uribe M, Afif N, Dahan E, Sparsa L, Haby C, Sibilia J, et al. Exposure to abatacept or rituximab in the first trimester of pregnancy in three women with autoimmune diseases. Clin Rheumatol. 2013;32(5):695–700.
140. Fischer-Betz R, Specker C, Schneider M. Successful outcome of two pregnancies in patients with adult-onset Still's disease treated with IL-1 receptor antagonist (anakinra). Clin Exp Rheumatol. 2011;29(6):1021–3. Epub 2011/12/14.
141. Sangle SR, Lutalo PM, Davies RJ, Khamashta MA, D'Cruz DP. B-cell depletion therapy and pregnancy outcome in severe, refractory systemic autoimmune diseases. J Autoimmun. 2013;43:55–9. Epub 2013/04/24.

Part XIII
Thyroid Disease

Chapter 14
Thyroid Disease

Mae Whelan and Geetha Gopalakrishnan

Introduction

Thyroid disease is fairly common among pregnant women. Pregnancy itself can affect thyroid gland and function. The three categories of thyroid disorders that will be covered in this chapter are hyperthyroid, hypothyroid, and thyroid nodules/cancer. Thyroid dysfunction can impact both maternal and fetal outcomes and, therefore, must be recognized and treated appropriately.

Background/Definition

Thyroid-stimulating hormone (TSH) is produced by the pituitary gland. It stimulates the thyroid to synthesize tetraiodothyronine (T4) and triiodothyronine (T3). The thyroid generates 100 % of T4 and 20 % of T3 in circulation. Peripheral conversion of T4 to T3 is responsible for the remainder of T3 production. The biological activity

---

M. Whelan, M.D.
Endocrinology Fellow, Department of Internal Medicine,
Rhode Island Hospital, Providence, RI, USA

The Warren Alpert Medical School of Brown University, Providence, RI, USA
e-mail: mwhelan@lifespan.org

G. Gopalakrishnan, M.D. (✉)
OB Medicine-Endocrinology and Diabetes in Pregnancy, Women's Medicine Collaborative,
The Miriam Hospital, Providence, RI, USA

Hallett Center for Diabetes and Endocrinology, Rhode Island Hospital, Providence, RI, USA

The Warren Alpert Medical School of Brown University, Providence, RI, USA
e-mail: ggopala@lifespan.org

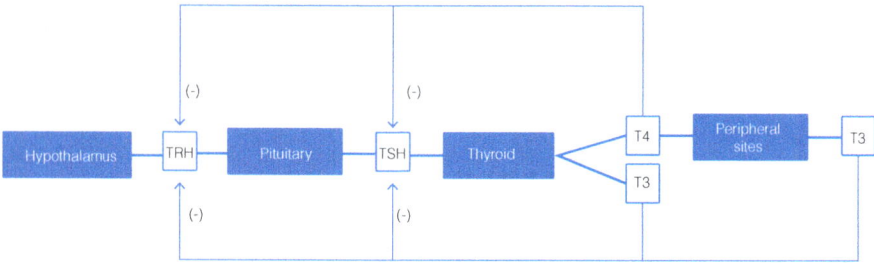

Fig. 14.1 Thyrotropin-releasing hormone (TRH); thyroid-stimulating hormone (TSH); tetraiodothyronine (T4); triiodothyronine (T3)

of thyroid hormone is mediated predominantly by the intracellular generation of T3 in peripheral sites. The formation of T4 and T3 is tightly regulated by TSH. Both T4 and T3 can feedback on the hypothalamus and pituitary to impact TSH production. The hypothalamus produces thyrotropin-releasing hormone (TRH) which stimulates the pituitary to produce TSH (refer to Fig. 14.1).

Conditions that increase T3 and T4 production result in hyperthyroidism and those that decrease production result in hypothyroidism. Iodine is an essential element of thyroid hormone (i.e., tetra*iodo*thyronine and tri*iodo*thyronine), and consumption of food or supplements rich in iodine content is critical for thyroid hormone production. Deficiency of iodine can result in hypothyroidism and goiter formation (i.e., enlargement of the thyroid gland). In general, primary disorders originate within the thyroid gland, and secondary disorders have an alternate source of pathology, such as the hypothalamus or pituitary gland. Disorders of function (i.e., hypothyroidism or hyperthyroidism) can result in overt or subclinical disease. Abnormal laboratory findings with minimal/no symptoms characterize subclinical disease. Growth of the thyroid gland can be diffuse or nodular (i.e., solitary or multinodular) in nature. Although nodules can be malignant, the majority of thyroid nodules are benign. Differentiated thyroid cancers (i.e., papillary and follicular thyroid cancers) are slow-growing tumors of the follicular epithelium with excellent prognosis. Other cancers of the thyroid include medullary and anaplastic.

Epidemiology

Women can present with a preexisting thyroid condition or develop a new thyroid problem during pregnancy and the postpartum period. An estimated 1–3 % of pregnancies experience gestational hyperthyroidism, 0.1–1 % are complicated by Graves' disease (i.e., autoimmune hyperthyroidism), and another 4.1 % develop postpartum thyroiditis (PPT) [1–3]. The incidence of overt (OH) and subclinical hypothyroid (SCH) in women of childbearing age is 0.3–0.5 % and 2–2.5 %, respectively [4]. These rates are anticipated to be higher with iodine deficiency. In iodine-sufficient regions, autoimmune hypothyroidism is the leading etiology with 50 %

of women with SCH and 80 % of women with OH presenting with detectable antibodies [4]. Although the prevalence of thyroid nodules in pregnancy can range between 3 and 21 % with mild to moderate iodine deficiency, thyroid cancer is relatively uncommon in pregnancy [5]. An estimated 14.4 thyroid cancers per 100,000 pregnancies are reported in the literature with papillary thyroid cancer being the most common type [6].

Normal Physiologic Changes

Fetal thyroid develops by 12 weeks of gestation and is fully functional by 18 weeks. The fetus is dependent on maternal thyroid hormone until 18 weeks and maternal iodine throughout pregnancy. In addition, thyroid physiology in pregnancy changes as a result of maternal factors. As estrogen levels rise in pregnancy, the liver production of thyroid-binding globulin (TBG) increases and the clearance of TBG is reduced. TBG binds thyroid hormone in the circulation and reduces the availability of free or bioavailable thyroid hormone. Further reductions in free thyroid hormone levels are precipitated by placental deiodinase, an enzyme that metabolizes maternal thyroid hormone. As a result, the production of T4 and T3 needs to increase by as much as 50 % during pregnancy [7]. The higher demand for thyroid hormone not only increases iodine requirements in pregnancy but also increases the size of the thyroid gland by as much as 10–20 % [7]. Increased renal clearance and fetal thyroid hormone production also contribute to higher iodine requirements in pregnancy.

B-human chorionic gonadotropins (B-hCG) can weakly bind TSH receptor and stimulate T4 and T3 production. B-hCG levels increase during the first trimester of pregnancy, peak by 8–12 weeks, and then decline. B-hCG stimulates the thyroid to produce thyroid hormone and subsequently lowers TSH levels during the first trimester of pregnancy. As a consequence of the above factors, thyroid function tests can be altered in pregnancy, and trimester-specific normal ranges for TSH and FT4 should be established by each laboratory. If it is not available, utilization of TSH reference range (refer to Table 14.1) and measurement of FT4 by equilibrium dialysis or liquid chromatography/tandem mass spectrometry should be considered. Typically, total T4 and T3 levels are elevated in pregnancy due to elevated TBG, but free levels (i.e., FT4) are within the normal range.

Table 14.1 Trimester-specific normal range [8]

Trimester	TSH (mIU/L)
First	0.1–2.5
Second	0.2 3.0
Third	0.3–3.0

Hyperthyroidism

Effect of Pregnancy on Hyperthyroidism

Gestational hyperthyroidism is the most common cause of thyrotoxicosis in pregnancy. It typically presents in the first trimester with the rise in human chorionic gonadotropin (hCG) and resolves by the second trimester. Approximately 10–20 % of normal women have suppressed TSH in the first trimester [9]. In conditions associated with exaggerated B-hCG production (i.e., molar pregnancy, hyperemesis gravidarum, multiple pregnancies), thyrotoxicosis (i.e., excess T3 and T4 levels) can ensue. Approximately 50 % of women with hyperemesis will have elevated FT4 and suppressed TSH [9].

Additionally, thyroid autoantibody titers can increase during the first trimester of pregnancy and postpartum period. Often antibody titers resolve by the second and third trimester. Under these circumstances, autoimmune-mediated disorders like Graves' disease and PPT can manifest themselves according to the underlying autoantibody status. If thyrotoxicosis is not adequately treated, stress events like labor, infection, and trauma can precipitate a thyroid crisis called thyroid storm. Thyroid storm is an endocrine emergency presenting with mental status changes, hyperthermia, and cardiometabolic decompensation. Mortality rates as high as 50 % are noted in nonpregnant patients.

Effect of Hyperthyroidism on Pregnancy

Uncontrolled overt hyperthyroidism (e.g., Graves' disease) can result in adverse pregnancy outcomes including low birth weight, prematurity, spontaneous abortion, preeclampsia, placental abruption, maternal congestive heart failure, pregnancy-induced hypertension, and thyroid storm. Subclinical hyperthyroidism (i.e., low TSH and normal FT4) has not been shown to cause adverse pregnancy outcomes. T4 can cross the placenta and cause fetal tachycardia, heart failure, and growth retardation. Treatment of thyrotoxicosis with antithyroid drugs needs close monitoring. Since these drugs can cross the placenta, fetal hypothyroidism and goiter formation are a potential complication.

Fetal thyroid is also affected by maternal T4 and thyroid autoantibodies. Excess T4 can interfere with the development of fetal hypothalamic-pituitary-thyroid axis and cause central congenital hypothyroidism in the infant. Patients with a history of Grave's disease (even after treatment with thyroidectomy or radioiodine ablation) can continue to produce thyroid autoantibodies. TSH receptor antibodies (TRAbs) can cross the placenta and precipitate fetal Graves' disease, which can manifest as fetal tachycardia, goiter, heart failure, hydrops, accelerated bone maturation, and growth retardation.

Diagnosis

Symptoms

Symptoms of hyperthyroidism include anxiety, heat intolerance, palpitations, hand tremors, and weight loss or failure of appropriate weight gain during pregnancy (refer to Table 14.2). Diffuse (e.g., Graves' disease) or nodular goiter (e.g., toxic nodule or toxic multinodular goiter) can be palpated on exam. Graves' disease can manifest unique clinical findings including ophthalmopathy (i.e., gritty feeling in eyes, diplopia, exophthalmos (proptosis), periorbital edema, limited eye movement), infiltrative dermopathy (i.e., orange peel-textured papules, pretibial nonpitting edema), and thyroid acropathy (i.e., clubbing, periosteal new bone formation in metacarpal bones). It is often associated with other autoimmune conditions such as vitiligo, alopecia, celiac disease, and pernicious anemia.

Gestational hyperthyroidism is typically asymptomatic. It can be associated with hyperemesis gravidarum and present with severe nausea and vomiting symptoms that can result in a weight loss of more than 5 %, ketonuria, and dehydration. Hydatidiform moles and choriocarcinomas arise from trophoblastic epithelium of the placenta. Patients present with an enlarged uterus, vaginal bleeding, pelvic pain, and hyperthyroidism. Symptoms specific for thyroid conditions that can present in pregnancy are highlighted in Table 14.3.

Table 14.2 Clinical features of hyperthyroid

General	Weight loss or failure of adequate weight gain despite increased appetite, rapid or pressured speech
Eye	Stare, lid lag
Neck	Diffuse or nodular goiter
Cardiovascular	Palpitations, systolic hypertension, atrial fibrillation, heart failure, cardiomyopathy
Respiratory	Shortness of breath, dyspnea on exertion, tracheal obstruction from large goiter
GI	Hyperdefecation, malabsorption, dysphagia due to goiter, abnormal liver function tests
Renal	Urinary frequency
GU	Menstrual disorders, infertility, gynecomastia, erectile dysfunction
Endocrine	Heat intolerance, glucose intolerance
Skin	Increased perspiration, edema, skin moist and warm, thinning of hair, loosening of nails from nail bed (Plummer's nails)
Musculoskeletal	Proximal muscle weakness, myopathy, osteoporosis, hypercalcemia
Neuro	Tremor, hyperreflexia
Hematologic	Anemia
Psych	Anxiety, emotional liability, psychosis, agitation, depression, insomnia

Table 14.3 Differential diagnosis for thyrotoxicosis

Differential diagnosis	Predisposition to a particular trimester	History and exam	TSH	T3 and T4	Ultrasound	Other studies	Treatment in pregnancy
hCG-mediated hyperthyroidism (i.e., gestational hyperthyroidism, hyperemesis gravidarum, trophoblastic disease)	Gestational hyperthyroidism presents in first trimester and resolves by second trimester	Nausea, vomiting, weight loss, dehydration, ketonuria with hyperemesis gravidarum; trophoblastic disease can present with enlarged uterus, vaginal bleeding, and pelvic pain	Low	Normal or high	Evaluate for trophoblastic disease (i.e., molar pregnancy and choriocarcinoma)	Exaggerated hCG levels	IV fluids in severe cases as well as antiemetics; surgical excision recommended for trophoblastic disease
Graves' disease	Activates in first trimester and postpartum period. Typically improves in second and third trimester	Ophthalmopathy, infiltrative dermopathy, thyroid acropathy, features of other autoimmune conditions	Low	Normal or high	Diffuse goiter	TRAb positive; fetal ultrasound if high TRAb titers (>3× normal)	ATDs; thyroidectomy if intolerant to ATDs
Thyroiditis (i.e., postpartum, lymphocytic, subacute thyroiditis)	Up to 12 months postpartum	Painless thyroid exam with postpartum thyroiditis (pain with subacute thyroiditis)	Low	Normal or high	–	–	Self-limiting

Condition		Exam	TSH	T4	Other findings	Additional test	Treatment
Multinodular goiter	–	Nodular goiter on exam	Low	Normal or high	Multiple nodules	–	ATDs; thyroidectomy if intolerant to ATDs
Solitary nodule	–	Single nodule on exam	Low	Normal or high	Single nodule	–	ATDs; thyroidectomy if intolerant to ATDs
Struma ovarii (i.e., ovarian tumor with thyroid tissue)	–	Abdominal mass, pelvic pain, ascites	Low	Normal or high	Ovarian teratoma	–	ATDs followed by surgical removal of ovarian tumor
Exogenous intake of T3 or T4	–	Access to thyroid hormone or diet medications	Low	Normal or high	–	Thyroglobulin suppressed	Stop exogenous intake
Pituitary tumor	–	Headache, visual field defect, signs and symptoms of other pituitary hormone defects	Normal or high	High	–	MRI of pituitary	ATDs; surgical excision in high-risk patients (i.e., vision loss)

Thyroid-stimulating hormone (TSH), tetraiodothyronine (T4), triiodothyronine (T3), thyrotropin receptor antibodies (TRAb), antithyroid drugs (ATDs; propylthiouracil in the first trimester and methimazole in the second/third trimester). Surgery can be considered in patients who are intolerant to ATD or are at high risk for complications

Differential Diagnosis

A range of medical conditions associated with thyrotoxicosis can manifest in pregnancy. Although hCG-mediated hyperthyroidism (i.e., gestational hyperthyroidism, hyperemesis gravidarum, and trophoblastic disease), autoimmune Graves' disease, and postpartum thyroiditis are associated with pregnancy, other etiologies should also be considered (refer to Table 14.3).

Thyroiditis is an inflammatory process that results in the release of stored thyroid hormone and thyrotoxicosis initially (refer to Table 14.2). This results in the suppression of TSH and endogenous thyroid hormone production, which can manifest as hypothyroidism after a few weeks to months (refer to Table 14.4). Eventually, the thyroid restarts thyroid hormone production and euthyroid status is established. This self-limiting condition can last 6–12 months. Other conditions in the differential diagnosis include TSH-secreting pituitary tumor, ovarian teratoma with thyroid tissue (i.e., struma ovarii), exogenous intake of thyroid hormone, toxic nodule, and toxic multinodular goiter.

Diagnostic Evaluation

TSH is the initial test in the evaluation of thyroid disorders. If abnormal, then free T4 (FT4) and total T3 (TT3) should be ordered. Suppressed TSH (<0.1 mIU/L in first trimester) associated with an elevated T4 and/or T3 is diagnostic of primary hyperthyroidism. Secondary hyperthyroidism (i.e., pituitary tumor) manifests with

Table 14.4 Clinical features of hypothyroidism

General	Fatigue, weakness, weight gain, slow speech
HEET	Hoarseness, decreased hearing, enlarged tongue, periorbital edema, loss of lateral eyebrow
Neck	Diffuse or nodular goiter
Cardiovascular	Bradycardia, diastolic hypertension, pericardial effusion
Respiratory	Shortness of breath, dyspnea on exertion, heart failure, pleural effusion, tracheal obstruction from large goiter, sleep apnea
GI	Constipation, decreased taste, dysphagia due to goiter, abnormal liver function tests, ascites
Renal	Decreased GFR
GU	Menstrual disorders, infertility, galactorrhea, decreased libido, erectile dysfunction
Endocrine	Cold intolerance, hypothermia, growth failure, hypercholesterolemia, hyponatremia
Skin	Dry skin, coarse hair, brittle nail, nonpitting edema,
Musculoskeletal	Slow movement, myopathy, myalgia, arthralgia, carpal tunnel
Neuro	Cognitive dysfunction, delayed deep tendon reflex
Hematologic	Anemia, bleeding due to hypocoagulable state,
Psych	Depression, emotional liability, psychosis

elevated TSH and T3 and T4 levels. In subclinical disease, TSH is suppressed, but T3 and T4 levels are normal. Other studies to consider in pregnancy include hCG, TSH receptor antibody (TRAb), thyroglobulin, and ultrasound (refer to Table 14.3).

Multinodular goiter and Graves' disease are noted to have higher T3/T4 ratios and can present with isolated T3 thyrotoxicosis. Thyroiditis is associated with higher T4/T3 ratio. Unlike other etiologies of thyrotoxicosis, thyroglobulin levels are low with exogenous intake of thyroid hormone. Documentation of TRAb confirms Graves' disease. Exaggerated hCG levels (i.e., higher than normal pregnancy) are noted with trophoblastic disease. Ultrasound of the ovary (i.e., struma ovarii), uterus (i.e., trophoblastic disease), and thyroid (i.e., nodular disease) may help narrow the diagnosis and can be used in pregnancy. Radioactive iodine (RAI) uptake and scan is probably the best test to differentiate among the different etiologies of thyrotoxicosis, but the test is contraindicated in pregnancy, since the RAI crosses the placenta and can be taken up by fetal thyroid tissue. It can be considered in the postpartum period with breastfeeding interrupted for several days after the scan. A radioactive iodine scan can localize uptake in the ovary (struma ovarii) or thyroid (i.e., diffuse for Graves' disease, patchy for nodular goiter, single focus for toxic nodule). A low uptake is associated with an inflammatory process (i.e., thyroiditis) or exogenous intake.

Management/Treatment

Antepartum Management

Patients with gestational hyperthyroidism are asymptomatic and generally do not require any treatment. Symptomatic patients with hyperemesis gravidarum often need electrolyte and fluid management especially if weight loss is noted. Treatment for thyrotoxicosis in pregnancy includes antithyroid drugs (i.e., propylthiouracil (PTU) and methimazole (MMI)) and thyroidectomy. Both antithyroid drugs (ATDs) block thyroid hormone synthesis. PTU has an additional benefit of reducing peripheral T4 to T3 conversion. Allergic reaction occurs in 3–5 % of patients on ATDs [10]. Congenital malformations such as dysmorphic facies, esophageal or choanal atresia, and aplasia cutis have been linked to MMI therapy. Although PTU is not known to have any teratogenic effects, the major adverse effect of PTU is liver toxicity leading to death. Therefore, thyrotoxicosis in pregnancy is generally managed with PTU during the first trimester and MMI thereafter. PTU is dosed three times a day (starting 50–300 mg daily) and is generally reserved for patients in the first trimester of pregnancy, individuals intolerant of MMI, and patients at risk for thyroid storm. MMI is typically a once-a-day drug (starting 5–15 mg daily) and is the preferred agent starting in the second trimester of pregnancy and in the postpartum period. The conversion factor for PTU to MMI is approximately 10–1. Once treatment is started, FT4 should be monitored every 2–6 weeks with the goal of maintaining FT4 at or slightly above the normal range.

Beta-blockers such as propranolol (20–40 mg q 6–8 h) can be used for symptomatic treatment. However, they should ideally be stopped once T4 levels are close to the normal range to avoid adverse effects of beta-blockers on the fetus over time (e.g., fetal bradycardia and hypoglycemia). Radioactive iodine treatment is contraindicated in pregnancy. Therefore, thyroidectomy may be considered in patients who cannot take ATDs due to side effects or noncompliance. Ideally, thyroidectomy should occur in the 2nd trimester to minimize risk to fetus. Before undergoing surgery, patients should be treated with a beta-blocker to alleviate symptoms and a short course of potassium iodide (50–100 mg/day) to block thyroid hormone release.

Adverse fetal outcomes in patients with Graves's disease include both neonatal and fetal hypo- and hyperthyroid. These complications are usually a result of high TRAbs (fetal and neonatal hyperthyroidism), high doses of ATDs (fetal or neonatal hypothyroidism), and uncontrolled maternal hyperthyroid (i.e., transient central hypothyroidism). Therefore, monitoring FT4 levels throughout pregnancy is imperative. Because all ATDs cross the placenta, the goal is to use the lowest effective dose possible and to avoid overtreatment which can result in fetal hypothyroidism. Most patients with Graves' disease have worsening symptoms in the first trimester, followed by improvement in the second and third trimesters. Some patients (20–30 %) may be able to stop ATDs in the second and third trimesters [11].

In women with a history of Graves' disease, the prevalence of fetal and neonatal hyperthyroidism ranges between 1 and 5 % and can lead to neonatal and fetal mortality if not addressed appropriately [12]. Therefore, TRAb should be measured at 20–24 weeks gestation in all patients with a history of Graves' disease. Serial fetal ultrasound and consultation with a maternal fetal medicine specialist is recommended if uncontrolled hyperthyroidism and/or high TRAb titers (i.e., more than 3 times normal) are noted. ATDs are generally continued until delivery in patients with high TRAbs. If fetal goiter is detected in a Graves' disease patient on antithyroid drugs, cordocentesis can be considered to determine the etiology. It can differentiate between drug-induced fetal hypothyroidism and TRAb-mediated fetal Graves' disease.

Peripartum Management

Thyroid storm is a rare but serious emergency. This usually occurs in patients with uncontrolled hyperthyroidism and may be precipitated by labor. Aggressive management including ICU admission, steroids, beta-blockers, ATD, and iodine might be necessary. PTU is generally the preferred agent in thyroid storm due to its additional benefit of blocking peripheral T4 to T3 conversion.

Prevention

Preconception counseling for women with thyrotoxicosis is of the utmost importance. Pregnancy should be avoided until a euthyroid state is established. Options for the treatment of prepregnancy include radioactive iodine ablation, antithyroid drugs, or thyroidectomy. If a patient has high TRAb titers and is planning pregnancy, radioiodine (RAI) therapy should be avoided. RAI therapy can further increase antibody titers. Antibodies can cross the placenta and impact fetal thyroid status. Therefore, TRAb should be measured in all patients in the third trimester with a history of Graves's disease irrespective of treatment modality employed.

In general, pregnancy should be avoided for 12 months after radioiodine therapy. Although radioiodine has no fetal effects in the first trimester, it can cross the placenta and destroy fetal thyroid after 12 weeks gestation. Therefore, RAI is contraindicated in pregnancy. The effect of radioiodine given 3 month prior to pregnancy is minimal and the real concern is the fetal effects of maternal hypothyroidism. Therefore, thyroid hormone replacement should target TSH below 2.5 mIU/L prior to pregnancy. Surgery is a reasonable option for patients who are unable to wait 12 months to achieve euthyroid status. ATDs can also be considered, but risk-benefit should always be discussed with patients. MMI can be prescribed prepregnancy to achieve remission, but it must be switched to PTU in the first trimester of pregnancy.

Postpartum

Many patients with Graves' disease will have exacerbation of their symptoms in the immediate postpartum period. ATD doses usually need to be increased postpartum. Methimazole is now the recommended ATD postpartum. A dose of 20–30 mg/day is safe for lactating mothers. PTU (300 mg/d) is the second-line agent. Radioactive iodine therapy can be considered once breastfeeding is complete. It is the definitive treatment for toxic nodule, toxic multinodular goiter, and even Graves' disease.

Postpartum thyroiditis (PPT) is a more common cause of thyrotoxicosis than Graves' disease postpartum. This period resolves without intervention. Patients will often become hypothyroid before returning to a euthyroid state by 3–12 months. However, 10–20 % of patients remain permanently hypothyroid [13]. Women with thyroid antibodies (i.e., thyroglobulin (Tg Ab) and thyroid peroxidase (TPO Ab) antibody) have a much higher likelihood of developing PPT. Other conditions associated with increased prevalence of PPT include type 1 DM, systemic lupus erythematosus, Graves' disease, viral hepatitis, and other autoimmune conditions. Patients are usually more symptomatic during the hypothyroid phase but may have mild symptoms during the thyrotoxic phase as well. Data from some studies indicate a possible association between PPT and postpartum depression. Therefore, TSH, FT4, and TPO Abs should be checked in women with postpartum depression. Thyroid hormone replacement is recommended for symptomatic patients who are in the hypothyroid phase especially if they are attempting pregnancy or have postpartum depression. Beta-blockers (i.e., propranolol) can be considered for symptomatic thyrotoxicosis. Women with PPT are at risk of developing permanent hypothyroidism; therefore, TSH should be monitored every two months until one year postpartum and then yearly thereafter. Risk factors for permanent hypothyroidism include high TPO Ab titers, maternal age, multiparity, miscarriage, and severity of hypothyroidism.

Hypothyroidism

Effect of Pregnancy of Hypothyroidism

Iodine requirements increase in pregnancy as a result of maternal urinary excretion, increased maternal thyroid hormone production, and fetal demand. During pregnancy, higher iodine requirements are necessary to maintain normal thyroid status. If deficient, maternal thyroid preferentially produces T3 instead of T4. T3 is not accessible to the fetus and, therefore, fetal development is impaired. Maternal and fetal hypothyroidism as well as goiter formation are noted with iodine deficiency.

Thyroid hormone levels increase in pregnancy as a result of TBG and placental deiodinase. TSH and hCG stimulate the thyroid to produce the required hormone. However, patients with hypothyroidism prepregnancy are often not able to increase the production of thyroid hormone to keep up with metabolic demand of pregnancy. Levothyroxine (LT4) dose as well as iodine supplementation often needs to increase during pregnancy.

Effect of Hypothyroidism on Pregnancy

Adverse effects of hypothyroid on pregnancy are reported in untreated overt hypothyroidism (OH). These include low birth weight, gestational hypertension, premature birth, and miscarriage. One study reported a 60 % risk of fetal loss with untreated OH [14]. OH may also negatively affect fetal neurologic development because T4 is involved in neuronal migration and neurogenesis. Fetal brain development occurs during 8–16 weeks gestation, during which time the fetus still depends on maternal thyroid function. Studies have shown delayed cognitive development as well as lower IQ scores in children born to mothers with inadequately treated hypothyroidism. OH which is adequately treated, however, has not been associated with any pregnancy complications. Data are inconclusive regarding whether subclinical hypothyroid (SCH) or isolated hypothyroxinemia adversely affects pregnancy outcomes or fetal development. Some studies have shown increased fetal loss among women with SCH and decreased IQ scores have been reported in children born to women with isolated hypothyroxinemia. More research is needed to elucidate the effect of SCH and isolated hypothyroxinemia.

Iodine deficiency can result in fetal and maternal hypothyroidism. Severe iodine deficiency results in miscarriages, still birth, and infant mortality. If a fetus is exposed to inadequate thyroid hormone throughout gestation, then the fetus is at risk for cretinism. Cretinism is characterized by neurodevelopmental delay, mental retardation, deafness, stunted growth, motor rigidity, and neonatal mortality. Severe iodine deficiency is the most prevalent cause of cretinism and mental retardation globally. Iodine supplementation programs can improve clinical outcomes and mortality.

Women with thyroid autoantibodies (TAb) are at risk for developing hypothyroidism during pregnancy and the postpartum period. Women with TAb (i.e., TPOAb or TgAb) with and without hypothyroidism are at increased risk for infertility, miscarriages, premature delivery, and prenatal death. Impaired motor and cognitive development in the fetus are also noted with high TAb titers. Treatment of Graves' disease with surgery or radioablation can result in hypothyroidism. These patients continue to produce antibodies (i.e., TRAb) that can cross the placenta and precipitate fetal Graves' disease.

Diagnosis

Symptoms

Symptoms of hypothyroidism are often nonspecific and difficult to distinguish from normal pregnancy (refer to Table 14.4). Symptoms include fatigue, weight gain, constipation, cold intolerance, and in severe cases myxedema coma. Myxedema is characterized by severe hypothyroidism associated with hypothermia, mental status change, and cardiopulmonary decompensation. Mortality rates can be as high as 50 %. Autoimmune conditions like vitiligo and alopecia are often associated with Hashimoto's hypothyroidism.

Differential Diagnosis

Although iodine deficiency is the most common etiology of hypothyroidism worldwide, autoimmune hypothyroidism is the most common etiology within the United States. Use of certain medications (e.g., lithium, amiodarone, PTU, and MMI), thyroidectomy, radioiodine therapy, thyroiditis, and secondary hypothyroidism are also in the differential diagnosis (refer to Table 14.5). TPO antibodies are detected in 50 % of pregnant women with SH and 80 % OH.

Diagnostic Evaluation

Primary hypothyroidism is defined by an elevated TSH above the pregnancy-specific normal range (>2.5–3.0 mIL/L). Overt hypothyroidism (OH) is diagnosed when TSH levels are above 10 mIU/L or when TSH is elevated with low FT4 levels. If TSH is elevated (2.5–10 mIU/L) and FT4 levels are normal, then patients are diagnosed with subclinical hypothyroid (SCH). If the TSH is normal, but free T4 decreased, then isolated hypothyroxinemia is diagnosed. In secondary hypothyroidism (i.e., pituitary or hypothalamic process), FT4 is also low with normal or low TSH levels.

Table 14.5 Differential diagnosis for hypothyroidism

Differential diagnosis	Pregnancy considerations	History	TSH	FT4	Other studies	Treatment in pregnancy	Monitor	Goal
Hashimoto's hypothyroidism	Can present in the first trimester and progress during pregnancy. Higher risk in the postpartum period as well	Other autoimmune conditions	High	Normal or low	US with goiter	LT4 replacement	TSH	Trimester-specific norms
Thyroiditis (i.e., postpartum, lymphocytic, silent or subacute thyroiditis)	Can present up to 12 mo postpartum	Symptoms of hyperthyroidism followed by hypothyroid. Painless thyroid exam with postpartum thyroiditis (pain with subacute thyroiditis)	High	Normal or low	–	LT4 replacement if trying to become pregnant, postpartum depression or other symptoms	TSH	Self-limited
Iodine deficiency	Higher iodine requirements in pregnancy and breastfeeding	Living in endemic regions or limited nutritional status	High	Normal or low	US with goiter	LT4 replacement and iodine replacement	TSH/FT4	Trimester-specific norms
After radioactive iodine ablation therapy or thyroidectomy	If history of Graves' disease, then TRAb needs to be checked 20–24 weeks	Other autoimmune disorders	High	Normal or low	–	LT4 replacement	TSH	Trimester-specific norms
Secondary hypothyroidism	–	Other pituitary disorders	Normal or low	Low	MRI of pituitary	LT4 replacement	FT4	FT4 in the upper end of normal

Thyroid receptor antibody (TRAb), levothyroxine (LT4), thyroid-stimulating hormone (TSH), free thyroxine (FT4), ultrasound (US)

14 Thyroid Disease

Both TSH and FT4 are recommended in pregnancy to identify abnormalities in thyroid function tests (TFTs) due to iodine deficiency. As discussed, iodine deficiency can shunt thyroid hormone production toward T3 and not T4. TSH in these circumstances can be normal but FT4 will be low.

Management/Treatment

Antepartum Management

Women with OH should always be treated during pregnancy. Recommended treatment is oral LT4. Other treatments, such as T3 or desiccated thyroid, should not be used. This is largely because fetal development requires LT4. Clinicians should aim to keep free T4 within pregnancy-specific reference range. The dose of LT4 usually needs to be increased in the first trimester due to increased metabolic requirements. Typically, a 25 % increase in dose is recommended as soon as pregnancy is confirmed, and the dose increases by as much as 50 % by the second trimester. It is recommended that TSH be checked in patients on LT4 every four weeks during the first half of pregnancy and once between 26 and 32 weeks.

There is lack of strong evidence to recommend for or against treating women with SCH who are TAb negative. There are some studies which have shown that women with SCH and TPO positive who are treated with levothyroxine during pregnancy have better outcomes than those who are not treated. Therefore, women who have SCH and are TPOAb + should be treated with levothyroxine during pregnancy. Patients with TAb but normal TFTs do not require LT4. However, these patients are at risk of developing hypothyroidism by the time of delivery. Patients with SCH or TAb who are not treated should have their TSH and FT4 checked every 4 weeks to evaluate for development of OH until 20 weeks of gestation and then once between 26 and 32 weeks. They will also need close follow-up after delivery as they have an increased likelihood of developing OH at some point. There are no data to support treatment of isolated hypothyroxinemia at this time.

Prenatal vitamins with iodine are recommended during pregnancy. These vitamins should be taken at least 2 h after LT4 so that absorption of LT4 is not impacted by iron or calcium found in the vitamin. Food rich in iodine content (i.e., seafood, egg, meat, poultry, milk, bread) and iodinated salts are recommended in pregnancy. In general, 150 mcg/day of iodine is recommended in women of reproductive years, and this goal increases to 250 mcg/day in pregnancy and breastfeeding.

Prevention

Universal screening of pregnant women for hypothyroid has been very controversial. Most guidelines suggest obtaining TSH early in pregnancy for women who are at higher risk of developing hypothyroidism (refer to Table 14.6).

Table 14.6 Risk factors for hypothyroidism

History of thyroid dysfunction (i.e., Graves' disease) or prior thyroid surgery
Age >30
Symptoms of thyroid dysfunction or goiter
TPOAb positive
Type 1 DM and other autoimmune disorders
History of miscarriage or preterm birth
History of head or neck radiation
Family history of thyroid dysfunction
Morbid obesity (BMI > 40)
Use of amiodarone, lithium, or recent exposure to iodinated contrast
Infertility
Living in area of iodine deficiency

Preconception

Women who are hypothyroid on LT4 and planning pregnancy should increase their dose of LT4 by 25–30 % after the first missed menstrual cycle. One option is to increase the number of doses weekly from 7 to 9. Providers should aim for a goal of a TSH <2.5 in hypothyroid women who are planning pregnancy. TAb (i.e., TPO Ab or TgAb) has been associated with pregnancy loss. Even though one study demonstrated decreased rate of miscarriages with LT4 replacement (3.5 % vs. 13.8 %), currently there is insufficient evidence to screen or treat euthyroid women with positive TAb [15]. However, these women are at risk for hypothyroidism during pregnancy and PPT. TFT should be monitored and LT4 started based on abnormal results.

Postpartum

Most patients can return to their dose of LT4 prepregnancy after delivery. However, if weight gain is significant, a higher dose is recommended until weight returns back to baseline. TSH should be checked 6 weeks after delivery to ensure results are within normal range. Women with TAb with residual thyroid function are at risk for PPT.

Thyroid Nodule and Thyroid Cancer

Effect of Pregnancy on Thyroid Nodules and Cancer

Depletion of maternal iodine, increased thyroid hormone requirement, and stimulatory effect of B-hCG can precipitate nodule formation and growth during pregnancy. Prevalence increases with increasing maternal age, parity, and iodine deficiency.

Although most nodules are benign, thyroid cancers can present in pregnancy. Papillary thyroid cancers are the most common followed by follicular. Overall, the outcomes of women with differentiated thyroid cancer (i.e., papillary and follicular) during pregnancy seem to be similar to those of nonpregnant patients. Pregnancy may result in progression of differentiated thyroid cancer (DTC) if present at time of pregnancy. However, women previously treated for DTC who are disease free at the time of pregnancy have not been shown to have increased recurrence rates. It is unknown how pregnancy affects outcomes of women with other types of cancer such as medullary.

Diagnosis

Symptoms

Most patients with thyroid nodules are asymptomatic. However, some patients can present with symptoms of thyrotoxicosis (see Section "Hyperthyroid"). Compressive symptoms (i.e., problems swallowing or breathing) can occur with large nodules. Malignancy needs to be considered if patients present with symptoms of rapid growth, cough, or hoarseness. Lymph nodes identified on neck exam should also raise the suspicion of malignancy.

Differential Diagnosis

Thyroid nodules can be functional or nonfunctional. Functional nodules are typically benign in nature and patients present with symptoms of thyrotoxicosis. Nonfunctional thyroid nodules are either malignant or benign. Papillary, follicular, and anaplastic cancers are derived from the follicular epithelium. DTC are generally slow-growing tumors with excellent prognosis. Anaplastic tumors are aggressive, undifferentiated thyroid cancers with a disease-specific mortality of 100 %. Medullary thyroid cancers (MTC) are tumor of the parafollicular or C cells of the thyroid gland. The production of calcitonin is a characteristic feature and correlates with tumor burden. Although most are sporadic, MTC are associated with multiple endocrine neoplasia type 2 (MEN2) syndrome.

Diagnostic Evaluation

The history should focus on risk factors for thyroid malignancy including history of radiation to the head or neck, family history of thyroid cancer, and history of MEN syndromes. Physical exam should include careful palpation of nodule and neck for enlarged lymph nodes. Thyroid function tests including TSH and free T4 should be obtained. Ultrasound is the best diagnostic test to evaluate thyroid nodules. If the nodule is <10 mm or has benign features on ultrasound, usually fine-needle

Table 14.7 Ultrasound nodule characteristics worrisome for thyroid cancer

Hypoechoic pattern
Irregular margins
Nodules that are taller than they are wide
Microcalcifications
Incomplete halo
Central vascularity

aspiration can be delayed until after pregnancy. If malignancy is suspected, fine-needle aspiration should be performed during pregnancy. Certain nodule characteristics (refer to Table 14.7), extracapsular growth, and lymph node involvement are suspicious of malignancy. Calcitonin should be measured in patients with history of medullary thyroid cancer or MEN-2. Fine-needle aspiration (FNA) is a safe procedure during pregnancy in all trimesters. No adverse effects to fetus have been reported. Radioiodine imaging and uptake scanning is unsafe in pregnancy and should not be performed.

Management/Treatment

Antepartum Management

If the nodule is found to be toxic, then antithyroid drugs should be initiated in pregnancy until a definitive treatment with radioactive iodine can be considered postpartum (see Section "Hyperthyroid" for management). For nodules over 1 cm with worrisome US characteristics, FNA should be performed in pregnancy. Nodules that are benign or "suspicious" by FNA usually do not need surgery during pregnancy. However, if these nodules cause compressive symptoms or if they begin to grow rapidly, surgery is recommended. LT4 therapy to suppress nodule growth is not recommended during pregnancy. Most thyroid nodules that appear "suspicious" for thyroid cancer on FNA are benign. Only 30 % of these "suspicious" lesions are malignant.

Surgery is the mainstay of treatment for differentiated thyroid cancer (DTC). If a DTC is diagnosed in the first trimester, it should be monitored with ultrasound and serum thyroglobulin every trimester. If cancer increases in size significantly by 24 weeks or if metastasis occurs, surgery is recommended. If the nodule is stable, thyroidectomy should be delayed until after pregnancy. For most patients with DTC diagnosed in the second half of pregnancy, surgery is delayed until delivery. If surgery is performed during pregnancy, it should be performed in the second trimester (before 22 weeks) to minimize risk to mother and fetus. Patients should be monitored and treated for postoperative hypothyroidism and parathyroid abnormalities. If the decision is made to delay surgery until after delivery, patients should be treated with LT4. In patients with a current and previous history of DTC, TSH goals in pregnancy are based on cancer risk (i.e., TSH <0.1 mU/L persistent cancer, 0.3–1.5 mU/L low-risk tumors). It is important to keep in mind that LT4

14 Thyroid Disease

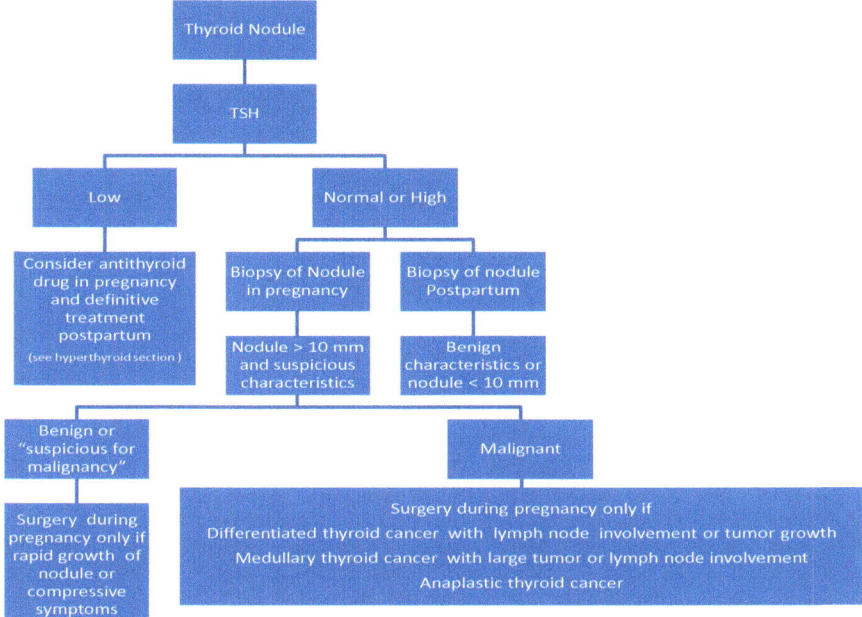

Fig. 14.2 TSH recommendations

dose requirements increase in pregnancy and, therefore, TSH should be monitored every 4 weeks until 20 weeks and once between 26 and 32 weeks gestation. Although medullary thyroid cancer and anaplastic tumors are rare, surgery is often recommended in pregnancy due to the aggressive nature of these tumor types (refer to Fig. 14.2).

Prevention

Patients with thyroid nodules identified prior to pregnancy should undergo ultrasound evaluation followed by biopsy if necessary. Malignant lesions often require thyroidectomy. RAI is generally reserved for high-risk patients with DTC. Pregnancy should be avoided for 6–12 months post-RAI treatment.

Postpartum

After delivery, women with thyroid cancer and thyroid nodules should have their treatment plans carried through according to the ATA guidelines [16]. Delaying definitive treatment until the postpartum period generally does not alter prognosis for most patients with low-risk DTC.

References

1. Goodwin TM, Montoro M, Mestman JH. Transient hyperthyroidism and hyperemesis gravidarum: clinical aspects. Am J Obstet Gynecol. 1992;167:648–52.
2. Patil-Sisodia K, Mestman JH. Graves hyperthyroidism and pregnancy: a clinical update. Endocr Pract. 2010;16:118–29.
3. Stagnaro-Green A. Postpartum thyroiditis. Best Pract Res Clin Endocrinol Metab. 2004;18:303–16.
4. Allan WC, Haddow JE, Palomaki GE, Williams JR, Mitchell ML, Hermos RJ, Faix JD, Klein RZ. Maternal thyroid deficiency and pregnancy complications: implications for population screening. J Med Screen. 2000;7:127–30.
5. Struve CW, Haupt S, Ohlen S. Influence of frequency of previous pregnancies on the prevalence of thyroid nodules in women without clinical evidence of thyroid disease. Thyroid. 1993;3:7–9.
6. Smith LH, Danielsen B, Allen ME, Cress R. Cancer associated with obstetric delivery: results of linkage with the California cancer registry. Am J Obstet Gynecol. 2003;189:1128–35.
7. Keely E, Barbour L. Thyroid Disorders. In: Rosene-Montella K, Keely E, Barbour LA, Lee R, editors. Medical care of the pregnant patient. Philadelphia: Sheridan Press; 2008. p. 253–70.
8. Stagnaro-Green A, et al. Guidelines of the American thyroid association for the diagnosis and management of thyroid disease during pregnancy and postpartum. Thyroid. 2011;21:1081.
9. Goodwin TM, Hershman JM. Hyperthyroidism due to inappropriate production of human chorionic gonadotropin. Clin Obstet Gynecol. 1997;40:32–44.
10. Mandel SJ, Cooper DS. The use of antithyroid drugs in pregnancy and lactation. J Clin Endocrinol Metab. 2001;86:2354–9.
11. Hamburger JI. Diagnosis and management of Graves' disease in pregnancy. Thyroid. 1992;2:219–24.
12. Zimmerman D. Fetal and neonatal hyperthyroidism. Thyroid. 1999;9:727–33.
13. Stagnaro-Green A. Clinical review 152: postpartum thyroiditis. J Clin Endocrinol Metab. 2002;87:4042–7.
14. Abalovich M, Gutierrez S, Alcaraz G, Maccallini G, Garcia A, Levalle O. Overt and subclinical hypothyroidism complicating pregnancy. Thyroid. 2002;12:63–8.
15. Negro R, Formoso G, Mangieri T, Pezzarossa A, Dazzi D, Hassan H. Levothyroxine treatment in euthyroid pregnant women with autoimmune thyroid disease: effects on obstetrical complications. J Clin Endocrinol Metab. 2006;91:2587–91.
16. Cooper DS, Doherty GM, Haugen BR, et al. Revised American thyroid association management guidelines for patients with thyroid nodules and differentiated thyroid cancer. The American thyroid association (ATA) guidelines taskforce on thyroid nodules and differentiated thyroid cancer. Thyroid. 2009;19(11):1167–281.

Index

A
Acquired disorders, 164
Acute asthma exacerbations, 238–239, 242, 243
Acute coronary syndrome, 5
Acute fatty liver of pregnancy (AFLP)
 clinical presentation, 121
 description, 118
 and FATMO, 120
 LCHAD, 119
 management, 121–122
 pathogenesis, 118–119
Acute hepatitis (AH), 106–107, 201
Acute liver failure (ALF), 106, 201
Acute renal failure, 265–266
AED. *See* Antiepileptic drug (AED)
Airway management
 hemodynamic monitoring, 25–26
 invasive monitoring, 26–27
 noninvasive monitoring, 26
 obesity, 24
 preeclampsia and eclampsia, 24–25
 in pregnancy, 23–24
 preoperative evaluation, 25
 regional anesthesia, 24
ALF. *See* Acute liver failure (ALF)
American Society of Hematology (ASH), 155
5-Aminosalicylates (5-ASAs), 100
Anemia
 chronic hemolytic, 111, 154
 iron deficiency, 151
 macrocytic, 151
 in pregnancy, 150
 sickle cell disease, 153
Angiotensin II receptor blockers (ARBs), 63, 183, 269, 270

Antidepressant
 benzodiazepines, 43
 birth weight, 40
 child development, 42–43
 congenital malformations, 41
 hypnotic benzodiazepine receptor agonists, 43
 medications, anxiety/insomnia, 43
 miscarriage, 40
 mood disorders, 39
 postnatal adaptation syndrome, 42
 PPHN, 41–42
 preterm birth, 40
Antiepileptic drug (AED)
 antepartum management, 228
 antipsychotic medications, 56–57
 breastfeeding, 229
 carbamazepine, 55–56
 folic acid supplementation, 229
 hemorrhagic complications, 229
 idiopathic epilepsy, 227
 lamotrigine, 56
 lithium, 54–55
 perinatal woman, 57
 pregnancy, 228–229
 seizures, 224
 teratogenic effect, 226
 valproate, 55
Antihistamines and anticholinergics, 96
Antiphospholipid antibody syndrome (APS), 135, 136
Antipsychotic
 breast-feeding, 57
 FGAs, 56
 SGAs, 57

Antiretrovirals therapy
  perinatal HIV prevention, 199
  postpartum period, 201
  pregnant woman, 200
  safety data, 209, 210
Antithrombin III deficiency, 135, 137, 143
APS. *See* Antiphospholipid antibody syndrome (APS)
ARBs. *See* Angiotensin II receptor blockers (ARBs)
Arrhythmias, 5
ASH. *See* American Society of Hematology (ASH)
Asthma
  African American and Hispanic women, 237
  babies, congenital anomalies, 237
  exacerbations, 237
  principles and management
    acute asthma exacerbations, 242, 243
    allergic rhinitis, 239–240
    care components, 238
    chronic asthma, 238
    classification, 239, 241
    ergotamine and ergot derivatives, 241
    GERD, 240–241
    medications uses, 239, 240
    multi-institutional prospective study, 239
    randomized controlled trial, 239
    stress dosing, 241
  randomized controlled trial, 237
  respiratory physiological changes, 236
  stress dosing, steroids, 241
Autoimmune hepatitis (AIH), 112–113
Azathioprine, 101

B

Bacterial pneumonia. *See also* Pneumonia
  aspiration risk and heartburn, 244
  categories, 242
  diagnosis, 244–245
  gingival hyperplasia, 244
  intrauterine infection, 244
  microbiology and epidemiology, 242–244
  obstetric complication, 244
BCSH. *See* The British Committee for Standards in Haematology (BCSH)
Behcet's disease (BD)
  clinical manifestations
    annual incidence, flares per patient, 299
    diagnosis, 298
    ISG criteria, 298–299
    morbidity and mortality, 296
    oral and genital ulcerations, 296, 299
    progesterone, 299
    renal disease and peripheral nervous system, 297–298
  epidemiology, 296
  impact, disease, 299–300
  postpartum management
    abatacept, 309
    anakinra, 309
    autoimmune diseases, 303
    azathioprine (AZA), 307
    biologic DMARDs, 308
    calcineurin inhibitors, 307
    corticosteroids, 307–308
    cyclophosphamide (CYC), 305
    FDA categorization, medications, 302, 303
    hydroxychloroquine (HCQ), 306
    immune-modulating medications, 302
    leflunomide, 304–305
    methotrexate (MTX), 304
    mycophenolate mofetil (MMF), 305
    rheumatologic diseases, 302
    rituximab, 310
    sulfasalazine (SSZ), 306–307
    tocilizumab, 309
    tumor necrosis factor inhibitors (TNFIs), 308–309
  preconception counseling, 302
  treatment, 300–302
Benzodiazepines, 43
Beta agonists
  asthma, 240
  dobutamine, 28
  dopamine, 28
  epinephrine, 28
B-hCG. *See* B-human chorionic gonadotropins (B-hCG)
B-human chorionic gonadotropins (B-hCG), 323, 324, 336
Bipolar disorder
  component, 50
  definition and prevalence, 51
  diagnosis, 51
  effect of pregnancy, 51
  postpartum period, 52–54
  on pregnancy, 52
  type I, 51
  type II, 51
Bleeding disorders, 159–161
Breastfeeding
  ACE inhibitors and ARBs, 269, 270
  anti-TNF agent, 103

Index

and delivery, 208
and diabetes medication, 74, 75
lactating patients, 86
and renal transplant medications, 269, 270
sulfasalazine and mesalamine, 100
thalidomide, 102
The British Committee for Standards in Haematology (BCSH), 155, 158

C
Cardiac disease
 antepartum management, 14–15
 CARPREG study, 4
 congenital and acquired, 4
 diagnostic evaluation, 12
 differential diagnosis, 12
 epidemiology, 9
 fetal considerations, 13–14
 management/treatment, 13
 NYHA, 13
 peripartum management, 15–16
 physiologic changes, 10
 postpartum recommendations, 16
 pregnancy, 10–11
 pregnant patient, 3
 prevention, 16
 risk classification, 4
 risks and management, 5–9
 signs and symptoms, 12
Cardiomyopathy, 8, 11, 189
Cardiovascular risks
 gestational hypertension or preeclampsia, 190
 hypertension, 180
Cerebral vein thrombosis (CVT), 138, 141, 143
CH. See Cluster headache (CH)
Chicken pox. See Varicella pneumonia
Chronic asthma, 238
Chronic hypertension
 diagnosis
  components, 180
  evaluation, secondary causes, 180, 181
  screening, 180, 181
 management
  ACE inhibitor, 183
  antihypertensive therapy, 182
  B-blockers, 183
  hydralazine, 183
  hydrochlorothiazide, 183
  labetalol, 182, 183
  methyldopa, 182, 183
  nifedipine, 183

 risk in pregnancy, 179–180
Chronic renal disease (CKD)
 complications risk, 266
 ESRD, 266
 follow-up, fetal growth, 267–268
 obstetric complications, 267
 prepregnancy creatinine and pregnancy outcome, 267
 superimposed preeclampsia, 267
 urinary tract infection, 267
 worsening hypertension, 266–267
CKD. See Chronic renal disease (CKD)
Cluster headache (CH), 220, 221
Coagulation, 163
Congenital heart disease, 4
Congenital varicella syndrome (CVS), 247–248
Corticosteroids, 100–101
CVS. See Congenital varicella syndrome (CVS)
CVT. See Cerebral vein thrombosis (CVT)

D
dcSSc. See Diffuse cutaneous systemic sclerosis (DcSSc)
Deep vein thrombosis (DVT), 138–141
Depression
 definition and prevalence, 35
 DSM-5 diagnostic criteria, 35, 36
 EPDS, 35, 37
 MDD (see Major depressive disorder (MDD))
 non-pharmacological treatment, 44–45
 PHQ, 36, 38
 postpartum blues, 45
 PPD (see Postpartum depression (PPD))
 screening measurement, 35
Diabetes
 calcium channel blockers, 63
 contraception, 75–76
 diabetic gastropathy, 64
 DKA, 64
 epidemiology, 62
 fetal and perinatal risks, 64–66
 GDM, 66
 hyperglycemia treatment, 67–68
 IHD, 64
 internist and obstetric offices
  fetal growth assessment, 71
  obstetrical prenatal care, 68
  preconception assessment, 69–70
  screening, 69, 70
 labor and delivery, 71–73

Diabetes (cont.)
  microvascular and macrovascular disease, 63
  pathobiology, 62
  postpartum, 74–75
Diabetes mellitus (DM)
  and GDM, 62
  labor and postpartum, 71–73
  microvascular and macrovascular disease, 63
Diabetic ketoacidosis (DKA), 64
Dialysis, 268
DIC. See Disseminated intravascular dissemination (DIC)
Diffuse cutaneous systemic sclerosis (DcSSc), 283–284, 294
Disseminated intravascular dissemination (DIC)
  acute fatty liver, 158
  bleeding disorders, 159, 160
  diagnosis, 156
  thrombocytopenia, 158
DM. See Diabetes mellitus (DM)
Dobutamine, 28
Dopamine, 28
DVT. See Deep vein thrombosis (DVT)

E
Edinburgh Postnatal Depression Scale (EPDS), 35, 37
Electroencephalogram (EEG), 227, 228
Endoscopic retrograde cholangiopancreatography (ERCP), 86
End-stage renal disease (ESRD), 266, 267

F
Factor V Leiden, 166, 168
Factor V Leiden mutation (FVL), 135, 137, 143
Factor XI deficiency, 163
Fatty acid transport and mitochondrial oxidation (FATMO), 120
Fetal and perinatal risks
  hyperglycemia, 64
  maternal hyperglycemia, 65
  obstetrical caregivers, 66
  Pederson hypothesis, 65
  pregnancy, 65
Fetal morbidity, 184, 185, 264, 286
Fetal mortality, 16, 122, 157, 202
First generation antipsychotics (FGAs), 56
FVL. See Factor V Leiden mutation (FVL)

G
Gallstone disease, 114
Gastroesophageal reflux disease (GERD), 239–241
  diagnosis, 90
  heartburn, 90
  lifestyle modification and diet, 91
  pharmacological intervention, 91
Gastrointestinal disease
  abdominal pain, pregnancy, 88–89
  chronic liver disease, 107–124
  diagnosis and management, 88
  endoscopy
    fetus, 86
    indications, 86
    recommendations, American Society, 86, 87
  GERD (see Gastroesophageal Reflux Disease (GERD))
  IBD, 83, 98–104
  imaging and radiation, 87–88
  IOM, 82, 83
  laboratory values, pregnancy, 81, 82
  LFTs, 105–107
  nutrition requirements
    alcohol and fish, 85
    BMI, 83
    calcium, 85
    folic acid, 84
    iron deficiency, 83–84
    omega-3 polyunsaturated fatty acid, 84–85
    omega-6 polyunsaturated fatty acid, 84
    vitamin D, 84
  NVP and HG, 91–98
  pregnancy, maternal gastrointestinal functions, 81, 82
  protein synthesis, 81
GDM. See Gestational diabetes (GDM)
GERD. See Gastroesophageal reflux disease (GERD)
Gestational diabetes (GDM)
  cardiovascular disease, 74
  and hypertension, 101
  postpartum, 74
  and pregestational diabetic patients, 68
  risk factors, 66
Gestational hypertension, 178, 179, 190
Gestational thrombocytopenia, 155
GFR. See Glomerular filtration rate (GFR)
Glomerular filtration rate (GFR), 54, 262–263
Goiter
  and Graves' disease, 329
  and hypothyroidism, 322

Index   345

Graves disease
    multinodular goiter, 329
    ophthalmopathy, 325
    placenta and precipitate fetal, 324
    and postpartum thyroiditis, 328
    and PPT, 324
    surgery/radioablation, 333

H
HBV. *See* Hepatitis B virus (HBV)
HCV. *See* Hepatitis C virus (HCV)
Headaches
    debilitation, 230
    definition, 220
    diagnosis and management, 222–223
    epidemiology, 220
    pathobiology, 221–222
HELLP. *See* Hemolysis, elevated liver enzymes, low platelets (HELLP)
Hematological malignancies, 168–169
Hemoglobinopathies
    sickle cell disease, 152–154
    thalassemias, 154
Hemolysis, elevated liver enzymes, low platelets (HELLP)
    acute renal insufficiency/failure, 266
    bleeding disorders, 160
    complications, 123–124
    description, 122
    diagnosis, 156
    hypertensive disorders, 178
    LCHAD mutations, 119
    maternal and fetal mortality, 157
    maternal complication, 120
    steroids, 124
    symptoms, women, 123
    thrombocytopenia, 123
    treatment, 158
Hemolysis, elevated liver enzymes, low platelet (HELLP) syndrome, 122–124
Hepatitis, 93
Hepatitis B virus (HBV)
    counseling, 204
    epidemiology
        DNA virus, 202
        Hepadnavirus family, 202
        2011 HHS action plan, 203
        immunoprophylaxis, 203
        infection, 203
        United States, 203
    liver disease
        antiviral therapy, 208–209
        delivery and breastfeeding, 208
        HBsAg-positive patient, 205–207
        hepatitis B core antibody (HBcAb), 206
        immunization failure, 207–208
        safety data, antiviral therapy, 209–210
        serological markers, 206
        vertical transmission, 207
    pregnancy outcomes, 205
    screening and diagnosis, 204
Hepatitis C virus (HCV)
    autoimmune diseases, 210
    chronic infection, 210
    description, 210
    fetal/maternal complications, 211
    Filoviridae family, 210
    insulin resistance, 210
    liver function tests, 211
    management, 212
    preconception counseling, 211
    risk factors and screening, 212
    RNA single-stranded virus, 210
    sexual transmission, 211
    vertical transmission, 213
Hepatitis E virus (HEV)
    clinical course, 202
    in developing counties, 202
    Hepeviridae, 202
    HEV, 202
    management, 202
    RNA virus, 202
HEV. *See* Hepatitis E virus (HEV)
HG. *See* Hyperemesis gravidarum (HG)
HIV. *See* Human immunodediciency virus (HIV)
HIV medication, 198, 201
HIV prevention, 199, 200
HIV testing, 198, 199, 201
Human chorionic gonadotropin (hCG), 92
Human immunodediciency virus (HIV)
    definition, 197–198
    diagnosis, 199
    early and effective antiretroviral therapy, 201
    epidemiology, 198
    management/treatment, 200–201
    pathobiology, 198–199
Hyperemesis gravidarum (HG)
    acupressure/acupuncture, 95
    congenital malformations, 94
    dietary treatment, 95
    electrolyte and fluid management, 329
    PUQE scoring system, 93–94
    treatment, 95
    in women, 93

Hyperglycemia
  euglycemia, 67
  GDM, 67
  long-term effects, 67
  pharmacokinetics, insulins, 67, 68
Hypertension
  chronic (*see* Chronic hypertension)
  clinical presentations, 178
  definition, 177
  long-term risk, 190
  pathophysiology, 179
  postpartum, 188–189
  preeclampsia, 184–188
  in pregnancy, 177
  prevention, 189–190
Hypertensive disorders. *See* Hypertension
Hyperthyroid
  clinical features, 325–327
  neonatal and fetal hypo, 330
Hyperthyroidism
  antepartum management, 329–330
  diagnosis
    clinical features, 328
    diagnostic evaluation, 328–329
    symptoms, 325–327
  fetal thyroid, 324
  gestational hyperthyroidism, 324
  peripartum management, 330
  postpartum, 331
  prevention, 330–331
  thyroid storm, 324
Hypothyroid
  adverse effects, 332
  antepartum management, 335
  diagnosis
    diagnostic evaluation, 333, 335
    differential diagnosis, 333, 334
    symptoms, 333
  iodine
    deficiency, 332
    requirements, 332
  postpartum, 336
  preconception, 336
  prevention, 335–336
  TAb, 333
  thyroid hormone levels, 332
Hypothyroidism. *See* Hypothyroid

I
IBD. *See* Inflammatory bowel disease (IBD)
Idiopathic thrombocytopenia (ITP), 155, 156
IHD. *See* Ischemic heart disease (IHD)

Immune thrombocytopenia purpura (ITP), 155, 157, 160
Immunosuppressive therapy, 301, 302, 310
Inflammatory bowel disease (IBD)
  antibiotics, 102
  antitumor necrosis factor alpha agents, 103
  5-ASAs, 100
  azathioprine/6-mercaptopurine, 101
  breastfeeding, 100
  corticosteroids, 100–101
  cyclosporine, 102
  effect of pregnancy, 99
  fertility, 98
  management, 99
  methotrexate, 101
  natalizumab, 103–104
  symptoms, 98
  thalidomide, 102
  women, 99
Influenza pneumonia
  descritpion, 250
  diagnosis, 251
  epidemiology, 250
  pharmacotherapy, 251–252
  preterm delivery, 250–251
  prevention and vaccination, 252
  risk, adverse fetal outcomes, 250
  supportive management, 251
Institute of Medicine (IOM), 82, 83
Insulin
  and crystalloid replacement, 64
  glyburide, 74
  labor and delivery, 71
  pharmacokinetics, 67, 68
  pregnancy and glucose control, 67
  treatment, 67
Intensive care unit (ICU), 98, 244, 252, 277
Intrahepatic cholestasis of pregnancy (ICP)
  description, 114
  diagnosis, 115–116
  epidemiology, 115
  maternal and fetal complications, 116–117
  monitoring, 116
  pathogenesis, 115
  ursodiol, 117
IOM. *See* Institute of Medicine (IOM)
Iron deficiency anemia, 151
Ischemic heart disease (IHD), 64, 190

L
Listeria infection, 85
Lithium, 54–55

Index

Liver disease
    AIH, 112–113
    complications, pregnant patient, 109
    conception outcomes, 108
    fertility and pregnancy outcome, 113
    Gallstone disease, 114
    ICP (see Intrahepatic cholestasis of pregnancy (ICP))
    maternal outcomes, 108
    MELD, 109
    mycophenolate mofetil, 114
    portal hypertension and variceal bleeding, 109–110
    prednisolone, 113–114
    pregnancy outcomes, 108
    Wilson's disease, 111–112
Liver function tests (LFTs)
    and AH, 106–107
    asymptomatic moderate elevation, 105–106
LMWH. See Low-molecular-weight heparin (LMWH)
Low-molecular-weight heparin (LMWH), 15, 142, 144, 166–167

M

Macrocytic anemias, 151
Major depressive disorder (MDD)
    anxiety and stress, fetus, 38
    effect of pregnancy, 37
    infant and child, anxiety and stress, 39
    on pregnancy, 37
    risk factors, 37
    untreated prenatal, effects, 39
Maternal
    diabetic gastropathy, 64
    fetal and perinatal risks, 64–66
    and fetal health, 61
    hyperglycemia, 71
    insulin, 62
    renal function, 63
Maternal morbidity, 28, 97, 110, 124, 229
Maternal mortality, 16, 108, 109, 122, 139, 150, 202, 292
MDD. See Major depressive disorder (MDD)
6-Mercaptopurine (6-MP), 101
Methotrexate, 101
5,10-methylenetetrahydrofolate reductase (MTHFR) gene, 135
Metoclopramide, 96
Model for end-stage liver disease (MELD), 109
Mood disorders
    antidepressant, 39
    antipsychotic, 54–57
    bipolar disorder, 50–54
    depression, pregnancy, 35–39
    PPD, 45–49
    pregnancy outcomes, 40
Mycophenolate mofetil, 114

N

Natalizumab, 103–104
Nausea and vomiting of pregnancy (NVP)
    antiemetics, 96
    antihistamines and anticholinergics, 96
    gestational vomiting, 92
    ginger, 95
    hCG, 92
    and HG, 91–98
    hydration and nutritional support, 97–98
    metoclopramide, 96
    ondansetron, 97
    on pregnancy outcome, 92–93
    pregnant women, 91
    pyridoxine/doxylamine, 96
    risk factors, 91
Nervous system
    headaches, 220–223
    neurological disorders, 219
    pregnant patients, 219
    seizures, 223–230

O

Obstructive sleep apnea (OSA). See Sleep-disordered breathing (SDB)
Ondansetron, 97
Ovarian vein thrombosis, 167–168

P

Patient health questionnaire (PHQ), 36, 38
PE. See Pulmonary embolism (PE)
Perinatal HIV transmission, 200
Persistent pulmonary hypertension of the newborn (PPHN)
    etiologies, 41
    risk factors, 41
    SSRI, 41–42
PGM. See Prothrombin gene mutation G20210A (PGM)
Platelet function disorders, 159
Pneumonia
    bacterial (see Bacterial pneumonia)
    influenza virus, 250–252
    management/treatment

Pneumonia (cont.)
    acute respiratory distress network studies, 245
    antibiotic therapy, 246
    bicarbonate, 246
    early intubation, 245
    fetal monitoring, 245
    ICU, 246
  varicella, 246–249
Post-exposure prophylaxis, 207
Postnatal adaptation syndrome, 42
Postpartum, 74–75
Postpartum depression (PPD)
  antidepressants and breast-feeding, 48
  definition and prevalence, 45–46
  etiologies, 47
  non-pharmacological treatment options, 48
  pharmacotherapy treatment, 47–48
  risk factors, 46
  risks of untreated, 47
  screening measurement, 46
Postpartum hypertension, 188–189
Postpartum psychosis
  risk factors, 53
  symptoms, 52
  women, 52, 53
Post-thrombotic syndrome (PTS), 139
PPD. See Postpartum depression (PPD)
PPHN. See Persistent pulmonary hypertension of the newborn (PPHN)
Preconception assessment, 69–70
Prednisolone, 113–114
Preeclampsia
  clinical manifestations, 184, 185
  description, 184
  diagnosis, 184, 185
  management
    acute severe hypertension, 188
    algorithm, 186–187
    fetal morbidity, 185
    placenta, 185
    severity of disease, 186
    steroids, fetal lung maturity, 185
  risk factors, 184
Pre-exposure prophylaxis, 199, 200
Pregnancy
  and diabetes (see Diabetes)
  physiology
    cardiovascular changes, 22–23
    description, 21
    gastrointestinal changes, 23
    respiratory changes, 21–22
    thyroid disease (see Thyroid disease)
Protein C deficiency, 135, 137

Protein S deficiency, 135, 137, 143
Prothrombin gene mutation, 166, 168
Prothrombin gene mutation G20210A (PGM), 135, 137, 143
PTS. See Post-thrombotic syndrome (PTS)
Pulmonary arterial hypertension (PAH), 286, 292–295
Pulmonary embolism (PE), 138, 140–141
Pyridoxine/doxylamine, 96

R
RA. See Rheumatoid arthritis (RA)
Renal
  acute failure, 265–266
  ARBs, 269, 270
  blood flow and GFR, 262–263
  breastfeeding and ACE inhibitors, 269, 270
  calculi, 264–265
  CKD, 266–268
  dialysis, 268
  physiologic changes, 262
  physiology, 262
  renal stones, 264–265
  transplant, 269, 270
  UTIs, 263–264
Rheumatoid arthritis (RA)
  clinical manifestations, 280–281
  epidemiology, 279–280
  impact of disease
    fertility, 281
    pregnancy outcomes, 281–282
  preconception counseling, 282–283
  treatment, 282

S
Scleroderma. See Systemic sclerosis (SSc)
Scleroderma renal crisis (SRC), 285–286, 291–294
SDB. See Sleep-disordered breathing (SDB)
Second generation antipsychotics (SGAs), 57
Seizures
  antiepileptic drugs, 224
  causes, 224
  definition, 220, 223
  diagnostic evaluation, 228
  differential diagnosis, 227–228
  effect of disease on pregnancy, 226–227
  effect of pregnancy on disease, 225
  epidemiology, 224
  epilepsy, 223
  management/treatment, 228–230
  pathobiology, 224–225

physiologic changes, 225
SGAs. *See* Second generation antipsychotics (SGAs)
Sickle cell disease, 152–154
SLE. *See* Systemic lupus erythematosus (SLE)
Sleep-disordered breathing (SDB)
   description, 253
   management/treatment, 254–255
   neonatal outcomes, 253–254
   pregnancy and fetal, 253–254
   screening, 253
Snoring, 253, 254
SRC. *See* Scleroderma renal crisis (SRC)
SSc. *See* Systemic sclerosis (SSc)
Superimposed preeclampsia, 178, 179, 190
Systemic lupus erythematosus (SLE)
   antiphospholipid antibodies, 277
   clinical disease activity, 278
   clinical manifestations, 276–277
   disease management
      azathioprine, 279
      corticosteroids, 279
      dexamethasone, 278
      fetal M-mode echocardiography, 278
      fetal monitoring, 278
      high-dose prednisone, 279
      hydroxychloroquine, 279
      trimester laboratory tests, 278
   epidemiology, 276
   highest maternal risk, 277
   intrauterine growth restriction, 277
   neonatal lupus, 278
   preconception counseling, 279
   preterm labor (PTL), 277
   serologic activity, 278
Systemic sclerosis (SSc)
   clinical manifestations, 283–284
   epidemiology, 283
   impact, pregnancy outcomes
      case-control series, 287
      conception, 287–288
      decidual and placental vasculopathy, 288–289
      fetal loss, 288
      maternal death, 287
      preterm delivery, 288
      retrospective and prospective studies, 287
   interactions, pregnancy
      cardiac output, 285
      digital ulceration, 287
      gastro-esophageal reflux disease, 285
      nitric oxide (NO), 284–285
      PAH, 286
      physiologic hemodynamic and vascular changes, 284
      Raynaud phenomenon, 285, 287
      renin angiotensin-aldosterone system, 285
      SRC, 285–286
   management
      anesthesia considerations, 290
      mode of delivery, 290
      PAH, 292–293
      risk assessment, 289
      special considerations, 290–291
      SRC, 291–292
   noninflammatory vasculopathy, 283
   obstetric and neonatal care, 296
   postpartum management, 295
   preconception counseling and planning, 293–295
   renal crisis, 296

T
TAb. *See* Thyroid autoantibodies (TAb)
Tension-type headache (TTH), 220, 221
Thalassemias, 154
Thalidomide, 102
Thrombocytopenia
   BCSH, 155
   causes, 159
   DIC, 158–159
   differential diagnosis, 155, 156
   HELLP, 157–158
   immune thrombocytopenic purpura, 155, 157
   TTP, 158
Thromboembolism
   clinical scenario, 144
   coagulation factors, 164, 165
   risk, pregnancy, 164
Thrombophilia
   coagulation factor levels, 164, 165
   definition, 134–135
   diagnosis, 137–138, 166, 167
   epidemiology, 135
   Factor V Leiden, 166
   guidelines, 167
   LMWH, 166–167
   National Commission on Radiation Protection, 166
   pathobiology, physiologic changes, 135
   pregnancy
      anticoagulant medication, 136
      APS, 136
      diagnosis, 136–137

Thrombophilia (cont.)
　　placenta-mediated complications, 136
　　prothrombin gene mutation, 166
　　Virchow's triad, 164, 165
　　VTE, 166
Thrombosis
　　definition, 138
　　diagnosis
　　　　CVT, 141
　　　　DVT, 141
　　　　PE, 140–141
　　　　VTE signs and symptoms, 140
　　epidemiology, 138–139
　　management/treatment
　　　　acute thrombosis, 141–143
　　　　issues, 143
　　　　VTE prophylaxis, 143–144
　　pathobiology, physiologic changes, 139
　　pregnancy
　　　　DVT, 139
　　　　PTS, 139
　　　　UK Confidential Inquiry on Maternal Mortality, 139
Thrombotic thrombocytopenic purpura (TTP)
　　bleeding disorders, 160
　　diagnosis, 156
　　TTP-HUS, 157–158, 265
Thrombotic thrombocytopenic purpura–hemolytic uremic syndrome (TTP–HUS), 157–158, 265, 266
Thyroid autoantibodies (TAb), 324, 333, 335, 336
Thyroid-binding globulin (TBG), 323, 332
Thyroid cancer. See Thyroid nodule
Thyroid disease
　　B-hCG, 323
　　definition, 321–322
　　epidemiology, 322–323
　　fetal thyroid, 323
　　hyperthyroidism (see Hyperthyroidism)
　　hypothyroidism, 332–336
　　TBG, 323
　　thyroid nodule and thyroid cancer, 336–339
　　trimester-specific normal range, 323
Thyroid nodule
　　antepartum management, 338–339
　　diagnosis
　　　　diagnostic evaluation, 337–338
　　　　differential diagnosis, 337
　　　　symptoms, 337
　　maternal age, parity and iodine deficiency, 336
　　postpartum, 339

　　prevention, 339
TTH. See Tension-type headache (TTH)
TTP. See Thrombotic thrombocytopenic purpura (TTP)
TTP-HUS. See Thrombotic thrombocytopenic purpura–hemolytic uremic syndrome (TTP–HUS)

U

UFH. See Unfractionated heparin (UFH)
Unfractionated heparin (UFH), 15, 142, 144, 166
Urinary tract infections (UTIs)
　　antibiotic prophylaxis, 263, 264
　　asymptomatic bacteriuria, 263
　　organisms infecting, 263
　　pyelonephritis, 264
Ursodiol, 117
UTIs. See Urinary tract infections (UTIs)

V

Valvular disease, 9, 10
Varicella pneumonia
　　changes, physiology and immunity, 247
　　CVS, 247–248
　　description, 246–247
　　diagnosis, 248
　　epidemiology, 247
　　infection in babies, 248
　　management/treatment, 249
　　passive immunization, 249
　　preterm delivery and low birth weight, 247
Vasculitis, 297, 298, 303, 310
Vasopressors
　　dobutamine, 28
　　dopamine, 28
　　shock, 27
Venous thromboembolism (VTE)
　　diagnosis, 140
　　management, 141, 143
　　peripartum risk factors, 134
　　pregnancy, 135, 138, 139
　　prophylaxis, 143–144
　　signs and symptoms, 140
　　thrombophilia, 135
Viral infections
　　acute hepatitis, 201
　　HBV infection, 202–210
　　HCV, 210–213
　　HEV, 202
　　HIV, 197–201

Index

Viral load
  antepartum management focuses, 200
  HBsAg-positive patients, 207
  HBV, 205, 206
  HIV infection, 199
  intravenous zidovudine, 201
  risk, perinatal transmission, 199
Viral pneumonia
  influenza virus, 250–252
  varicella, 246–249
von Willebrand disease (vWD)
  and bleeding disorders, 159–161
  characteristics and laboratory findings, 161–162
  congenital disorders, 160
  DDAVP, 162–163
  description, 161
  epidural anesthesia, 162
  estrogen levels, 162
  FVIII, 162
  treatment options, 161
VTE. *See* Venous thromboembolism (VTE)
vWD. *See* von Willebrand disease (vWD)

W

Wilson's disease, 111–112

CPSIA information can be obtained at www.ICGtesting.com
Printed in the USA
LVOW02s2055091114

412764LV00003B/18/P